the GARDEN of EDEN COOKBOOK

Recipes in the Biblical Tradition

the
GARDEN
of EDEN
COOKBOOK

Recipes in the
Biblical Tradition

Devorah Emmet Wigoder

1817

HARPER & ROW, PUBLISHERS, SAN FRANCISCO

Cambridge, Hagerstown, New York, Philadelphia, Washington
London, Mexico City, São Paulo, Singapore, Sydney

THE GARDEN OF EDEN COOKBOOK.

Copyright © 1988 by Devorah Emmet Wigoder.

FIRST EDITION

Designer and Illustrator: Brad Greene

Library of Congress Cataloging-in-Publication Data

Wigoder, Devorah.
  The garden of Eden cookbook.

  Includes index.
  1. Cookery, Israeli. I. Title.
TX724.W5 1987   641.595694   87-45200
ISBN 0-06-069402-5

88 89 90 91 92 **KRU** 10 9 8 7 6 5 4 3 2 1

To my family, Meir, Shimshon, and Michal Aviad,
each of whom is a very good cook,
and to my grandson, Itamar,
and to my husband, Geoffrey,
who only asked for a poached egg on toast.

CONTENTS

❧ ❧ ❧

ACKNOWLEDGMENTS

I wish to thank my family and friends for their encouragement in the course of writing this book. I remember with affection Bea Wiggs, of blessed memory. I also wish to express my appreciation to Yehuda Feliks, professor of biblical botany, for his inspirational assistance; to the Armenian community in Jerusalem; to the staff of the Hadassah Seligsberg School; and to the many people who have shared their treasured recipes with me.

I would particularly like to mention my friends who have offered hospitality to me to work on the manuscript: Selma Spitzer and Heni Levi; Raif Elias; and to Mildred Devor especially. I wish to thank the management and staff of the Ecumenical Institute at Tantur for their assistance and the use of the library facilities; and Dorothy (Hadassah) Weisbrod, whose understanding and faith in me have been the hallmarks of our long friendship.

Chicory

PREFACE

❧ ❧ ❧

My journey into Jewish life started as a protest. It was 1946; World War II had ended. The age-old accumulation of insults, accusations, betrayals, and blood libels had finally led to the mass murder of six million Jews. With this tragic wartime fate of European Jewry came the realization of the total human responsibility for it.

I was then Jane MacDwyer, an Irish-American lass reared in Catholic schools. I had many questions.

Why were the Christian values of Western civilization not potent enough to stem the tide of anti-Semitism? Because anti-Semitism is well rooted in Christian theology. It springs from a long-held premise that so long as Jews continued to reject Jesus as the Messiah, and refused to convert to Christianity, God's wrath would visit them for many generations.

Why had the self-proclaimed "enlightened" forces of socialism and communism not done more to protest the menace of Nazism? Were not the principles of human dignity and the right to social justice being violated? Or was the protection of human rights a privilege reserved for Christians only, without reference to Jews, gypsies, and homosexuals? Who would dare to claim that the twentieth century has marked a milestone in human social progress?

Why, then, did Jews remain Jews? Why didn't they obligingly convert to Christianity in large numbers, if for no other reason than just to stay alive? Of course Hitler knocked out that escape route. Men and women in the thousands were murdered in concentration camps without knowing in some measure they were Jewish (not a few of them were observing Christians).

In an attempt to seek out answers to these questions, I began a careful search into recorded Jewish history. I was both a student and a secretary at the New School for Social Research in New York, and had easy access to its well-stocked library. I also had my choice of courses dealing with the Jewish presence in many countries of the world; courses about Jews in organized labor or in politics, science, and the arts. There was no shortage of books dealing with the history of anti-Semitism.

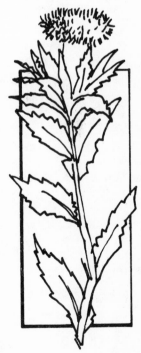

Safflower

A whole new world opened up to me: fascinating, revealing, and enlightening. I became involved in long conversations with my Jewish contemporaries in the student body, and with the emigré Jewish scholars who were teaching at the New School. Reluctantly, they told me their stories. They expressed their fear and fury in the period prior to their escape from Europe, as well as the shock they experienced upon seeing civilization threatened by the rule of tyranny and savage dictatorship. Each person's experience was dominated by an ingrained compulsion to survive, set against an uncanny mixture of chance, timing, courage, and disbelief.

At the New School I met a woman who was to become a dear friend, Dorothy Weisbrod. From her I learned much about Jewish life in New York City, especially on the East Side. I was fascinated by the faces I saw there. They bore the strain of hard work, but not despair. I was puzzled by my attraction to a people who were history's scapegoats, the bearers of so much bad luck. Yet I was drawn to look in the windows of the faces I saw there: into eyes that shone out of the depths of a seemingly secret world. Why did they shine so? Was it inner confidence, despite their position on the social ladder?

I felt I must have overlooked a crucial point. I had not yet found the secret of Jewish continuity. What was the special cohesive force that made the Jewish people a people bound together? Was it the painful experiences they held in common? Surely it took more than the accumulation of negative factors to bind a people.

Ironically, I had overlooked the factor of religion! In parting with the faith of my fathers and my Irish-Catholic education, I had put God on hold. Understandably, I was slow to overcome my inertia and seek out the meaning of Jewish survival and solidarity on religious grounds. Yet, if I was so moved as to join the Jewish people and to become entangled in their fate, then I had to explore the God-dimension of their history. To what kind of Jewish identity could I, in honesty, commit myself: a Jewish Communist; a Socialist; an agnostic; a contributor to causes; a Jew by any definition of being Jewish? Or as a practicing Jew?

"Where do I go from here?" I asked Dorothy. "Speak to Wolfe Kelman," she replied, "the rabbinical student with whom we worked in the United Jewish Appeal students' campaign. He can help you, especially because he knows you."

In a truly rabbinical manner, Wolfe discouraged me. "Look," he said, "you don't have to become a Jew to achieve salvation, or if your intention is to befriend Jews. With a name like Jane MacDwyer, your help could have special significance."

I made it clear to him that I did not wish to become a mere window-gazer into Jewish life: I wanted to experience it. I wanted to know where and how to explore the roots of Jewish survival. His direction and guidance brought me to courses in the Jewish Theological Seminary and a lot of reading-homework, lectures, and synagogue services. I was confronted with the multiple facets of Judaism: It was a religion; a way of life; a covenant between people and God; a culture.

I met Jews from many worlds of Jewish experience. They certainly did not seem bound together solely because of their common experience with discrimination. They were conscious Jews, educated in Jewish values. They were joyous Jews. They were Jews by choice and not by chance.

My ongoing education brought me to the door of Rabbi Milton Steinberg's study. I had read his books, and I knew that he was the person who would understand my quest for answers to Jewish survival. No less so, he would appreciate my compulsion to go beyond making a protest. He would accept the positive action I contemplated: to personally replace one of the six million Jews lost in the Holocaust.

I had great difficulty coming to terms with Jewish prayer. To help me over this hurdle, Rabbi Steinberg suggested that Morton Leifman, a rabbinical student, should guide me through the massive jungle of Jewish ritual observance. Mortie was the right person—his attitude toward prayer came close to a Chasidic love-language between God and humanity. Guileless and generous, Mortie had a pocketful of Jewish jokes and anecdotes that improved with age and telling. (How well I understood that trait! I was reared in an Irish storytelling family, and I knew that great storytellers lean heavily on humorous license. They can never tell the same tale in the same way twice.)

Mortie was patient with my tendency to disagree with common prayer forms, especially their repetitive quality. "Mortie, these prayers try to pin God down, asking him to be both a Santa Claus and a referee in the battles people wage against each other." It seemed to me that relying on the answer to prayers was an easy way out of one's personal commitment to moral responsibility. "Is not our greatest gift our free will?" I asked.

Rabbi Steinberg encouraged me to go beyond the study of prayer. "Try praying," he said. "You may tap levels of personality unknown to yourself. Remember that much of Jewish observance developed when Israel was in exile. It became a way to preserve Israel as a Promised Land, and to keep the Covenant of Jews with God alive." I wondered fleetingly if living in Israel would exempt me from praying!

Finally, I came to realize that most of Jewish prayer is much more than petition and supplication. Hymns and praises encourage men and women to appreciate their inherited blessings and to be grateful for their special status among the creatures of this earth. We are elevated to a position far above the common stance of being beggars.

Beyond prayer, the roots of Judaism constituted a lifeline to the survival of the spirit in spite of the ever-present physical threat to generations of Jews. Those roots emerged from an agrarian reality constituted in the three-dimensional proposition God had offered to Abraham, the first convert to Judaism (Genesis 12:5). Abraham was gently but firmly urged to abandon his devotion to many gods. He was advised that, in fact, there was only one God. One God who belonged to all people. Poor Abraham! He must have been confused by the thought of one God. The same God for all his family and good neighbors—and for all his enemies too? How could that be?

If that was not enough to confuse Abraham, God next commanded him to, "Get out of this country, go into the Land of Canaan. There I will make you a great nation." He was commanded to give up his nomadic life; to take his herds of goats and sheep, his silver and gold treasures, and move on to another land. He was commanded to make his peace with the soil. Abraham must have been bewildered. The soil he knew was dry, desert sand on which but a few weeds grew. He was being asked to do so many things. Why? What reward was there in store for him?

Reading his mind, God said, "Abraham, look to the heavens . . . count the stars. So too shall your seed be. You will sire a great nation." To a man without children, this surely was an inducement to do as he was commanded. And in so doing, Judaism was conceived to stand on three pillars of identification: monotheism, the land, and peoplehood.

No previous religious culture had been so constituted. In my Catholic rearing, the concept of God for all people and all nations was overshadowed by the personal importance of Christ, the Son of God. No less so was the infallibility of Catholicism stressed as the only way to salvation. Fellow believers were referred to as Catholics, but Protestants were called Christians! Jews—as nonbelievers—were lost.

To me, the momentous impact of the monotheistic concept was like a comet heralding the dawn of civilization which would unify the human race. I thought, surely, if people had thoroughly understood this there would have been fewer crusades in the name of Christian honor.

I wanted to belong to this people whose faith and way of life was based on a God-image that embraced the wholeness of humankind. Granted, there are tribal and national signposts in Judaism; but it is universal in concept. Much more than a denomination, it is a dimension in the life of a people. The major events of the Jewish calendar relate to the cycle of creation and human partnership with nature.

And so the great day arrived, a day apart from all others. This day I made my way to the Jewish Theological Seminary not to explore Rashi's commentaries, nor to learn Hebrew, nor to dine in the cafeteria. Within a short time I would face the *Beth Din*,* the rabbinical court, then go on to the *mikveh*, the ritual bath. Toward this moment I had traveled a long way. I was thrilled and frightened at the same time, and particularly conscious of my aloneness. Of course, other people would witness my entrance into the House of Israel. But the commitment I was about to make was between God and myself.

Thousands of Jews had undoubtedly lived and died without ever standing as naked before God; nor had their wholeness been reconstructed. I was about to make a beginning. The *Beth Din* was not nearly as formidable as I had expected. A quiet prevailed which it seemed even language could not disturb. The judges and I were participants in a moment of formal ceremony, accommodating a historical, rabbinical tradition. They were witnessing one woman's changeover of religious commitment. Yet I was sure each one realized that no person was eligible to judge the worthiness of a proselyte's intention, nor could

*This and other terms are defined in the Glossary (pages 307–309).

anyone measure the basic caliber of a soul. Who could dare to define the moment when a Jew-by-choice, as I was, could be declared a finished product! Becoming a Jew meant to be a traveler, stopping continually at learning stations along the line of Jewish life experience.

I stood in the *mikveh* before three witnesses to my complete submersion, and to the symbolic washing away of all other alignments. I went down once, and for the second and third time. Then, my name now Devorah Emmet bat (daughter of) Abraham, I joined the rounds of remembering, and the thousands of voices lifted throughout the ages to echo human enlightenment. I spoke the historical words of faith: *Shema Yisrael Adonai Elohenu Adonai Echad:* Hear, O Israel, the Lord our God, the Lord is One.

the GARDEN of EDEN COOKBOOK

Recipes in the Biblical Tradition

1 GOING UP TO JERUSALEM

My decision to settle in Israel was inevitable. The recent rebirth of the State of Israel opened up the way for the realization of the return to Zion for all those who would choose to come, and for the thousands who had no other choice. The dynamics of the push or pull to Israel was not always clearly defined; but the chance to make Jewish history, instead of constituting a historical reference, belonged to each new immigrant.

The pull for me was not singular. I had already committed myself to replacing one Jew who had not survived the Holocaust, and whose place in Jewish continuity I would try to fill. Where better could this challenge be accomplished than in the birthplace of Judaism and Jewish history? My conversion to Judaism had passed from a protest-statement to an identification with a people whose roots were linked to an agrarian lifestyle. Settling in Israel seemed logical and natural. I could not see myself sitting in Greenwich Village praying for rain in Jerusalem! I wanted to go, Bible in hand, along those pathways where prophecy had illuminated humanity's partnership in the creative process. Who knew? Perhaps reclamation of the Land of Israel might one day constitute the Third Commonwealth of the Jewish People. Would not a food-pregnant land of trees, flowers, and fruits more than equal a rebuilt Temple? Does prayer demand a domicile?

So off I went, back to the beginning, to that small stretch of land upon which so much human history has been experienced. My chapter in the contemporary chronicle began with my marriage in 1948 to Geoffrey Wigoder, a rabbinical student whom I had met at New York's Jewish Theological Seminary.* It took place on a rooftop in Tel Aviv, under a cloudless blue sky that crowned the *chuppah* (the canopy under which the marriage ceremony takes place). One vow Geoffrey was unwilling to take, however, was to be a farmer or a *kibbutznik*. His Jewish identity was firmly linked to the written word and

Fenugreek

---

*The complete story of my transition from an Irish-Catholic upbringing to a commitment to Judaism, and my journey to Jerusalem are told in full in *Hope Is My House* (Englewood Cliffs, N.J.: Prentice-Hall, 1966).

to the scholarly interpretation of Jewish history. I was sure, given time, that I could convert him—but as of this writing I have not succeeded!

In the beginning of 1950 we moved into a rented flat in Talbieh, Jerusalem. These early years necessitated many adjustments for both of us. Geoffrey maintained that we had settled down long before we settled up—if, in fact, we ever had.

I had little opportunity to try my hand and hoe at tilling the soil. We received water every ten days—barely enough to maintain our Western standard of cleanliness. No drop of water could be used for gardening or houseplant culture. In fact, if not for an ancient water-collection system, Jerusalem may not have survived the War of Independence or any other of the many sieges which had threatened her.

Rainwater collection began in the Middle and Late Bronze Ages. It was particularly suited to the hilly areas of the Land of Israel, of which Jerusalem was one. Underground cisterns were cut out of the rocky limestone foundations upon which Jerusalem stands. Drains, leading down from rooftops and other high places, directed the rainwater into the cisterns through a narrow shaft. In time, Jewish settlers improved the cisterns by covering the walls with a lime-based plaster. This protective coating prolonged the time water could be stored and impeded seepage. Almost no newly built house was without its private cistern, which served through the hot summers until the winter rains came.

Such a cistern existed under the house in which we were living. It was from this source of water and from other cisterns in the city that a water-rationing system served the whole of Jerusalem, supplying water to those neighborhoods where cisterns did not exist. So we really had no complaint.

In any case, before I could introduce myself to the holy earth of Jerusalem—except, of course, as a curious and appreciative pilgrim—there were challenges to meet. Not the least of them was to find a job and learn Hebrew. These were no mean targets for a greenhorn from New York City.

Theoretically, I knew that I would be living in a country that was recuperating from a war, but it did not really come home to me until we set up housekeeping in Jerusalem. Our limited time spent in Tel Aviv and a short stay in a *kibbutz* were only minor exposures to an existence more frugal than I had ever experienced. Living in Jerusalem was a shock. Beyond learning Hebrew and looking for a job, I also had to face the continual pursuit of food. The jungle of bureaucracy contained in the postwar rationing system was a constant battle. Shopping was a time-consuming, strenuous chore. My Greenwich Village lifestyle was no preparation for queuing for a live chicken, carrying it to the *shochet* (the ritual slaughterer of animals), then finding someone to pluck it.

There was an alternative to this, which many people preferred. They took their live chicken ration—distributed every three months—and raised it for eggs. Our whole neighborhood resounded with the crowing and cackling of chickens, especially at the crack of dawn. It was like living on one big chicken farm. People kept few house pets in those days. Lost-and-found signs in the neighborhood did not seek dogs or cats, but those winged early risers who often flew the coop in search of better food scraps around the corner.

This didn't seem an alternative for us. I couldn't see Geoffrey as a poultry raiser, or the one to take the chicken to the *shochet*. So we usually gave our ration as a contribution to a communal Sabbath meal. We felt it was better to eat a smaller portion of chicken in good company, and a welcome change from the usual frozen cod fillet.

Ways of cooking cod, the only available unrationed protein, challenged the most inventive homemakers. Not a few of them reported the frequency of fish forms in their dreams! Cod was the butt of many jokes. One jingle went like this: How odd of God to choose the cod, frozen, for God's chosen.

The brutal reality of austerity contrasted with the breathtaking backdrop of Israel's capital city. The rise and fall of its natural beauty was awesome; its staircases of ancient surviving terraces lured the walker to climb them. I was impelled to embrace them, to press my body against their hardness. The limestone buildings changed color as the slow movement of the sun reflected on them; shadows seemed to lengthen into human shapes. The ringing of church bells sounded the hours for prayer; the cry of the *muezzin* (the Arab town crier who calls the faithful to prayer) echoed from across the hill upon which the Old City walls of Jerusalem stand.

The war rubble had not been entirely cleared away. Warnings were everywhere: Danger. Stop. Border. How could there be danger in a city so beautiful? How could warfare blight the City of Peace, gleaming under a brilliantly blue sky? To this urban American, who had never experienced neighborhood, homefront warfare, it was incongruous.

I was overwhelmed by the multitude of divergent impressions related to the human condition and history of Jerusalem. I wanted to shout, "Stop! I have not absorbed the last minute's thunderbolt!"

It was true that the Arabs got the Old City, but we got the view to it. And on that first day of discovery of the eastern section of the city, the sky was cloudless. No mist rose up from the Dead Sea to mar the view of the Mountains of Moab. They seemed almost within handshake. I wanted to call out, "I know you. It was in your midst that Ruth the Moabite, grandmother of David, lived. You're as beautiful as poets have described you. Your fields were tilled in joy and rhythmic shouts; the poor came to them for their share of the gleanings which your viable soil allowed. One day I will visit you, for my first contact with the Bible was reading the Book of Ruth, long ago, in the days when Catholics were forbidden to read the Old Testament."

I heard a small voice in my ear: "Lass, enough of your dreaming. It's time now to pick up this month's rations—before they run out." And so it was: two pounds of sugar, per person, per month! I measured it in my mind: eight glasses—one cup of sugar a week. Fortunately, we didn't take sugar in our tea or coffee. We could keep our ration for breakfast cereal, puddings for Geoffrey's sweet tooth, and the occasional Sabbath cake.

It took extra sugar to cancel out the taste and smell of kerosene, which permeated most of our cooking before gas was discovered in Israel. (After that discovery we only used the odorous kerosene for heating stoves.) Every time the *neft* (kerosene) man sounded his presence with a loud clanging, we rushed out with empty cans and a queue was formed. In America I had done public relations for the New School for Social Research. That experience set me thinking about the supplier, the world-famous Shell Oil Company, with its multimillion-dollar advertising budget. Here was this quaint driver, surely a descendant of lines of Levis or Cohens, whose long beard waved in the wind and went white in the winter snow, leading a donkey-pulled makeshift delivery tank marked in bold red letters: SHELL. He was indeed a reassuring sight, especially on a cold day.

It was obvious that rationing was the only fair way to cope with the gigantic job of feeding the hundreds of thousands of newly arriving immigrants. In fact, every boatload and planeload of new immigrants was cheered. Likewise, the helping hand of world Jewry was applauded for making possible Operation *Kibbutz Galuyyot* (the Ingathering of the Exiles).

Yet our willingness to do our share was sometimes shaken when the larder was depleted. We learned to manage with the streamlined rations: two pounds of fat and two pounds of flour per month. Potatoes did not grow in Israel then, and they were rarely available; lentils, dried peas, and pearl barley were seldom attainable. One had to think carefully about the best use of the ration of two eggs per week. We had no cholesterol problem in those lean days! But sesame paste, which I first thought was peanut butter, was in good supply. It allowed for an additional protein count.

Modern methods of broiling and roasting were almost unheard of. Many men created makeshift barbecue grates and placed them over charcoal fires. Not a few Middle Eastern Jews had wood-burning ovens in their courtyards, in which they baked bread and long-cooking casserole-type foods. Small, compact electric ovens also existed. They were used for making pastries and cakes. But the star of the early period of settlement was the Wonder Pot. And indeed, one could do wondrous things in them: cakes, potatoes, *kugels*, and breads.

The Wonder Pot was brought to Palestine in the 1930s by German Jewish immigrants. It was easily copied locally, and became a prized kitchen utensil. This all-purpose pot, which is still in use today, looks like a chiffon-cake pan. It is round, with a funnel (larger than a sponge-cake pan), and a perforated lid. It sits on a metal ring over an open flame. You can bake a cake in about fifty minutes this way, potatoes or macaroni in less time.

Bread and beans remained in good supply, but meat was almost invisible — the ration of half a pound per month was only slightly increased for a festival. When Geoffrey's parents came from England to visit us for Rosh Hashanah, the Jewish New Year, they too were allotted ration coupons. Alas, when I went to buy the meat, I inadvertently handed over the month's rations. The rest of the month we were vegetarians, except for the intrepid odd cod. We only had a shower, so I could not imitate the prevailing custom of buying fresh carp on Wednesday, then using the bathtub as an aquarium until cooking time Friday morning. Nor did the ice man always cometh. A salty goat cheese, however, often saved the day. Rolled in flour and fried, it went well with salad as a light evening meal. (Israelis, as do their Mediterranean neighbors, eat their main meals in the middle of the day, and serve a light dairy meal in the evening.) The most used and varied standby, almost all year round, was the eggplant. In fact, there is a saying that a good Jerusalem housewife knows how to cook this beautiful purple vegetable twenty ways and more. According to Geoffrey, I achieved that goal—except that every dish ended up tasting like eggplant!

Geoffrey and I were classic examples of innocents abroad. But if Geoffrey was inadequately trained for doing plumbing jobs or repairing household breakdowns, he did arrive with a literate command of the Hebrew language. Unfortunately, his biblically and liturgically based vocabulary was not particularly useful for shopping. Not a few of the tradesmen looked at this Hebrew-speaking immigrant as though he might well be a prophet in disguise. To be on the safe side, they treated him with muted respect and a measure of inquiry.

Fortunately for me, British rule in Palestine encouraged people to learn English. My own suspicions that Israelis would resist using English when the British left were unfounded. Actually, the siege of Jerusalem had left many Jerusalemites hungry and emotionally spent. They were out of breath, out of supplies, and awed by achieving statehood! How long would their newly won independence last against the multiple improbables facing it? People like Geoffrey and myself, who had come to Israel not as survivors of the Holocaust, but out of personal commitment as Zionists, signaled for many of them faith in the future of the newly reborn state. We were welcomed and willingly helped—with furniture, pots and pans, and a gracious measure of friendship. When my halting Hebrew broke down, their excellent English came to the rescue.

We had no plastic bags in the early days of marketing in Israel, and very few brown paper bags. I was soon taught how to make cloth bags into which the shopkeepers would dole my ration of sugar, flour, rice, powdered milk, and eggs. When I expressed my shock at seeing the fish ration wrapped up in Hebrew newspapers, I was soon told off: "Miss, if you prefer having your fish wrapped in English print, bring along your old newspapers." When I tried to convince the fishmonger of the seeming insult to the Holy Tongue, philosophically he replied: "Thank God we've got something in which to wrap the fish."

I tried my hand at freelance writing and continued my conquest of the Hebrew language. Learning it was much more than a linguistic exercise, such as learning French or Spanish. Here was an ancient language in which first-year schoolchildren were being taught, and yet it was little changed from the original language in which prophets, priests, and farmers had communicated thousands of years ago. A sense of awe impeded my pursuit of the language, partly because my first contact with Hebrew had been in learning my prayers. It was difficult for me to employ it to express mundane matters.

Above all, learning Hebrew against the dramatic backdrop of Jerusalem was unsettling. Did I have the right to speak this language that was so tied up with biblical injunction? I struggled against a racial perception, as if the language belonged to a long line of inheritance no less significant than the line of land inheritance particular to a chosen people and their promised land. Maybe converts were not supposed to master the holy tongue too easily? Was there some ancient Jew backstage giving me the wrong cues? Or could it be that I just was not linguistically endowed? Its format was logical, based on the seven grammar tenses. Learning them first made me realize how poor my English grammar was, and later how much more I understood the structure of the English language.

But the sense of belonging I felt in Israel was mine. It was personal. I felt related to every stone in the neighborhood. Every narrow path had a first-person presence for me; every archeological tell (mound) was a magnet. I yearned to know the secrets buried under it. Was the Hebrew language also a tell, filled with ancient treasures? Could I unearth it? Would that be a comparable exercise to making peace with the soil of Israel?

2 MAKING IT ON THE LAND

In the spring of 1954 we moved from Talbieh to Beit HaKerem, a garden suburb of Jerusalem just a few miles west of the city's main sector. It had been founded some thirty-five years earlier by a group of scholars and teachers connected to the Beit HaKerem Seminary. Small, red-tiled cottages bordered by pine trees along narrow winding streets gave the community a rustic quality. It was just the environment I had hoped for. Situated among the seven hills of Jerusalem, the fresh mountain air was pure and invigorating. No smog or pollution intruded.

Jerusalem's brilliance has inspired endless poetic expression. It has the highest intensity of light of any city in the world, largely because of the interaction of the city's 3,000-foot elevation and its proximity to the Judean desert. These factors also influence the city's soil and vegetation, and greatly contribute to the character of Jerusalem—especially in the awakening hours of dawn and in the golden hours of eventide. Small wonder that no other city in the world is as coveted, defended, and endangered as Jerusalem, the capital of Israel and center of the universe.

Coming to live in Beit HaKerem gave me the deepest sense of coming home. I knew that in this place I would find myself. From the terrace of our living room we could look across to the approaches of Bethlehem where the Mar Elias, the Franciscan monastery church tower, rose clearly into view. A sense of timelessness stretched across the hills of Judea, not unlike the effect of the horizon of the sea. "Enjoy it while you can," Geoffrey remarked. "In a few years the view will be replaced by huge housing projects!"

Few private gardens graced Jerusalem in the 1950s, and fewer gardens of flowers. Housing units were landscaped after the builders cleared away the rubble. A sprinkling of flower gardens indicated where plant enthusiasts lived. But, in the main, landscaping was designed for limited maintenance and utilized perennial shrubs, climbers, geraniums, and hardy rosemary bushes. Most of the gardens were cared for by hired gardeners.

In the older sections of Jerusalem, however, every patch of viable earth was used for planting—especially edible plants used in salads and cooking. The

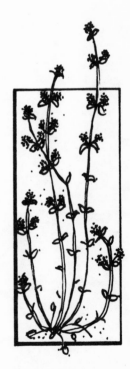

Syrian Marjoram

shortage of water and the limited number of household cisterns in the poorer areas made flower growing a luxury. But lettuce, parsley, mint, radishes, scallions, garlic, dill, and Jerusalem artichokes were commonly grown and carefully tended by the menfolk.

Religiously observant Jerusalemites followed the ancient rabbinical injunction that a Jew was forbidden to live in a city in which there were no gardens. The reference was to food-producing plants. However, today we are much wiser about the great number of flowering plants that are both edible and highly nutritious. The family cottage gardens in semirural areas like Beit HaKerem were large enough to include fruit-bearing trees such as almond, olive, pomegranate, and lemon.

Our apartment was—and is—located in the first cooperative housing unit built in the newly developing area. It was the forerunner of the three-story buildings that changed the rural ambiance of the neighborhood. Following an accepted pattern, housing units were mainly landscaped front and rear and tended by a house gardener. Small patches of land along the sides of the housing were allotted to each family. In these small plots families could grow plants of their choice, including flowers and kitchen greens.

Our neighbors represented a cross-section of Jews from many countries, mainly European, but there were Israel-born families as well. In fact, we were the only newcomers to the country. Being greenhorns, we were initially spared serving on the house committee, which decided how the coop would be administrated.

The first meeting of the house committee determined that there was not enough money in the kitty to landscape both the front and rear of the building. Not surprisingly, the view to the front was considered more important, since it would be seen by visitors and passersby. The committee decided that landscaping the rear of the house would have to wait. Unfortunately for us, our apartment faced the rear!

We waited. After some years had passed and there was no sign of landscaping, I became impatient. Our sons, Shimshon and Meir, were growing up. I had more free time, and decided to confront the house committee. "Look, I came to Israel as a Zionist," I told the committee. "I didn't come here to face a jungle of weeds, snakes, and scorpions. If there is no budget for cultivating the rear of the house, I propose to cultivate it myself." With not much more than a shrug of the shoulder, the house committee agreed.

I felt it was a great day for the Irish—and a challenge for this transplanted biblical Jew. Unlike Adam, who was born in a garden, our Garden of Eden would have to be created from scratch—or, more realistically, from stones. A showplace garden to mirror *House and Garden* standards was not my intention. But I would certainly change the look of what Americans call a back yard into a garden where the children of the house could play and enjoy a view to natural beauty. Later on, when they grew older, they could help me.

I decided that I would try to give the garden a biblical character, knowing full well that many of the trees and plants in Adam's garden would not grow well in the special growing conditions particular to Jerusalem. Not the least of these was the hilly topography of the Judean hills, which had seriously challenged the tribes of Judah and Benjamin in their early settlement in the Promised Land.

It was time, then, to evaluate the area beyond our terrace and living room. With Beit HaKerem now connected to the main Jerusalem water supply, our job would be greatly eased. The use of water would be regulated not just by need, but also in consideration of the nation's limited water resources; but it was a long stride beyond the ten-day water ration we had earlier experienced.

So the four Wigs, as yet without a cabbage patch, began an inventory of nature's bounty. What of it could be included in our design? What should be uprooted and discarded? Also, what of the existing landscape would influence the shape of our green growing to come?

Alas, twelve fast-growing eucalyptus trees stood as sentries over our scheming. When our neighborhood was not connected to the municipality's drainage system, they had been welcome suckers-up of the sewage. But as they stretched their leafy arms in a possessive challenge to our gardening efforts, it was clear there would be trouble in paradise. They were asserting their land rights. It was only a matter of time before they would invade our living room, joining us for afternoon tea! Would that we could have destroyed those even-dozen demons! But trees are the sacred cows of Israel: they could not be uprooted. Chalk one up for the Jobian exercise of learning to live with that which cannot be changed.

Barbed-wire fencing separated our housing properties—not simply for demarcation, they were required security measures. Gracious, green stretches of lawn carpeted properties closer to the Mediterranean Sea; but the rolling, green lawns of suburban American landscaping would only reach Israel much later—and then rarely in Jerusalem. Luckily for Jerusalem, we had an edible cover-up: the spreading blackberry bush (*Rubus scantus*). What a welcome climber—especially for the children, who loved to pick the berries and eat them without fuss one by one, or on their breakfast cereal.

This thorny climbing bush has been identified with the biblical *sneh*, which Moses saw as "a burning bush that was not consumed" (Exodus 3:1–4). We certainly would not uproot that respected food-giving veteran. In my travels I have seen it in the peninsula area of San Francisco, and fighting for its place in the sun among the limited green growing patches in that city's Mission district. On family trips to the western coast of Ireland, we were excited to see that nature had also blessed the green Isle with the rampant bramble. We had to admit, however, that Jerusalem's blackberries were sweeter. They were more sun-kissed.

In another corner of the garden I was happy to see a succulent plant with flat, fleshy leaves that looked familiar. It was the French-prized purslane! Mixed with sorrel and parsley leaves, purslane gives *bonne femme* soup its special character. A cherished companion to all that goes into Indian and Persian stews, purslane belongs to the large *Portulaca* family. Considered a weed by some non-cook gardeners, it has been extolled by many botanists for its medicinal advantages. You squeeze out the mucilage in the stems, mix it with honey or sugar, then take it to relieve colds. The juice is applied externally for bruises and as a cooling agent on hot foreheads.

Purslane was no less revered in the *Mishna*, the early rabbinical literature, which speaks of its seeds being collected, dried, and used in bread and gruel making. Some gardeners curse the plant's propagative habit of taking over the garden, especially because of its long flowering period (April through October). As much as I appreciate the rabbinical advice to use the seeds in making bread, I did hope that we would not have to resort to purslane seed powder to make our daily bread.

I found another member of the family growing in the garden, *Portulaca grandiflora*. This charming rockery plant was brought to Israel during the British Mandate period. The children call it *boker tov*, "good morning." It is not good for cutting, because it closes up when taken indoors; but it can brighten up a poor growing area.

Many of the wild plants of Israel bear lovely blue flowers. Among the daintiest of these is the chicory plant (*Cichorium intybus*). I discovered it growing under one of the side balconies in a suitably shaded spot. When I asked an old-timer about the food value of the plant, he looked at me in amazement: "That's not worth eating in a salad—unless, of course, you like dandelions." I do. He continued, "It's the root which is used as one of the five bitter herbs upon which you can perform the *mitzvah* of eating a bitter herb in the Passover Seder."

That was a bit of a blow. I was using the leaves in salads before the flowers appeared. I had hoped my sixth-generation neighbor might tell me how I could successfully dig up the roots, then dry them to use in coffee so I could stretch our coffee allotment. However, from another neighbor I did learn the special method of digging up the long taproots. I washed them and then roasted them in the cherished Wonder Pot on top of the kerosene burner until they were hard and brittle. When they were thoroughly cooled I ground them. No one in the family liked the straight chicory-brewed drink, claiming that the bitter herb taste overwhelmed any suggestion of coffee. Mixed with imported Maxwell House coffee, however, the blend was more successful.

I had surveyed the jungle outside our home, and selected from it those gifts of nature that we would include in our plan for a Bible-based garden. It was now time to tackle the task of making it on the land. But this was not ordinary land: it was land among the hills of Judea; a mountainous region standing almost three thousand feet above sea level; a natural stronghold befitting a capital city—Jerusalem.

The hill-country ecology played an important role in the early history of the Land of Israel, seemingly a proving ground for agricultural pursuits. If the nomadic tribes could be transformed into farmers, then they would be rewarded with land holdings in the more fertile areas in the lowlands. But if hill-country settlement guaranteed political independence, surviving in its rocky terrain was close to embattlement. The limestone foundation of Jerusalem is only slightly enriched by the country's commonest type of soil, *terra*

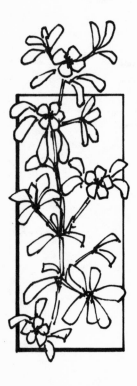

Purslane

rosa. Wind, rain, and soil erosion mark the winter season, and dry, arid conditions prevail during the long summer months.

We must wonder, then, how did the Israelite people transform the formidable, desolate mountain tracts into viable agricultural land? How did they manage to produce enough food to support thousands of people?

They were helped by the country itself, which was blessed with native agricultural products. To these the Israelites came heir when they arrived in the Promised Land: barley and wheat, and grapevines, olive, pomegranate, date, and fig trees. The produce from these seven species contain basic nutrients important to good health, but not without the accompaniment of other nutritious foods. To meet these needs they had to develop a larger food base. But where?

The answer lies in the Judean hillside. Actually, the Israelites' greatest agricultural innovation was in terrace agriculture. Three-fifths of the Judean hills were covered with manmade terraces. It took one to three years of backbreaking labor to turn three-quarters of an acre into farmland. It has been said that bringing forth bread from the soil was not the major problem; bringing soil out of the stone was the great accomplishment.

The remains of terracing along the slopes in the Hills of Judea, in our immediate neighborhood filled me with a mixture of awe and sadness. Clearly, they are landmarks of the determination of a people, in the First and Second Temple periods, to create womblike nests of soil out of which needed food would grow. In them, food plants flourished. Retaining walls were strong enough to hold back the fierce, cascading winter rains from sweeping away precious soil into the lowlands; the falling rain was absorbed where it fell. Their determination to create stretches of viable earth was fired not only by necessity, it was motivated by God's promise to them that one day they would inherit the lush lands of the Canaanites—providing, of course, they passed the test of terrace husbandry. They succeeded.

My sense of sadness sprang from the prophetic words of Ezekiel 38:20: "If the terraces are neglected, the steep places and terraces will fall; every wall shall fall to the ground." And so it happened when the Israelites were forced into exile.

We were spared the task of building terraces, because we had access to a tract of flat land. We weren't much more experienced than the Israelites. But just as they had learned on the job, observing the experienced Canaanites work their lands, we would have the advantage of their historical direction. And no small shortage of neighborly advice, even if most of the neighbors were as green as ourselves!

And if our motivation was not as religiously oriented as that of our farming forefathers, nor as accelerated out of necessity (the supermarket was too close for us to face hunger if our food crops failed), we were grateful for the opportunity to work the land. I was still moved by the biblical injunction that "cultivation of the soil was the destiny and duty of man from the beginning," and Isaiah's wisdom, which declares that only agricultural pursuits will bring peace to humankind.

In fact, serious agricultural pursuits were beyond the limitations of our soil-realm, but we did envision growing produce to eat: pulses, kitchen greens, herbs, fruit trees, grapes, and flowers for the Sabbath table. So, even if we did not have a large land holding, we were encouraged by the adage that "he that has a little garden of his own and fertilizes it, digs it, and enjoys its produce, is far better off than one who works a large garden according to shares."

We launched our conquest according to the Hebrew agricultural calendar: at the end of summer, in the time prior to the Jewish New Year. Following the long, dry, hot summer, the earth must be prepared for planting. It is then that the prayer and hope for rain stir farmer and urban dweller alike. The shorter, cold wet season would be welcomed. A brief spell of spring follows the rains. It is in this typically Mediterranean climate that human and plant life are conditioned in the Land of Israel.

The Israelite farmers were advised of the importance of opening the soil to fresh air in anticipation of the rains, which they hoped would fall in the end of October. Once the rains had permeated the earth it would be enlivened and easier for the farmer to work.

After we had thoroughly weeded the earth, we started the tough job of turning it. With no ox-goad or a mule-drawn plough, we were unable to follow the exact biblical methods for ploughing. However, with the metal tools in our possession—pick-axe, rake, spade, and hoe—we made a brave attempt. I reserved the right to use the hoe after the male Wigoders tried their hands on the more formidable agricultural implements. When we had not achieved the biblical rule of thumb to dig down three "breadths," the proper depth of penetration for good aeration, the children suggested we use a tractor. But not only would this mean cheating on the ground rules we had set for ourselves, it would have been impossible for a tractor to turn around in our land strip without ripping up part of the house. Instead, what we accomplished was similar to the modern method of double digging. The open earth looked wonderful. If particles of earth could talk, I was sure they would have said, "Thanks for the breath of fresh air."

In Isaiah 28:24 it is explained that the soil was twice ploughed before being sown. The first ploughing opened the hardened, dry earth. This allowed the rain to soak into the soil instead of running off. The second ploughing made leveling the ground much easier. Rabbinic literature lists four ploughings: the first in summer after harvesting; the second after the first rains. Spaces were then left between the furrows in the ground to divert the rain, which could cause erosion. The third ploughing ensured aeration and soil texture in preparation for sowing. After sowing, there was a light ploughing to cover the seed.

These instructions could more easily be followed in the plains of Israel. The rocky, limestone earth of Jerusalem was a major challenge to the Israelite settlers. In fact, turning Judea's mountain-forest soil into viable agricultural land and gardens is considered ancient Israel's unmatched agricultural achievement.

We soon realized that making peace with the soil must have challenged the faith and backs of the neo-farmers. Muscle fatigue taxed us as we worked to open up the earth from its long, deep sleep. Especially so when one of us would strike a massive limestone rock. If Judean rocks were diamonds, the financial history of Israel may well have been different. It seemed we had unearthed enough rocks to build the Third Temple!

"I think we'd better use them to build a rockery," Geoffrey suggested. So we did. It was a great success—we called it the laughing wall! We made soil nests among the stones. In them we planted hardy geraniums, Shasta daisies, and flowering bulbs. Ground-hugging rosemary carpeted the base of the rockery.

When the going got rough, I tried to encourage my planting partners by reminding them that our ancestors too had worked hard. In fact, the harder the task the greater would be the joy of harvest. Meir was not easily impressed: "I hope we'll have something to eat before the harvest. We haven't even planted anything yet."

I realized it was time to put our labors into a more historical light. I remembered an exciting archeological discovery, the tenth-century B.C. Gezer Calendar. "Tea time," I called out to my weary workers, who were happy for a break. I opened a book on Israelite agriculture, which included a photograph of the calendar. "Who can read the inscription on the picture?" Shimshon and Meir made a brave effort to decipher the lettering. "Looks like a lot of sevens to me, or some funny kind of Hebrew," Shimshon said. Meir was silent. "Of course they can't read it," Geoffrey commented. "It's written in an ancient script, long before modern Hebrew developed."

Then, as Geoffrey slowly read it out loud, the children looked over his shoulder:

> Two months picking olives
> Two months planting grain
> Two months late planting
> One month flax harvest
> One month barley harvest
> One month wheat harvest and feasting
> Two months vine pruning
> One month picking summer fruit and drying

The fact that not a few scholars consider it to be the work of a schoolboy seemed relevant to the two junior members of our workforce. The calendar, which dates back to the period of the Judges (which Shimshon was studying), is engraved on a limestone tablet. It lists a brief but exact description of the cycle of agricultural operations throughout the year according to seasons. It is written in verse, which can't be duplicated in translation. Whether or not the author is a schoolboy, the inscription provides a view to the scientific standard of agriculture the Israelites had reached in the time of the Judges.

Perhaps now my operational plan for the garden might be better appreciated; if not for the type of food plants mentioned, at least for our target—good husbandry. In any case, for me it was the doing that was important; the target was less important. We laughed, ached, quarreled, and worked together.

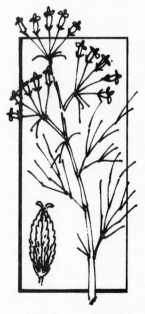

Cumin

Although there is no word in the Bible for fertilizer, in rabbinic literature dung is compared to precious stones. The Israelites gathered sheep manure by enclosing sheep in a temporary hold to collect their droppings. They mixed it with organic materials to create a soil improver—a viable fertilizer.

Quite clearly, the Hebrew farmers were advised to put back into the earth a goodly portion of what they had taken out of it. The soil improver was such a measure. It ensured the soil's fertility. They had no large tracts of farming land, so the Hebrew farmers were pushed to seek innovative ways to achieve the maximum results from their laborious efforts. They were also motivated by a sense of being on trial. Their husbandry was in the service of God. They feared his wrath lest they did not fulfill their role as keepers of his vines and tillers of his soil. Their former tribal loyalty had been based primarily on fear of the enemy and the unknown. They were now moving into a communal social experience with responsibility to God.

Beyond the practice of improving the soil, how else could farmers preserve the vitality of their limited land holdings? After extensive experimentation, the idea of farming by a system of crop rotation emerged. They changed the position of various crops each year, so that related plant types did not follow one another two years in succession. Root and leaf crops were alternated, as were grains and pulses. The remaining stalks and vines of harvested food crops were turned back into the soil, in time becoming green manure.

The advantages of crop rotation soon became visible, especially in better returns. Rotational cropping also proved to be a natural, organic form of pest control. Not all plants harbor the same potential pests, so alternating crop positions prevented leftover pest bacteria from germinating. It would seem that even the ancient Hebrew farmers were aware that preventive action was much better than trying to find a cure.

A further innovation aimed at preserving the vitality of the soil developed out of crop rotation: the Sabbath to the land. If it was commanded that man, his servant, and his beast should rest one day a week, on the seventh day, so too must people allow the land and the fields to rest once in seven years. (The Sabbatical year to the land is observed in Israel today in the religious *kibbutzim* and *moshavim*.)

The small holdings of the farmers made adherence to the principles of crop rotation and allowing the land to lay fallow difficult. But because their agrarian lifestyle was so founded on a religious code of rules, reflecting the will of God, they observed every commandment. Their feasts and festivals followed an agrarian calendar related to their agricultural labors.

Long before it was clear we would be working our land strip, I had started a compost heap—under the biblical injunction to utilize waste and because the dire period of austerity and rationing here had heightened my awareness of saving and recycling. Not a few people—mainly neighbors—were violently opposed to the creation of a compost heap. "Who needs a pile of garbage in a hot climate like ours? It will just provide incubation for all manner of flying pests, rats, scorpions, and snakes! This isn't a *kibbutz*. You can't smell up the place with rotten tomatoes! Commercial fertilizers are excellent. Why don't you use them?"

There was no compost heap in the neighborhood to which I could point to refute their negative arguments. And when I explained I was an organic gardener and wished to build an organic compost pile fashioned along biblical lines, I received neither applause nor agreement. "But this is the twentieth century," one man replied, adding, "the Israelites didn't have access to commercial fertilizers." That comment provoked me into sharper resolution. I would not yield to protests without the chance of proving my point: the importance of practicing conservation, not just in large-scale farming, but in home gardens as well. The fact that I had never made a compost heap was a well-guarded secret. Otherwise, I would have no chance of composting.

Finally, we reached a truce: we agreed upon a trial compost heap. If it stank or brought an immigration of unwelcome pests to our surroundings, I would bury the lot into the ground.

I found a good location for the great experiment in a sheltered spot against the fence, on a slight slope where the rain could easily run off. We loosened the ground, then scooped the earth out to achieve a pit-like basin. Into it we piled kitchen and garden waste; then we covered the pile with a layer of earth and watered it. I also added blood left from koshering.

The compost heap developed with many additions of organic matter and soil. We turned it once a week. When it was partially decomposed, we shoveled it down to the lower part of the slope for final decomposing. We began a new cycle of composting in the upper layer. I watched the growing heap like a mother hen. Mostly, I was on the lookout for any threatening pests. But when I saw the first worm, I called out: "Hallelujah, we've made it!" It was our heap of gold at the bottom of the garden.

In time, the doubting Thomases accepted the composted eminence within our midst. They too contributed kitchen waste and were happy to take compost to fertilize their houseplants. I was as proud as I was thrilled with the end results. Not infrequently, when asked out to dinner, I brought a bag of Wigoder compost, wrapped with a bright ribbon, as a substitute for a bottle of wine.

I have asked Geoffrey to add the following to my tombstone: "Here lies a woman who had the best compost pile in Jerusalem." Some might argue that such a boast was easily won, since there are so few compost heaps in Jerusalem.

With the soil dug and in good crumbly condition, we were ready to fortify it with our prime compost. We worked in teams of two, digging in the organic matter. No smell of manure marred our efforts. The compost smelled as fresh as old-fashioned laundry soap. I picked up a handful of the dug-up earth to examine it. It was good Jerusalem earth. We could plant in it.

As I held the earth in the palm of my hand, my thoughts raced back to another period in my life, when I stood at the graveside during the burials of my two brothers, Edmund and Robert Emmet. They had died accidentally within three years of each other. They were both in their twenties and I a teenager. Seeing each of them lowered into the cold, wet earth in St. John's cemetery had ripped open the seams of my being. The finality of their fate, before they had barely experienced life, filled me with fear and foreboding. "Tragedies run in threes," my mother was wont to say. Who, then, would be the third loss in our family? Would it be me? I hated the earth then. I threw none of it into their graves.

My hand closed on the dug-up earth it held. It didn't feel like the earth of death. It was earth teeming with life . . . millions of minute organisms moving in it. Never would I dishonor it by wearing gloves as I worked it. We would be partners. Together we would bring about a healthy garden of goodness for Zion's sake.

"What are we waiting for? Let's get on with the planting!" It was a beginning.

Not unlike the Hebrew people—who, when they had leaped out of the frying pan of the desert into the fire of the Promised Land, had faced the formidable challenge of making it on the land—I too had doubts as to whether I could achieve even a meager measure of making peace with the soil along biblical injunctions. They did, at least, inherit some guidelines from the Canaanite experience. By the time the four Wigs began their cultivation of the soil, the recently established State of Israel was well on its way to advanced innovative methods of agriculture, earning world acclaim. This was mainly accomplished in the areas of the country's milder climates, in less rocky soil than we had in Jerusalem. For me, visiting them was more inspirational than useful. They were well entrenched in the twentieth century, successfully employing modern methods of land husbandry; the Wig foursome, however, had decided to be faithful to the ground rules of ancient agriculture related to small-holdings gardening.

More than a few times I saw myself facing the three males of our family in situations not unlike Moses must have experienced when he had difficulty restraining a disgruntled lot. The Israelites apparently continued to talk about their hunger for the onions and leeks they had enjoyed eating in Egypt, adding to the day's ration of complaints about their boring diet of manna and more manna. Granted, Moses had to cope with a tribe, while my reluctant diggers were but three. Of the three, Shimshon—perhaps in association with his name (the Hebrew for Samson)—was the best digger (usually to get something out of his system). Meir, three years younger, was creative, but not short of criticism. "*Ima* (mother), can't we have a gardener like our neighbors do?" On occasion he would throw in a piercing question as to whether in New York City I had studied gardening. His skepticism about our success was apparent.

Geoffrey was the scholar in residence, to the encyclopedia born. He was a good mediator and defended my mission, even though he thought it was quite unnecessary to defend my status as a new Jew by digging up the roots of Judaism—especially so, since it involved Meir, Shimshon, and himself in a back-breaking exercise! He didn't realize how much my quest for the agrarian roots of Judaism had propelled me toward experiencing contact with the soil as a partner.

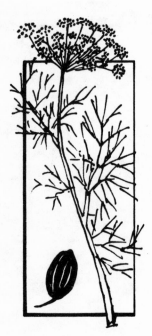

Dill

What was the divine implication inherent in the marriage of people and the land? Surely, it must be more than that the land and not the stars had given them sustenance. Beyond the seven species which the early Hebrews found in the Holy Land, there were masses of wild edible flora, just for the picking. Why were moral issues so intermingled with working the land and eating of the fruits of one's labor? Part of my coming to Israel was to find that out. I now had three people with whom I wanted to share that search.

Meanwhile, our neighborhood was experiencing radical changes. These events represented part of the post-War of Independence build-up. The small cottages of the pioneering academic elite were being replaced with cooperative housing blocks. Each morning dynamite charges, used to break up the stubborn Judean rocks, resounded like thundering alarm clocks. The thunder continued intermittently through the day until four o'clock, when the last blast went off and the workforce went home. The old-timers in the neighborhood were relieved that the deafening noise heralded progress and not the sporadic cross fire of war.

When the foundations of the housing units were laid, the next step in the construction process began: the establishment of land markers involving a long-standing Jerusalem security ploy, the erection of barbed-wire fences. (Wire did not exist when Joshua and his fellow Hebrews began their settlement on the land. Then divisions of land were marked off by stone fencing. Unearthed stones were piled one on top of the other to create both borders and enclosures to keep wandering animals at bay. No camouflage was necessary; the rich colors of the radiant limestone rocks sparkled in the sunlight.)

Barbed-wire fencing may have been necessary for security, but it did not mean that we had to live with their naked ugliness. So when Wig Planters, Limited met for our first planning session, we agreed that our first task was to cover up the barbed-wire fences. This decision was not immediately accepted by the boys, who enjoyed separating the wires as part of their strategic war games. They feared the cover-up foliage would interfere with a fast retreat (never mind that they ripped their trousers in the jump).

The question was, which biblical plants would suit the part? These choices would have to be determined by what existed on the other side of the wire demarcation—that is, in our neighbor's garden. For instance, in the area facing east a parade of domineering pine trees confronted us and our scheming. Planted by the early Beit HaKerem settlers, they were selected as sunshades. Alas, their prize pine nuts never fell in our direction; only their acid pine needles carpeted our ground. Our choices would have to be able to survive as greenies only, or with some color. Acid-demanding plants could not be utilized, either because they were not biblical plants or because they couldn't tolerate hot weather. Showoffs like camelias, azelias, and rhododendrons rarely survive here.

My working partners were rather short on patience, mostly because they had other plans or just wanted to get on with the job. How fast- or slow-growing an eligible climber, shrub, or bush was soon became a factor. My declared principle to grow plants from seeds in true horticulture practice was another even more important consideration, because we were establishing a biblically based garden. The Israelites planted from seeds or from cuttings; no instant methods existed for them.

The exchange of glances among the three reluctant diggers was grave. If I hoped to sustain the group gardening idea, a compromise was inevitable. "Perhaps you might ask among your friends for some cuttings or seedlings. I would accept that," I said. Toward this goal Shimshon and Meir set out on a treasure hunt, explaining with some embarrassment that their mother wouldn't agree to buy ready-to-plant seedlings from a nursery. Their social contacts came in good stead (helped along by the years their friends had enjoyed my cakes and biscuits). It was a bartering binge: plants for toys or costumes for Purim, Israel's dress-up holiday, and, of course, a promise of their mother's gold compost.

It wasn't long before we had a treasure-trove of cuttings, seedlings, and bulbs—not all identified, but welcome nevertheless. "We can start our own plant nursery," Shimshon suggested. The cover-up action could now begin. I tried to separate them according to season and happy-state growing, so that the wire fences would show color all year round. We prepared the soil and then planted yellow winter jasmine (*J. nudiflorum*), passion fruit (*Passiflora grandilla*), trumpet flower (*Bignonia grandiflora*), paper flower (*Bougainvillea glabra*), honeysuckle (*Lonicera japonica*), English ivy (*Hedera helix*), and morning glory (*Ipomoea purpurea*). They all held their ground against the giant pine trees and stately cypresses.

The real challenge was to find plants that would stand up to the chief garden thief, the eucalyptus trees (*E. camaldulensis*). It was our bad luck that this pompous "euc," one of the most popular trees in the world, had been planted in our garden. A veritable social climber, eager to rise in the world, given the right conditions it could stretch up 80 to 120 feet. When it passed my height, 5 feet 10 inches, and Geoffrey's 6 feet, I was tempted to resort to insecticide to stunt its growth. Alas, we had inherited a baker's dozen of these monsters! Not only are they water drunks, they are in perpetual motion—dropping their leaves all over the place, spitting out their kernels, and then shedding a shower of yellow fuzz all over a newly raked area.

Every couple of years, in the ongoing effort to make things grow in the area of the "eucs," Geoffrey and the lads labored to dig up their roots, sawing them into segregation. We only slightly stunted their growth in that exercise. However, it was an opportunity to aerate the soil and to pitch out the rocks among the roots of plants near by. Seeing so many rocks and stones in varying sizes and shapes, we hit upon the idea of making rockeries at the foot of the "eucs."

Actually, I saw the opportunity to imitate the historical method that had been employed by the early Israelites in their dramatic hill terracing. The difference lay in the formation of our rockeries, which consisted of stones removed from the earth. The hill terracing had been accomplished by hollowing out the natural stepped limestone surfaces to form foundations for the terraces, which in turn were reinforced by a retaining wall. Behind the wall were nested layers of gravel and soil.

Terracing had been conceived out of a dire necessity to minimize hillside erosion caused by the heavy rains, which otherwise would run down into the sea. Without terracing, edible flora could not have grown, nor would the inhabitants of Judea have been free from hunger.

We, on the other hand, used shapely rocks to achieve a vertical dimension in the garden's composition. And because, from an early age, Meir expressed his view of life visually, the rockeries were saved from looking like a pile of discarded stones and we achieved a sculptured grouping. We carefully positioned the large, age-old rocks. We filled the empty spaces between the rocks with a planting mixture of sand, compost, and earth. We created raised-bed planting nests, not unlike those used in terracing. Shimshon suggested planting small plants in the many deep holes of the ancient rocks. Here small flowering succulents jutted out like a nosegay.

After we constructed three rockeries, we rested. In our next planning session we chose plants to grace the rocky sculptures. We agreed to use herbs and spices mentioned in the Bible. We would not attempt to group them according to the purest approach; how they looked in the rockery was of prime importance for Meir and myself, and also how they would fare. So we chose the candidates without consideration of their culinary or medicinal use, or perfumed scent.

Geoffrey's talent for game making cast the physical chores into the realm of sportsmanship. With a list of potential candidates, I began the roll call of herbal old-timers. Geoffrey interrupted, "Wait, let's try selecting a herb and a spice related to a biblical description of its growing habit or folklore association."

"What do you mean exactly?" asked Shimshon.

"Well, let's see, what about a herb you enjoy eating almost every day with *tahini* and *hummus?*" No response.

"What do Arab farmers eat in the fields for their morning break, like Western people enjoy coffee or tea and cake?" I asked.

"Oh, you mean *za'atar*," Shimshon and Meir answered in unison.

"That's it—and in English it is hyssop." Geoffrey continued, "And what about its growing style?"

"Was it Solomon who spoke about the stately cedars of Lebanon and the hyssop that springeth out of the wall?" Shimshon asked.

"But they are different," Meir remarked, "The cedar is so tall and hyssop is a lowly plant. Was he saying that small things are also big? After all, cedars are not native to Israel, really, and you can't eat them. But *za'atar*, everyone loves to eat that."

So that earned hyssop a distinguished location in the rockeries, placed high up so it could jut out as it does together with the other six wild plants growing in the Western Wall. Then came coriander, second only to salt in biblical importance. "But it smells like soap," Meir groaned. "So don't smell it," advised Geoffrey, who also disliked coriander. (I had anticipated hostility toward this plant. It was only by camouflage and deception that I managed to sneak this parsley-like plant into cooking, especially Chinese cooking, which the family enjoyed. Eventually, I revealed that it was the fresh coriander— Chinese parsley—which gave the food its special taste.)

Chickpea

"But beyond an unpleasant smell, with what do you associate it?" Geoffrey continued. "I guess manna, but who knows what that is. We learned in school that manna tasted like coriander seed," Shimshon answered. "I don't mind the seeds," Meir replied. "It's the stinky leaves that smell up the refrigerator."

Not without more criticism, I did manage to win that choice. The game of herbs and spices and their biblical association continued until we cast the rockery plants in dramatic settings suitable to their growing habits. And in time they grew well and multiplied, and seasoned our meals.

Today, the cast of characters in our Herb and Spice Rock Show includes sage, caraway, thyme, garlic, chives, wild fennel, scented pelargonium, lavender, mint, nasturtium, and sorrel.

Not long after we planted the rockeries, my attention was drawn to a bush that seemed more weed than worthwhile plant. From time to time I had cut it down, but now it was growing along the row of eucalyptus trees. This must be a stubborn shrub, I thought. None of our neighbors could identify it. "If it bothers you, we can uproot it," Geoffrey suggested. I hesitated, probably out of respect for the plant's capacity to survive in spite of the greediness and shade of the "eucs." When it grew to the point of shading the second story of the neighboring block of flats, it became, for me, a protected species. I decided to have a word with it. "Listen, nameless, it seems you are happy growing here, so I have decided to welcome you to this problem-ridden garden. Be my guest! You'll be one more tree to cope with."

One day, after a heavy rainfall I noticed that our guest was adorned with clusters of small, yellow flowers—obviously, it was producing a bouquet of appreciation of my formal acceptance of its presence. Upon inspecting the flowers, I became aware of a fragrance that was pungent yet slightly sweet. Crushing a leaf between my palms, I became excited and called to Geoffrey, "It's a bay leaf tree and it's flowering!" How it arrived in the garden, I don't know. The *Laurus nobilis* does seed, as we saw. The flowers are followed by purple berries, but were unlikely to germinate except very slowly. And although the tree tends to sucker easily, I had not planted a sweet bay sucker. Whichever course brought it to the garden, it was truly welcome. Later, I successfully planted suckers in a container and pruned it into a formal shape. It joined the growing cover-up crowd, plucked for use in many culinary dishes: soups, stews, spaghetti sauce, and stuffings. We gave ribbon-tied branches as gifts to hang up in the kitchen.

We continued the cover-up action by planting a row of bushes in front of the covered wire fences. Old-fashioned hollyhocks (*Alcea rosea*) joined the cover-ups in the rear of the garden. Their pink, red, and white flowers bloomed in late summer when color was needed. Along the same line they blended with the oleander (*Nerium oleander*), which some people reject because the plants are poisonous when eaten. Israeli children are soon taught not to taste the milky white substance contained in their stems. They were fine looking in front of the pine trees, and grew tall enough so that their flowers blocked out the sight of dry, dying pine branches.

Continuing on that side of the garden we also planted a sumac tree (*Rhus coriaria*). It takes some time for the tree to produce seeds. These are mixed with *za'atar* for a biting taste, in contrast to the sesame seed-*za'atar* mixture.

The English ivy evergreen vine has served us well, covering fences and as a ground cover in places where no other plants grew. Always green and attractive in hanging baskets on a terrace, it also covers poorly finished outside building walls. So, in time, we did achieve a thriving green background, accented by flowering bushes and climbing roses—and, of course, our old friends the blackberry vines.

The wilderness that had greeted us was slowly taking on a groomed and cultivated look. Contributing to the landscape were the fruit trees we had planted before we embarked on the Bible belt. Geoffrey's first choice was an unbiblical peach tree, which we planted together. The lads were too small then to be of much help—except, of course, in eating the peaches. My choice was a lemon tree. I wanted to experience the excitement of going out to pick a lemon. I cooked with lemons and lemon juice, and used the leaves in preserves, stews, and cooked stuffed vine leaves. Later we planted an olive and fig to round off the five fruit trees belonging to the Seven Species. Earlier, the House Committee had planted pomegranate trees and one date palm. It has never born fruit; I suppose it is sex-starved because of its single state.

Meir wanted to plant a loquat tree (*Eriobotrya japonica*) from the seeds he had saved and potted. It seemed unlikely that it would do more than send up a few shoots. We were proved wrong. Though slightly acid, the fruit was nicely aromatic and sweet enough to eat. The tree branches were heavy with big leaves, and we learned that it was necessary to prune so light could enter the interior of the tree. The decorative leaves in flower arrangements are especially attractive because the berry clusters contrast with the leathery leaves. We also planted native white mulberry (*Morus alba*), Japanese quince (*Cydonia vulgaris*), and more grapevines trained over a trellis.

In the mid-1960s I was writing my book, *Hope Is My House*, in the studio of Ruth Levin, the Israeli painter. Her small, charming, limestone house was in the village of Ein Karem, just outside Jerusalem, where many immigrants from North Africa and Yemen had settled. One November morning I heard an impatient loud knock on the door. It was Ezra, a neighbor. "Devorah, come quickly, I need your help." I sensed the urgency of his request, and followed him in the direction of his house; but he made it clear we were going further on.

When we reached a clearing along an old terrace hill, he pointed to a hoe: "Look, it's going to rain tomorrow or the next day. I must get these lentils planted before the rain comes. Please help me." Handing me the hoe, he said: "I've dug up the ground once, now make a furrow along the marked line. I will follow and plant the seed!"

I was twice his size, so I suppose he thought I was twice as strong. As I started hoeing, he coached me. "Not so deep, just keep opening the soil and pushing it aside. I'll plant the seeds." I did as I was instructed, feeling some back-breaking aches. Later, I raised my head and saw that he didn't have a small packet of seeds—he had a sizeable sack! "Ezra, let's change jobs; my back is aching." Reluctantly, he agreed.

The next morning I heard another knock. It was Ezra, full of smiles: "You see, it's raining. Your good deed brought down the rain." He offered me a small glass of brandy to bless the event, and gave me a bag of green lentils.

I cut short my writing that day, and when the children came home from school I related the story. I made a quick meal in the blender to keep their hunger at bay, and then said, "Come on, fellow planters, there's a break in the rain; we can plant the lentils." They caught the excitement. Out we went to plant the green lentils. The ground had already been prepared, so we were able to work quickly, finishing the job in one hour. Just as we were entering the house, the rain started again. I looked up at the sky and shouted, "Thanks, all contributions gratefully received!"

In the days to come, we planted chickpeas and broad beans, plants that did not need seed-box incubation. We were well on our way with another portion of the biblical plant project. However, we had not as yet started at the beginning: that is, seed planting. I consoled myself that Moses too must have made a few strategic detours in his shepherding of the Hebrew people across Sinai. I would have to be forgiven for allowing the male trinity of the Wig Planters, Limited to lead me down the garden path away from the basic principles of gardening from scratch—in this case, seeds. Catching the mood of personal disappointment, the boys chimed in, saying, "We have planted a lot and it meant working hard. You should feel happy and not guilty."

They were right. Our garden was beginning to have character and composition. The lentil shoots were showing, chickpeas were asserting themselves, and millet was making an effort to get into the act. The barbed wire was less visible, and all manner of tree world seemed to bask in contentment.

"Well, gentlemen, if you want to help me overcome my sense of guilt as diagnosed by Shimshon (the future psychologist), let's go back to the planning board and move on to the next stage. It must start with seeding in preparation for planting vegetables." Geoffrey and Shimshon volunteered to do the digging when the seedlings were ready. This left Meir and myself with the responsibility for getting boxes to start the seed process.

We didn't find commercially prepared flats; but when we took a walk through the neighborhood in search of throwaways, we collected an assortment of discarded kitchen-cabinet drawers, orange crates, and broken boxes. They were far from the conventional oblong fourteen-by-twenty-four-inch shallow boxes; but Meir was game to convert them into seed containers resembling photos he had seen in a magazine.

Of course, this entailed buying some work tools not included in our sparse tool chest. From then on, the sound of sawing was heard in the air, followed by a driving hammering as Meir made holes for drainage. Actually, I found that double egg trays made very effective seed containers. Once I pushed a small nail through the porous material, the trays were vented enough for drainage. They were also deep enough for the small seeds of such herbs as dill, cumin, and garden cress.

Fig

We prepared our own seed mixture using one part garden earth, one part sand, and one part well-sifted compost. It was all well mixed in a bucket and ready to use. It smelled deliciously fresh. We were then set to fill the boxes. We followed the accepted practice of lining the boxes with newspapers. A good part of our newsprint, including the prestigious London *Times*, found its way into the compost pile. We also lined the seed flats with newspapers. The next step was to sift the seeding mix into the seed box. Meir then firmed it with a strip of wood until it was evenly flattened. Now we carefully broadcast the seeds over the surface and pressed them in gently with the strip of wood. We soaked the filled flat in water and then let it drain off. We planted the seeds in shallow furrows and pressed them into the soil, mindful that the furrows should be of the right depth to accommodate the size of the seed, and placed them well apart for quicker germination. We covered the flat with a double sheet of newspaper and placed it in a protected place.

We watched the seedlings develop, and at a given point we thinned them out. Meir wasn't entirely convinced that this was a good idea. He was sure the remaining seedlings would suffer. I reminded him that biblical commentary was replete with references pertaining to the successful farming methods employed by the early Israelites. They planted fewer seeds in one furrow than their neighbors ever seeded. In addition, they thinned out the seedlings according to fixed percentage rates of thinning. This method ensured that the remaining seedlings would be strong and viable. (Later, when we planted lettuce, we enjoyed the thinnings and used them for last-minute garnish.) So there we were, right on track. When the seedlings were strong enough, we transplanted them into the garden.

Transplanting was tricky. It took a few failures before we learned the best way to transfer seedlings from the seed box to the open ground with some of our gold compost. First we tried using a cake spatula to separate the seedlings, but this didn't work for me. I found that gently taking the seedlings out of the box with my fingers (I enjoy the contact with the earth) worked best. Even though some earth was lost in this way, the roots were less disturbed. Meir liked to firm the soil around the root with an unsharpened pencil, once he had dug a bedding hole. We scooped out some of the earth around the planted seedling to create a basin for watering. For me, this was the nicest part of gardening. It was like following a complicated cooking recipe. I'm sure the early Israelites prayed for good growing. I did too—and said aloud, "Well, greenies, you're on your own now. Good luck." We had good luck in planting cabbage, chard, lettuce, cucumbers, herbs, melons, turnips, gourds for fun, sunflowers, and radishes. From tubers and bulbs we grew Jerusalem artichokes and members of the onion family: scallions, garlic, shallots, chives, and leeks.

The jubilant excitement that attended each harvest in ancient times was not possible for us, since the limitations of our garden space did not allow us to grow barley or wheat. However, we had enjoyed the fruits of our labor in an ongoing parade of pickings. Some of them we consumed raw, and others enriched the cuisine of the Wigs of the biblical cabbage patch. Fresh herbs especially and newly picked vegetables brought to the cooking cauldron an almost indescribable flavor. Eating our first fruits from the pomegranate tree and sharing them with friends enriched us beyond any monetary value. Also, we knew that what we were eating was wholesome and spray-free. What we produced may not have won us prizes in gardening competitions, but considering our handicaps we felt like winners.

Probably the most satisfying harvest we experienced was picking the five bitter herbs from our garden on Passover eve. At the seder we offered our guests a choice of one or more of the bitter herbs listed by the rabbis as valid.

In our attempt to create a Bible-based garden, we benefited from the hard-earned experience of the Hebrew people—especially in the concept that if a thing is worth doing, it is worth doing properly. No shortcuts were acceptable in successful soil and plant management. Poor harvests and diseased crops were the only returns.

The Wigs too soon learned that you only realize results in proportion to your input. How much more this applied in small planting areas! We looked back on the Israelite history of crop rotation, and found two systems that easily applied to our gardening situation. First, following every harvesting or picking, we could turn discarded stalks and vines back into the soil as a form of green manure. Second, crop rotation had proved effective in two ways: one, annually changing the position of various crops, especially those soil-improving plants, was a form of fertilizer; two, not all plants share the same potential pests. Changing planting locations prevented leftover bacteria from germinating. We did this with our root vegetables, which rarely suffered disease or pests.

I used garlic, nasturtiums, and tegettes in pest control. It didn't bother me to mix plants, vegetables, and flowers. The visual effect was charming, and the vegetables benefited from the floral pest deterrent in their midst. When we could we left a plot or two to rest, only digging in compost.

As the trunks of the "eucs" developed their middle-aged spread, the roots underneath them reached out for moisture and nutrients, attaining giant proportions. The trees waved in the wind and cracked their nuts all over the place. One winter we were blessed with two snow storms. Meir photographed the snow-laden branches, which even I had to admit were beautiful to behold. During the night the high wind rose to alarming proportions. A terrible cracking sound outside our window ended in a crash. Rushing out to the terrace to observe what had happened, we saw that two enormous eucalyptus branches had fallen. One had landed on a neighbor's fence and the other lay prostrate across our garden. "Hallelujah!" I called out.

"What happened?" the lads asked.

"Behold," I answered, "the enemy has suffered a serious blow."

We "mercifully" finished off two of the monsters. However, there were still ten left. From then on, I prayed for snow.

Eventually, unlike the ancient Hebrew people, we stumbled on container gardening. We placed the containers in the eucalyptus area and on our terrace, which was big enough to accommodate a selection of fairly large pots and containers. The controlled healthy environment in the containers lowered weather risks and eliminated the problem of intruding roots.

I was and am a heavy user of herbs and spices in cooking, and I wanted them to be within easy reach for picking near the kitchen. The kitchen terrace window ledge was long enough to support a selection of culinary herbs: mint, parsley, garlic chives, onion, shallots, sage, coriander, and lemon balm. The larger herbs and spices did well in the garden. We dried and bottled them to sit on the kitchen shelf.

Container gardening is a wonderful remedy for people who live in apartments and dream of having a herb garden. You can do it even if your windows face north. Good lighting during four or five hours a day is a must for many culinary and ornamental herbs. But plants like chervil, mint, and lemon balm manage well without sun but in good light. If resting space is not available but sunlight comes through a kitchen window, put the plants in a basket hung from the ceiling or a wall bracket. The plants will thrive if the ventilation is good and the plants are fertilized once in ten days.

We live on the ground floor, surrounded by trees. Our light is poor. I use ordinary fluorescent light to grow shade-loving plants in the living room and in the bathroom, which doesn't receive continuous light. Wandering Jew (*Zebrina pendula*), cast iron plant (*Aspidistra elatior*), and snake plant (*Sansevieria trifasciata*) all do well (in fact, Wandering Jew seems to have settled down in Israel!). They certainly brighten the rooms. I sometimes jazz them up with colorful dried flowers. Giving the plants an airing from time to time also encourages their growth. So much oxygen is removed from our habitats. There's no substitute for fresh air which, after light, is the lifeline for thriving plants. An important advantage of container gardening is mobility. Containers placed on wheel-bases can easily be moved to better light.

Almost every home garden has better or lesser areas of productivity, depending on factors the home gardener cannot always control. We experienced results that disappointed us, but which we had to accept. Even industrialized agriculture using modern methods does not always succeed. So what is the alternative? Surrender and allow nature to take over the garden undisturbed? Let the weeds win out?

A visitor to our garden once exclaimed, "Devorah, how charming. It's like a forest here!" I wanted to throw a stinkweed in her direction, but demurely replied, "Thanks, we're trying to grow vegetables!" To some extent, however, she was right. Especially in the evening, when the garden was illuminated, one had the feeling that nothing existed beyond the eye's view. No visible boundaries, only woods beyond the geraniums at the foot of the garden.

In time we even planted a lawn, although of no English carpeting quality; in fact, as the "eucs" became more aggressive, we eventually had to resort to *Dichondra carolinensis*, which was not a hardship (just not as good for rolling in as Bermuda grass).

About that time calls went out from the Ministry of Agriculture to discourage home vegetable growing. Agriculture was doing well in the country. "So, ladies, buy your greens rather than grow them!" Of course, that might have

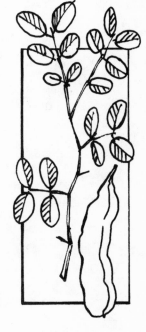

Carob, Locust Bean

been a legitimate out for some people. However, the wise men in the ministry overlooked the fact that one doesn't necessarily grow greens for the purpose of saving money.

They were probably desk-bound decision makers allergic to the earth and green growing things. They missed the point of personal satisfaction one enjoys in gardening, and the exhilarating experience of going out in a lovely morning to pick garden-fresh spinach, parsley, scallions, or berries for breakfast. All these are grown by the gardener with loving care in a good marriage with nature.

We did, of course, adjust our list of priorities, still holding on for the most part to biblically identified plants. After all, our initial intention to make a viable, Bible-based garden had been realized. We were not committed to continuing the exercise for life. In fact, some members of the Wig Planters, Limited were quite ready to abdicate in favor of outside hired labor, namely, a gardener. To support their request they would pledge themselves to shop for fruit and vegetables.

Their point was not taken because we had failed, although in some instances we did. We failed to understand that nature had a will of its own. And it would seem that certain higher elements in the hierarchy had not been briefed concerning a special project in progress down there on earth, outside the City of Jerusalem, in Beit HaKerem. There a spirited woman, her two sons, and her husband were trying their hands at making peace with the soil, in a manner that another group of *nouveau* farmers had tried during the ancient Israelite settlement. But it had been expected that in view of the group's good intentions and their lack of know-how, some consideration should be given them, particularly in the variables of wind and rain.

One day, out of the blue—in this case, out of an assembly of threatening black cloud formations—there sounded an angry clap of thunder. The neighborhood of Beit HaKerem was alarmed. And more so when the accompanying rainfall bordered on the torrential. Our newly planted garden stretch was flooded beyond recognition; the young seedlings of cress, dill, and cumin were washed into the sewer. It was of no consolation to the Wig Planters that the seasonal rainfall was premature, nor that the velocity of the wind had made history in that subtropical climate. The mother sharecropper nearly went into shock.

The next time round we took a low iron frame (once the base of an impractical glass-topped coffee table) and set it over the new seedlings. We fastened a net cover over it. When rain seemed ruinous, we added an awning-type covering.

In time, we realized that the conditions of our cabbage patch were best suited to sturdy root vegetable crops, plus the onion range of vegetables. We planted delicate herbs in containers; the robust herbal plants like hyssop, rosemary, lavender, and sage we planted in borders. We fortified cucumbers and melons by growing them against fences and house walls.

Hardy vegetables weren't among the lads' favorites anyway. Not wanting to use the hackneyed ploy, "Eat them, they're good for you," I reminded them instead that we had grown them and that they were biblical. Eventually, I learned to cook turnips in six enticing ways.

With all our ups and downs, our garden was a success. Each of us discovered a viable connection with the land and our own roots. For me, it was a personal objective linked to my conversion and attraction to the agrarian roots of Jewish life. I would love to have lived in the early Israelite period, when a moral social structure seemed to be developing parallel with human husbandry and especially respect for the soil.

Geoffrey would never be a farmer, but he was sympathetic to my motivation in introducing our sons to an exercise in creating by hand a land of green, growing things. They would learn from this some of the earth's secrets and how we, the planters, could communicate with it, being as we are between heaven and earth. Adam and Eve were placed in a garden, not on a satellite, and the story went on from there.

Each one in some way experienced a sense of partnership with the natural order of living things, and their value. We sensed the seasons and their return; the constant and the unexpected; the incongruous riddle of why some seeds in a row germinate and others do not, even though the prevailing conditions are constant. In gardening there is the gentle reminder of one's minor role in the greater scheme of continuity, and yet the calamity if one had missed being party to that meager role.

We did more than plant a Bible-based garden in the City of Jerusalem: We planted ourselves in it, and we rooted each one of us to the other.

3 HERBS AND SPICES

❦ ❦ ❦

Better a meal of herbs where love is, than a fatted ox and hatred therewith.

(Proverbs 15:17)

A nation's historical past is not only ascertained in remnants of its pottery, sculpture, woven fabrics, and paintings, it is also measured by the character of its flora. Biblical references to plants number but 100; but the rabbinical work the *Mishna*, compiled in Palestine in the second century, mentions 180 plants belonging to 115 families. Among them are herbs and spices long associated with the human history of the Land of the Bible.

Herbs are described botanically as one of the herbaceous plants which are used as a flavoring, scent, or for medicinal purposes. These include annuals and perennials whose leaves, blossoms, and soft stems are edible. Their primary use in biblical times was medicinal, with specific use as cures and preventive applications. Even today in Israel, if you ask an old-timer about a particular herb or spice, the first response will deal with the plant's capacity to aid digestion, improve concentration, cleanse blood, or regulate the bowels.

According to the Book of Jubilees 10:12, the angels revealed special remedies to Noah, who recorded them in a book. In olden times, books of remedies were kept by families who had learned from generation to generation which plants, trees, and roots were available for specific applications. In rabbinical commentary, as many as seventy plants were indicated as having medicinal use. These included plants that were also food providers: olives, dates, pomegranates, and quinces; garlic, beets, hyssop, cumin, and fennel-flower.

The Bible does not give a specific word for spices. Biblical commentary also does not clearly define spices, except as "food improvers." This is a far cry from today's identification of spices as being aromatic vegetable products derived from the bark, root, fruit, or berry of perennial plants, used as a flavoring or a condiment in foods and drinks.

Most of the important spice trees do not grow in Israel. Cinnamon, nut-

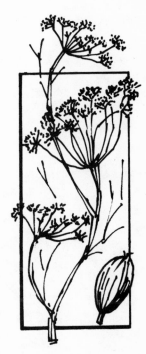

Fennel

meg, and clove trees demand a hot, wet habitat (in contrast to Israel's climate, which is either hot and dry or cold and wet).

Spices are used for religious purposes, especially as incense. The Temple itself was perfumed with aromatic spices. Spices were stuffed into the carcasses of animals being offered for sacrifice to counter the smell of burning flesh, which was thought to be offensive to God. It was customary to inhale fragrant spices to round off a meal, not unlike the way smokers enjoy smoking a cigar or cigarette at the end of a meal.

When meat, poultry, or cheeses were absent from a meal, the cook embellished the vegetables with seasonings to give the illusion of a richer meal. Of course, the role of spices in food preservation was significant. Salt was the greatest ally, and gave rise to all sorts of recipes for pickling and salting meat, poultry, fish, and vegetables. Later, an acquired taste for pickled food led people to preserve food out of choice.

Rabbinical commentary refers to "food-improvers," which both preserve and improve the taste of foods. This was often necessary in a land of scanty resources to mask the taste of food that had spoiled. Gradually, more emphasis was put on flavoring and condiments for their own sake.

Not infrequently, conquering armies came to the Holy Land accompanied by their chefs, who brought their preferred spices and herbs and seeds to plant. In addition to the locally available flavoring stocks, they could cultivate their own favorites. The Romans came with a storehouse of seeds suitable for a Mediterranean climate, but not indigenous to the Holy Land. The Romans were quick to boast that they had no need of doctors; their knowledge of herbs and spices for medicinal purposes was sufficient for cures. Basil and oregano were among the seeds they brought.

The Persians brought the cultivated rose, called *Varda*. They made rose water, rose syrup, and rose petal jam from a choice variety of red and pink roses.

Let us now look at the aristocrats: the herbs and spices popular in the Land of the Bible. They have been around for centuries, and many of them are used today. Not a few of them have found their way to other lands and kitchens.

A SHORT LIST
OF HERBS AND SPICES

Allspice (*Pimenta diocia*)

Allspice is not native to Israel, but it is one of the most important spices in Middle Eastern cooking. It is native to Jamaica, and is one of the few spice trees to have originated in the Western hemisphere. The dried and unripe fruit of this tree, also called "green pimenta," tastes like a mix of cinnamon, cloves, and nutmeg. Allspice combines with foods to yield an aroma that enhances the taste of the dishes prepared with it. As the aroma fills the kitchen, impatience grows to taste the contents of the pot.

In Israel allspice is especially popular in rice-based dishes, particularly rice-stuffed vegetables. In fact, any long-cooking dish benefits from allspice. It is less used in puddings and pies; but the returning Jews to Israel, whether from the Far East or the West, reach for allspice-enhanced chutney or genuine ketchup as an accent to eating.

Anise (*Pimpinella anisum*)

The authorized version of the translation of Matthew 2:23 speaks of "Tithe of mint and anise and cumin." However, the botanists conclude that anise is a mistranslation, and that the reference applies to dill (*Anethum graveolens*). Certainly, at a later period, anise was cultivated and even grew wild in the Holy Land. Its leaves are used in salads, and its seeds for flavoring cookies, pastries, and confections. Anise is the flavor that distinguishes Arak, one of the most popular drinks in Israel and throughout the Middle East.

Basil (*Ocimum basilicum*)

There are dozens of different species of basil, annuals and perennials, flowering in colors ranging from white to purple. The well-known sweet basil grows easily in gardens or in containers on terraces (but don't fertilize the plants, because in so doing flavor is lost). Basil has become associated with tomatoes and tomato sauces; it sweetens tomatoes during cooking.

The treasured perennial oriental basil, whose scent and taste far exceed that of sweet basil, is sold in Israeli markets on Wednesdays. It was brought to Israel in the pockets of Yemenite Jews, who were part of an airlift operation called the Magic Carpet during the early days of Israel's statehood: The husbands carried the old family possessions related to religious observance; the women filled their pockets with their treasured spices and seeds. One of the seeds was for beautiful flowering basil plants to decorate their homes on the eve of the Sabbath, in case the "Promised Land" did not include them. In time, neighbors and friends were fortunate enough to receive a supply of these seeds. The lucky ones eventually discovered the use of this basil in cooking.

Bay Leaves (*Laurus nobilis*)

The edible bay leaf comes from the laurel tree, mentioned in Isaiah 44:14, which grows happily in the hilly areas of Israel. Though not indigenous to Israel, bay leaf is a seasoning of major importance.

Bay leaves have long been used for flavoring and preserving, and are essential in a bouquet garni. They are slow to emit their oils and so are valued in slow-cooking dishes such as soups, casseroles, and stews. A bay leaf at the bottom of a paté basin, a meat loaf pan, or in a pan used to roast poultry, gives a special aroma to the meat. Also, its pungent scent will ward off the disapproval of those people who dislike the smell of certain kinds of fish. Scattered over barbecue coals, bay leaves will enhance the flavor of foods on the grill.

Finely ground bay leaves improve the flavor of custards and milk puddings. They are recommended for sick or convalescent people whose appetite has to be encouraged.

Capers (*Capparis spinosa*)

The flowering caper plant is of rare beauty, displaying a prism of colors on string-like petals. It grows among the rocks and walls of Israel, including the Western Wall, and in mountainous terrain. Ecclesiastes 12:5 speaks of the caper's fruit: "And the almond-tree shall blossom . . . and the caperberry shall fail; Because man goeth to his long home . . ." This symbolizes the shortness of human life, because soon after the plant blossoms the seeds are scattered and the flowering part of the plant dies.

Fortunately, the plant produces new fruit every day. One picks the flower buds when they are quite young, and pickles them in salt and vinegar. When the plant completes its flowering it develops a small, cucumber-type fruit pod, which is also pickled and considered a delicacy.

Caraway (*Carum carvi*)

The caraway plant is in the parsley family. It was known to the early rabbis as a vegetable whose leaves and roots were eaten. Their pungent taste is not as sharp as that of the seeds, which today are more prized. Some people use them as an aid to digestion.

Caraway seeds can flavor preparations as disparate as soups and liqueurs. Jewish rye bread in particular owes its special taste to caraway seeds. *Kummel* is the German name for the seeds introduced by German immigrants to Israel.

Cardamom (*Elettaria cardamomum*)

Amomum, a plant similar to cardamom that belongs to the ginger family, is mentioned in commentaries on the Bible as belonging to the group of spice-greens. The cardamom seed belongs to a tropical East Indian plant, and is one of the oldest known spices.

Cardamom seeds are associated with cakes, apple pies, and desserts in many countries; in Israel their main use is to flavor Bedouin coffee. Cardamom is an indispensable ingredient of curry, and is used in Middle Eastern cooking, especially with fruit. Cardamom seeds are often the second most expensive spice in the world, second only to saffron. The high cost of the spice arises because the pods that encase the seed have to be picked off by hand with the aid of scissors. It is a slow process, which at best yields a limited return. But the haunting aroma of freshly ground cardamom seeds, for whatever use, make good cooks grateful for the hands that pluck the pods.

Cayenne (*Capsicum annuum*)

This perennial plant is not mentioned in the Bible, but in Israel it grows in abundance. It produces red, orange, and yellow pods, which when ground are known as chili pepper or cayenne pepper. Garlands of the young peppers are hung on terraces and kitchen windowsills to dry in the sun. Many people use them instead of black peppercorns, which are considered an unnecessary extravagance.

Israeli Jews from India, Yemen, and Morocco use cayenne pepper to give

Caper

a characteristic sharpness to their sauces. The fresh, green cayenne peppers, whose pods are less fiery, can be picked and served whole with olives and radishes as an hors d'oeuvre, to get the digestive juices going.

The plant is sometimes confused with *Capisicum minimum*, a highly pungent fruit that is milder than cayenne. It is used in a favorite Lebanese spice bouquet, which combines two parts sweet pepper, paprika, and *Capisicum minimum* with two parts cinnamon.

Cloves (*Eugenia caryophgllata*)

Cloves are the name of the unopened flower bud of a small evergreen tree belonging to the myrtle family. The buds are gathered by hand, dried, and sold whole or ground for culinary purposes.

The clove tree grows wild in the Spice Islands. It is not mentioned in the Bible, but it has long served the peoples of the Land of the Bible both in medicinal and culinary use. Unfortunately, many people associate the scent and taste of clove with dentists and doctors because clove oil is a local anesthetic.

Called "nail" in some languages, cloves have been used to season cakes and spike wines, and in marinades for game and poultry and pickled fruit. Clove-studded oranges are used as pomanders to give forth a fragrant odor capable of repelling insects and perfuming cupboards.

Coriander (*Coriandrum sativum*)

Biblically, coriander is second in importance only to salt. It is probably the oldest recorded herb, going back to 5000 b.c. Its seeds are likened to manna in Exodus 16:31 and Numbers 11:7. Coriander is indigenous to the Holy Land. In ancient times coriander seeds were exported, and used as barter against the import of spices not indigenous to Israel.

Coriander belongs to the parsley family. Many people are familiar only with the seeds, which are used in curry powders, perfume, cordials, and candy. But the pungent leaves, which may initially put some people off, are used in soups and stews, and to garnish many dishes. It is very important in Chinese, Indian, and Mexican cooking, and has long been praised as an aid to digestion.

Cumin (*Cuminum cyminum*)

An ancient plant of the parsley family, cumin was one of the popular herbs exported from the Land of Israel, being of superior quality to cumin grown in neighboring countries. "It was important enough to pay the tithe" (Matthew 23:23). Essentially, it was used for medicinal purposes, especially to stop bleeding caused during circumcision.

Although cumin has long been associated with caraway seed, it has a distinctly different taste and appearance. Generally held as the best appetizer flavoring of all condiments, it enhances a wide variety of foods and liqueurs: cheeses, cabbage, rice, curries, and salads. Probably the most used spice in Israel, cumin is added to ground beef for kebabs and in rice and vegetable stuffing. Cumin competes with sesame seeds as a topping for baked pastries and bread doughs.

Dill (*Anethum graveolens*)

The origin of dill is not known, but it is described in a papyrus dating back to 1536 B.C., where it is suggested as an aid against headaches. It is thought that dill seeds were brought by the Israelites to the Promised Land after the Exodus from Egypt. Dill is not an easy plant to grow, but is worth including in your herb garden. Actually, its popularity today is so great in Israel that vegetable suppliers keep the supply coming throughout the year. Dill freezes well after being rinsed and patted dry, and can then be used in soups and sauces.

Dill's distinctive flavor is a mixture of anise, parsley, and celery, with a stimulating aroma that suggests mint, citrus, and fennel. No wonder it has a secure place in culinary tradition! In Scandinavia, Central Europe, and the Mediterranean area, it is used for pickling.

To store fresh dill, place branches of dill in an airtight container in the refrigerator. It will remain fresh for weeks.

Fennel (*Foeniculum vulgare*)

Fennel is related to dill; it grows wild in Israel. It was used extensively in the time of Jesus, when its young, feathery leaves were gathered for salads. However, it is the seed that has served humankind for centuries and given inspiration to poet and prophet. Seeds, leaves, and root have been used to make a refreshing broth to ease indigestion and improve stomach complaints. There is a firm belief among herbalists that a strong fennel infusion imbibed regularly actually helps weight reduction. Also, a facial pack made of fennel brewed with honey is supposed to arrest the development of wrinkles.

In the kitchen, fennel brings a freshness to baked and broiled food, especially duck, chicken, and fish. Its scent and flavor enhance apple pie and compotes. Not a few Israeli women scatter fennel seeds on bread dough and rolls before baking, and even on seafood casseroles. It is a popular contention that fennel seeds added to leftovers casts them in a completely new role.

Fennel Flower (*Nigella sativa*)

"Black cummin" and "black caraway" seeds are names given for the fennel flower mentioned in Isaiah 28:25 and 27, and in rabbinical commentary of the time of Jesus. The seeds and oil of this annual plant have a strong fragrance and are used in cooking and perfume. For centuries fennel flower seeds have been used in tobacco snuff.

Cooks sprinkle the seeds on bread, like poppy seeds, or put them into cakes and wine. They are also mixed with other fragrant spices, such as cinnamon and ginger, to flavor fruit conserves.

Fenugreek (*Trigonella foenumgraecum*)

Fenugreek is identified in biblical commentaries as a vegetable and a spice-green. Medicinally, it was said to keep the body strong and aid digestion. Its high protein and vitamin content serve vegetarians well, and it is especially popular in India. Fenugreek seeds are an important part of many mild curries.

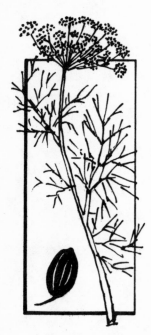

Dill

Halva, the sesame-seed sweetmeat so popular in Israel and in other Middle Eastern countries, is flavored with fenugreek seeds. In America the seeds are used to flavor imitation maple syrup.

The leaves of the young plant are used in mixed green salads, to which they give a pungent flavor. The leaves can be quickly blanched in boiling salted water and used in a salad of cooked greens served with a mild curry sauce. Fenugreek seed sprouts may also be added to salads.

Ginger (*Arum dioscoridis*)

The popular ginger plant does not grow in Israel, but the ginger-like *Arum dioscoridis* grows wild. The leaves are spectacular, resembling the black cala lily (Solomon's Lily), and were eaten as a vegetable in times of food shortages.

Ground dried ginger root can be used in many ways: in ginger cakes, chutneys, cookies, and candy. Perhaps the most treasured delicacy is crystallized ginger, processed from the fresh green rhizome. Middle Eastern vegetables and stews are frequently seasoned with ginger, and it is an important ingredient of curry powders.

Horseradish (*Armoracia rusticana*)

Horseradish, a perennial herb, is related to the mustard family and is sometimes called German mustard. It is grown mainly for its roots, which in former times were used medicinally as an antiscorbutic. It is not indigenous to Israel, but is grown plentifully here—to the point of annoyance in some areas! It is best grown in a vessel, with a piece of the root partially covered by water. When the leaves sprout, they can be used to season salads or for cooking. The flavor is not as sharp as that of the roots.

Horseradish is associated with Eastern European Jewish cooking—especially gefilte fish (pages 264–65). It is mixed with beetroot and oil to make a sharp sauce. It was commonly used in Eastern Europe as a substitute for one of the five bitter herbs in the Passover Seder service. For Passover, grated horseradish root is mixed with lemon or vinegar and salt and eaten with matzo. Cold and hot horseradish sauces are good accompaniments to meat and fish.

Hyssop (*Hyssopus officinalis*)

Hyssop grows wild in the hills, especially among the rocks and crevices in stone walls. It is one of the most important spices mentioned in the Bible, both for food and seasoning. There has been much confusion and controversy concerning hyssop, because at least seven varieties can be found growing wild.

In the Bible, the hyssop plant is contrasted with the majestic cedar of Lebanon (1 Kings 5:13). Hyssop symbolizes humility, while the cedar tree stands tall as pride itself. Hyssop and cedar branches were combined for purposes of purification in the preparation of the ashes of the red heifer (Numbers 19:6), and also in the water for purification of the leper (Leviticus 14:4).

Hyssop is also associated with the paschal sacrifice. The ancient story tells of using a hyssop branch to sprinkle blood on the doorsteps of the houses of the children of Israel in their sojourn in Egypt, during the plague of the firstborn.

In John 19:29 it is written that when Jesus complained he was thirsty, "A bowl full of vinegar stood there; so they put a sponge full of vinegar on hyssop, and held it to his mouth."

Hyssop has long been used as an aromatic herb. Being rich in oil and perfume, it was greatly valued. It was one of the first spices to be eaten. Today, Middle Eastern Jews and local Arabs use hyssop (za'atar) extensively; they put it into hot water for a tissane to clear congestion of the chest, and to help expectoration of the phlegm. Mainly, however, hyssop is combined either with sumac or sesame seed, and sprinkled on dough to be baked or over the chickpea paste hummus (page 101). Not a few Israelis dip pita bread (pages 56–57) in olive oil and then in hyssop as a breakfast food to start the day right. Stronger than marjoram, hyssop improves the flavor of tomato sauces, eggplant dishes, barbecued food, and even pizza.

Mace and Nutmeg (Myristica fragrans)

Mace and nutmeg go together like a hand and glove, because they are from the same plant. Mace is usually sold in "blades," portions of the fruit of the Myristica fragrans tree stripped off from the husk and dried. Sometimes smaller fruits are dried whole. Inside the mace is a fragrant pit called nutmeg. Both mace and nutmeg are strongly aromatic and pungent. Mace has the stronger taste of the two, and is more often used in long-cooking dishes, court bouillon, and marinades.

Though not mentioned in the Bible, nutmeg is common to Middle Eastern cooking and Jewish Eastern European cuisine. Iranian spinach dishes depend on nutmeg to lift up the taste. Passover cooking would be flat without the inclusion of the sweet-sharp taste of nutmeg in soups, matzo balls (page 52), and desserts.

Mint (Mentha species)

Mint is a perennial plant mentioned in rabbinic literature. Both spearmint and peppermint are native to Israel. The apostles Matthew (23:23) and Luke (11:42) write about paying tithes in quantities of mint, along with anise and cumin. Mint leaves are associated with hospitality. Its medicinal virtues have been highly praised, especially as a stomach-ache soother.

In Western cuisine, mint is generally limited to candy, medicines, and mint sauce for lamb. In Israel, however, it is used as a flavoring in many stuffings for vegetables, and with yogurt in a summer salad dressing. Persian influences are responsible for a delightful mint-based drink. Mint, vinegar, and sugar are brought to a boil, cooled, then diluted with ice-cold water and served garnished with fresh mint leaves.

Mustard (Brassica species)

Three kinds of mustard grow here, all of which have biblical identification. Leaves of the field mustard (Sinapis arvensis) are cooked with spinach and Swiss chard for a piquant dish. The seeds of white mustard (*Sinapis alba*) and black mustard (*Brassica nigra*) are used in medicines and in seasoning. Ground mustard seeds are mixed with turmeric to make an excellent sauce, which accompanies many Israeli dishes. Most of the mustard's sharp and brightening flavor comes from its oil, whose taste resembles that of the onion and green garlic.

In the New Testament, the grains of mustard carry comparisons concerning the Kingdom of God: "It is like a grain of mustard seed, which, when sown in the earth is the smallest of all the seeds on earth" (Mark 4:31). Also, "If you have faith as a grain of mustard seed, you will say to this mountain, 'Move hence to yonder place,' and it will move; and nothing shall be impossible to you" (Matthew 17:20).

Parsley (*Petroselinum sativum*)

The parsley grown in Israel and in most of the Middle Eastern countries has flat leaves, unlike the curly French parsley, *Petroselinum crispum*. Although it is less decorative for a garnish, cooks prefer to use flat-leaved parsley because its flavor is stronger. In the United States it is often called "Italian parsley."

Parsley has been identified in rabbinic literature as the "celery growing in the rivers of the land." It's not an easy plant to grow; sometimes it takes almost two years to come to fruition (long after you have forgotten where you planted it!).

Parsley is basic to the daily diet here, both in raw vegetable salads and in cooking. One of the things a bride must learn quickly is to chop parsley, especially for a salad of sliced tomatoes and parsley. Many people think that a daily dose of raw parsley, which is naturally high in vitamin C, is a preventive measure against a cough and infection. Unlike the discarded parsley garnish of the West, which is usually thrown down the drain, here the parsley garnish is eaten with pleasure.

Many herbalists have applauded parsley seeds as being the most important ingredient in the family medicine cupboard. It has been suggested that chewing parsley seeds after a rich meal will prevent indigestion.

Rosemary (*Rosmarinus officinalis*)

Rosemary, a perennial, grows very well in Israel both as a ground cover and as a tall shrub up to 5 feet tall. Because it endures poor soil and hot sun, it is a popular landscape plant. Although rosemary is native to the Mediterranean region, it is not mentioned in the Bible nor does rabbinical commentary mention it. Even so, sprigs of rosemary are commonly used in the Havdalah ceremony to mark the end of the Sabbath and the beginning of the new week.

Legends connected with rosemary abound in Greek and Roman stories, and in associations connected with the life of the Virgin Mary in the Holy Land. Rosemary flowers, it is said, received their color when she washed her blue cloak and hung it over a rosemary bush to dry. In her flight to Egypt, she is said to have taken cover behind a sprawling rosemary bush.

Medicinal attributes of rosemary are legion: Its fragrance is considered a disinfectant; when used as a flavoring it aids digestion; it is said to stimulate the brain when worn as a bracelet or garland; and to overcome constipation when taken as a tissane. It was Shakespeare who wrote, "Rosemary, that's for remembrance."

The culinary virtues of rosemary have long been appreciated by Mediterranean peoples; and with the increasing interest in and consumption of Italian foods, its special characteristics have become widely appreciated. Rosemary is well known to gourmet chefs, some of whom put a sprig in a bottle of vinegar to impart more flavor to vinegar-based salad dressings and marinades. It also goes well in a sauce for lamb or in a seafood salad. In Israel, we throw sprigs of rosemary over the red-hot coals of a barbecue fire just before roasting chicken is done. The scented smoke imparts a special flavor to the meat. Not a few Israeli chefs prefer rosemary-flavored tomato sauces to those flavored with basil, especially because rosemary is more accessible here than basil.

Saffron (*Crocus sativus*)

Saffron grows wild in Israel. It is mentioned in the Song of Songs (4:14). Long before coal-tar dyes came into use, and before many other flower dyes became known, saffron was used for coloring. Ancient kings were anointed with oils perfumed with saffron, and today meals flavored with saffron are considered food for kings.

Saffron is considered to be the most expensive spice in the world. It takes 225,000 stigmas—saffron's delicate flavoring agent—to make up a single pound when dried. Saffron is sold whole rather than ground, to avoid adulteration. The dried threads can be crushed with a mortar and pestle, then soaked in the stock or sauce, or added to hot cooking oil.

The use of saffron in cakes and biscuits, more common in European cuisines, is not widespread. In Israel it is used in festive rice dishes. Many people substitute the less expensive turmeric for saffron in cooking, although the flavor is somewhat different.

Sage (*Salvia* species)

Dozens of plants in the *Salvia* family are commonly called sage. Local sage grows wild in the hills of Jerusalem, and has both Old and New Testament references. Sage has a long history, more concerned with medicinal values than cookery. Sage, *miriamya*, is especially important to Arab Christians. It is considered a refreshing remedy for many sicknesses, but particularly colds and sore throats.

Throw some sage leaves on your charcoal-burning stoves or open fireplace to cleanse the air and impart a fresh fragrance. Place branches of sage on your grill and barbecue fire to add flavor to grilled fish and kebabs.

The Western use of sage leaves in stuffings is less common in Israel, although it is used to flavor certain sausages. In summer sage gives a sharp dimension of taste to summer squash, tomato sauces, and ratatouille.

Saffron

Salt

Biblical references to salt are manifold, and it is called one of the nine essentials of life. It was taken from the waters of the Dead Sea and the Mediterranean, then spread in beds and pans to evaporate. Lot's wife was turned into a pillar of salt (Genesis 19:26).

Jewish life from biblical periods onward included the presence of salt both in ritual and symbolism. No sacrifice was offered without salt (Ezekiel 43:24), nor was a meal to be eaten without it. In time, it became customary to sprinkle salt on the bread over which grace before meals was to be said. Symbolically, one's table became an altar before the Lord. The dietary laws of *kashrut* are based on the use of salt as an agent to draw out the blood of an animal. Salt was considered a purifier and preserver, as well as an important flavoring. Today, salt is less significant as a flavoring in Middle Eastern cooking. Lemon juice is more commonly used, either in flavoring salad dressings mixed with oil, or added to foods at the end of cooking.

The "covenant of salt," frequently mentioned in the Bible, symbolized permanence (2 Chronicles 13:5 and Numbers 18:19). It denotes friendship and hospitality. A person who spoke with wisdom and perception was considered one "who salted his words" (Colossians 4:6).

Dead Sea salt is very strong. It contains potassium chloride, which is used in fertilizers, but is also included in ordinary salt. One grain of it in salt might be harmful if it got into one's eyes, so it became obligatory to wash one's hands before meals (this was in addition to the statutory ruling of washing hands). The salt of Sodom's Salt Sea was also part of the incense used in the Temple during the Second Temple period.

Christian commentary contains many references to salt, especially in the sayings of Jesus—"Have salt and keep the peace with each other" (Mark 9:50). Salt was considered a necessary ingredient to further harmonious relations between human beings. One of the best compliments comes from Matthew 5:13, when he describes a person as "the salt of the earth."

In modern Israel, it has become the custom for the Mayor of Jerusalem or one of the city's elders to greet an honored guest at the gates of the city with an offering of bread and salt.

Sesame (*Sesamum orientale*)

The oil from sesame seeds (representing 50 percent of the seed's content!) was used in ancient times as fuel in lamps. Today, of course, it is widely used as a healthful cooking oil. It is a summer plant whose seeds taste like nuts and are used in place of crumb topping on casseroles, in seasoned flour for frying, and sprinkled on savory pastries.

Arabs and Jews alike enjoy a thick paste called *tahini* (pages 212–13) made from sesame seeds. Roasted sesame seeds are often eaten like nuts. They are considered an excellent substitute for animal protein and are popular among vegetarians.

Thyme (*Thymus* species)

Thyme was mentioned in rabbinic times. It grows wild among the rocks in hilly areas and is often mistaken for hyssop. Long esteemed as a medicinal plant, it symbolizes courage and well-being. Oil of thyme—thymol—is considered a powerful bactericide.

Our local *Thymus capitatus* is a different species from the common thyme described in European herbal and culinary books. The distinction is more in its appearance and its habitat in the Middle East.

Today *Thymus capitatus* is also cultivated and is used as a ground cover and for landscaping effects. Its fresh or dried leaves can be used (ground thyme can also be used, but less effectively) to season vegetable juices, stuffed vegetables, and meat loaves. Fish stews particularly are improved by a good measure of thyme, although in general one has to use thyme sparingly.

The strong scent of fresh thyme, especially in warm climates, is confirmed by the attraction of bees to it. Beekeepers here move the hives near thyme and orange blossoms, when the strongly scented plants are flowering.

Turmeric (*Curcuma domestica*)

Turmeric is often called "Indian saffron." It is not indigenous to Israel, but is widely used in place of the more expensive saffron. A sharp-flavored member of the ginger family, turmeric's major contribution to cuisine is to lend color, a virtue which in ancient times was used in dyestuffs.

It colors rice and stews, chicken soup, mustard, and cheese spreads. Sometimes a plate of bland food can be given more eye appeal with the use of turmeric. Mashed potatoes combined with chopped chives, for instance, will be enlivened with a dash of turmeric, as will a cream sauce for fish. But easy does it, or a bitter taste may spoil the color's effect.

Vanilla (*Vanilla planifolia*)

This climbing plant of the orchid family does not grow in Israel. It is indigenous to Central America, where hot, humid tropical conditions prevail. It produces pods that can be dried or made into a liquid extract.

Vanilla is quite popular in Israel. A relative of the vanilla plant, *Orchis* species, grows wild in Israel, and is referred to by the early rabbis. Its root is eaten and has been used for seasoning. Ground orchid root is the base of an Oriental custard—like the *sahlab* drink popular in the Middle East, which is served hot in winter and cold in summer. (*Sahlab* powder is exported from Israel and is available in specialty shops. It is scented with rose water, an important flavoring in local cooking for many dishes.)

DRYING AND FREEZING HERBS

How to Dry Herbs

It is easy to dry herbs according to this ancient method: tie together branches of herbs and flowers, and hang them upside down in a warm, dry, airy place. Some of the color and scent will be lost this way, but the method's simplicity gives it high marks. Also, in so doing, you can decorate your kitchen or breakfast corner. In about two weeks, the herbs will be ready to store in containers with close-fitting tops.

Another way to dry herbs is to place the herbs on wire racks or cardboard egg trays (punch holes in the egg sections), or wrap the herbs in brown paper bags that have been punctured for ventilation. Place them in an airy cupboard, in the plate-warming compartment of an oven, or in a passageway that is warm and well ventilated. Either method is also useful for drying flowers to be used in a potpourri.

How to Freeze Herbs

Freezing is suitable for soft-leaved herbs which do not dry well: mint, chives, parsley, fennel, basil, dill, and sorrel, in particular. Freeze the herbs in small quantities for handy use. If the herbs are intended for use within two months, it is not necessary to blanch them. Just wash them, shake them dry, and freeze in plastic bags. Once whole leaves are frozen, they are easy to crumble for use.

To blanch, tie the herbs in bunches. Dip them first in boiling water, then in cold water. Remove the leaves from the stem, chop them, pack in plastic bags, and freeze.

If you prepare a number of small flavoring bouquets in advance, they will be in easy reach when you need them. Try 2 or 3 sprigs of parsley; 1 sprig of rosemary; and 1 bay leaf or sweet basil leaf. Or combine chopped leaves of parsley, chives, and dill.

To use frozen herbs, remove from the freezer and add them still frozen to the food you are cooking. You must defrost them first for use in salads or other cold foods (they will not retain their fresh appearance, but will taste as good!).

4 GRAINS

As humanity developed and the gap narrowed between hunters of animals and gatherers of food plants, grains began to replace meat in the daily diet of the Semitic peoples. Barley, wheat, millet, and rice were the mainstays.

BARLEY (*Hordeus sativum, vulgare*)

Barley is probably the world's oldest grain crop. It is a small white grain with a thin brown line running down the center to separate each grain into two sections. The pearl-like grains called pearl barley emerge when the hull, bran, and germ are rubbed from the barley kernel by an abrasive stone. Both types of barley were eaten in ancient times.

Barley, which adapts itself to poor soil and areas of low rainfall, is indigenous to Israel. It is one of the seven species with which the Land of Israel was blessed (Deuteronomy 8:7–8). Fields of barley greeted the Hebrew people, led by Joshua, when they emerged from their desert wanderings and entered the Promised Land.

Barley is the first of the grains to ripen, and in ancient times the barley harvest heralded the first signs of spring (Ruth 1:22). It usually coincides with the beginning of the Passover festival. According to Jewish tradition, the first sheaf offered in the Temple at Passover time was a sheaf of barley.

Barley was a staple in the diet of the Hebrew people. From it bread and porridge were made. David's army was fed daily barley bread (2 Samuel 17:28). Later, during the construction of Solomon's Temple, the hewers of timber in Lebanon were kept strong by a nutritious diet that included barley (2 Chronicles 2:9). The miracle of the loaves and fishes in John 6:9, 13 refers to loaves of barley.

Wheat, a finer grain, later replaced barley in the diet, especially in making bread; but barley remained the poor people's staple. It was commonly used to make beer, as it is today, in Israel and in many parts of the world.

Coriander

Basic Barley

❦ ❦ ❦

Barley does not need to be soaked overnight. It will cook in boiling water in 20 to 30 minutes, depending on the quality of the grain. You can roast barley in an iron skillet over a high flame until slightly browned to reduce the cooking time, although this reduces the vitamin content.

3 cups water
1 cup pearl barley
salt, to taste

1 teaspoon butter or oil
chopped fresh parsley, for garnish

1. In a saucepan, combine the water and barley. Bring to a boil, cover, and simmer for about 30 minutes. Season with salt to taste toward the end of the cooking time.   2. Remove the cover and add the butter or oil. Continue cooking, uncovered, until the barley is tender. Serve garnished with chopped parsley. *Serves 2 to 4*

To Steam Barley

In a large pot, bring 4 quarts of water to a boil. Add 1 cup medium pearl barley, rinsed. Return water to boiling; cook barley over moderate heat for 20 minutes. Drain. Place barley in a metal colander and rinse under running water. Place colander over a pan of boiling water. Cover with a cloth and a lid and steam the barley for about 25 minutes, or until tender and dry. *Makes 3 cups*

Clear Barley Water

❦ ❦ ❦

You may add raisins or dried figs to prepared barley water to make a delicious fruit drink.

2 tablespoons pearl barley, rinsed
rind and juice of 1 lemon

2 cups boiling water
sugar, to taste

1. Put the barley in a saucepan and cover with cold water. Bring to a boil and strain.   2. Place the barley in a jug with the lemon rind and juice. Pour in boiling water, stir, and add sugar.   3. Cover jug and leave to cool. Strain and serve. *Serves 6*

Summer Minted Barley Soup

We usually think of barley soups as warm winter foods. But barley is a light grain, and combined with mint and yogurt it makes a refreshing summer soup. Serve the soup with a salad and fruit for an easy hot-weather supper.

½ cup pearl barley	½ teaspoon allspice
1 large onion, chopped	2 tablespoons fresh parsley, chopped
2 tablespoons vegetable oil	2 tablespoons fresh mint, chopped
2 cups vegetable stock	3 cups yogurt
½ teaspoon salt	chopped fresh mint, for garnish

1. Rinse the barley and soak in 2 cups water. 2. In a soup pot, fry the onion in the oil. Add the stock and the water in which the barley was soaked. Bring to a boil. 3. Add the barley; return to boiling and simmer over a low flame for 1 hour. 4. Add the salt, allspice, parsley, and mint. Continue cooking for 3 minutes. 5. Remove the soup from the stove and let it cool. Add some of the cooled soup to some of the yogurt and stir until well mixed. Return the mixture to the soup, add the remaining yogurt, and blend until smooth. Serve chilled or at room temperature. You may also serve it hot, but be careful not to let the soup boil—it will curdle. Garnish with chopped mint. *Serves 4*

Barley Casserole

1 cup uncooked barley	¼ teaspoon black pepper
2 onions, chopped	¼ teaspoon nutmeg
2 tablespoons butter *or* vegetable oil	2 eggs, beaten
½ pound mushrooms, sliced	chopped fresh parsley, for garnish
½ teaspoon salt	

1. Cook the barley according to the directions on page 44. 2. Brown the onions in butter or oil and add to the cooked barley. Sauté the mushrooms with salt, pepper, and nutmeg in the same skillet. Mix into barley and onions. 3. Add beaten eggs and mix well. Pour the mixture into a greased baking dish. Bake in a preheated 350° oven for 30 minutes or until set. Serve garnished with chopped parsley. *Serves 4*

Barley Salad

3 tablespoons lemon juice
1 tablespoon salt
½ cup olive oil
3 cups steamed barley
¾ cup chopped fresh parsley
¾ cup chopped fresh dill

½ cup chopped scallions
4 tablespoons chopped fresh mint
lettuce leaves
baby radishes, sliced, for garnish
sliced tomatoes, for garnish

1. In a small bowl, combine the lemon juice and salt. Slowly add the olive oil, dribbling it in, and beat with a fork until dressing is well combined.   2. In a large bowl, toss the hot barley with the dressing. Add the parsley, dill, scallions, and mint. Cover the bowl and chill for one hour.   3. Serve on lettuce leaves on individual plates, or mound the barley salad on a large round platter lined with cut-up lettuce or endive. Decorate with thinly sliced radishes or chopped tomatoes. *Serves 6*

Unleavened Barley Bread and Cabbage

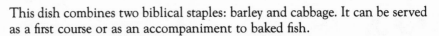

This dish combines two biblical staples: barley and cabbage. It can be served as a first course or as an accompaniment to baked fish.

2 cups shredded white cabbage
2 eggs, beaten
2 tablespoons chopped fresh parsley
1 cup buttermilk
½ teaspoon salt
½ teaspoon sugar

1 cup barley flour
1 tablespoon melted butter *or* margarine
1 tablespoon cumin seeds *or* sesame seeds

1. Wash and blanch the shredded cabbage; drain. Mix with the beaten eggs. Line a greased oblong ovenproof dish with the mixture, and top with parsley.   2. Combine the buttermilk, salt, and sugar in a bowl. Stir in the flour and blend until smooth. Add the butter or margarine. Spread the batter over the cabbage leaves. Sprinkle the cumin or sesame seeds on top. Bake in a preheated 425° oven for 30 minutes or until lightly browned. Serve hot with butter or yogurt. *Serves 4*

Cumin

Note: Barley flour and barley flakes are available in health food shops; 1 cup of barley flour equals 2 cups of regular all-purpose flour.

Baby Barley (*Belila*)

The Sephardic Jews of Spanish origin serve *belila* to celebrate a baby's first tooth. It is an excellent dessert dish, or you can serve it with coffee and tea instead of cake. If you replace the sugar with 1 teaspoon each of salt and oregano, *belila* becomes a flavorful savory dish.

½ cup pearl barley, washed and
    drained
1 cup sugar (or to taste)
2 or 3 tablespoons rose water
½ cup blanched almonds, lightly
    fried

¼ cup raw peanuts, chopped
¼ cup pine nuts
fresh mint

1. Cook the barley according to directions on page 44 and drain.   2. Add the sugar and stir until dissolved. Add the rose water, almonds, peanuts, and pine nuts.   3. Mound on a round platter and garnish with chopped mint leaves. *Makes 6 small portions*

Spiced Barley-flake Cookies

1 cup sifted all-purpose flour
1 teaspoon cinnamon
1 teaspoon nutmeg
1 teaspoon baking powder
½ teaspoon salt
¾ cup shortening

1 cup brown sugar
2 eggs
⅓ cup milk
2 cups barley flakes
1 cup raisins

1. In a mixing bowl, sift together the flour, cinnamon, nutmeg, baking powder, and salt.   2. Cut in the shortening. Add the sugar, eggs, and half of the milk, and stir; fold in the remaining milk, barley flakes, and raisins.   3. Drop the dough by the teaspoonful onto a greased baking sheet. Bake in a preheated 350° oven for 12 to 13 minutes or until lightly browned. *Makes 48 cookies*

WHEAT (*Triticum*)

Two species of wheat are grown in Israel: hard durum wheat, called "dark" wheat, suitable for pasta; and "white" wheat, used for making bread and cakes. Their origins date back many centuries. Of the five species of grain particular to the Land of Israel, wheat was considered the most valuable. In biblical times wheat was sown at the beginning of the winter, before the rains fell, and ripened in early summer (Exodus 9:31).

An abundance of wheat in a harvest was said to symbolize well-being and peace (Psalm 81:17). In fact, legend holds that the Tree of Knowledge in the Garden of Eden was in fact wheat. In the early days of Hebrew settlement "only the rich of the land ate wheat" (Josephus, *Wars* 5:427). Later, when agriculture was more developed, wheat became the common food of all. The rabbis said, "One who grows wheat is sure of his bread, but one who buys wheat in the market, his future is doubtful."

The most common use of wheat flour today is still in the making of bread. In Israel, no meal is considered complete without bread, over which Jews say a special blessing. Bread made from whole wheat flour, including wheat germ and bran, constituted the "staff of life." The Rabbis said that clean bread, fat meat, and old wine strengthened the spine of man. Ironically, clean bread was made from partially refined flour, whereas coarse flour contained bran. Today, of course, many people hold that bran is much more beneficial to good health and weight control than refined flour!

Perhaps no other food has been so universally important to human survival as our daily bread. Biblical references to bread abound, and the word "bread" was used in a general sense to mean food ("Give us this day our daily bread"—Matthew 6:11; Luke 11:3). Bread and water were considered the minimal needs for human survival.

Bread has played a major role in religion, war, and politics. *Lehem*, the Hebrew word for bread, contains the same root letters as the Hebrew word for war. The implication is that people fought over bread. *Bethlehem* means the "house of bread."

No discussion of bread in biblical times would be complete without mention of manna, which the Israelites described as "bread from heaven" (Exodus 16:14). Actually not a bread at all, manna was white and sweet, looking like coriander seed but tasting like "wafers made with honey" (Exodus 16:31). Though the Israelites in the wilderness initially puzzled over what exactly *did* descend on them from heaven—the folk etymology of the word manna relates to the Hebrew for "what is it?"—they discovered that manna could be ground, pounded like meal, boiled, and made into cakes (Numbers 11:8). The monks in St. Catherine's monastery at the foot of Mount Sinai have held since the fourth century that manna originated from the secretions of insects on the branches of tamarisk trees, and many modern scientists agree.

Though misleading, the term "bread from heaven" testifies to the life-sustaining properties of bread, for manna fed the Israelites for forty years. From the unleavened *matzo*, to the pocket *pita*, to the rich egg bread *challah*, Israelis have perfected the art of breadmaking.

Unleavened Bread

The origins of unleavened bread go back to early human history, long before fermentation and leavening agents had been discovered. Unleavened bread was to be offered up with sacrifices on the altar of the Temple (Leviticus 24:5–6). Yet only grains capable of fermentation were to be used, such as those included in the five species: wheat, barley, spelt, rye, and oats (the last two did not grow in Israel). Special precautions were laid down so that wheat did not ferment before it was milled and the dough for unleavened bread did not ferment in preparation. One estimated how long it would take a dough mixture of wheat and water to ferment by the time it took a man to walk a Roman mile (1,482 meters)—between 18 and 24 minutes.

Why all these precautions? Because leaven was considered to be a symbol of impurity. In rabbinical literature it was written that "yeast in dough prevents us from performing the will of God." In the New Testament leaven symbolized the presence of evil in society: Paul contrasted the "leaven of malice and evil," which had to be purged out, with "the unleavened bread of sincerity and truth" (1 Corinthians 5:8).

During the eight days of Passover, observant Jews do not eat leavened bread. They eat *matzot*, unleavened bread, to symbolize the bread made by the Israelites at the time of their departure from Egypt. The unleavened bread of Passover was eaten by Jesus and his disciples at the Last Supper. It passed into Christian ceremony as the wafer of communion. *Matzot* are still used in Jerusalem in the Roman liturgy for the Eucharist.

Remnants of the ancient type of unleavened bread are seen today not only in *matzot* but in the Mexican *tortilla*, the Indian *chapati*, the Chinese *pao ping*, and the Bedouin *pita*. Isaiah 44:19 and 1 Kings 19:6 tell us that flour was made into dough, baked like "a cake on hot stones," or baked in improvised ovens. Contemporary Bedouins make a simple dough of whole wheat flour and water to which they add a little oil and salt. They form the dough into a thin, flat round about the size of a hen's egg, then bake it over hot coals on a tin cover, or directly on top of a hot stone. In minutes the black-spotted flat bread is ready.

The simplicity of making the dough and the good taste of the bread when hot makes it perfect for cooking when camping out or at a barbecue.

Unleavened Bread

❦ ❦ ❦

½ cup whole wheat flour
½ cup white flour
1 teaspoon salt
½ cup water, or as needed

flour or cornmeal
1 tablespoon vegetable oil for
    greasing pan
melted butter

1. Combine flours and salt. Slowly add water until dough sticks together.
2. Knead until dough is soft and elastic. Cover with a damp cloth and let rest on a floured surface for 30 to 45 minutes.

To cook on a stove: 1. Divide the dough into 12 small lumps. Dust your hands with flour, pat lumps flat, and gently stretch the dough until it is about a 6-inch round. 2. Flour the rounds (you can use cornmeal if you wish) and lay one at a time on a smoking-hot oiled frying pan over moderately high heat. When the bread bubbles turn it over and cook briefly on the other side. When the dough has puffed up, turn it over again. Keep turning until both sides are flecked with black spots (about 3 minutes). 3. Brush lightly with melted butter while bread is hot. Rounds can be kept warm in a low oven: brush with butter and cover with a damp towel. *Makes 12 rounds*

To cook on a campfire: 1. Mix and form dough as above. 2. Build a fire and allow it to die down. Put a greased metal baking sheet or frying pan over the red-hot coals. (Traditionally, a concave iron pan similar to a wok is used, bottom up.) 3. When the surface is smoking hot lay the rounds on it one at a time and cook until bubbles form. Turn it over and cook briefly on the other side. 4. Place the bread on a wire grill directly over the fire. When the dough puffs up, turn it over. Keep turning until both sides are flecked with black spots. Brush with melted butter. *Makes 12 rounds*

Matzo Meal Biscuits

4 cups matzo meal	½ cup olive oil
2¼ cups sugar	½ cup rendered chicken fat
1 tablespoon cinnamon	any sweet wine, as needed

1. Mix the matzo meal, sugar, and cinnamon together. In another bowl, blend the olive oil with the softened (but not melted) fat.   2. Combine the two mixtures and moisten with wine until the dough is pliable.   3. Roll the dough ¼ inch thick, and cut the biscuits out with a small glass or demitasse cup. Place the biscuits on an ungreased cookie sheet. Bake in a preheated 350° oven for 15 minutes. *Makes 36 biscuits*

No-bake Matzo Layer Cake

Many Israeli women make this seven-layer cake during Passover. It was one of the first Passover cakes I learned to make.

3½ ounces bittersweet chocolate	2 tablespoons brandy
½ cup butter *or* margarine	8 whole matzot (square or round)
1 cup sugar	1 cup any sweet wine
4 eggs, beaten	1 cup walnuts *or* almonds, chopped

1. Melt the chocolate in the top of a double boiler over hot but not boiling water. Add the butter or margarine and sugar.   2. Add the eggs slowly and beat with a wire whisk or hand-held electric beater over moderate heat until mixture thickens.   3. Remove from fire, add brandy, and continue beating until the mixture again thickens. Allow to cool.   4. Pour the wine into a large shallow dish. Gently dip the matzot one at a time into the wine just to moisten, not to soak.   5. Place one matzo on a serving plate and coat it with a layer of chocolate mixture. Continue this process until the eighth matzo is on the top. Use the remaining chocolate to frost the top and sides. Garnish with nuts.   6. Let sit 10 minutes at room temperature, then refrigerate for several hours. Cut into small squares and serve. *Makes 1 cake*

Fennel

Passover
Carrot-Matzo Meal Cake

1 cup butter *or* margarine
2 cups sugar
4 eggs, slightly beaten
1 cup matzo meal
¼ cup potato flour*
1 teaspoon baking powder
¼ teaspoon salt

1 teaspoon cinnamon
juice and rind of 1 lemon
juice and rind of 1 orange
1 pound carrots, grated (about 4 cups)
1 cup walnuts, chopped
1 cup raisins
confectioners' sugar

1. In a large bowl, cream the butter and sugar together. Add the eggs.   2. In another bowl, mix the matzo meal, potato flour, baking powder, and salt. 3. Combine with the butter and sugar. Add the cinnamon, juices, and rinds, and mix well. Stir in the carrots, nuts, and raisins.   4. Pour into a greased ring mold or a cake pan with removable sides. Bake in a preheated 350° oven for 45 minutes or until the edges of the cake pull away from the sides of the pan. Unmold carefully onto a plate. Dust with sugar. *Makes 1 cake*

*Potato flour is available in kosher markets or in markets with kosher sections, but if you can't find it, increase matzo meal by ½ cup.

Matzo Meal Balls

2 eggs
2 tablespoons chicken fat *or* margarine
½ cup fine matzo meal
½ teaspoon ground ginger
½ teaspoon ground nutmeg

salt and pepper to taste
2 teaspoons fresh parsley, chopped (optional)
2 teaspoons grated onion (optional)
6 cups water *or* stock

1. Beat the eggs until very light. Add the fat. Slowly fold in the matzo meal, ginger, nutmeg, salt and pepper, and optional ingredients. The dough should be soft. Add more matzo meal if the dough does not firm up. Do not handle the dough too much. Cover and refrigerate for at least 1 hour.   2. Wet your hands and form dough into small balls a little more than 1 inch in diameter. Drop balls into six cups of salted boiling water or stock. Reduce heat when all the balls have been dropped in. Cover and allow to simmer for 20 minutes or until the balls have become swollen and light and the centers are cooked. Serve in soup. *Makes 20 balls*

Yeasted Bread

Bread has long symbolized humanity's roots in nature. No wonder today's search for roots has in some measure expressed itself by a return to making bread at home. Refined, chemically bleached flours are frowned upon in favor of less eye-appealing whole-grain flour containing the important ingredient: wheat germ. The experts on making bread insist that the best bread is made with home-ground whole wheat flour.

Failing this heroic measure you may use stone-ground whole wheat flour, which is available in health shops and many supermarkets. Remember to refrigerate whole wheat flour to prevent rancidity.

Following a few basic rules will guarantee excellent bread. Here are the main points to remember:

1. Yeast is a living organism and works best in a warm room. You may use either dry yeast or compressed yeast. To test the freshness of compressed yeast, crumble it between your fingers. If it does not crumble easily, it is not fresh. (Yeast stored in the freezer will keep indefinitely.)
2. Before you begin, assemble all the necessary equipment and ingredients.
3. Use a good-quality flour that is rich in gluten.
4. Fat gives bread its basic flavor. You may use vegetable oil, butter, or margarine.
5. The sweetener you use is another important flavoring agent. Sugar, malt, honey, brown sugar, or molasses can alter the flavor to suit your taste.
6. Eggs add richness to the dough and give it color and lightness.
7. Oil your hands lightly before you knead the dough.
8. Water and milk are the basic liquids in bread making. It is better to heat milk gently than to scald it—which tends to destroy the phosphates both in the grain and the milk. Bread made with water alone resembles French bread; the crust is heavier and crisper than that of a milk dough.

Sabbath Bread (*Challah*)

The most important bread, in a religious sense, was and remains the Sabbath bread. Women, historically, were considered in a special category because it was their duty and privilege to make *challah* for the Sabbath. *Challah* bread is so named because a small portion of the dough (called the *challah*), about the size of an olive, was removed from the dough and burned, in memory of the burnt offerings in the Temple. The loaves of *challah* bread are placed on the Sabbath table to symbolize the two portions of manna distributed on Fridays to the children of Israel during the Sinai exodus from Egypt. The bread initially was sprinkled with cumin or fennel flower seeds as a further reminder of the manna eaten in the Sinai exodus. Today in Israel sesame seeds are more often used.

There are many shapes of bread for the Sabbath and festivals. The three-braided bread symbolizes that the world is upheld by three forces: truth, peace, and justice. The round festival loaf is connected to the major planets, implying that just as the world revolves around the sun, so too, does Jewish life revolve around eternal traditions. A second interpretation emphasizes our need to be aware of the continuity of creation. (On a practical level round loaves were baked because they baked more evenly in less time.)

1 package (1 tablespoon) active dry
    yeast
1¼ cups lukewarm water
2 teaspoons sugar
4½ cups sifted all-purpose flour
2 teaspoons salt

2 eggs, beaten
2 tablespoons vegetable oil
1 egg yolk mixed with 1 tablespoon
    water
sesame seeds

1. In a large bowl, dissolve the yeast in ¼ cup warm water. Stir in the sugar and let the mixture stand for 5 minutes.   2. Sift the flour and salt into the bowl. Stir in the eggs one at a time; add oil and remaining water. Beat with a wooden spoon until dough becomes smooth and pliable. When the dough is too stiff to mix with a spoon, turn out onto a large, floured board and knead well, adding more flour if necessary to make a smooth and elastic dough.   3. Place the dough in a greased bowl and brush the top lightly with oil. Cover the bowl and put in a warm place to rise for about 1 hour. Punch the dough down and let it rise again until double in bulk.   4. Divide the dough into two parts. (It is at this point that religious women take off a piece of the dough, make the blessing over it as described on page 53, and place it in the oven to burn when the bread is baking.) On a slightly floured board, shape each half into three equal portions. Flour your hands and roll the portions into strips of equal length to make braids. Braid the strips together, narrowing the braids at each end, then press the edges together.   5. Place each loaf in the center of a greased baking pan. Cover with a towel and let the loaves rise until double in bulk. Brush the loaves with the egg yolk and water and sprinkle with sesame seeds. Bake in a preheated 375° oven for about 50 minutes. *Makes 2 loaves*

Sesame

Basic White Bread

¼ cup warm water
1 package (1 tablespoon) yeast, dry or
    compressed
2 cups milk, warmed

2 tablespoons melted margarine *or*
    vegetable oil
2 teaspoons salt
2 tablespoons sugar
6½ cups sifted all-purpose flour

1. Pour the water into a large mixing bowl. Add the yeast and stir until it is dissolved. Stir in the milk, add the butter or oil, salt, and sugar. Continue stirring until the mixture is blended. 2. Stir in one cup of flour at a time. After the fourth cup beat firmly with a wooden spoon until the dough becomes smooth and pliable, about 10 minutes. Mix in the fifth cup of flour. When the dough is too stiff to mix with a spoon, turn it out onto a large floured board and knead, adding more flour until the dough is smooth and elastic. Fold the dough toward you and then push it away with the heel of your hand. Add more flour if necessary until the dough is smooth and doesn't stick. A good deal of kneading is essential to allow the gluten in the flour to develop and to give the finished product lightness and texture. 3. Place the dough in a greased bowl and grease the top slightly. Cover the bowl and put in a warm place (about 85°F) to rise. Allow dough to rise for about 1½ hours or until it has doubled. A sure test for well-risen dough is to insert two fingers about ½ inch into it—if the two holes remain, the dough is ready to be shaped. 4. Make a fist, punch it into the dough, and allow the air bubbles to be released. Grasp the dough, squeezing out the air bubbles, divide it in two, and reshape each portion into a loaf. Hold one portion in one hand, and with the second hand pinch the center seam. Put each loaf pinched seam down in the bottom of a well-greased 5¼ × 9¼-inch or 4½ × 8½-inch loaf pan. 5. Cover pans and allow bread to rise in a warm place until nearly doubled. Bake in a preheated 375° oven for about 45 minutes. *Makes 2 loaves*

Sweet Bread

For many years I had no success in making bread. Along came a friend who said, "I have an easy bread recipe for you, and if you don't succeed with this recipe you had better give up writing a cookbook!" Thus challenged, I tried the recipe. It turned out to be both easy and delicious.

½ cup plus 2 tablespoons butter *or*
   margarine
1 egg
6 tablespoons sugar
1 package active dry yeast
2½ cups all-purpose flour
½ teaspoon salt
1 cup soda water
½ cup flour

Filling:

1 tablespoon sugar
1 teaspoon cinnamon
1 cup raisins

Topping:

1 egg yolk mixed with 1 tablespoon
   water
sesame seeds *or* poppy seeds

1. Melt the butter or margarine and allow to cool. Beat the egg with the sugar until the sugar dissolves and mix in the crumbled yeast. Beat this mixture and allow to stand. 2. In a large bowl, mix the 2½ cups of flour and salt. Stir the egg mixture into the flour with a fork, and pour in the soda water. Mix slightly, cover with a plate, and refrigerate for 12 hours or overnight. 3. Prepare a 9¼ × 5½-inch loaf pan. Remove the dough from the refrigerator and give it a good punch (this is excellent for releasing aggressive feelings!) and add ½ cup flour. Knead on a floured board. Roll out dough in a ¼-inch-thick rectangle as for a stollen. Fill with sugar, cinnamon, and raisins according to taste. Brush with egg yolk and water top with sesame seeds or poppy seeds, or dust with icing sugar when bread is recovered from the oven. Bake in a preheated 375° oven for 30 to 40 minutes. *Makes 1 loaf*

Pita Bread

Although many women in the Jewish, Christian, and Muslim communities of Israel bake their own bread, few of them make homemade *pita*. Often they make the dough at home and then bring it to a local bakery that specializes in *pita* baking. The cost is small, and the opportunity to sit and chat while waiting for the bread to bake is a welcome rest from household chores.

    Pita bread has become well known in many Western countries, where supermarkets stock frozen or fresh "Arab" flat bread. *Pita* bread cut in half to form two rounds makes an easy base for homemade pizza; when cut in half the two sides separate to form pockets, which can be filled.

6 cups all-purpose flour, sifted
1 tablespoon coarse salt
2 tablespoons sugar
1 package (1 tablespoon) active dry
   yeast

2½ cups warm water
2 tablespoons vegetable oil
¼ cup cornmeal

1. In a bowl, combine the flour, salt, sugar, and yeast. Stir in the water and oil

and knead the dough until it is soft and pliable. Continue to knead the dough on a floured board for 15 minutes, or until it is smooth and elastic and no longer sticks to your fingers.   2. Lightly oil the inside of the mixing bowl. Put the kneaded dough into it and turn once or twice so that the oil coats the dough. Cover the bowl with a cloth and set in a warm place to rise. Let it rise until double in bulk (1½ to 2 hours).   3. Punch down the dough and knead again for a few minutes. Divide the dough into 12 equal pieces, and form each one into a ball. Flatten each piece on a floured board. With a slightly floured rolling pin, roll each round ¼ inch thick. Dust them with flour and place on a cloth-covered board in a warm place and allow to rise once more.   4. Preheat the oven to 425° for 20 minutes. Place the rounds of dough on hot, oiled baking sheets or on ungreased pans sprinkled with cornmeal. Dampen surfaces with cold water to keep them from browning too fast. Bake 8 to 10 minutes. (Don't open the door during baking time—it will lower the heat and the *pitas* will not puff properly.) Cool on racks. *Makes 12 rounds*

PASTRIES

Just as apple pie is a hallmark of American baking, savory and sweet pastries made of paper-thin layers of pastry distinguish Middle Eastern cuisine. Though *filo* pastry predominates the scene, many doughs are used. Women seldom labor to make *filo* pastry. They leave that to the bakeries specializing in the paper-thin leaves, or use the puff pastry available in specialty shops and supermarkets. It is generally agreed that making the fillings for *boreka* and *baklava* delicacies entails enough work!

Basic flan and flaky pastry are made at home, as is *sanbusak* dough (which dates back centuries, and is the general name given for pastry). It is not as crisp or as refined as *filo* pastry, but the simplicity of making it and its usefulness has earned *sanbusak* a special corner in home baking. When you make flaky pastry choose a cool day or a well-aired kitchen. Keeping one's cool is the order of the day!

Mallow

Basic Pastry for Pies, Dessert Tarts, and Flan Cakes

❦ ❦ ❦

2 cups all-purpose flour
½ teaspoon salt

½ cup butter *or* margarine
¼ cup ice water, or as needed

1. In a mixing bowl, sift the flour and salt together. Cut the butter or margarine into the sifted flour and work it with your fingers until the mixture is pea-sized. Slowly add the water and blend with a fork until the dough forms a ball. It

should be moist but not soggy. 2. Turn the dough onto a floured board and knead lightly. Roll it out for immediate use or wrap it in wax paper or foil and chill for at least 2 hours. *Makes pastry for 1 9-inch pie, 1 flan case, or 8 fruit tartlets*

Boreka

❦ ❦ ❦

This flaky pastry is the homemade substitute for *filo*:

4 cups all-purpose flour, sifted
1 teaspoon salt
1 cup ice-cold water

2 cups butter *or* margarine
1 egg beaten with 1 tablespoon water
sesame seeds

1. On a marble-topped table or pastry board, sift the flour and salt. Make a well in the middle. Slowly add the water with one hand, and quickly mix it into the flour with the other. When the dough forms a ball, put it into a glass bowl. Cover with a clean cloth and refrigerate for 20 minutes. 2. Cut the butter or margarine into pieces with a chilled knife. Work it to a spreadable consistency without letting it become too soft. 3. Roll out the dough on a floured surface until it is a rectangle about 24 inches long by 8 inches wide, and about ¼ inch thick. Now spread the butter over half the dough. Fold the other half of the dough over the butter, allowing for a margin of about 1 inch. Pinch the edges closed. 4. Roll out the dough lengthwise, being careful that the butter doesn't squeeze out. If there is a break in the dough, patch it quickly. Fold the pastry into three parts, starting from the far side: fold one end into the center, then fold the other end into the center point. Chill in the refrigerator for 15 minutes. 5. Roll out the dough from right to left into a long strip. Fold as before into three sections and chill. The more often the dough is rolled out and chilled the flakier the pastry will be. Patient pastry makers aim for six performances! 6. Roll out thinly and shape into squares or rounds (there are those who think the rounds are better and bake faster). Make either shape smaller if you intend the *borekas* to be eaten by hand or larger if you plan them to be eaten with a fork. 7. Place a heaped teaspoon of filling* in the center of the portions of dough and fold the dough over to form a half-moon shape. Pinch the edges of the dough with a fork. Baste with the egg and water and sprinkle them with sesame seeds. Bake in a preheated 425° oven for 3 minutes, then reduce heat to 350° and bake for 30 minutes until pastries are golden brown. Serve warm.

* See Savory Fillings, pages 62–63.

Baklava

❧ ❧ ❧

For this recipe you will need commercially prepared *filo* dough.

2 pounds nuts: walnuts, almonds, or
    pistachios, or a mixture of two
    (about 4 cups)
¼ cup sugar
1 teaspoon cinnamon
2 pounds *filo* pastry, room
    temperature
2 cups unsalted butter, melted

Syrup:

2 cups sugar
1 cup water
2 tablespoons lemon juice
2 tablespoons orange-blossom water
    or orange liqueur mixed with
    water

1. Grind the nuts coarsely in an electric blender, a few at a time. Mix with the sugar and cinnamon.   2. Line a large, deep baking pan with a single layer of *filo* dough and brush it with butter. Keep the unused dough covered with a moistened towel to prevent it from drying out. Repeat until you have six layers.   3. Sprinkle with some of the nut mixture, add two more pastry sheets, and butter each one. Repeat this process until the nut mixture is used up, and finish with at least two layers of *filo* dough.   4. Butter the top. Trim the edges and cut into diamond shapes with a sharp knife.   5. Bake in a preheated 375° oven for 30 minutes. Then reduce the temperature to 350° and bake 30 minutes more or until golden.   6. While the pastry is cooking, prepare the syrup. In a saucepan, mix the sugar, water, lemon juice, and orange-blossom water or liqueur and water. Heat to boiling, making sure sugar is completely dissolved. Allow to cool before spooning over hot pastry. *Makes 42 pieces*

Mock *Baklava*

❦ ❦ ❦

The dough for mock *baklava* is easy to make. The traditional filling of nuts, sugar, and cinnamon can be varied with apples and raisins. Another delicious filling would be a selection of dried fruits, chopped and soaked in wine.

4½ cups all-purpose flour
2 teaspoons baking powder
½ teaspoon salt
2 cups sweet butter *or* margarine
2 eggs
1 cup milk
1 egg yolk mixed with 1 teaspoon
    water

Filling:

2⅔ cups almonds *or* walnuts
2 tablespoons sugar
1 teaspoon cinnamon

Syrup:

syrup from *baklava* recipe (page 59)

1. Sift the flour with the baking powder and salt. Cut the butter or margarine into the flour mixture and work with hands until pea-sized.   2. In a small bowl, lightly beat the eggs and add most of the milk. Add the egg-milk mixture to the flour gradually, and knead lightly until the dough forms a soft ball.   3. Divide the dough into two portions, wrap each one in wax paper, and refrigerate for 10 minutes.   4. Grind the nuts coarsely in an electric blender, a few at a time. Mix with the sugar and cinnamon.   5. Roll out one portion of dough to fit a 16-inch-diameter round baking tray, or a 13 × 18-inch tray. Sprinkle the nut mixture evenly over the dough. Roll out the second portion of dough and place on top. Brush the top with the egg yolk mixture and cut pastry into diamond-shaped pieces.   6. Bake in a preheated 400° oven for about 35 minutes. Pour cooled syrup over the pastry and serve. *Makes 48 pieces*

Trovados

This is the Sephardic version of sweet *sanbusak* pastry (pages 61–62).

4 cups all-purpose flour
1 tablespoon sugar
1 cup butter *or* margarine
⅝ cup red wine

Filling:

1¾ cups ground almonds
1 cup castor sugar (fine, granulated sugar)
2 tablespoons rose water

Syrup:

¼ cup water
½ teaspoon lemon juice
1 cup sugar

1. In a bowl, sift the flour and sugar together. Cut in the butter or margarine and work it with your hands until pea-sized. Slowly add the wine and blend with your hands until the dough is well mixed and quite wet. Refrigerate for 20 minutes. 2. Roll the dough out about ⅛ inch thick and cut it into 2-inch rounds with a cookie cutter or a glass dipped in water. 3. To make the filling, combine the ground almonds, castor sugar, and rose water. Put a teaspoonful in the center of each round and fold over to make a half-moon shape, pressing the edges together. 4. There are several methods of cooking *trovados*. You may bake them in a preheated 350° oven for about 30 minutes, or until they are light pink. They can also be shallow-fried in butter or oil, or deep fried in vegetable oil. 5. To make the syrup, heat the water, lemon juice, and sugar in a saucepan and bring to a boil, making sure the sugar is completely dissolved. Let cool and pour over the *trovados* when ready to serve. *Makes about 24*

Sanbusak

An easier and more traditional Middle Eastern pastry that combines butter or margarine with oil, *sanbusak* is used for savory dishes. The pastries are baked in a moderate oven or are deep fried in oil.

½ cup vegetable oil
½ cup butter
½ cup warm water
1 teaspoon salt

1 pound sifted all-purpose flour
1 egg beaten with 1 tablespoon water
sesame seeds

Mix oil and butter in a Pyrex bowl placed over a hot pan of water. Heat until butter has melted, then mix in the warm water and salt. Pour into a large mixing bowl, add the sifted flour gradually with one hand, and mix the dough with the other until the mixture forms a soft ball. Add more flour if necessary to achieve a pliable dough. Roll out the dough and cut into circles. Put a generous teaspoon of filling (see Savory Fillings, pages 62–63) in the center of each circle and fold over to make a half-moon shape, pressing the edges together. Place on an ungreased baking pan. Baste with the egg and water and sprinkle with sesame seeds. *Makes about 30 medium-sized pastries*

SAVORY FILLINGS

Cheese Filling

2 cups cottage cheese
½ pound cheddar cheese, grated
1 egg, beaten
salt and pepper to taste

1 tablespoon caraway seeds
1 egg beaten with 1 tablespoon water
sesame seeds

In a bowl, mix the cottage cheese and cheddar cheese; add beaten egg, seasonings, and caraway seeds. Fill pastry circles with filling. Fold over and seal by pressing edges with a fork. Brush with the egg and water; sprinkle with sesame seeds. Bake in a preheated 375° oven for 40 minutes or until lightly browned, or fry in hot oil until brown. *Makes about 24 pastries*

Eggplant Filling

1 pound eggplant, unpeeled, cut into
    cubes
salt
2 tablespoons olive oil *or* vegetable oil
2 green onions, cut on the slant

2 tomatoes, chopped
½ teaspoon black pepper
juice of half a lemon
1 teaspoon dried rosemary

Sprinkle salt on eggplant cubes; leave to drain in a colander for 15 minutes. Rinse and drain. In 2 tablespoons olive or vegetable oil fry the green onions lightly. Add the eggplant cubes and fry until soft. Add tomatoes, pepper, lemon juice, and rosemary. Cover pan and simmer until vegetables are nearly cooked, then mash the vegetables to a paste. Fill pastry circles with filling. Fold over and seal by pressing edges with a fork. Bake in a preheated 375° oven for 40 minutes or until lightly browned. *Makes 24 pastries*

Spinach and Cheese Filling

2 tablespoons olive *or* vegetable oil
   (*or* one of each)
1 medium-sized onion, finely chopped
1 10-ounce package frozen chopped
   spinach, thawed and drained, *or*
   1 pound fresh spinach, stems
   trimmed, steamed and chopped
8 ounces feta cheese, crumbled

½ cup cottage cheese
1 egg, lightly beaten
1 tablespoon all-purpose flour
½ teaspoon ground nutmeg
¼ teaspoon freshly ground black
   pepper
1 egg beaten with 1 tablespoon water
sesame seeds

In a skillet, heat the oil; sauté the onion until soft. Add the spinach and cook, stirring, until liquid evaporates. Remove from the heat. In a bowl, mix the feta cheese, cottage cheese, beaten egg, flour, and seasonings, and add the spinach-onion mixture. Fill pastry circles with filling. Fold over and seal by pressing edges with a fork. Brush with egg and water; sprinkle with sesame seeds. Bake in a preheated 375° oven for 40 minutes or until pastry is lightly browned. *Makes 24 pastries*

Mushroom and Walnut Filling

3 tablespoons butter *or* margarine
1 tablespoon vegetable oil
1 large onion, finely chopped
1 pound fresh mushrooms, cleaned,
   dried, and chopped
2 garlic cloves, minced
6 rocket leaves, chopped

1½ cups chopped walnuts
salt and pepper to taste
1 teaspoon nutmeg
1 teaspoon sour cream *or* nondairy
   vegetable cream
sesame seeds

In a skillet, heat the margarine and oil; sauté onion until soft. Add the mushrooms, garlic, and rocket. Cook until liquid evaporates. Cool. Stir in walnuts, seasonings, and cream. Fill pastry circles with filling. Fold over and seal by pressing edges with a fork. Sprinkle with sesame seeds. Bake in a preheated 375° oven for 40 minutes or until pastry is lightly browned. *Makes 24 pastries*

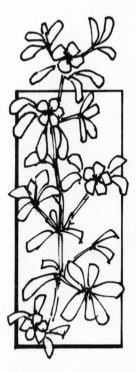

Purslane

CAKES AND SWEET BISCUITS

Aviva Vardi's
Jerusalem Almond Cake

3 eggs, separated
1¼ cups sugar
3 eggs, lightly beaten
1 cup ground almonds

4 ounces unsweetened chocolate,
    grated and hardened in the
    refrigerator

1. Beat the egg whites until they form stiff peaks. Gradually add the sugar. Beat in the egg yolks, then add the lightly beaten eggs. 2. Fold in the nuts and the chocolate. 3. Grease a round spring-form pan, pour in the batter, and bake in a preheated 350° oven for 25 or 30 minutes. Allow the cake to cool before cutting. *Makes 1 cake*

Shoshana Cohen's
Cognac and Nut Torte

Torte:
6 eggs, separated
1¼ cups sugar
½ teaspoon baking powder
½ teaspoon vanilla extract
¾ cup all-purpose flour

Filling:
1 cup almonds, ground
1 cup peanuts, ground
1 cup sugar
½ cup cognac *or* brandy
1 cup lemon juice
rum to taste

Topping:
10 egg whites
1 cup sugar

1. To make the torte, beat the egg whites until the mixture forms stiff peaks. Gradually add the sugar, yolks, baking powder, vanilla, and flour. 2. Pour batter into 3 greased and floured layer pans and bake in a preheated 350° oven for about 30 minutes. (If you don't have 3 layer pans, you can bake one large layer and cut it into 3 rounds when cool.) 3. To make the filling, combine the almonds, peanuts, and sugar and set aside. In a small bowl, combine the cognac or brandy, lemon juice, and rum. 4. Turn the first layer onto a cake dish.

Sprinkle with half of the juice and cognac mixture, then spread with half the nut and sugar mixture. Place the second layer over this and repeat the process. Cover with the third layer.   5. To make the topping, beat the egg whites and sugar until they form soft peaks. Spread this topping over top and sides of the cake. Refrigerate for 24 hours and serve. *Serves 6*

Almond Sponge Cake

This cake keeps well in a cake tin for two weeks, or in the refrigerator for a month—unless a sweet-toothed husband or child gets to it first!

1 cup self-rising flour	4 eggs
1 tablespoon cornstarch	1 teaspoon almond extract
½ teaspoon salt	1 teaspoon ground ginger
½ cup ground almonds	confectioners' sugar *or* lemon curd
1 cup butter *or* margarine	(page 143)
1 cup sugar	

1. In a small bowl, sift the flour, cornstarch, and salt together. Add the ground almonds.   2. In a large bowl, cream the butter or margarine and sugar together until fluffy. Add the eggs one at a time and beat thoroughly.   3. Add the flour mixture in four equal portions and mix until smooth. Add the almond extract and ground ginger, and mix with a spoon until well blended.   4. Spoon the mixture into a well-greased cake tin or pan with a removable bottom. Bake in a preheated 350° oven for 1 hour. Test for doneness. Allow the cake to cool; wrap it in plastic wrap and store in a cake tin or in the refrigerator. Serve with confectioners' sugar or lemon curd. *Makes 1 cake*

Devorah's Basic Orange Cake

¾ cup butter *or* margarine	¼ cup orange juice
¾ cup sugar	2 tablespoons orange marmalade
grated rind of one orange	¼ cup chopped almonds
2 eggs, separated	orange icing sugar spread (page 82)
2½ cups self-rising flour	

1. Cream the butter or margarine and sugar until fluffy. Mix in the orange rind. Add the egg yolks one at a time and beat until smooth. Beat in the flour

alternately with the orange juice. Add the orange marmalade and mix in the almonds by hand. Fold in the stiffly beaten egg whites.   2. Pour the batter into a round greased and lightly floured cake tin with removable sides. Bake in a pre-heated 350° oven for 1¼ to 1½ hours. Test for doneness.   3. When the cake is cool ice it with orange icing sugar spread. *Makes 1 cake*

Sheila Moser's
Baba Annie Butter *Bulkes* (Buns)

❧ ❧ ❧

2 packages (2 tablespoons)
   active dry yeast
⅓ cup sugar
½ cup warm water
5 cups all-purpose flour
1 cup sugar
pinch of salt
½ cup melted butter
4 eggs
1 cup sour cream

Topping:
1 cup sugar
2 tablespoons cinnamon

1. Dissolve the yeast and sugar in the warm water and set aside for 10 minutes.   2. In a large bowl, sift together the flour, sugar, and salt. Make a well in the middle of the mixture and pour in the butter, eggs, sour cream, and yeast mixture.   3. Mix with your hands to form a soft dough, and knead until smooth and elastic. Put the dough in a lightly greased bowl, cover, and let rise for 2 hours. Punch the dough down and allow it to rise again for 2 hours.   4. To make the topping, mix the sugar and cinnamon together and spread evenly on a board. Form handfuls of the dough into sausage shapes and roll them in the topping.   5. Place the buns side by side on a greased pan and let them rise once more for 30 minutes. Bake in a preheated 350° oven for 45 minutes. *Makes 24 buns*

No-bake
Refrigerator Cake Roll

Slices of this chewy, healthful roll can be served in place of cake as a sugar-free dessert. They look lovely on a slice of orange from which the peel has been removed.

2¾ cups raisins
rind of 1 orange
¼ cup sesame seeds
¼ cup honey

½ cup ground coconut
½ cup wheat germ
½ cup orange juice, approximately
1 teaspoon cinnamon

1. Grind the raisins and orange rind in a blender or food processor. Add the sesame seeds. Empty mixture into a bowl.   2. Add the honey, coconut, wheat germ, and some of the orange juice. Blend well with a fork until the mixture is firm. Add the cinnamon and more juice if needed.   3. Separate the mixture into two pieces. Place each piece on a length of wax paper and roll the paper over the mixture to form a 1-inch-wide roll. Refrigerate until cold and firm, then slice into rounds. *Makes 1 cake roll*

Pastry-based Cheesecake

1 unbaked pie shell (pages 57–58)
2 cups cottage cheese
3 eggs, separated
½ cup sugar

½ cup heavy cream
½ cup mixed candied fruit peels
1 teaspoon vanilla

1. Prepare a pastry shell and keep it cool while you start the cheese filling.
2. Push the cottage cheese through a sieve into a bowl. Blend the egg yolks, sugar, and cream in an electric blender, on low speed at first and then increasing to high. Or you may use a hand beater.   3. Stir the blended mixture into the cheese and add the candied peels and vanilla.   4. Whip the egg whites until they form stiff peaks and fold into the cheese mixture. Pour the batter into the pie shell and bake in a preheated 350° oven for 40 minutes. Turn off the heat and allow the cheesecake to cool in the oven. Chill in the refrigerator before serving. *Makes 1 cake*

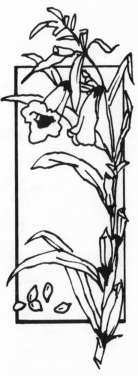

Sesame

Pastry-based Fruit Cheesecake

Pastry:

4 tablespoons butter *or* margarine
2 egg yolks
½ teaspoon salt
2 tablespoons lemon juice
1½ cups sifted all-purpose flour
1 teaspoon baking powder
2 or 3 teaspoons cold water

Filling:

1 cup uncreamed cottage cheese
1 cup thick sour cream
⅓ cup sugar
½ teaspoon salt
3 eggs, well beaten
1 teaspoon grated lemon rind
1 egg white, slightly beaten
1 cup canned crushed pineapple
½ cup seedless raisins, chopped or whole

1. To make the pastry, cream the butter or margarine and add the egg yolks, salt, and lemon juice. Gradually add the flour and baking powder. Knead the mixture with enough of the water to make a smooth dough. Press into a pie plate or spring-form pan until the dough is about ¼ inch thick.   2. To make the filling, rub the cheese through a sieve into a bowl. Add the sour cream, sugar, salt, eggs, and grated lemon rind. Mix well.   3. Brush the pastry shell with egg white to seal it and spread the pineapple and raisins over it. Pour the cheese mixture evenly over the fruit. Bake in a preheated 450° oven for 10 minutes. Then reduce the heat to 350° and bake 20 minutes longer, or until the cheesecake begins to brown. Cool and serve cold. *Serves 6*

Easy Crumble Cake

Pastry:

1 cup sugar
1 cup butter *or* margarine
2 cups all-purpose flour
2 cups self-rising flour
2 eggs, lightly beaten

Filling:

2 cups jam
1 cup sugar
1 teaspoon cinnamon

Topping:

1 cup hazelnuts *or* almonds, chopped fine

1. In a large bowl, cream the sugar and butter or margarine until fluffy. Gradually add the flour and mix in the eggs until a soft dough is formed. Refrigerate

for 30 minutes. 2. Divide the dough into 2 pieces. Wrap 1 piece in plastic wrap and put it in the freezer. Pat the other portion into a greased rectangular pan. 3. To make the filling, combine the jam, sugar, and cinnamon in a small bowl. Spread the filling over the dough in the pan. 4. Remove the second piece of dough from the freezer and grate it coarsely over the filling until crumbs cover the whole surface. Top with the nuts and bake in a preheated 350° oven for 30 to 40 minutes. *Makes about 24 large or 48 small portions*

Shortbread Lemon Squares

1 cup butter *or* **margarine**	**2 teaspoons grated lemon rind**
½ cup confectioners' sugar	**6 tablespoons lemon juice**
1 egg	**1 teaspoon baking powder**
2½ cups all-purpose flour, sifted	**4 tablespoons confectioners' sugar** *or*
3 eggs	**3 tablespoons grated coconut**
2 cups sugar	

1. Cream the butter or margarine and confectioners' sugar until fluffy. Add 1 egg and mix well. Gradually mix in 2 cups of flour. 2. Spread this dough evenly over the bottom of a well-greased rectangular baking pan and bake in a preheated 350° oven for 20 minutes until partially baked. 3. Beat 3 eggs until they are thick and yellow. Add the sugar gradually. When well mixed, add the lemon rind and juice, the rest of the flour, and the baking powder. Beat until the mixture is well blended. 4. Pour the lemon mixture over the partially baked shortbread dough and return it to the oven. Bake for 20 minutes more or until the top is slightly browned. Remove from the oven and sprinkle the top with confectioners' sugar or grated coconut. Cut into small squares while still warm. Cool and serve in small paper cups arranged on a large cake tray. *Makes about 24 squares*

Garden Sorrel

COOKIES

Mrs. Rittersporn's
Hazelnut Cookies

1 cup dry sugar
4 egg whites
1 cup walnuts, broken into pieces
½ cup hazelnuts, chopped

1. To dry the sugar, put it in a clean pan and place it in a warm oven which has been turned off. Leave it there for about 10 minutes. Use the sugar when it has cooled.   2. Beat the egg whites until they form stiff peaks. Add the dry sugar gradually. Fold in the nuts slowly, making sure not to break down the consistency of the egg whites.   3. Drop the cookie batter by the teaspoonful onto a greased cookie sheet.   4. Preheat the oven to 400°. Turn off oven and put in the cookies. Leave them in the oven for a few hours with the door shut. *Makes 40 cookies*

Christmas Bars

¾ cup butter *or* margarine
1½ cups sugar
1 egg yolk
1 teaspoon lemon juice
2½ cups all-purpose flour, sifted
½ teaspoon salt

1½ cups nuts, chopped fine
4 egg whites
½ teaspoon lemon extract
1 teaspoon vanilla extract
1 cup marmalade *or* blackberry jam *or* blueberry jam

1. Cream the butter or margarine with ½ cup of the sugar until fluffy. Add the egg yolk and lemon juice. Mix in the flour, salt, and ½ cup of the nuts. Pat evenly onto a greased cookie sheet and bake in a preheated 350° oven for 15 minutes.   2. Beat the egg whites until stiff peaks form. Add the remaining sugar slowly. Mix in the lemon extract, vanilla, and remaining nuts. Spoon this mixture over the partially baked dough and spread jam over the entire surface.   3. Return the dough to the oven and bake 30 minutes more. Cut into fingers or bars while the cookie dough is still warm. Remove from pan when cooled. *Makes about 60 bars*

Armenian Easter Cookies

❦ ❦ ❦

1 cup butter *or* margarine, softened
½ cup confectioners' sugar, sifted
1 whole egg, beaten
¼ cup whipping cream
2 tablespoons banana cordial *or*
    orange liqueur

4 cups flour, sifted
1 teaspoon baking powder
¼ teaspoon salt
1 whole egg beaten with 1 tablespoon
    water
½ cup grated almonds

1. Cream butter or margarine with sugar until light and fluffy. Add the egg, whipping cream, and liqueur. Mix well. 2. Sift the flour, baking powder, and salt into a large mixing bowl. Mix gradually into the creamed mixture until a soft dough is formed. Pat circles out of 2 tablespoons of dough and brush with the egg and water. Sprinkle with grated almonds. Bake in a preheated 375° oven for about 30 minutes or until golden brown. *Makes about 40 cookies*

BATTERS

Blintzes (Crepes)

❦ ❦ ❦

Blintzes are probably so-called because the first Zionist pioneers hankered for the Russian *blinis* to which they were accustomed. In time, *blini* pancakes became known as *blintzes*. You may serve them as a light dinner with sour cream or cinnamon sugar, made by mixing ½ teaspoon cinnamon into ⅓ cup fine sugar. Seasoned applesauce also makes a nice accompaniment for *blintzes*.

Batter:

4 eggs
1 cup water
salt
2 tablespoons vegetable oil
1 cup all-purpose flour
oil for frying

Cheese Filling:

2 cups cottage cheese
1 tablespoon flour
½ teaspoon salt
1 tablespoon butter *or* margarine,
    melted
2 tablespoons sugar
½ cup raisins (optional)

1. In a large bowl, mix all the batter ingredients by hand; or pour into the container of an electric blender and blend until smooth. 2. Lightly grease a 7-inch skillet and heat over medium-high heat. Pour about 2 tablespoons of the batter into the skillet and tilt in all directions so that the batter covers the bottom of the pan in a thin, even layer. When the underside is lightly browned,

carefully turn it out onto a large napkin or tea towel, browned side up. Continue to make pancakes, piling them one on top of the other, until all the batter has been used. Cover with plastic wrap and fill later, or continue with filling. 3. To make the filling, beat all the filling ingredients together until well mixed. (If you serve *blintzes* for dessert you may add ½ cup raisins.) 4. Spread a heaping tablespoon of filling along one side of a pancake, fold in both ends, and roll up. Continue until all *blintzes* are filled. Fry the *blintzes* in oil or butter or bake them in a preheated 425° oven until browned. *Makes about 20 blintzes*

Batter for Deep-fried Vegetables and Fish

Use this batter with recipes in the Vegetable and Fish sections.

1 cup all-purpose flour
1 teaspoon ground cumin *or* ground oregano
¼ cup melted butter *or* margarine *or* 2 tablespoons vegetable oil
½ teaspoon turmeric (optional)

½ cup milk *or* half water and half milk *or* flat beer *or* white wine
salt and pepper, to taste
1 egg, beaten
¼ cup chopped parsley (optional)

1. Put the flour and cumin or oregano in a bowl and stir in the butter, margarine, or oil. (You may add turmeric to the flour to enhance the color.) Add the liquid and stir to a smooth consistency. Add salt and pepper, the beaten egg, and parsley if so desired. Allow the batter to rest for at least 1 hour. *Makes about 1 cup*

Syrian Marjoram

CRACKED WHEAT (Bulgur)

Cracked wheat is wheat that has been prepared for cooking and eating raw by cracking, steaming, and toasting. It is easily digested and has long been esteemed for its high nutritional content. It is readily available toasted and untoasted in health food shops and in shops that carry Middle Eastern food. Toasted bulgur is preferred for eating uncooked, as in *tabouleh* salad (pages 74–75).

Bulgur Dumplings

❧ ❧ ❧

The Old World heartiness associated with dumplings (when getting enough to eat rather than dieting was the daily pursuit) is an important factor in many national cuisines. In the Middle East cracked wheat, semolina flour, and matzo meal are common denominators. Filled or plain, dumplings reinforce soups and stews. The important factors are good taste and lightness—"sinkers" are definitely out.

1½ cups fine bulgur
¾ cup all-purpose flour
½ teaspoon ground coriander
¼ cup chopped fresh parsley
½ teaspoon black pepper
½ teaspoon allspice
1 teaspoon salt
¼ cup cold water, approximately

1. Wash the bulgur in hot water and drain. Wrap in a towel and allow to dry.   2. Put bulgur in a bowl and mix with the dry ingredients. Add enough of the water to make a stiff dough. Allow the dough to stand in a cool place for about 30 minutes.   3. On a floured board, form the dough into marble-sized balls. Moisten your hands to make the job easier. Drop the balls into boiling water or soup. Simmer uncovered for about 20 minutes or until dumplings have expanded and are cooked through. Serve with hot soup or stew. *Serves 12*

Note: These dumplings are good with oxtail soup (pages 230–31) and sheepshead meal-in-a-bowl (pages 229–30). If you serve them with a plain soup, fill the dumplings with a mixture of chopped beef and onions fried together.

Armenian Bulgur Pilav

This dish is a good accompaniment to stews. It is often served with hard-boiled eggs.

2 cups coarse bulgur
2 onions, chopped
1 cup oil *or* melted butter
salt and pepper, to taste

½ teaspoon allspice
2 cups soup stock *or* water with 1
    bouillon cube

1. Wash the bulgur and soak it in water. Fry the onions in half the oil or butter. Drain the bulgur and add it to the onions. Stir and fry for 10 minutes. Season the mixture with salt, pepper, and allspice.   2. Add stock or water to cover the bulgur. Mix well, bring to a boil, then lower the heat. Cover the pot and simmer for 10 minutes.   3. Pour the remaining oil or melted butter over the partially cooked bulgur. Cover the pot tightly, placing a cloth between the pot and lid to lock in the steam. Cook the bulgur over very low heat another 30 minutes. *Serves 4 to 6*

Tabouleh Salad

The traditional method of eating *tabouleh* salad is to scoop it up with lettuce leaves. You can also eat it with *pita* or rye bread as a light lunch or as part of a summer dinner. It travels well for picnic fare.

1½ cups bulgur
1 cup chopped fresh parsley
1 cup chopped fresh mint
1 cup chopped scallions
½ cup chopped parsley stems
3 tablespoons olive oil
½ cup fresh lemon juice
salt and pepper, to taste
1 tablespoon ground cumin

1 cup sliced violet leaves (optional)
1 head lettuce, washed and drained,
    separated but not cut up
3 tomatoes, chopped
2 cucumbers, peeled and diced
paprika
2 hard-boiled eggs, chopped
violet flowers (optional)

1. Pour hot water over bulgur to wash it. Drain, add 3 cups cold water, and allow bulgur to soak for 30 minutes.   2. Marinate the parsley, mint, scallions, and parsley stems in the olive oil and lemon juice while the bulgur is soaking. Add the salt, pepper, and cumin and mix well.   3. Drain the bulgur, mix with herb mixture, and allow it to stand for 60 minutes.   4. Serve the *tabouleh* mounded up in a large bowl. You may wish to sprinkle chopped violet leaves on top of

the salad. Insert the lettuce leaves around the sides of bowl and add the tomatoes and cucumbers, but do not mix. Garnish with paprika, chopped egg, and violet flowers. *Serves 10*

Bulgur-based Dough
(*Kibbi*)

❦ ❦ ❦

The making of cracked-wheat dough, *kibbi*, is almost a cult. Moslem and Christian Arab communities cook many varieties of ground lamb or beef *kibbi*, and Kurdish Jews excel in vegetarian *kibbi*. Sephardic Jews, having learned from their Arab neighbors, claim their own method of making *kibbi* dough. They substitute matzo meal for bulgur during Passover week.

Folklore holds that men have been attracted to women because of their skill in making delicious *kibbi* in a variety of ways. A woman's skill is made easier in the execution of *kibbi* dishes if she is blessed with a long index finger (using an implement to make a hole in the *kibbi* dough is unacceptable!). In fact, there are as many ways to make *kibbi* as there are fingers on two hands.

Raw Bulgur Paste
or Dough (*Kibbi Nayya*)

❦ ❦ ❦

Raw meat and bulgur combine to make an exotic dish. You squeeze lemon juice over the dough, scoop it up in a lettuce leaf, and enjoy! Be sure to use only the best-quality meat for *kibbi nayya*!

1½ cups fine bulgur	¼ teaspoon allspice
1 pound lean lamb *or* beef, ground 3 times	¼ teaspoon nutmeg
	lettuce leaves
1 large onion, finely chopped	2 lemons, quartered
salt and pepper, to taste	

1. In a bowl, soak the bulgur in cold water for 10 minutes. Drain the bulgur in a sieve, using a potato masher to press out the excess water, until dry. Return it to a dry bowl and combine it with the ground meat.   2. Add the onion and seasoning, and grind the mixture again until very fine.   3. Moisten your hands with cold water and knead until smooth.   4. Mound the *kibbi* dough on an attractive glass or china plate lined with lettuce leaves and quartered lemons. *Serves 4*

Stuffed Bulgur Shells I
(*Kibbi Bissaniyyeh*)

Shells:

1 recipe *kibbi nayya* (page 75)

Filling:

1 or 2 large onions, finely chopped
2 tablespoons vegetable oil
½ pound chopped lamb *or* beef
⅛ cup pine nuts
salt and pepper, to taste
½ teaspoon cinnamon
½ teaspoon ground cumin
2 tablespoons stock *or* water

1. Make dough for shells as described in recipe for *kibbi nayya*. Refrigerate while you prepare the filling.   2. Cook the onions slowly in oil until soft and golden. Add the meat and pine nuts and cook, stirring, until the meat changes its color. Add the seasonings and stock or water and mix well. Turn off heat.   3. Wet your hands in a bowl of cold water. Pull off a handful of *kibbi* dough and form it into an egg shape. Hold this in your left hand. Carefully make a hole in the shell with the index finger of your right hand. With the fingers of your left hand, ensure that the dough remains firm. If the dough cracks, firm it with a little water. Carefully fill the hole with 1 tablespoon of filling, and pinch the *kibbi* over the hole to enclose the filling.   4. Fry the *kibbi* "eggs" in two inches of hot vegetable oil over moderate heat until they are browned on all sides. Remove with a slotted spoon and drain on a rack or on paper towels. Serve with *tahini* sauce (pages 212–13). To keep *kibbi* warm, wrap them in foil or put them in a covered dish in a warm oven. *Serves 6*

Stuffed Bulgur Shells II

This dough is made with bulgur and flour, and without the ground meat. It is easier to make because you only need to grind the ingredients once.

Shells:

1¼ cups fine bulgur
1 onion, finely chopped
salt and pepper, to taste
1 cup all-purpose flour
1 egg (optional)

Filling:

2 medium onions
2 tablespoons olive oil
1 pound ground lamb *or* beef
¼ cup pine nuts
2 tablespoons stock *or* water
¼ teaspoon ground cumin
¼ teaspoon allspice
salt and pepper, to taste

1. In a bowl, soak the bulgur in cold water to cover for 10 minutes. Drain the bulgur in a sieve, using a potato masher to press out excess water, until dry. Return it to a dry bowl and combine it with the onion, salt, and pepper. Grind the mixture and return it to the bowl.   2. Add the flour and the egg, if you wish. Moisten your hands and knead the dough until it is smooth. Refrigerate for at least 30 minutes to make shaping easier—this dough is more fragile than dough made with meat.   3. To make the filling, cook the onions slowly in oil until soft and golden. Add the meat and pine nuts, and cook until the meat loses its color. Add stock, cumin, allspice, salt, and pepper, and stir. Turn off heat. 4. Shape, fill, and cook shells as described in stuffed bulgur shells I, step 3 (page 76). Serve with *tahini* sauce (pages 212–13). *Serves 6*

Mushroom-stuffed Bulgur Dough

❦ ❦ ❦

Shells:

1 recipe stuffed bulgur shells II (page 77)

Filling:

2 medium onions, finely chopped
2 tablespoons oil
1 pound raw mushrooms, chopped
¼ cup pine nuts
salt and pepper, to taste
1 tablespoon ground, dried mint leaves
½ teaspoon ground cinnamon

1. Make 1 recipe stuffed bulgur shells II.   2. Cook onions slowly in oil until soft and golden. Add the mushrooms, pine nuts, salt, pepper, mint, and cinnamon. Stir until mushrooms are cooked.   3. Shape, fill, and cook shells as described in stuffed bulgur shells I, step 3 (page 76). Serve with *tahini* sauce (pages 212–13). *Serves 6*

Baked Bulgur in a Tray

❦ ❦ ❦

This variation uses the non-meat dough in stuffed bulgur shells II. You may fill it with lamb, beef, or mushroom filling.

1 recipe stuffed bulgur shells II (page 77)
1 recipe lamb *or* beef *or* mushroom filling (pages 75, 78)

¼ cup salted butter *or* margarine, melted

1. Prepare dough and your choice of lamb, beef, or mushroom filling.   2. Pat half of the dough smoothly into the bottom of a 9-inch round baking pan. Spread the filling over this, and top with the rest of the *kibbi* dough. Slice into small diamond-shaped portions, brush with butter or margarine, and bake in a preheated 375°oven for 1 hour. Serve hot as an hors d'oeuvre with cocktails, or with a mixed salad as a luncheon dish. *Makes about 48 pieces*

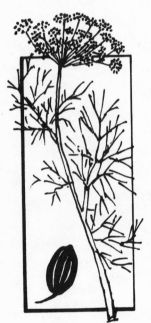

Dill

SEMOLINA

Semolina is derived from the hard particles in the interior of the wheat grain, especially durum. A special milling process produces a very white, coarse flour, rich in gluten.

In biblical times semolina was considered choicer than regular wheat flour, and the finest cakes were made from semolina. Showbread—"bread of display"—was offered in the Temple (Exodus 25:30; 1 Samuel 21:7; 1 Kings 7:48; 2 Chronicles 4:19). A meal offering of twelve loaves, corresponding to the twelve tribes of Israel, was arranged on the table in two rows of six loaves. The Showbread loaves were made of unleavened bread and were decorated with frankincense (Leviticus 24:7). In some Catholic communities in Jerusalem the Eucharist is made of semolina flour.

Because of the high quality of semolina flour it is used in making pasta. It is also used to thicken soup, and in breakfast cereals, puddings, *pita* bread, and cakes. The famed North African dish *couscous* is made of semolina grains.

Couscous

Couscous is a revered dish that dates back to the fifteenth century. It originated in the Maghreb countries of North Africa, but its fame has spread worldwide. Cooking methods vary according to family traditions. North African Jews serve it almost every day.

Couscous can be milled to the degree of fineness preferred. In Israel and in specialty shops that stock Middle East foods partially prepared *couscous* is packaged in fine and medium grind. Lighter than rice, it is suitable for summer eating.

Couscous belongs to the world of food for large families or gatherings (some people don't consider it worth the effort to make *couscous* for less than ten people!). The ingredients can number as few as fifteen and as many as fifty, depending on whether you are serving a meat-, chicken-, or fish-based *couscous*. The recipe that follows contains fish, but you can easily substitute lamb, beef, or chicken.

Making *couscous* involves two cooking operations, which are done in a two-part vessel: The upper part is called the *keskes*, the bottom the *couscousier*. You can use a large double boiler with a metal steamer lined with cheesecloth on top. To ensure a tight fit, insert a towel between the two parts.

½ cup olive oil

2 cups chickpeas, soaked overnight and cooked, *or* 1 16-ounce can chickpeas

1 4-ounce can tomato paste

3 pounds mixed vegetables in any combination: carrots, onions, potatoes, cabbage

2 to 3 pounds firm white fish (grey mullet, grouper, sea bass), cut into steaks

salt and black pepper, to taste

2 cups *couscous*

a handful of raisins

1 teaspoon ground cumin

½ teaspoon cinnamon

1. Heat the olive oil in the base of the *couscousier* or pot. Add the cooked chickpeas, tomato paste, and 5 cups of boiling water. Bring to a boil and add the vegetables: carrots and onions, cut in halves; peeled potatoes, cut in halves. Cook slowly for 5 minutes, and add the cabbage cut into wedges, the fish, salt, and pepper. Raise the heat so that the fish and vegetable stew will steam.   2. Moisten the *couscous* with a little cold water and put it into steamer or *keskes*, then place it over the lower pot or *couscousier*. (The fit between the two sections of the double boiler must be tight so that the steam will not escape.) When the steam rises, remove the *keskes*. Put the *couscous* into a bowl, and gently stir the grains with a fork until they are separated. Return the *couscous* to the *keskes* and place it over the *couscousier*.   3. Allow the steam to rise and cook the *couscous* for another 10 to 15 minutes. Ladle some of the sauce over the *couscous*. Mix carefully, adding the raisins, cumin, and cinnamon. Pile the *couscous* onto a platter, spoon the fish and vegetables over the top of it, and pour the sauce into a bowl or sauceboat. If you prefer a really hot sauce, harissa sauce (below) is excellent. *Serves 6 to 10*

Harissa Sauce

This red-hot oil sauce is traditionally served with *couscous*. You can buy pre-pared harissa sauce in Middle Eastern shops.

4 tablespoons dried red-pepper flakes

6 tablespoons water

2 tablespoons olive oil

1 teaspoon ground coriander

1. Combine the pepper flakes and water in a saucepan, bring to a boil, and stir well.   2. Remove the pan from the stove, add the oil and ground coriander, and mix well. *Makes ½ cup*

Semolina-Sesame Seed Bread

4 cups fine semolina	1½ cups warm water
6 packages active dry yeast (1½ ounces)	4 tablespoons olive oil *or* vegetable oil
½ teaspoon sugar	1 to 2 tablespoons lard *or* margarine *or* chicken fat *or* lamb fat
1½ teaspoons salt	3 tablespoons sesame seeds, roasted
1 teaspoon allspice	1 egg, beaten

1. In a bowl, combine the semolina, yeast, sugar, salt, and allspice. Stir in the water and oil and knead the dough until it is soft and pliable. Continue to knead the dough on a floured board until it is smooth and elastic and no longer sticks to your fingers.   2. Lightly grease the inside of a mixing bowl with one of the fats. Put the kneaded dough into it and turn once or twice so that the grease lightly coats the dough. Cover the bowl with a warm cloth and set in a warm place to rise. Let it rise until double in size (1½ to 2 hours).   3. When dough has doubled, punch it down and add the sesame seeds. Shape the dough into a smooth ball. Squeeze the dough in the middle to divide it into two small loaves.   4. Arrange the loaves on an oiled baking sheet. Cover with a cloth and allow them to rise again in a warm place until almost doubled (about 45 minutes).   5. Brush the loaves with the beaten egg and bake in a preheated 450° oven for 15 minutes. Lower the heat to 350° and continue baking for 20 minutes more or until browned. Remove from the oven and cool on racks.
Makes 2 loaves

Semolina Dumplings

Semolina dumplings are eaten in colorful vegetable-based soups such as carrot, tomato, and pumpkin, and are served with dairy meals. They also accompany carrot and pumpkin casseroles called *tzimis*. The dumplings are well seasoned to offset the blandness of the pumpkin and the semolina flour.

½ cup semolina flour	¼ teaspoon allspice
½ cup self-rising flour	2 eggs
1 teaspoon salt	4 tablespoons butter *or* margarine, melted *or* chicken fat, rendered, for a meat casserole
pepper, to taste	
¼ teaspoon nutmeg	

1. In a small bowl, combine the semolina, flour, salt, pepper, nutmeg, and all-spice. In a large bowl, beat the eggs and add the melted butter or fat. Beat the

Fig

dry mixture into the eggs and mix well. Cover and refrigerate for 8 hours or overnight. 2. Bring two quarts of salted water to a boil in a large pot. Wet your hands and roll balls of the dough to make dumplings (smaller balls ensure lighter dumplings). Drop the dumplings into the boiling water, cover, and cook for 45 minutes. Shake the pot every so often during cooking so that the dumplings will not stick to the bottom of the pot. 3. Remove the dumplings from the pot with a slotted spoon. If you serve them with a casserole, add them to the casserole during the last 15 minutes of baking. Add them to soups and stews and cook for about 15 to 30 minutes. *Makes 8 dumplings*

Semolina Sweet Cake

1 cup melted butter *or* margarine
1 cup sugar
5 eggs, beaten (6 if milk is not used)
1 cup semolina
2 cups chopped blanched walnuts
    or almonds
1 cup all-purpose flour
2 teaspoons baking powder
½ cup milk (optional)
1 cup coarsely ground walnuts
    or almonds

Syrup:
2 cups sugar
1 cup water
1 teaspoon lemon juice *or* orange
    blossom water

1. In a large bowl, combine the melted butter and sugar and add the eggs. Fold in the semolina, chopped nuts, flour, baking powder, and milk. Pour into a greased, rectangular baking pan and top with the ground nuts. Bake in a pre-heated 350° oven for 45 minutes or until golden. 2. Carve the cake into diamond-shape portions, but do not cut all the way through. 3. Now make the syrup. In a saucepan, cook the sugar and water together for 15 minutes. Add the lemon juice or orange blossom water and cool. 4. Pour the syrup over the warm cake. Cover the cake with foil and let it sit in the warm oven (with the heat turned off!) for 1 hour. Then remove the cake and cut all the way through the diamond pattern. Turn each piece upside down onto a serving plate—this looks very nice and distributes the syrup evenly. *Makes 36 pieces*

Filled Semolina Cakes
(*Ma'amoul*)

Dough:
2 cups medium semolina
1 cup all-purpose flour
1 cup melted margarine *or* oil
1 cup sugar

Filling:
1 cup finely chopped almonds *or*
    walnuts
½ cup sugar
1 teaspoon ground cinnamon
1 tablespoon rose water *or* 1 teaspoon
    vanilla extract

1. Mix all the dough ingredients together and let rest for 1 hour. Form the dough into large egg shapes.   2. Mix all the filling ingredients together. Make a well in each dough shape with your thumb, then fill and pinch the dough closed over the filling. Press down lightly with a fork on the tops of the cakes to make a pattern. Bake in a preheated 350° oven for 25 minutes. When cool, sprinkle with sugar. *Makes 30 cakes*

Semolina Marzipan

½ cup fine semolina
¼ cup sugar
1 cup confectioners' sugar
pinch of salt
1 egg white

1 teaspoon almond extract
¼ teaspoon lemon juice
3 tablespoons ground almonds
1 teaspoon cocoa powder

1. Mix the semolina, sugar, confectioners' sugar, and salt with the egg white to make a heavy paste. Add the almond extract, lemon juice, and almonds.   2. Shape the paste into small balls and roll them in cocoa to coat. *Makes 16 balls*

Summer Semolina Pudding

1 cup water
2 cups orange juice
¾ cup medium semolina
1 cup castor sugar
grated rind of 3 lemons

½ cup lemon juice
tangerine sections (optional)
1 teaspoon ground cinnamon
   (optional)

1. In a saucepan, bring the water to a boil. Combine the orange juice, semolina, and sugar, and add them to the boiling water. Return the mixture to a boil, stirring.   2. Pour this mixture into a bowl. Add the lemon rind and lemon juice, and beat the mixture with a hand-held beater until it cools. Pour into a serving dish and chill. Garnish with tangerine sections, or sprinkle with cinnamon. *Serves 6*

Winter Semolina Pudding

3 cups water
3 cups sugar
1 teaspoon lemon juice
1 cup fine semolina

½ cup unsalted butter
1 teaspoon cinnamon
1 cup heavy cream, whipped

1. In a saucepan, combine the water, sugar, and lemon juice. Simmer it until it thickens into a syrup.   2. Fry the semolina in the butter for 5 minutes. Add the syrup, stirring carefully with a wooden spoon. Allow the mixture to rest. Serve in small, warm dessert dishes and sprinkle with cinnamon and a topping of whipped cream. *Serves 6*

Carob, Locust Bean

MILLET (*Miliaceum*)

Millet is mentioned in the Bible (Ezekiel 4:9), and is also referred to by the rabbis in the time of Jesus. The cereal is mainly grown in warm climates, because it is tolerant of arid conditions. It is a summer crop that has served humanity from ancient times.

Three varieties of millet are cultivated: proso, pearl, and foxtail. The foxtail type is a small seed variety that is sometimes ground and used to decorate bread and cakes. In the United States, 90 percent of the millet grown is the foxtail variety, which is harvested for poultry and birdcage seed—lucky birds!

Millet was used in the Land of the Bible in areas where wheat could not be grown. Traditionally, it served as a cereal and was disdained as a food for the poor. Today's trend toward whole foods has put a higher value on vitamin-rich millet. Combined with vegetables and herbs, millet enriches stews, soufflés, and baked casseroles. When cooked, millet is fluffy and soft.

How to Cook Millet

1 cup coarse millet *or* 1 cup regular
    millet
3 cups boiling water

1. In a saucepan, combine 1 cup coarse millet with 3 cups of boiling water (or 1 cup of regular-grind millet with 2 cups boiling water). Turn down the heat, cover tightly, and cook for 20 minutes.   2. When the cereal is cooked, you can serve it as a porridge with sugar or honey and milk. *Serves 2 to 4*

Herbed Millet and Yogurt

1 cup cooked millet
½ cup chopped onions, fried
½ cup blanched and roasted almonds
½ teaspoon allspice

½ teaspoon cinnamon
½ teaspoon prepared curry powder
½ cup raisins

1. Mix all the ingredients together when the millet is at room temperature. Serve with yogurt or sour cream. *Serves 2 to 4*

Millet and Sunflower Seed Loaf

Loaf:
1 cup cooked millet
3 tablespoons finely chopped onion
1 teaspoon salt
2 teaspoons lemon juice
1 cup ground sunflower seeds
1 teaspoon soy sauce
1 cup matzo meal *or* bread crumbs
1 cup grated yellow cheese
1 cup milk
1 egg

Tomato Sauce:
1 teaspoon olive oil
1 onion, chopped
2 cloves garlic, crushed
1 pound ripe tomatoes, washed and
 peeled
½ green bell pepper
1 bay leaf
2 tablespoons chopped fresh parsley
1 teaspoon oregano
1 teaspoon basil
salt and black pepper, to taste
½ cup dry red wine

1. Combine the ingredients for the loaf. Bake in a greased loaf pan in a preheated 350° oven for 1 hour. 2. To make the sauce, heat the olive oil in a heavy frying pan or electric skillet (you may wish to make the sauce at the table) and sauté the onion and garlic. 3. Purée the tomatoes and green pepper in a blender and add to the pan. Stir in the bay leaf, parsley, oregano, basil, salt, and pepper. Bring the sauce to a boil, lower the heat, and simmer slowly for at least 30 minutes. Add the wine before serving. 4. Slice the loaf and serve topped with the tomato sauce. It is also good served plain, with butter. *Serves 6*

Millet Vegetable Stew

1 cup millet
1 tablespoon sesame oil *or* soy oil
1 cup sliced onions
½ cup sliced carrots
½ winter squash, sliced

1 teaspoon ground coriander
3 cups water
1 teaspoon soup seasoning (prepared
 herbal mix)
2 teaspoons soy sauce

1. Roast the millet by stirring it in a hot frying pan. 2. In a pressure cooker, heat the oil and sauté the onions and vegetables. Remove from the fire and allow the pot to cool. Add the millet, coriander, water, soup seasoning, and soy sauce and close the pot and raise the heat. When the pressure rises, lower the heat and cook for 20 minutes. Allow the pressure to drop slowly before you remove the lid. *Serves 6*

Double-boiler Millet Bread

❦ ❦ ❦

This bread is good for breakfast or a light meal. You can make this bread part way the night before, then finish cooking in the morning.

1 cup whole wheat flour	2 tablespoons honey
1 cup millet meal	¾ cup raisins
2½ teaspoons baking powder	2 tablespoons melted butter
1 teaspoon salt	1½ cups milk

1. Bring the water in the bottom portion of double boiler to a boil while you prepare the dough.   2. Sift the dry ingredients and add the honey and raisins. Combine the butter and milk and pour it over the dry ingredients, stirring until a dough is formed.   3. Butter the upper portion of double boiler and spoon the dough into it. Cover and cook for about 2 hours (add water to bottom pot as needed).   4. Spoon the bread into a bowl, pack it down, then turn it upside down onto a breadboard. Cut the bread into wedges and serve with butter and date or fig syrup (page 127). *Makes 1 loaf*

RICE

Rice was introduced to the Land of Israel in the Second Temple period. The subtropical conditions of northern Israel were suitable for growing rice, especially in the Baneas area of the Dan Valley. The quality of rice that was grown then was a superior type suitable for export.

Rice is a cereal grain, an annual summer crop grown in water after careful sowing preparation. Instead of plowing the earth, farmers simply stirred it with water. It was ready to eat after the husk had been removed by threshing to loosen the hulls, and the skin of the seed had been removed by pounding. Rice is more productive than wheat, and the comparative ease of processing made it a major crop.

Modern attempts to grow rice in Israel have not proved very economical. Limited space for planting has been a factor. In addition, rice is bereft of gluten and unsuitable for bread making unless flour is added. These factors have combined to influence the decision not to grow rice.

Rice cultivation may no longer exist in Israel, but rice consumption is high. Rice is to Middle Eastern cuisine what potatoes are to Irish cooking or pasta to Italian cooking.

Of the three basic types of rice in use today—long grain, medium grain, and short grain—the long grain *basmati* or *patna* rice and imported converted rice are most popular in Israel. Brown rice is becoming more popular, especially among the younger generation of health food enthusiasts. Whatever you use, rice is rice when it is served simply, or pilav when included with other ingredients. A mainstay of the daily Israeli diet is rice-stuffed vegetables.

How to Cook Rice

❦ ❦ ❦

Although most of the rice available today in the Western world has been so thoroughly milled that washing is unnecessary, rinsing rice before cooking is customary in Israel. If you use packaged rice, follow the package directions. If not, use one of the following three cooking methods:

Method 1.

Put 1 cup of rice in a heat-proof bowl and pour boiling water over it. Stir it well to remove any impurities and drain in a metal colander. Rinse well with cold water until the rice is clean. Put the washed rice into 2 cups of boiling salted water, and allow it to boil briskly for a few minutes. Then lower the heat, cover the pot, and cook for 10 minutes. Add 2 tablespoons of oil, cover the pot, and allow the rice to absorb the oil. *Serves 2 to 4*

Method 2.

Wash and rinse the rice according to method 1. In a pot, heat 2 tablespoons of oil. Sauté the rice until the grains have been coated with oil. Add 2 cups of boiling water and cover the pot tightly. Boil for about 20 minutes. Turn off the heat and allow rice to rest, covered, for 10 minutes. *Serves 2 to 4*

Method 3.

Wash and rinse the rice according to method 1. Combine it with 2 cups of water and boil on medium heat until most of the water has been absorbed. Remove the pot from the heat, cover it with a clean napkin, and place a tight-fitting lid on top. Allow the rice to stand for 20 minutes until all the water has been absorbed. *Serves 2 to 4*

Saffron Rice: Add ¼ teaspoon of powdered saffron or ½ teaspoon to the rice in method 2.

Herbed Rice: To 2 or 3 cups of hot, cooked rice, add 2 tablespoons of chopped fresh parsley and 2 tablespoons of chopped chives or scallions.

Almond Rice: Garnish cooked rice with ½ cup of blanched and lightly fried almonds and a sprinkle of chopped fresh parsley.

Upside-down Rice

❦ ❦ ❦

This is a main dish for a buffet supper. Accompanied by a salad of tomatoes, peppers, and parsley, and finished off with fresh fruit or a light sweet, it makes an easy, entertaining menu. The presentation is effective.

2 pounds eggplant *or* summer squash
1 pound chopped lamb *or* beef
vegetable oil for frying
¼ teaspoon allspice
¼ teaspoon black pepper

¼ teaspoon cinnamon
3 bay leaves
1 large onion, halved
2 cups rice, washed and drained
fried nuts *or* parsley, for garnish

1. Peel the eggplant and slice into ⅓-inch-thick rounds. Salt the pieces evenly and put them into a colander to drain. (If you are using squash, slice but do not salt and drain.) 2. Brown the meat in oil in a pressure cooker or heavy saucepan. Add the rest of the ingredients, cover with cold water, and bring to a boil. Skim the scum off the top of the water before you close the lid. If you are using a pressure cooker, cook according to instructions for the type of meat used. Allow the cooker to cool before removing the lid. If you are using a saucepan, cover the meat and cook until it is fork-tender. 3. While the meat is cooking, prepare the eggplants. Rinse off the salt, press out the excess moisture, and pat dry. Fry them in oil until they are light brown on all sides (it is not necessary to cook them completely). Drain on a rack. 4. Strain the cooked meat and discard the onion and bay leaves; save the cooking juices to be used later. 5. In a heavy saucepan, place half the fried eggplant in the bottom of the pan. Cover with the cooked meat, and top off with the remaining eggplant. 6. Add the rice and 3½ cups of combined meat juices and water. Bring to a boil, lower the flame, and place a wire rack or heat-proof pad under the pot. Cover and cook for 20 minutes. Turn off the heat and let it rest, covered, for 15 minutes. Do not open the lid. Turn the dish out onto a large round platter and decorate with fried nuts or parsley. *Serves 4 to 6*

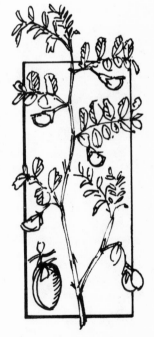

Chickpeas and Rice

❦ ❦ ❦

½ cup oil *or* butter *or* margarine
1 green pepper, chopped
½ pound onions, chopped
1 cup chickpeas, soaked overnight
salt and pepper, to taste

1 teaspoon ground cumin
1 teaspoon soy sauce
2 cups long-grain rice, washed and
    drained

Chickpea

1. Heat the oil or fat, add the green pepper and onions, and sauté until soft. Add the chickpeas and enough water to cover. Season with salt, pepper, cumin, and soy sauce. Bring to a boil, cover, and simmer about 1 hour, or until the chickpeas are tender.   2. Measure the remaining liquid in the pot of chickpeas. Add water to make two cups. Bring it to a boil, add the rice, and mix well. Cover the pot, lower the heat, and simmer for about 20 minutes. Allow the chickpeas and rice to rest in the covered pot for 10 minutes more. Serve as is or with harissa sauce (page 80). *Serves 2 to 4*

Rice with Noodles

Rice with noodles is often served as a luncheon dish with yogurt and a cucumber salad. You can make it in the morning, and keep it in a warming oven until ready to serve. In Israel, when a warming oven is not available, it is customary to wrap the pot of cooked rice (without opening the lid to look into it!) in newspapers and an old blanket or pullover sweater. The rice will remain warm for hours. Some people put the wrapped-up rice under the covers if it will be a long time before the rice is eaten. This is a great idea for cooking in a bed-sitter; of course you have to remember to take out the pot before going to bed!

1 cup long-grain rice	2 cups boiling water
¾ cup vermicelli noodles	1 bouillon cube *or* 2 teaspoons
2 tablespoons cooking fat *or* Indian	chicken or beef flavoring
ghee or vegetable oil	2 teaspoons salt

1. Wash the rice in boiling water. Put it into a metal colander and rinse well with cold water until rice is clean. Drain.   2. In a heavy saucepan, fry the noodles in oil or fat until they are light brown. Add the rice and stir until the rice is coated with fat.   3. Add the boiling water along with the bouillon cube or flavoring and salt. Let boil, covered, without stirring until almost all of it is absorbed. Lower the flame and place a wire rack under the pot. Leave to simmer about 20 minutes, until the rice is dry and fluffy. *Serves 2 to 4*

Moroccan Rice Salad

❦ ❦ ❦

½ pound long-grain rice
1 tablespoon olive oil *or* vegetable oil
2 tomatoes, chopped
2 cucumbers, chopped and drained
4 tablespoons chopped fresh parsley
3 tablespoons chopped fresh mint *or*
    1 teaspoon dried mint

6 scallions, chopped
salt and pepper, to taste
1 teaspoon ground cumin
½ teaspoon dried chili pepper, grated
juice of ½ lemon
olives, black or green, pitted and
    sliced, for garnish

1. Prepare and cook rice according to method 1 or 2 on page 88, using 1 tablespoon of vegetable oil.   2. Allow rice to cool slightly and add the rest of the ingredients. Garnish with olives. The rice salad should be prepared shortly before serving. If left to sit too long it will become too moist. *Serves 12*

5 LEGUMES AND PULSES

❧ ❧ ❧

Pulses, the edible seeds of a selection of leguminous plants, include the dried lentils, beans, and chickpeas that have served humankind for centuries. Legumes have constituted the protein balance to an early diet of cereals and cereal-pastes. These ancient foods have experienced new popularity in our health-conscious times—they are nutritious, filling, and fat-free.

FAVA BEANS OR BROAD BEANS (*Vicia faba*)

Several species of beans are listed in ancient Jewish sources. The most popular was the fava or broad bean, *pol* in Hebrew and *ful* in Arabic.

Many folktales are told about the fava bean. Greek tales suggest that fava beans disturb one's sleep and should not be eaten by prophets who need an undisturbed sleep. (Paradoxically, fava beans are said both to calm one's soul, and to disturb one's sleep because they are not easily digested.) Many people, especially those whose ancestors were from areas around the Mediterranean, are allergic to them. However, these hearty beans have served pharaoh, priest, and poor alike.

Fava beans cook slowly. (A Greek variety of broad beans, available in Greek specialty shops, needs less cooking.) It is best to cook the beans in unsalted water. Drain the water after an hour's cooking and replace it with fresh water. This method reduces the gaseous content of the beans.

Fava
(Broad Bean)

Boiled Fava Beans

This is a favorite supper dish in winter, seasoned with prepared ground hyssop and red sumac, and served with *pita* bread or whole wheat bread to scoop up any remaining juices on the plate.

1 pound fava beans, soaked overnight	6 hard-boiled eggs
2 cloves garlic, crushed	½ cup chopped fresh parsley
1 teaspoon olive oil	1 lemon, quartered
salt and pepper, to taste	

1. In a saucepan, bring a large quantity of water to a boil. Add the beans and return the water to a boil. Reduce the heat, cover the pot, and simmer for about 2 hours. Drain.   2. In a large bowl, toss beans with garlic, oil, salt, and pepper. Serve with halved hard-boiled eggs and garnish with parsley. Squeeze a little lemon over the beans if you like. *Serves 4 to 6*

Cholent

Jewish religious law prohibits work on the Sabbath, including cooking or heating food. However, dishes prepared in advance of the Sabbath and kept warm may be eaten.

In order to ensure a hearty meal for the Sabbath lunch, countless Jewish women in communities throughout the world have devised variations on the one-pot meal. To achieve this they have relied heavily on beans, potatoes, and barley, depending on family tradition and taste. The basic recipe uses food that not only stands up to the long hours of cooking, but is improved by slow, even cooking.

Cholent is a traditional Sabbath dish. This Yiddish word is thought by some to have been derived from the Yiddish for synagogue, namely, *shul*. "*Shul ende*" means *shul* is ended. It was then that a small child was sent to the local bakery to take the *cholent*, which had been placed there on the previous day when the fires were banked for the night.

Cholent is also called *hamin*, which means "hot" in Hebrew. Brisket or stewing meat can be added to the main ingredients. Many Jews from Muslim lands use whole chickens. Sometimes they remove part of the skin of the chicken and fill it with highly seasoned chopped meat.

3 onions, chopped
2 tablespoons chicken fat *or* vegetable
    oil
1 clove garlic, crushed
3 pounds brisket *or* stewing meat

8 medium red potatoes, halved and
    peeled
salt and pepper, to taste
¼ teaspoon ground ginger
1 cup fava beans, soaked overnight

1. In a Dutch oven, sauté the onions in the fat until they are brown. Add the garlic. Put in the brisket or stewing meat and brown. Add potatoes, salt, pepper, and ginger. Cover with boiling water and bring to a boil. Add the beans. Cover the pot, reduce the heat, and simmer on top of the stove for 1 hour.   2. Transfer to the oven and bake for 24 hours in a preheated 250° oven; or bake the *cholent* more quickly in a preheated 350° oven for 4 to 5 hours. Serve with cucumber salad or mixed greens. *Serves 6*

LENTILS (*Lens esculenta*)

The lentil plant was among the first plants cultivated by the peoples of biblical lands. Remains of the plant have been unearthed in archeological digs dating back three thousand years. The Bible credits lentils with being an important source of nourishment. They are said to be the plate of "red pottage" for which Esau sold his birthright to Jacob (Genesis 25:29–34). Ezekiel, the prophet, was commanded to eat for 390 days a lentil-and-bread mixture (Ezekiel 4:9–10). In 2 Samuel 17:28, we learn that lentils were a substantial part of the diet of David's army. Interestingly, the magnifying "lens" is so called because of its resemblance to the special shape of lentil seeds.

Lentils were considered the poor person's standby for centuries. However, as nutrition information became better known, the high protein content of lentils raised their status. Many people think of lentils as the basis for a substantial soup, and rarely eat them as a "side dish." But the diet of many people in Israel and the Middle East includes lentils as an important main dish. Vegetarians especially depend on lentils.

Lentils absorb sharp spices easily. In fact, the inclusion of spices is important for more than taste alone. They overcome the strong breath odor lentils sometimes produce.

Lentil Soup
with Spinach and Lemon

❦ ❦ ❦

1½ cups green or brown lentils,
    rinsed and picked over
8 cups water *or* 2 cups soup stock
    plus 6 cups water
1½ pounds spinach *or* Swiss chard
2 medium onions, finely chopped
3 cloves garlic, crushed
4 tablespoons olive oil *or* vegetable oil

4 freshly milled coriander seeds *or* 1
    tablespoon ground coriander
½ teaspoon salt
¼ teaspoon pepper
¼ teaspoon ground cumin
2 tablespoons lemon juice
sliced lemons, for garnish

1. In a large soup pot, bring the lentils and water (or stock and water) to the boil. Cover and simmer.   2. Prepare the spinach by washing it well, draining, and shredding the leaves. Add the spinach to soup and simmer for 45 minutes.   3. Shortly before the soup is finished cooking, sauté the onions and garlic in oil until soft. Add the coriander, salt, pepper, cumin, and lemon juice. Add this to the soup and simmer for 10 minutes. Serve with slices of lemon. *Serves 8*

Oriental Lentils

❦ ❦ ❦

2 cups lentils, rinsed and picked over
1 onion, chopped
3 tablespoons olive oil
1 teaspoon salt
1 16-ounce can tomatoes
¼ cup olive oil

3 cloves garlic, crushed
1 bay leaf
1 teaspoon black pepper
1 teaspoon ground cumin
parsley *or* 2 hard-boiled eggs, sliced,
    for garnish

1. Cook the lentils in 4 cups of water with the chopped onion and oil for 45 minutes. Add the salt and stir. Add the tomatoes with their juice, olive oil, garlic, bay leaf, pepper, and cumin. Simmer uncovered for 20 minutes, stirring occasionally so that lentils don't stick to the bottom of the pot.   2. Remove the bay leaf and transfer the lentils to a warmed casserole. Serve garnished with parsley or sliced hard-boiled eggs. *Serves 4 to 6*

Lentil

Herbed Lentil Casserole

❦ ❦ ❦

Serve this casserole as a first course, or with salad as a luncheon dish.

½ cup red or brown lentils, washed
    and rinsed
2 eggs, beaten
½ pound tomatoes, chopped
2 onions, chopped

1¼ cups grated cheese
1 teaspoon brewer's yeast
2 tablespoons chopped fresh parsley
1 teaspoon garlic granules
2 teaspoons powdered hyssop

1. Cook the lentils in boiling water until tender. Drain off surplus water.
2. Mix the eggs, tomatoes, onions, grated cheese, yeast, and herbs with the lentils. Place in a greased baking dish and cover with foil. Bake in a preheated 400° oven for about 45 minutes. *Serves 6*

Lentils and Rice
(*Megadarra*)

❦ ❦ ❦

This lentil-and-rice dish is still known today as Esau's favorite. Served hot, it is very popular in many Middle Eastern communities as a substantial dish for winter. During the summer months serve it at room temperature accompanied by yogurt.

    Generally, the proportions between the rice and lentils are equal; but either the rice or the lentils may be increased. The fried onions are the crowning touch.

1 cup lentils, washed and picked over
salt, to taste
1 onion, grated
3 tablespoons olive oil
black pepper, to taste
1 teaspoon ground coriander

1 cup long-grain rice, washed
2 onions, finely chopped, *or* 4
    tablespoons prepared fried
    onions
yogurt (optional)

1. Soak the washed lentils in cold water for about 30 minutes. Discard the water and boil the lentils in fresh water for about 1 hour or until they are tender. Add salt during the last 5 minutes. Drain, saving the cooking water.
2. Fry the grated onion in 1 tablespoon of olive oil until golden. Add to the lentils and season with pepper and coriander. Stir well. Add the rice, 1 cup of water, and 1 cup lentil-cooking liquid. Bring the mixture to a boil, cover the pot, and cook undisturbed for about 20 minutes. Turn off heat and allow rice

and lentils to rest. 3. Fry the chopped onions quickly in 2 tablespoons of hot oil until thoroughly browned, stirring constantly. (You may use prepared fried onions heated in oil for a few minutes.) Serve in a shallow serving bowl, garnished with the fried onions and accompanied by yogurt, if you wish. *Serves 6*

Lentil Patties

1½ cups lentils, washed and picked over
2 cups beef stock *or* chicken stock
2 teaspoons cornstarch *or* potato flour
½ cup onions, finely chopped
⅓ cup fresh parsley, chopped
1 teaspoon turmeric

2 tablespoons fresh dill, chopped
1 teaspoon garlic powder
salt and freshly ground black pepper, to taste
1 egg, beaten
2 cups fine bread crumbs
vegetable oil for frying

1. Cook the lentils in the stock for about 50 minutes. Blend the cornstarch or flour with a little water and add to the lentils. Cook uncovered over medium heat until most of the moisture has evaporated. Mash the lentils with the onion, parsley, turmeric, dill, garlic powder, salt, and pepper, or purée the mixture in a blender. Refrigerate until chilled. 2. Form into flat patties about 6 inches in diameter. Dip them in beaten egg and coat with bread crumbs. Refrigerate until chilled. 3. Brown patties in oil on both sides and drain on paper towels. Serve garnished with tomato slices, as an accompaniment to stewed beef or roasted chicken. *Makes 12 patties*

Variation: For a firmer and more piquant patty, mix the cooked lentils with 1 package of Israeli *felafel* mix and 1 beaten egg. Form into smaller patties suitable for hors d'oeuvres. Fry as directed above. *Makes 24*

Lentil Paste

Spread lentil paste on crackers to accompany cocktails, or on toast topped with a poached egg for lunch.

½ pound green lentils, washed and
   picked over
¼ cup butter *or* margarine
2 teaspoons dried parsley
1 teaspoon ground coriander

1 teaspoon soy sauce
¼ cup finely ground bread crumbs
3 slices onion, boiled
salt and cayenne pepper, to taste
hot clarified butter

1. Cook the lentils until tender. Drain and rub them through a sieve. Add the butter, parsley, coriander, and soy sauce, and mix well. Add the bread crumbs and onions, and blend to a smooth paste with a wooden spoon. Mix in the salt and cayenne pepper. Or, put all ingredients in a blender or food processor and process until you have a thick paste.   2. Place the lentil paste in a small, sterilized jar. Cover with hot clarified butter and refrigerate. *Makes 1 cup*

Indian Lentils and Chicken

Many Jews from India have settled in the *moshavim*, Israel's cooperative farms. They have adjusted their traditional dishes to the produce grown there, with a few purchased additions. This is a characteristically substantial dish.

1½ cups lentils, washed and picked
   over
3 onions, sliced
¾ cup *ghee or* margarine
2 whole cloves
3 cloves garlic, crushed
1 teaspoon ground ginger
2 teaspoons salt

1 teaspoon *garam masala* (see Note,
   page 100)
2 pounds chicken legs and thighs
1 medium eggplant, cubed
2 large tomatoes, chopped
½ pound frozen spinach, *or* 1 pound
   fresh spinach, cut up

1. In a large saucepan, cook the lentils in enough water to cover.   2. In a frying pan, sauté the onions in the *ghee* or margarine for 5 minutes. Add the cloves, garlic, ginger, salt, and *garam masala*. Sauté the chicken for 2 minutes in the same pan over a high flame until brown. Transfer the chicken to a warm plate. 3. Add the eggplant, tomatoes, and spinach to the fried onions and cook for 10 minutes. 4. Stir the lentils and blend them into their cooking liquid to

Lentil

make a sauce. Add the vegetables and stir until thick and stew-like. Return the chicken to the pot, cover, and simmer until the chicken is well done. *Serves 6*

Note: *Garam masala* is available in specialty shops that sell Middle Eastern and oriental seasonings, but you can easily make it at home. In a frying pan over a high flame, roast the following ingredients:

½ cup cardamom seed
2 tablespoons ground cumin
½ teaspoon ground cinnamon

¼ teaspoon cloves
2 tablespoons mace

Grind the roasted spices in a spice grinder or coffee grinder. Store in an airtight jar.

CHICKPEAS (*Cicer arietinum*)

Chickpeas are among the oldest known pulses. They are mentioned in Isaiah 30:24 (incorrectly translated as "provender"). Farmers in Israel and in other countries appreciate the special character of the chickpea. Unlike most plants, chickpeas enrich the soil in the course of growing.

Chickpeas grow in warm climates and are known by different names: *garbanzos*, in Spain and Mexico; *pais chiches* in France; *ceci* in Italy; *hamitz* or *afun* in Hebrew; and *hummus* in Arabic. They have long been hailed by nutritionists for their high protein content, and are often recommended as a substitute for meat.

The people of the Bible have prepared chickpeas in ways that accentuate the nut-like flavor. In Israel, many people use canned chickpeas, but more often they buy chickpeas in bulk for home consumption, since the method of cooking them is easy.

How to Cook Chickpeas

Cooked chickpeas are ready for many uses. Serve them with rice, meat, or stews.

2 cups dry chickpeas
salt to taste

1. In a large pot, soak the chickpeas in water to cover. Bring to a boil and simmer for at least 3 hours, loosely covered; or pressure cook for 50 minutes.   2. Drain, and add salt to taste. *Serves 4 to 6*

Salted Chickpeas

❦ ❦ ❦

These crunchy chickpeas can be served in a bowl and eaten like peanuts.

1½ cups raw chickpeas, soaked,
    cooked, and drained, *or* 1
    16-ounce can chickpeas

2 tablespoons vegetable oil *or* melted
    butter
salt, to taste

1. Spread chickpeas on a baking sheet. Pour the oil or butter over them and mix well.   2. Bake in a preheated 350° oven for 2 hours, stirring occasionally. Sprinkle with salt. *Makes about 3 cups*

Chickpea Paste (*Hummus*)

❦ ❦ ❦

Hummus is a wonderful dip for sliced *pita* bread or raw vegetables.

2 cups raw chickpeas, soaked and
    cooked, *or* 1 16-ounce can
    chickpeas
juice of 2 lemons
3 cloves garlic, crushed
⅔ cup *tahini* sauce (pages 212–13)

salt and pepper, to taste
¼ teaspoon ground cumin
1 tablespoon olive oil
1 teaspoon paprika
2 tablespoons chopped fresh parsley

1. Pour some of the cooking water and the lemon juice into the bowl of an electric blender or food processor. Add half of the chickpeas, and the garlic and *tahini*. Blend until smooth. Add the remaining chickpeas (save a few for garnish), salt, pepper, and cumin. The resulting creamy paste should be slightly thicker than mayonnaise.   2. Spread in a large flat dish or individual small plates sprinkled with oil, paprika, and parsley. *Makes 2 cups dip*

Israeli Chickpea Patties
(*Felafel*)

🍂 🍂 🍂

Felafel—spiced chickpea patties—are very popular in Israel. Although a pre-pared *felafel* mix is available in the United States, you can easily make your own. You may serve *felafel* as an hors d'oeuvre with *tahini* sauce (pages 212–13) or in a *pita* bread sandwich: Split a *pita* (see pages 56–57) in half to form two pockets. Fill up half-way with *felafel* balls, add cut-up tomatoes, lettuce, or vegetables of your choice, and top with *tahini* sauce.

**2 cups dried chickpeas, soaked and
    cooked, *or* 1 16-ounce can,
    drained**
1 large onion, chopped
1 egg, lightly beaten
**2 tablespoons finely chopped fresh
    parsley**
1 teaspoon salt
1 teaspoon garlic powder
1 teaspoon red pepper *or* chili pepper
1 teaspoon ground cumin
½ teaspoon baking powder
1 cup all-purpose flour
1 cup bread crumbs
vegetable oil for frying

1. Process the chickpeas, onion, and egg in an electric blender or food proces-sor until fairly smooth but not paste-like. Add the parsley, salt, garlic powder, red pepper, cumin, and baking powder and blend 1 minute more. Remove the contents from the blender container and mix in enough flour to make a pliable dough. 2. Moisten your hands and form the mixture into small balls. Roll the balls in bread crumbs. In a hot frying pan, drop the balls into enough hot oil to allow them to float. As the balls rise to the top, turn them over with a fork. When they are golden, drain them in a colander or on paper towels. *Serves 6 to 8*

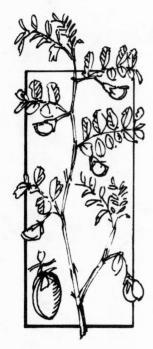

Chickpea

Oriental *Hamin*

This hearty, slow-cooking meal will fill your kitchen with a tempting aroma while it cooks overnight.

1½ pounds stewing beef	1 teaspoon cinnamon
1 calf's foot, cut into pieces *or* ½ pound beef marrow bone	salt and pepper, to taste
4 cloves garlic, peeled	½ pound chickpeas, soaked and drained
2 onions, chopped	6 eggs, in the shell
1 teaspoon Tabasco or chili sauce	

1. In a large casserole or pot, brown the beef. Add the calf's foot or marrow bone and continue to brown. Add the garlic, onions, hot sauce, cinnamon, salt, and pepper, and brown lightly. Stir in the chickpeas. 2. Cover with water to the top of the casserole. Wash the eggs and carefully place them in the pot. Put a piece of aluminum foil between the pot and the lid so that the pot is tightly sealed. Simmer gently overnight on a pilot light on top of the stove, or bake overnight in a preheated 250° oven. The eggs will be browned. *Serves 6*

Chickpeas and Rice

½ cup vegetable oil *or* butter *or* margarine	salt and pepper, to taste
1 green pepper, chopped	1 teaspoon ground cumin
½ pound chopped onions	1 teaspoon soy sauce
1 cup dry chickpeas, soaked overnight	2 cups long-grain rice, washed and drained

1. In a pot, heat the oil and cook the green pepper and onions until they are soft. Add the chickpeas, salt, pepper, cumin, and soy sauce and cover with water. Bring to a boil, cover, and simmer until chickpeas are tender, about 1 hour. 2. Measure the liquid in the pot of chickpeas and add water to bring it up to 2 cups. Bring to a boil, add the rice, and mix well. Cover the pot, lower the heat, and simmer for about 20 minutes. Add salt if necessary. Allow the chickpeas and rice to rest in the pot for 10 minutes more. Serve with harissa sauce (page 80). *Serves 4*

Chickpeas and Chicken Salad

3 cups cooked chickpeas
3 cups cubed cooked chicken
1 cup diced red bell pepper
⅓ cup chopped fresh parsley
⅓ cup sliced scallion
lettuce, chopped

Dressing:
⅓ cup *tahini* sauce (pages 212–13)
1 teaspoon salt
½ teaspoon black pepper
½ cup lemon juice
2 tablespoons water
2 cloves garlic, crushed

1. In a bowl, combine the chickpeas, chicken, red pepper, parsley, and scallion.
2. Mix all ingredients together to make the dressing. Toss the chicken salad with the dressing and chill. Serve on chopped lettuce or shredded escarole.
Serves 4 to 6

Variation: You may omit the chicken and *tahini* dressing, and serve with a caper dressing: Mix 4 ounces capers and their juice, 1 tablespoon olive oil, and 2 cloves garlic, crushed. Mound on leaves of iceberg lettuce, or pile the salad on a platter and scoop it up with *pita* bread.

6 THE FRUIT TREES

❦ ❦ ❦

And God said, "Let the earth bring forth . . . [the] fruit-tree bearing fruit
after its kind, wherein is the seed itself . . . "   (Genesis 1:11)

The fruits of Israel are rich with symbolic associations. The olive, fig, grapevine, date, and pomegranate all evoke images of mystery and wonder. What's
more, they're delicious to eat!

THE OLIVE (*Olea europaea*)

The olive tree is not the first tree mentioned in the Bible, but it is second to
none. More references link it to humankind and nature than any other fruit
tree. Its beauty and uses are manifold, reflecting the singular composition of
the tree itself with its silvery green leaves, its branches, its fruit, its pits, and
its oil. Each one in turn is the subject of high praise. Beyond serving humanity
in many useful ways, the olive tree symbolizes some of our highest ideals and
aspirations, as we learn in the book of Genesis.

After Adam and Eve's fig leaves, the olive leaves are the second to be mentioned. Genesis 7:6 tells the story of Noah. Noah, it is written, waited forty
days after the flood and then opened up the window of the ark. He released
a raven to ascertain if the waters had abated; but the raven did not return.
Noah was concerned. Later, he sent out a dove "to see if the waters were abated
from off the face of the earth." But the dove could not "rest the sole of her foot,"
and returned. After seven more days, Noah again sent forth the dove. "The
dove came in to him at eventide, and lo, in her mouth was an olive leaf it
plucked off. And Noah then knew that the waters had subsided from the earth."

Why, of all the winged creatures among those in the ark, did Noah send
out the dove? And why did he not send out the dove first? The homing instinct
of the dove must have been known to him, likewise its resting places. Doves
not only build their nests in cliff openings, caves, and the eaves of buildings,

Olive

they also nestle in olive trees. And so the dove found a resting place in the branches of this ancient evergreen tree, whose broad branches had in the past sheltered her from sun and storm. From it she plucked a leaf and returned to the ark. It was this leaf which gave Noah a clue as to the level of the flood waters. And so began a new day for Noah and his family and all manner of living things. God had made peace with them.

(As I was writing about Noah and the dove, I became aware of a cooing sound outside the window of my study. When I rose to investigate the sound I saw a dove. She was sitting on the windowsill under an umbrella of leaves and flowers. The moment the dove's rolling-ball eye spotted me she flew off, leaving bare the eggs she had been hatching. I left the room, and when I returned I saw that she had resumed her perch. She appraised me but made no move. From time to time I looked up from the typewriter and saw her watching me. Quietly, I moved to the window screen. She now seemed unafraid of me and I dared to speak: "It's all right, I won't hurt you or disturb the eggs. I'm also a mother. Actually, I'm writing about one of your biblical ancestors." The next morning she and the eggs were gone.)

Many homilies and interpretations have been written on the story of Noah and the ark, the dove and the olive branch. Common to them all is the factor of human sin and punishment, and God's magnificence in not only forgiving our corruption but giving us a second chance. Also common to them all is the symbolism of the dove as a homing bird, who brings the message of peace in the branch of an olive tree.

In artistic representation, the olive branch has been used to express individual and national hope for peace among peoples. The official emblem of the modern State of Israel is the *menorah*, a seven-branched candelabrum with an olive branch relief on both of its sides. The Great Seal of the United States of America is composed of a large eagle with an olive branch in its right talon and arrows in its left. The spacecraft that carried the first astronauts to the moon also bore the American insignia with an olive branch (the arrows, however, were omitted from the eagle's claws).

Rabbinic tradition holds that the dove brought back the olive leaf from the Mount of Olives, in Jerusalem, and also that in the end of time the Messiah will ascend the Mount of Olives. There Elijah shall blow his trumpet, announcing the resurrection of the dead (in consideration of this, it is an honor to be buried in the graves on the hillside of the Mount of Olives).

According to Christian tradition it was at the foot of the Mount of Olives that Jesus and his disciples spent the night before his arrest. From the top of the Mount, Jesus ascended to heaven after being crucified and resurrected. Accordingly, the Mount of Olives is regarded as a holy site. There the footprint of Jesus marked the last spot where he was seen by man as he passed to heaven. Similarly, Christian tradition holds, he will be seen there on his return.

There are four hundred species in the olive family, many of them wild. We do not know when the olive tree was domesticated; but evidence dating back to 3700 B.C. supports the conclusion that the ancient Land of Israel nurtured the cultivated tree, *Olea europaea* (the botanical term *olea* is taken from the

Latin and the Greek, *elain*). In the West *Olea* is used more for the oil than for the olive itself.

The olive tree was an image of fertility, so solemn concern regulated its preservation and survival. Felling the trees was only permitted under very special circumstances mainly related to its age, the presence of decay, or if the tree was past its fruit-bearing cycle. When trees were cut down they were usually lopped off at ground level. The roots were left intact so that new suckers would develop, thus guaranteeing regeneration. This cycle of renewal gave rise to the importance of the olive tree as a symbol of spiritual rebirth and nature's habit of regeneration.

The recent discovery (through a carbon-14 dating test) that olive trees growing in the Garden of Gethsemane (which is Hebrew for "olive press") at the foot of the Mount of Olives are over two thousand years old attests to the stamina of this ancient evergreen. When old age sets in, the tree's trunk broadens and becomes hollow inside.

When the first rains fall in late October and early November, the olive tree begins to ripen. Its fruit is left on the tree to ripen fully and is harvested only after the second rains, which improve the skins.

Harvesting of the fruit was done in two ways: by beating the branches with sticks, or by hand picking. In the latter, pickers drew their fingers down the branches in a milking motion, using a gentle pressure to release the olives into the picker's hand. In so doing the olives remained whole and were better for preserving. The first method was quicker, but the olives were bruised by the beating and many branches would fall off. This in turn caused less fruit in later harvests.

From time to time I have sought quiet in the hostel of the Sisters of Zion, in Ein Karem (the traditional birthplace of John the Baptist). There a beautiful mixture of colorful flowers, edible plants, and trees surround the convent and hostel. The nuns, both out of conviction and a tight financial budget, do not employ hired labor; they tend the gardens themselves. (When one of their community dies, they themselves dig the burial grave, as a special honor to the deceased. Only then is a priest summoned to officiate at the graveside.) However, when quick action is called for to save a harvest, the nuns do not object to volunteer help. It was on such an occasion that I and other volunteers assisted in picking the olives. We were allowed to employ the faster method. The nuns followed with the slower hand-picking method recommended in Bible times. We were amply rewarded with pickled olives and a bottle of first-class olive oil.

In Bible times, after the harvesting, pickers were forbidden to go over the boughs again. The fallen branches "shall be for the stranger, for the fatherless and for the widow" (Deuteronomy 24:20). This custom also applied to other harvests: "Gleanings, forgotten produce, and the corners of the field" (Deuteronomy 24:21) were also left for the poor to use. In ancient Israel the size of an olive was a main standard of measurement—even though different species varied in size.

Although olives were appreciated as a gift of nature and (in their pickled form) for their long storage value, the prime use of the olive was for the production of oil. Almost every phase of life was touched by olive oil, the only oil used in Bible times. It was utilized in Temple offerings (Numbers 28:5); in lighting in homes and in the Temple lamps; as a medicine (Isaiah 1:6; Luke 10:34); as an anointing oil for priests and for the crowning of kings; and to enrich cosmetics and tonics.

Many verses of the Bible describe ceremonial uses of oil. Jacob "poured oil upon the stone" (Genesis 28:18) that had been his pillow. In the way that salt was used in a covenant, oil too sealed a contract.

People in biblical times processed the oil from the olives by crushing and then squeezing them. A large stone wheel was set on edge, pivoted on a circular heavy beam, then turned on top of a circular stone basin, which held a supply of olives. Even a few turns of the wheel were effective enough to crush the olives. An alternate method involved pounding the olives to a pulp in mortars, or treading upon them (Micah 6:15).

The finest oil was made by placing the pulp in wicker baskets and straining the oil through them. This was considered the "first oil," and was used as fuel for the Temple's lamps, home lighting, and in daily oil offerings. The remaining soft, paste-like pulp was squeezed under pressure, and the resulting crude oil was stored in vats. In the course of time the sediment and water settled, and pure oil rose to the top. This in turn was carefully stored for future use. The second grade was produced by heating and further processing the pulp.

Workers added aromatic substances to the boiling oil, making it suitable as a protection for the skin against the hot sun. As a salve, oil-based anointment was used to sooth aching ears and throat. Perfumed oil was considered as precious as silver and gold (1 Chronicles 9:29; 27:28). Mixed with rose water, it had many cosmetic uses, including soap and skin tonic.

Today's latest research praises the high value of olive oil. It is a mono-unsaturated fat, which in our cholesterol-conscious times is the "best" fat. Not only does mono-unsaturated oil decrease cholesterol levels, but olive oil also decreases the level of damaging HDL (high-density lipoprotein) cholesterol. It is therefore recommended as a substitute for other oils and fats.

Olive oil is not recommended for deep frying, because it burns. But it makes the best salad dressing and adds a special flavor to steamed vegetables and gently poached fish fillets.

Although olive wood is very hard and beautifully grained, its uses are limited. It cannot be used in construction or in the manufacture of household furniture, but it is widely used to make small articles and a variety of religious artifacts made by Christian Arabs in Bethlehem and Nazareth. In old age, the olive tree's trunk broadens and becomes hollow inside. Olive tree trunks are often hollowed out further into decorative fruit bowls, carving boards, and key chain holders by local craftsmen.

The roots of olive trees spread out in shapes that have inspired their use as agricultural implements, especially the plow. The shape of the roots actually creates the design. The type of plow used by Arab peasants today is not very different from the plow of Bible times. It is beautiful to behold. Once I was driving near the town of Nablus (the Shechem of the Bible), and suddenly saw on display a collection of such plows. I stopped the car and asked the Arab owner if they were on sale. "Of course," he said, "we use tractors now." I delightedly purchased one, carefully packed it in my car, and when I got home proudly hung it up on my terrace wall, where it never ceases to intrigue visitors. A pity the Arab did not have an ass for sale, or I might have been tempted to buy one to pull the plow in my garden!

Tapenade (Olive Spread)

Spread this tangy olive mixture over lamb chops and hamburgers, or use it as a topping for quiche and pizza. You can also mix it with cream cheese for a cocktail cracker spread.

½ cup drained canned pitted black ripe olives
¼ cup drained capers
2 teaspoons prepared mustard

5 canned anchovy fillets, drained
¼ teaspoon crumbled bay leaves
¼ teaspoon dried thyme
1 clove garlic, pressed

1. Combine all the ingredients in a food processor or blender. Process until the mixture is finely chopped but not puréed. *Makes about 1 cup*

Olive, Almond, and Beet Salad

1 small head of lettuce, torn into bite-size pieces
1 cup cooked beets, cut into ½-inch cubes
2 tablespoons chopped scallions

1½ tablespoons red wine vinegar
¼ teaspoon Dijon-style mustard
¼ cup olive oil
salt and pepper, to taste
⅓ cup chopped almonds

1. In a salad bowl, combine the lettuce, beets, and scallions.   2. In a small bowl, combine the vinegar and mustard. Add the olive oil in a slow stream. Beat the dressing until it is well combined, and add salt and pepper to taste. Toss the salad with the dressing and sprinkle it with the chopped almonds. *Serves 4*

Walnut-Cheese Olives

❦ ❦ ❦

¼ cup butter *or* margarine
4 ounces cream cheese, softened
4 ounces blue cheese, softened
2 tablespoons minced shallots
2 teaspoons brandy

¼ teaspoon dry mustard
salt and white pepper, to taste
1 cup finely chopped walnuts, lightly
    toasted
24 pitted small green olives

1. In a bowl, combine the butter, cheeses, shallots, brandy, mustard, salt, and pepper. Cover the mixture and chill for 30 minutes. 2. Put the walnuts in a shallow dish. Pat the pitted olives dry with paper towels. Coat each olive with the cheese mixture and roll it in the walnuts. Transfer the hors d'oeuvres to a platter and chill them, covered, for 30 minutes, or until the cheese is firm. *Makes 24 hors d'oeuvres*

THE FIG (*Ficus carica*)

Fig

The identity of the Tree of Knowledge in the Garden of Eden remains a mystery. But many Bible commentators have held that because Adam and Eve covered their bodies with fig leaves after they had sinned, the tree must have been a fig tree. In the words of Rabbi Nehemiah: "It was the fig, the thing wherewith they were spoilt, yet were redressed by it. As it says: 'And they stitched a fig-leaf to make loincloths'" (Berakhot 40a).

One of the seven species with which the Land of Israel was blessed (Deuteronomy 8:8), the fig is often mentioned in the Bible together with the vine as the most important fruit of the country's fruit stock. The prophets warned against the destruction of the vines and fig trees (Jeremiah 5:17).

Dried figs dating from the Neolithic Age (5000 B.C.) were uncovered in the excavation at Gezer, in the lower hills of Judea. Ancient Egyptian inscriptions also confirm that the fig was grown in Israel, and refer to the destruction of the country's figs by its conquerors.

The many place names associated with the Hebrew words for fig attest to their widespread cultivation: Taanath-Shiloh (the Fig of Shilo, Joshua 16:6); Beth-diblathaim (House of Dried Figs, Jeremiah 48:22); Beth'phage (House of Unripe Figs, Mark 11:1); according to one interpretation, Bethany is a contraction of Beth-Te'ena, house of the fig.

Matthew 24:32 associates the coming of summer with the fig tree: "From the fig tree its lesson; as soon as its branches become tender and it puts forth its leaves, you know that summer is near." But a fig tree that failed to bear figs was cursed by Jesus (Matthew 21:18–19). This has been explained in Christian commentary as a possible symbolic reference to unbelieving Israel, destined to remain barren.

No small measure of the fig tree's importance was its acclimatization to dry farming agriculture characteristic of Mediterranean countries and to the rocky terrain of the hills of Judea. A deciduous tree capable of "cleaving to rocks," it can grow between fifteen and thirty feet tall, depending on its kind and care, and its thick leaves afford shade in the summer (John 1:48). In ancient times, it was sometimes trained as an espalier to spread out on a fence or trellis.

Figs also had medicinal use. King Hezekiah was cured when Isaiah administered a fig compress on his wound (2 Kings 20:7; Isaiah 38:2). The medicinal use of a fig compress to draw out infection continues today, especially among naturalists.

Rabbinical literature contains many expressions related to the fig tree and its special character. It discusses the early and late ripening of the fruit and the fact that the fig tree is dioecious, that is, that there are female trees and male trees.

The pollination of the female figs entails a complicated process and is only made possible by the presence of the fig wasp, *Blastophaga*. In other words—no fig wasps, no figs! To produce mature fruit the cultivated variety is subject to caprifigation. Flowering branches of a caprifig are hung in the tree so that the emerging wasps will carry caprifig pollen to the edible fig. The wasp deposits its eggs in them, and then, poor thing, it dies. Its body and eggs are absorbed by the developing fruit and only the eggs laid inside the caprifig fruit survive. What a creative death!

When warring conquerors sought to take over the land from the early Israelites, the agricultural base of the country was an object of assault. The special importance of fruit trees in supplying the diet of the people made them a high-priority target. Fig trees were among the first to be destroyed—and no wonder. The wholeness of the fig made it unique among fruits. Unlike most other fruits, the fig could be eaten in its entirety: skin, pulp, and seeds.

Ripe figs were anticipated, and relished when they matured. Every morning brought forth a new crop. When there were more figs than the people could consume, they were pressed into a honey-like mixture. This process continues today, especially in Arab villages. *Devalah*, the emerging fluid, is considered the honey of the fruit. And it was with this sweet fluid that the sages have identified the following passages: "a land flowing milk and honey" (Exodus 3:8); "honey out of the crag" (Deuteronomy 32:13); "honey out of the rock" (Psalm 81:16). Even in impoverished soil, fig trees developed their roots and bore fruit.

Some figs were dried, then made into cakes. They were valued as part of the presentation of the first fruits brought to the Temple. Strung like beads, they were decorative and more—their high sugar content guaranteed good storage and availability for eating during the fruitless seasons.

Fresh Fig Tarts
with *Sanbusak* Pastry

Fresh fig tarts are excellent brunch fare. You may serve them hot from the oven, just as they are. With whipped cream or vanilla ice cream they make a delicious dessert.

Sanbusak Pastry:

¼ cup vegetable oil
¼ cup butter *or* margarine
¼ cup warm water
1 teaspoon salt
½ pound all-purpose flour, sifted

Filling:

6 large *or* 12 small figs, stems
    removed
3 tablespoons sugar
4 tablespoons berry jelly *or* thinned
    marmalade

1. In a heat-proof bowl, mix the oil and butter. Place the bowl over a pan of hot water and heat it until the butter melts. Mix in the warm water and salt. 2. Pour the mixture into a large mixing bowl. Gradually add the flour with one hand and mix the dough with the other until it forms a soft, oil-moistened ball. Add more flour if necessary to make a pliable dough. Roll out the dough and cut it into 6 6-inch-wide circles. Place the pastry circles well apart on an ungreased rectangular pan. 3. To prepare the filling cut each fig into wedges. Lay the figs on the pastry circles in a star shape and sprinkle each tart with ½ tablespoon sugar. 4. Bake in a 400° oven for 20 to 25 minutes or until the crust is lightly browned. About 5 minutes before they are done, spoon 2 teaspoons of jelly or jam into the center of the star pattern on each tart. Bake 5 minutes more. *Makes 6 tarts*

Fig Bar Squares

Crust:

¾ cup butter *or* margarine, softened
1 cup brown sugar
1¾ cups all-purpose flour, sifted
½ teaspoon salt
1½ cups barley flakes *or* rolled oats

Meringue:

4 egg whites
dash of salt
10 tablespoons sugar
1 teaspoon lemon juice
1 teaspoon baking powder

Filling:

5⅓ cups (2 pounds) ripe figs, coarsely
     chopped
2 tablespoons lemon juice
½ cup sugar

1. To prepare the crust, mix all ingredients together thoroughly. Grease and flour two 13 × 9-inch pans and spread half the mixture in each one, flattening it with your hands so that the bottom of each pan is covered.   2. To prepare the filling, combine the figs, lemon juice, and sugar. (You can freeze it at this point for later use.) In a saucepan, cook the mixture over medium heat, stirring until it is thick and reduced to about 2 cups. As the mixture thickens reduce the heat to prevent scorching. When the fig mixture is cool, spread half of it over the pastry in each pan.   3. To prepare the meringue beat the egg whites and salt until fluffy. Beat in the sugar 1 tablespoon at a time until it is dissolved. Add the lemon juice and baking powder and beat until the meringue forms stiff peaks. Spread the meringue over the fig filling all the way to the end of crust so that it will not shrink. Bake in a preheated 350° oven for 25 minutes or until the meringue is golden.   4. When cool, cut the fig bars into squares. *Makes about 28 squares*

Figs in Honey and Port Wine

1 cup honey
⅓ cup port wine
3 cups figs, coarsely chopped

⅓ cup lemon juice
¼ teaspoon vanilla

1. In a large pan bring the honey and port wine to a boil. Add the figs and simmer for 10 minutes. Stir in the lemon juice and boil gently, uncovered, until

the sauce is reduced to ¾ cup. Let it cool slightly and drain the syrup into a small bowl. Stir in the vanilla.   2. Put the figs in a bowl and pour the syrup over them. Let the figs stand at room temperature overnight. The next day gently stir the syrup, without breaking up the figs. Serve just as it is or in small portions over ice cream. These figs will keep covered in the refrigerator for as long as 2 months. You can use any extra syrup for a fruit salad. *Makes 4 to 5 cups*

Pickled Figs

❦ ❦ ❦

10 pounds firm, ripe figs
about 10 whole cloves, to stick into
    figs
7 pounds sugar

1 quart citrus vinegar *or* white
    vinegar
1 tablespoon ground allspice
2 long cinnamon sticks

1. Wash the figs and leave them whole and unpeeled. Insert the cloves into figs.   2. In a large enamel or stainless steel preserving pan, mix together the sugar, vinegar, allspice, and cinnamon. Bring it to a boil, add the figs, and cook uncovered for 5 minutes. Remove the pan from the heat and allow it to cool. Cover and let stand at room temperature overnight.   3. The next day remove the figs from syrup. Bring the syrup to a boil, pour it over the figs, and let them stand at room temperature for 48 hours. Then remove the figs from the syrup, bring the syrup to a boil, and add the figs. Boil for a few seconds. Ladle the figs and syrup into hot, sterilized 1-pint jars. Seal at once. Allow the figs to pickle for 3 to 4 weeks before serving. *Makes 10 pounds*

After-dinner
Dried Fig Bites

❦ ❦ ❦

These morsels are wonderful with strong, after-dinner coffee.

½ pound dried figs, washed and
    drained

1 cup sherry wine
1 teaspoon cinnamon

1. In a medium-sized bowl, combine the wine and cinnamon. Add the figs and marinate for 1 hour. The figs should absorb all of the marinade so that they won't be runny.   2. Arrange them on a plate with a toothpick in each fig.
Serves 4

Passover Fruit Mortar
(*Charoses*)

This Middle Eastern dish is symbolic of the mortar the Hebrew people made as slaves in Egypt. It is served on matzo during the Passover Seder service, but it can also be served as a rich, sugarless dessert. Rolled into balls and coated with ground coconut it goes wonderfully with an assortment of cheeses.

20 dried figs and dates, finely
    chopped
4 tablespoons sesame seeds
2 teaspoons powdered ginger
½ cup matzo meal

dry red wine
juice of 1 lemon
rind of 1 lemon, finely grated
1 teaspoon paprika (optional)

1. In a large bowl, mix all the ingredients with a fork until well blended. The matzo meal is used to bind the ingredients, so add more if necessary. *Makes 1½ cups*

Dried Fig and Sherry Loaf

1½ cups ripe dark or light figs,
    coarsely chopped
¼ cup dry sherry
1⅔ cups all-purpose flour
½ cup chopped walnuts
1 teaspoon ground cinnamon

1 teaspoon baking soda
½ teaspoon ground nutmeg
½ teaspoon salt
1½ cups sugar
½ cup vegetable oil
2 large eggs

1. Combine the figs and sherry and let stand for at least 15 minutes. In another bowl, mix together the flour, walnuts, cinnamon, baking soda, nutmeg, and salt. 2. In a large bowl or electric mixer, beat the sugar, oil, and eggs. Blend in the flour mixture; stir in the figs and sherry. Pour the batter into a well-greased 5 × 9-inch loaf pan. Bake in a preheated 350° oven for 1 hour and 15 minutes. Let the loaf cool in the pan and then invert it onto a rack to cool further. Serve sliced. *Makes 1 loaf*

Fig

Festival Bars

¾ cup butter *or* margarine	4 egg whites
1½ cups sugar	½ teaspoon lemon extract
1 egg yolk	1 teaspoon vanilla extract
1 teaspoon lemon juice	1½ cups dried figs
2½ cups all-purpose flour, sifted	1 cup jam (marmalade, blackberry, or
½ teaspoon salt	blueberry)

1. Cream the butter with ½ cup of the sugar. Add the egg yolk and lemon juice. Fold in the flour and salt. Pat the dough evenly onto a greased cookie sheet and bake in a preheated 350° oven for 15 minutes until partially baked.   2. Beat the egg whites until they form stiff peaks. Slowly beat in the remaining sugar. Fold in the lemon and vanilla extracts and figs, and spoon the mixture over the partially baked dough. Spread jam over the entire surface. Bake in a preheated 350° oven for 30 minutes.   3. While the dough is still warm, cut it into fingers or bars. Remove them from pan when they are cooled. *Makes about 60 bars*

THE GRAPEVINE (*Vitis vinifera*)

Biblical tradition identifies vine growing with the beginning of agriculture and civilization. Noah is the first vinedresser mentioned—and he is also the first drunkard (Genesis 9:20).

Since as far back as the Bronze Age, the vine has been cultivated in Israel, Syria, and Egypt. Both the vine and the fig were considered the main fruit trees belonging to the domestic landscape. They served the Hebrew people well as they made their way in the Promised Land. Of the twelve spies sent by Moses to explore Canaan, only Joshua and Caleb brought back a favorable report of the land's bounty and fertility. To prove it, "They . . . cut down . . . a branch with one cluster of grapes, and they bore it upon a pole between two" (Numbers 13:23).

The Bible mentions the grapevine sixteen times. (Other vines are identified by their particular nomenclature, such as cucumber or melon.) Perhaps more than any other fruit mentioned in the Bible, the vine and the vineyard have inspired parable and poetry in an aura of youthful romance. In Amos 9:13, we read of God's special consideration of the vinekeeper: "And the treader of grapes shall overtake the sower of seed; and the mountains shall drop with sweet wine." As the first vintage of grape and wine were anticipated, the bounty and blessings of God were predicted for the future. In the New Testament the wine carried spiritual significance as described in John (15:1 ff.), when Jesus identifies himself with the vine.

A climbing shrub with long stems that bend and tendrils that curl, the grapevine's luxuriant foliage spreads out as if in a dance; it stretches upward or climbs onto the nearest object, enhancing every thing it nears. The untrained vine makes its way along the ground, soon becoming a massive ground cover. Inside the fruit, which is a berry, are two seeds in each of its two cells.

The vines that produced grapes for red wine were preferred in biblical times, but white-wine-producing vines were also planted. Only in modern Israel have the grapes for a dry white wine attained a position of importance.

In addition to grapes and raisins, juice and wine, vine leaves also have their uses—especially as wrappers for stuffings. The vine itself has structural uses. In a single year, if treated properly, it can produce enough growth to arch a walk, roof a trellis, cover a wall in leafy grandeur, or form an umbrella under which rest and meals can be taken. In biblical times the produce of the vineyard was a major contributor to the nation's economic wealth.

Isaiah's Song of the Vineyard (Isaiah 5) records the rightful method of tending a vineyard. The language is poetic, yet there is no loss of exactness in describing the cycle of agricultural operation in the vineyard. But woe to the vinekeeper who spared his time or strength at the expense of proper care of vine and grape! First the vinekeeper selected a field for planting; then proper clearing of thorns and thistles began, and large and small stones were removed. According to their size, these were used to make stone fences against roaming cattle trampling on the tender vines. Smaller stones were laid out in rows and covered with the uprooted thorns and thistles, to form a defense against the entry of smaller animals. ("Recycling" as a byword was not known to the early Israelites—necessity was the springboard to innovation.)

Careful attention to watering ensured juice and sweetness; moist roots were necessary during the whole of the growing season. But beyond the welcome winter's rainfall, from where did auxiliary irrigation come? The biblical text does not clearly explain the source. However, the long-established practice of collecting rainwater in cisterns, hollowed out of the rocks, surely applied in viticulture too. Even today, small water cisterns can be seen in the hills of Judea, located in the neighborhood of remnants of ancient wine presses and vineyard watchtowers.

In the process of making wine presses, large stones were hewn out of rock formations, and they in turn were used to build watchtowers. Building the watchtower was an important moment in the cycle of viticulture: it signaled the first vintage. Consisting of two stories, generally circular in shape, the watchtower gave the vinekeeper a good view of any approaching trespassers.

Much joy and excitement accompanied the gathering in of the grape harvest. Whether the vines yielded green, purple, or red grapes, and whether they would be eaten fresh, pressed, as sun-shriveled raisins, or consumed as juice or wine, the harvest constituted rich nourishment for the family and household. No wonder the vintage season was celebrated in gladness. It was in the vineyards that every summer the young maidens of Jerusalem, dressed in white, came out to dance in a special festival. The young men would look them over and select their brides. According to the rabbis, the vintage was the time when "The whole world and its fullness is like a vineyard. And what is the redemption? Abundance."

The vine juice was stored in vats or in new skin vessels for fermentation (Matthew 9:17). Now there would be wine enough for ceremonial uses in the calendar of feasts: for the Sabbath blessing over wine at the start of the meal; enough wine for the Havdalah ceremony at the end of the Sabbath, carrying the wish for a good week to come; enough wine for the four cups to be drunk at the Passover eve meal; two cups to drink to the bride and the groom at their wedding ceremony—and then in abundance at the ensuing festivities, as at Cana where Jesus ensured it could be drunk in plenty (John 2:1–11); then, when they would be blessed with a son, one cup of wine at the circumcision ceremony. There would be copious wine for the Purim festival, when it was considered meritorious to get at least a little drunk. And there would be enough wine to offer those who, God forbid, would have to be ready to perish and for those suffering bitterness in their souls (Proverbs 31:6). And of course there would be wine to toast the occasions of good fortune and good health with the traditional *"Le-Hayyim!"* ("To life!").

There are many joint biblical references to "corn, new wine, and oil" as the three important products of the land, while the vine and fig are partners in many descriptions of the good life that was and the hope for peace to come with every man sitting "under his vine and under his fig-tree" (Micah 4:4).

Bread and wine symbolized the basics upon which people could survive. Wine is described as "the blood of the grape" (Deuteronomy 32:14), and this concept is recalled in the words of Jesus over the cup of the Last Supper (Matthew 26:28–29). In time, bread and wine became the formula of the Eucharist (1 Corinthians 11:23–26).

Wine added to honey and pepper was a special dish, as was wine mixed with spices. The Persians introduced a "punch" of wine and pomegranate juice. In any case, a little wine was regarded as good for the stomach (1 Timothy 5:23). When old wine soured, it became vinegar. One might guess it was used as a tenderizer or pickling agent.

Jews were proficient vine growers, but many historical forces changed this, especially in the period of the diaspora. But because vine-keeping was so much of Israel's history, not a few attempts were made over the centuries to return to viticulture.

Vine-keeping was kept up over the centuries by the area's Arab inhabitants. When the Jews were able to return to the Land a century ago, viticulture was one of their pioneer enterprises. Because the Arab farmers cultivated table grapes, the Jewish farmers concentrated especially on wine grapes, using new varieties introduced from France. Soon Israel's wines became an export item; the sweet, sacramental wine was popular in Jewish communities around the world.

The industry developed greatly after the rebirth of the State of Israel, and various dry wines began to be cultivated. Wine growers complain that Israelis do not drink enough wine—the annual per capita consumption is less than 1 gallon, as compared with 32 gallons in Italy and 28 gallons in Spain! In general, Jews have not had a tradition of extensive wine drinking; and for the Moslem population, wine is forbidden. Many of the Christians, however, buy the sacramental and other wines produced in some of Israel's monasteries.

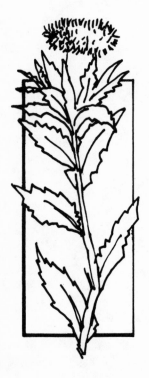

Safflower

Meat-stuffed Vine Leaves
with Egg-Lemon Sauce

½ cup short- or medium-grain rice
1 pound lean ground lamb *or* beef
    (or some of both)
1 8-ounce can tomato sauce
5 tablespoons lemon juice
1 medium onion, finely chopped
⅛ teaspoon cayenne
⅛ teaspoon black pepper
1 teaspoon salt

⅓ cup minced fresh parsley
40 fresh vine leaves (about a pound)
    or 1 16-ounce jar preserved vine
    leaves
olive oil
2 tomatoes, sliced (optional)
lemon wedges and chopped fresh
      parsley, for garnish

Egg-Lemon Sauce:

2 cups broth *or* water
3 eggs
3 tablespoons lemon juice

1. To prepare the filling, rinse the rice in cold water until the water runs clear; drain. In a large bowl, combine the rice with the meat, tomato sauce, and 3 tablespoons of the lemon juice. Mix well with your hands. Sauté the onions in oil until golden and limp and add them to the rice and meat mixture. Mix in the cayenne, black pepper, salt, and parsley.   2. To prepare the fresh grape leaves, bring about 6 cups of water to a boil. Separate the leaves and parboil them in the water for a few minutes. Remove the leaves and drain in a colander. To prepare preserved vine leaves, place them in a large bowl and pour boiling water over them, making sure the water penetrates all the layers. Let them soak for 20 minutes and drain. Then soak them in cold water and drain. Repeat the cold-water soaking once more to remove all the preserving salt.   3. To fill the vine leaves, put them in a pile with the rough side up and the stem toward you. Place one heaping teaspoon of filling at the base of each leaf. Fold the stem end over the filling, fold each side toward the middle, and then roll from the stem end to the top of the leaf until you have a firm cigar-shaped parcel.   4. Line a heavy skillet with extra or torn vine leaves and sprigs of parsley. Layer the stuffed leaves in a circle, sprinkling each layer with olive oil. Place sliced tomatoes on the top layer, if desired. Weight the contents with a heavy plate. Add 2 cups of water and a little salt, cover the pot, and bring the liquid to the boil. Add the remaining 2 tablespoons of lemon juice. Lower the heat and simmer for 1 hour, until most of the water has been absorbed. Allow the stuffed vine leaves to cool slightly in the pot. Carefully remove them from the pot, or invert the pot into a large, warm platter.   5. To prepare the egg-lemon sauce, bring the broth or water to a boil in a saucepan. Beat the eggs until frothy and add the lemon juice. Add some of the broth to the eggs, and then

gradually return this mixture to the broth, beating constantly until slightly thickened; do not boil. Pour into a sauce dish and serve hot with the meat-stuffed vine leaves. Garnish with parsley and lemon wedges. *Serves 4*

Meatless Stuffed Vine Leaves

2 onions, coarsely grated
½ cup long-grain rice, washed
2 cloves garlic, crushed
juice of 2 lemons
½ cup pine nuts
¼ cup fresh parsley, chopped
2 tablespoons fresh mint, chopped, *or*
    1 tablespoon crushed dried mint

½ teaspoon ground allspice
40 fresh vine leaves *or* 1 16-ounce jar
    preserved vine leaves
olive oil *or* safflower oil
2 tomatoes, sliced (optional)
salt and pepper, to taste

1. To prepare the filling, sauté the onions in oil until golden and limp. Add the rice, garlic, and lemon juice. Turn off heat and add the pine nuts, parsley, mint, and allspice. Mix well and cool. 2. To prepare and cook the vine leaves, see meat-stuffed vine leaves with egg-lemon sauce, steps 2, 3, and 4 (page 119). Refrigerate and serve at room temperature with a dollop of yogurt. *Serves 4*

Grape and Walnut Coffee Cake

½ cup butter *or* margarine
1 cup granulated sugar
4 eggs
1¾ cups all-purpose flour
¼ teaspoon salt
1 teaspoon baking powder
1 teaspoon grated lemon peel

½ teaspoon baking soda
½ teaspoon cinnamon
½ cup sour cream
1 teaspoon vanilla
3 cups seedless green grapes
1 cup coarsely chopped walnuts
⅓ cup firmly packed brown sugar

1. In a large mixing bowl, cream the butter and granulated sugar together until light and fluffy. Add the eggs one at a time, beating well after each addition. In another bowl, mix together the flour, salt, baking powder, lemon peel, baking soda, and cinnamon. Add half of this dry mixture to the butter mixture, beating until smooth. Mix in the sour cream, vanilla, and the remaining dry

mixture until smooth.   2. Spread the batter in a buttered 9- × 13-inch baking dish. Sprinkle the grapes evenly over the batter. Blend together the nuts and brown sugar and sprinkle over the grapes. Bake in a preheated 350° oven for 40 minutes, or until a toothpick inserted in the center comes out clean. Cut into squares and serve warm. You may refrigerate the leftovers and reheat them, uncovered, in a preheated 350° oven for 15 minutes. *Serves 6*

Grape Sorbet

Serve this refreshing sorbet in small dessert glasses topped with fresh whole or puréed grapes. For a color contrast serve with berries, thinned marmalade, or even a chocolate sauce.

1 tablespoon unflavored gelatin	grated rind and juice of 1 orange
3 tablespoons cold water	2 cups fresh grape juice *or* frozen
¾ cup sugar	concentrate, defrosted
1½ cups water	2 eggs, beaten

1. Soften the gelatin in 3 tablespoons cold water. In a small saucepan, bring the sugar and ¾ cup water to a boil. Boil until the mixture has thickened into a syrup. Add the gelatin to the syrup and simmer a few minutes. Stir in the orange rind and orange juice and grape juice.   2. Pour the mixture into an ice cube tray and freeze until it is mushy. Remove it from the freezer and cut it into strips. Put the frozen grape strips into a blender and process with the eggs. Pour the blended mixture into the ice cube tray and freeze.   3. When you are ready to serve the sorbet, put it through the blender one more time and freeze for 5 minutes. *Makes 1 quart*

Seedless Grapes
and Lemon Cream

1 egg yolk	1 tablespoon butter *or* margarine
2 teaspoons grated lemon peel	1 cup whipping cream
2 tablespoons lemon juice	4 cups seedless grapes, washed and
¼ cup sugar	halved, *or* blackberries
½ cup honey	

1. In the upper part of a double boiler or in a Pyrex bowl over hot water, mix the egg yolk, lemon peel, lemon juice, and sugar. Stir until the mixture comes to a boil. Add honey and butter or margarine; when the fat melts, turn off heat. Remove from the heat and allow to cool. Chill until thick.   2. Just before serving, whip the cream until stiff and fold in the lemon mixture. Serve over seedless grapes or blackberries. *Makes 2 cups*

Grape Upside-down Cake

2 cups seedless grapes rolled in sugar
12 glacé cherries
3 tablespoons butter *or* margarine
1 cup packed brown sugar
¾ cup margarine
2 cups sugar

4 eggs
3 cups sifted all-purpose flour
2 teaspoons baking powder
1 cup milk *or* water
1 teaspoon vanilla

1. Cover the bottom of a greased cake pan with the seedless grapes and dot with the cherries.   2. Blend 3 tablespoons margarine and brown sugar and sprinkle it over the layer of fruit.   3. Cream the margarine and sugar until they are light and fluffy. Add the eggs one at a time, beating between additions. Mix the flour and baking powder, and add to the batter alternately with the milk or water. Stir in the vanilla.   4. Pour the cake batter over the fruit and bake in a preheated 350° oven for about 50 minutes. Remove from the oven and invert immediately on a serving plate. *Makes 1 cake*

No-bake Refrigerator Raisin-Cake Roll

2¾ cups (1 pound) raisins
rind of 1 orange
¼ cup sesame seeds
¼ cup honey

½ cup grated coconut
½ cup wheat germ
½ cup orange juice
1 teaspoon cinnamon

1. Grind the raisins and orange rind in an electric blender or food processor. Add the sesame seeds, and put this mixture in a large bowl. Add the honey, coconut, wheat germ, and some of the orange juice. Blend well with a fork until it is firm. Add the cinnamon and more juice, if needed.   2. Separate the

mixture into two portions. Place each on a length of wax paper and roll the paper over it to form a 1-inch-wide log. Refrigerate. 3. Slice into rounds and serve in place of cake, or serve on a slice of orange from which the peel has been removed. *Makes 16 rounds*

THE DATE PALM (*Phoenix dactylifera*)

> The righteous shall flourish like the palm-tree; and grow like a cedar in Lebanon . . . They shall still bring forth in old age; they shall be full of sap and richness . . . (Psalms 92:13–15)

The date palm, dating back to the Neolithic Age, is one of the most ancient fruit trees indigenous to the Holy Land. A dioecious, evergreen tree, it has flourished along the course of the River Jordan, mainly near the Dead Sea. Considering the number of places that bear the Hebrew name for date-tree, *tamar*, and the fact that so many women were given the name Tamar, it is evident how important the date palm was in cultural and agricultural life during biblical times.

The palm tree has been ennobled in poetry and symbolism. In the Song of Songs 7:8–9, the beloved is said to be as stately as a palm tree. Deborah, the judge, sat under a palm tree when she judged the people (Judges 4:5). The tree's gracious and upright carriage has inspired people to emulate it and to gain confidence from the procreative strength of its vigor.

Growing to a height of 30 to 60 feet, it produces clusters both of male and female flowers and pinnate leaves 6 feet long. The pollination of the flowers of the palm tree is due to the wind. However, the Hebrew people observed that Egyptian agronomists used a more effective method of pollination. When the pollen of the male flower was ripe, a spiket of the male cluster was inserted into a fissure of the female palm flowers.

Even with careful assessment of the ovulation period of the female palm tree, it seems that there were occasions when pollination had not impregnated the tree. Not a few fruit tenders were wont to sense a measure of magic in the palm tree, particularly in the process of pollination itself. They were not surprised that not all male pollen was compatible with every neighboring female palm tree, and they accepted female rejection as a matter of course.

Much rabbinical commentary has been written about nature and our relationship to it. But they did not allow for the possibility, as suggested by some fruit tenders, that in fact there was actual communication both between people and trees and between trees and trees. They insisted that the silence of trees could be broken for one purpose only, to sing the song of praise unto their Creator: "Praise ye the Lord . . . Fruitful trees and all cedars" (Psalms 148:1–9). However, as it often happens fixed rules sometimes get out of hand, and behold—an exception shows up. In this connection, the story is told of one stately female palm tree in Emmaus. She was barren despite the fact that many attempts had been made to impregnate her with male grafts. One day, a tender of fruit trees offered his opinion: "That palm tree can see a tall handsome palm tree over there in Jericho. She nurses passion in her heart for it." And so a cutting was brought over from the Jericho male tree and this was grafted upon the heartsick female palm. In time she bore fruit.

We also read of the famous Rabbi Johanan Ben Zakkai who, it is reported, had a special talent for understanding the "speech of date palms." Skepticism of this talent was matched, however, with general praise for his outstanding accomplishments. As the story goes, "One windless day, so still that even when one spreads out a sheet of paper it does not stir, he who understands the speech of palms takes his position between adjacent palms. Then, carefully, he watches how their branches incline one towards another. It is in this moment that the gifted one can learn many things."

It is said of one medieval rabbi that he too was gifted in understanding the speech of palms. Because of that knowledge, "He was able to communicate great and wonderful things, the truth of which has been attested to by many." We know of inaudible sign language; perhaps one day the silent speech of palm trees will be understood by more people.

In Christian tradition, holiness and resurrection are associated with the palm tree. The Sunday before Easter, Palm Sunday, commemorates Jesus' entry into Jerusalem bestrewn with palm (Mark 11:8). The village of Bethany, where Jesus visited his friends Mary, Martha, and Lazarus (Luke 10:38–42; John 12:1–8), is the starting point of the traditional Palm Sunday procession which moves down the slope of the Mount of Olives to the Church of the Holy Sepulchre.

The palm tree also has many practical uses. In fact, no part of this majestic tree goes to waste. Its branches were used for housing in ancient times, and today for temporary booths in the desert. Its planed boards form ceilings, sleeping mats, donkey panniers, planting pots, and baskets. They play an important role in the Feast of Tabernacles, both in the synagogue ritual and to cover the temporary huts in which the Orthodox Jews spend the festival.

Due to enemy conquest and neglect, there were long bleak periods in the Holy Land when date plantations were few and far apart. "The city of palms"—Jericho—was bereft of fruit-bearing palms, to the dismay of travelers to the Dead Sea shoreland. In this century, date palm cultivation has been revived, and this important hot-weather fruit tree has been restored to the agricultural economy of the country. Once again the Jordan and Aravah valleys are bedecked with date palms which border the Dead Sea shores. Date cultivation too has returned to the southern coast, especially in the El Arish and Gaza areas. And so the daily diet is enriched with native dates, which crown the menus of festive occasions and national holidays.

Date Sherbet

¾ cup dates, pitted and chopped
3 tablespoons lemon juice plus
    pomegranate juice to make 1 cup
    liquid

2 large ripe bananas, cut into large
    chunks
1 8-ounce container plain, unflavored
    yogurt
¼ teaspoon ground nutmeg

1. In a food processor with a metal blade or in an electric blender, combine the dates and juices, and process until the dates are finely chopped. Add the bananas, yogurt, and nutmeg and process until smooth. Pour into a shallow pan, cover, and freeze. 2. Cut the frozen mixture into strips and process in the food processor or blender. Serve in individual dishes. *Makes 1 cup*

Steamed Date and Nut Pudding

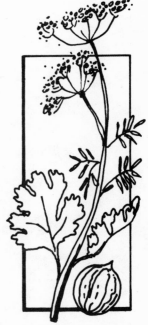

Pudding:

¼ cup margarine *or* butter
½ cup brown sugar
2 large eggs
2 cups soft bread crumbs
½ teaspoon salt
1 teaspoon baking soda
1 teaspoon baking powder
1 teaspoon ground allspice
1 teaspoon cinnamon
1 teaspoon nutmeg
½ teaspoon ground cloves
½ cup lemon juice
½ cup orange marmalade
1 cup chopped almonds
1 cup unpeeled, chopped dates

Hard Sauce:

⅔ cup margarine
½ teaspoon nutmeg
2 cups sifted confectioners' sugar
2 tablespoons brandy

1. In a food processor or blender, combine the margarine, sugar, and eggs. Add the bread crumbs, salt, baking soda, baking powder, allspice, cinnamon, nutmeg, cloves, lemon juice, and marmalade. Process until smooth. Put into a bowl and mix in the nuts and dates by hand. 2. Turn mixture into a greased, lightly floured 1-quart mold or heat-proof glass casserole, filling it ¾ full. Cover

Coriander

it tightly with foil and tie it with strong cord. Place the mold on a rack, and place the rack in a large pot half-filled with boiling water. Steam over constant heat about 2 hours, or until a toothpick inserted in the center of the pudding comes out clean. Check periodically and replenish water if necessary. Remove the foil to let out the moisture and serve immediately with hard sauce.   3. To prepare the hard sauce, cream the margarine and nutmeg until fluffy. Add the confectioners' sugar and brandy. Sprinkle additional nutmeg over each serving. *Serves 6*

Jellied Date and Nut Dessert

❦ ❦ ❦

2 tablespoons (2 ¼-ounce packages) unflavored gelatin
½ cup orange juice
½ cup boiling water
1 cup sugar
¼ teaspoon salt
1 cup pomegranate juice
½ cup sweet red wine
1 cup pitted dates, finely chopped
½ cup blanched almonds, slivered

1. In a large bowl, soak the gelatin in the orange juice. Combine the boiling water, sugar, and salt and add to the gelatin mixture. Mix the pomegranate juice with the wine and add to gelatin mixture. Refrigerate and chill until thickened.   2. Fold the dates and almonds into the chilled gelatin mixture. Pour into a slightly greased mold, refrigerate, and chill until firm. Unmold and serve with yogurt, whipped cream, or nondairy cream. *Serves 6*

Date Chutney

You can use this sweet and spicey chutney in curries, or add it to a lentil dish for a special flavor. It's also quite good combined with sauce for barbecued chicken. You may wish to preserve 3 cups of chutney and keep 1 cup, covered, in the refrigerator for everyday use.

1½ cups citrus vinegar *or* white
    vinegar
1 cup sugar
1 teaspoon dried garlic granules
    (available in herb and spice
    shops)

5 cups (2 pounds) chopped dates
1 cup raisins, chopped
¼ teaspoon freshly ground black
    pepper
1 teaspoon ground ginger
¼ teaspoon salt

1. In a saucepan, combine the vinegar, sugar, and garlic. Cook for 10 minutes or until it becomes a syrup. Add the dates, raisins, pepper, ginger, and salt. Stir well and cook for 15 minutes. Pack in hot, sterilized jars and seal immediately.
Makes 4 cups

Date and Cream Tart

Pastry:
1⅓ cups all-purpose flour
¼ cup sugar
½ cup cold margarine
1 egg yolk

Filling:
1 cup chopped, pitted dates
½ cup honey
¼ cup pomegranate *or* fresh orange
    juice
½ cup water

Brandy Cream:
½ cup honey
6 tablespoons all-purpose flour
1¼ cups milk
3 eggs, beaten
½ teaspoon grated lemon peel
¼ cup brandy
3½ tablespoons water

1. To prepare the pastry, stir together the flour and sugar. With a pastry blender, cut in the margarine until it is in small pieces. Then crumble the mixture with your fingers until it is mealy. With a fork, stir in the egg yolk until well blended, then work the dough with your hands until it holds together in a smooth ball. It should not be crumbly. Press the dough evenly over the bottom and sides of an 11-inch tart pan with a removable bottom. Bake in a preheated 300° oven

for 30 minutes or until golden. Cool.   2. To make the filling, combine the dates, honey, juice, and water in a saucepan. Cook over medium heat until it thickens. Cool and set aside. Spread the filling on the baked pastry crust. 3. Now prepare the brandy cream. In a pan, stir together the honey and flour. With a hand beater, gradually beat in the milk. Cook the mixture over medium heat, stirring until it boils. In a small bowl, beat the eggs. Stir some of this hot mixture into the eggs and return the mixture to the saucepan. Stir and cook just until it begins to boil. Then stir in the lemon peel, brandy, and water. Cool, cover, and chill.   4. Spoon the brandy cream over the date filling and chill the tart. Remove the pan sides before serving. *Makes 12 servings*

Marzipan-filled Dates

❦ ❦ ❦

Almond paste has long been associated with festivity and celebration. The combination of almonds and dates highlights the goodness of each—in fact, they are "fit for a king" . . . or queen!

1 pound pitted dates
grated coconut (optional)

Almond Paste:

3 cups (1 pound) blanched almonds
2 cups sugar
1 cup water
¼ cup plus 1 tablespoon orange juice
  or Kirsch
rose water (optional)
confectioners' sugar

Marzipan:

1 egg
1 cup almond paste
1½ cups sifted confectioners' sugar
lemon juice, as needed

1. To blanch the almonds, pour boiling water over shelled almonds and drain. Rinse in cold water, and rub off the skins. Grind the blanched almonds until they are very fine—at least three times, using the finest blade of a meat grinder, so the nuts will be oily. You can also use a food processor or electric blender.   2. In a small saucepan, boil the sugar and water to the end of the soft-ball stage. Add the ground almonds and orange juice or Kirsch and a few drops of rose water, if desired. Stir the ingredients until they are well blended and creamy. Cool. Dust your hands with confectioners' sugar and knead the mixture about 5 minutes. Pack the almond paste in a covered container and leave it a few days to "ripen."   3. To prepare the marzipan, whip the egg until it is fluffy. Work in 1 cup of the almond paste and add the sifted confectioners' sugar. Add a few drops of lemon juice if the paste gets too thick. If the paste becomes too oily, place the bowl over ice.   4. Wash, dry, and pit the dates, if

necessary. Mold the paste into small almond shapes and fit them inside the dates. Gently press the sides of the date together. You can roll the dates in grated coconut, if desired. Serve as is, or in small pastry cases such as those used for wontons. *Makes 1 pound*

THE POMEGRANATE (*Punica granatum*)

Of the five fruit trees mentioned in Deuteronomy 8:8 as being representative of the Land of Israel's bounty, the pomegranate is the most neglected in the Bible. Only in the Song of Songs does this veteran tree earn the praise it deserves. The beloved's cheeks "are like halves of a pomegranate behind your veil" (Song of Solomon 6:11), for only when the fruit is split open are its beauty and tempting, luscious pits visible. Elsewhere in the Bible it is the form of the pomegranate which provides inspiration. The golden bells which ornamented the Temple were inspired by the global shape of the tree's fruit, and the main garment of the High Priest was hemmed with a pomegranate-shaped ornament.

Early rabbinic references are more diversified. This can be seen, for example, in the homily that even in the most worthless and sinful Jews there is some good: "They are as full of good deeds as the pomegranate is of seeds"; or in the description of the Pentecost festival in the Temple, where, "They used to bring fresh fruits—olives, dates, and especially pomegranates." The number of seeds in the pomegranate is said to equal the 613 commandments derived from the Bible. Some pomegranate!

A deciduous tree, the pomegranate has been cultivated in the Holy Land for thousands of years. It grows both as a fruit tree and a shrub. The bush is widely used in container terrace gardening, where its bright red flowers are more desired than its fruit. The Hebrew name for pomegranate, *rimmon*, is found in many ancient place names in areas where these trees grow. As in the English word, which derives from the French *pomme-grenate* ("seedy apple"), the word in Hebrew has a double meaning. I was once startled when a *kibbutznik* with a faulty knowledge of English told me, "We have fruit plantations, specializing in growing hand-grenades."

In biblical times the seeds were eaten raw or mixed with date honey as a delicious dessert dish. They were also pressed into a refreshing juice, which was likened to wine in its richness. The fruit ripened at the end of summer when people were thirsting in their labors on hot days and longed to quench that thirst. Mixed with sweet wine, pomegranate juice produced a sweet-and-sour beverage worthy of use on special celebrations. Dried pomegranate seeds were used like raisins as flavoring agents.

People also used parts of the pomegranate medicinally. Its flesh and rind were both administered to fight respiratory ailments, stomach disorders, and internal worms. St. Jerome, writing in Bethlehem, called it "a kind of wine elixir for fevers of the stomach." Extracts of the rind and the bark of the tree also served dyers and tanners. Sometimes the extract was used as an ink (and

Pomegranate

a stubborn pomegranate stain on a white robe is as hard to remove as an ink stain).

Both the Hebrews and Canaanites adopted the pomegranate as an artistic motif, regarding it as a symbol of fertility and eternal life. Among peoples in the Middle East there was a legend that the Tree of Life was in fact the pomegranate. No small measure of biblical plantscape in art has its inspiration in the special shape and coloring of the red pomegranate fruit, blossoms, and flower. It appears in the design of mosaic floors, carved in stone on friezes, and in stone candelabra in ancient synagogues. It ornamented the curved column capitals of the Temple. It was depicted on ancient coins (and is reproduced on the coins of modern Israel). In early Christian art the multiple appearance of the pomegranate symbolized life everlasting. An example of the pomegranate in art (together with other fruits) can be seen on the floor of the cave of the Church of the Nativity in Bethlehem.

In the lingering veneration of village Arabs, it was considered to be a lucky tree with power against evil spirits. It was a tree under which one could sleep in safety and security. Legend holds that in each pomegranate fruit, one seed has come down from paradise.

The hilly regions are the traditional habitat of the tree, especially around Jerusalem, Bethlehem, and Hebron. However, it has been beset by pests: the pomegranate butterfly, trunk-boring beetle, and red mite have all caused leaf-drop and scale. And although pomegranate plantations are now to be seen in the Beisan Valley and in Arab groves in the hills around Nazareth, any dramatic development seems unlikely. Thanks to the juicer, pomegranates are still in demand. Pomegranate juice is a popular item, sold in Israeli street kiosks; and there have also been minor successful attempts to export frozen pomegranate pits. However, the fruit has become less important as a result of Israel's long strides in fruit cultivation, which has produced at the same season new varieties of peaches, plums, and apples, which are easier to open and to eat. But the exquisite flavor of the pomegranate remains worth the special effort to extract its juice.

Pomegranate Stew

½ pound ground lamb shoulder *or*
    veal *or* beef
vegetable oil *or* margarine
2 onions, sliced
½ teaspoon turmeric
½ teaspoon black pepper
1 teaspoon salt

1 pound mixed greens: scallion tops,
    fresh coriander, parsley, celeriac
    leaves
¼ cup fresh mint leaves, chopped
1 cup lentils
2 cups hot water
2 cups pomegranate juice

1. In a large pot, lightly braise the meat in a small amount of oil until slightly brown. Add the onions, turmeric, pepper, and salt.   2. Chop the vegetables and add them, along with the mint and lentils, to the pot of meat. Add the hot water, bring to a boil, and skim off the scum. Add the pomegranate juice, cover the pot tightly, and simmer for 1½ hours. Add water during the cooking if necessary; the stew should be soupy. Serve the stew over rice. *Serves 6*

Pomegranate-Ginger Sherbet

Serve this lovely pink sherbet garnished with sliced fruit, bananas, marinated raisins, or chocolate sauce.

1 tablespoon unflavored gelatin
3 tablespoons cold water
¾ cup sugar
1½ cups water
2 slices ginger root

grated rind of 1 lemon
juice of 1 lemon
2 cups pomegranate juice
2 eggs

1. Soften the gelatin in the 3 tablespoons of water.   2. In a small saucepan, boil the sugar and water until they become syrupy. Add the gelatin and the ginger slices to the syrup, and simmer a few minutes. Remove the ginger. Add the lemon rind, lemon juice, and pomegranate juice. Pour the mixture into an ice cube tray and freeze. Remove it when mixture becomes mushy.   3. In a blender, beat the eggs. Cut the frozen pomegranate mixture into strips and slowly add them to the eggs. Return the blended mixture to the ice cube tray and freeze until mushy. Remove and blend the sherbet once more. Freeze the mixture for 5 minutes and serve immediately. You can keep this sherbet for a month, covered, in the freezer. *Makes 1 quart*

Pomegranate

THE CAROB (*Ceratonia siliqua*, St. John's Bread)

Although the carob is not mentioned by name in the Bible, it is often referred to by the rabbis in the Second Temple period. They thought that the honey delicacy which Jacob sent as a gift to Egypt (Genesis 43:11) was made from carobs. Certainly the carob fruit can be made into a form of honey and the species particular to the Holy Land, *gedura*, is renowned for its sweetness. The saying, "He made him to suck honey out of the crag" (Deuteronomy 32:13) was also held by some to refer to the carob. Even today Arab villagers press the carob into a delicious kind of molasses called *debis* (which is the same word as *devash*, the Hebrew for honey).

References are also inferred from the New Testament. Luke 15:16 says, "He would gladly have fed on the pods that the swine ate; and no one gave him anything." The pods are thought to refer to the fruit of old carob trees used as animal fodder. And in the story of John the Baptist (Matthew 3:4), where we read, "He wore a garment of camel's hair and a leather girdle around his waist; his food was locusts and wild honey," the wild honey has been taken as coming from carob, hence the carob's second name—St. John's Bread. A similar story in Jewish tradition tells of the second-century sage, Rabbi Simeon bar Yohai, who with his son hid from the Romans in the caves of Galilee. They are said to have survived for twelve years on carobs alone!

A medium-sized evergreen, whose aggressive roots spread out almost as wide as its branch-stretch, the carob tree has a lot of personality. Its flowers are unisexual, males and females growing on different trees. They form spikes on old thick branches and eventually develop into many-seeded brown pods. The tree lives for centuries, and its girth is gross—"wider than the belly band of an ass," was a common village comment. A sentry tree in the early days of modern Israel, the carob was planted along open roadways to screen the view from enemy eyes.

However unfair it may seem that such a mighty veteran of the Holy Land fruit scene was not given biblical identification, the carob tree has stood the test of time. It sometimes takes ten years to fruit; but when it does, the product of its harvest is worth the waiting. Although it is not considered the choicest of fruits, the indigent ate it. Even today Arab and Israeli children with good teeth eat the fruit raw. Its timber was in demand for house furnishings and utensils. Israel Arabs still make a carpenter's glue from carob seeds, as Arab and Hebrew carpenters did in biblical times. Seeds were also used as shopkeepers' weights (hence our word "carats" for weighing gold and diamonds). Ground into a paste with flour, they produced a not unpleasant dish. After the Second Temple fell in ruins, poverty plagued all the Jews of the Land. Not a few more fortunate peoples around would mock and say: "Let us not be dependent on carobs like the Jews."

Ancient physicians held that carob fruit fortifies the intestinal process; it is said to be capable of checking phlegm, and is an aid in the treatment of gall bladder disorder. Today, milled carob pods are included in infant food preparations, as an aid to digestion, and for relief in stomach disorders. The pods are made into a syrup to soothe bronchial congestion.

In the early part of this century Aaron Aaronsohn (the discoverer of the mother wheat plant in Israel) introduced carob into the United States. American nutritionists have since proclaimed the carob fruit as a healthy substitute for chocolate. Low in protein, carob powder is also used in confections and milk drinks.

Glory, then, to the carob trees who in all their might now grace streets, divide gardens and plantations, and stand as sentries. They demand space, but little attention. They only occasionally need deep irrigation, when rain slackens. Perhaps research will someday reveal that carob trees, like chocolate, may carry aphrodisiac content. Imagine having your own home-grown sex symbols!

To Substitute Carob for Chocolate

For each square of chocolate called for in recipes, you may substitute three tablespoons carob powder and two tablespoons of milk or water.

Carob-Almond Cake

¾ cup melted margarine	½ teaspoon almond extract
1 cup honey	1½ cups whole wheat pastry flour
1 cup yogurt *or* sour milk	¾ cup ground brown rice
¼ cup apple juice	1 cup carob powder
½ cup water	1 tablespoon baking powder
1 teaspoon vanilla	

1. In a large bowl, combine the margarine, honey, yogurt, juice, water, vanilla, and almond extract. Sift the dry ingredients into the wet ingredients and mix well.   2. Pour into an oiled 9 × 9-inch pan and bake in a preheated 325° oven for 1 hour. *Makes 1 cake*

Carob,
Locust Bean

Carob-Apple-Banana Milk Shake

1 medium-sized apple
1 banana
2 cups milk

2 tablespoons carob powder
1 tablespoon honey
1 teaspoon vanilla

1. In a blender, combine all ingredients and blend until frothy. *Makes 3 cups*

Honey-Carob Cream

This recipe makes a nice drink or pie filling. If you do wish to use it for a pie filling, however, increase the arrowroot to ½ cup.

4 cups milk *or* soymilk
⅓ cup arrowroot
¾ cup honey

¼ cup margarine
⅓ cup carob powder

1. Blend all the ingredients together and pour them into a medium-size saucepan. Cook them over medium heat, stirring constantly, until the mixture begins to boil and thicken. Simmer 5 more minutes, stirring constantly. Remove from the heat and cool. *Makes 5 cups*

Raw Carob-Almond Icing

1 cup milk
¼ cup honey
2 teaspoons vanilla
⅛ teaspoon almond extract

¼ cup vegetable oil
1 cup carob powder
1 cup powdered non-fat dry milk

1. In a bowl, beat the milk, honey, vanilla, almond extract, oil, carob powder, and dry milk until they are smooth. *Makes 3 cups*

THE ALMOND (*Prunus amygdalus*)

The beautiful pinkish-white blossoms of the almond tree, which appear in January and February, are the first harbinger of spring. While other fruit trees are still bare, the almond tree is dressed in blossoms—long before its leaves appear. The fact that its blossoms appear so long before its fruit ripens was reflected in an old Hebrew proverb: "My son, be not hasty as the almond tree that blossoms before all trees but produces its fruit last, but be like the mulberry tree which blossoms last but produces its fruit first."

Almonds, like pistachios, were sent by Jacob to Joseph as a special delicacy of the Land of Israel (Genesis 43:11); in the desert Aaron's rod miraculously sprouted and produced ripe almonds (Numbers 17:8). Also in the desert, part of the ornamentation of the candelabrum in the Tabernacle was almond shaped (Exodus 25:33).

Two strains of almond grow in Israel: one produces pink blossoms and sweet fruit, the second produces white blossoms and bitter fruit. The latter grows wild in mountainous areas; the former does not grow wild and is regarded as a cultivated development, a result of grafting the original bitter almond (a sweet variety may have also grown wild in countries near Israel, where there are many species of wild almonds).

In the early part of the twentieth century, almost all the almond plantations were destroyed by the borer beetle. Almond cultivation was revived in recent decades, especially in the northern part of the Negev region, and now almond cultivation has again become an important part of Israel's agriculture.

Almond Paste

3 cups (1 pound) blanched almonds, coarsely chopped
3 large egg whites
¼ teaspoon salt
1 teaspoon vanilla
4 cups confectioners' sugar

1. Grind the almonds in a coffee grinder or meat grinder until they are finely powdered. Sift the powder into a large bowl. If any almond particles remain in the sieve, regrind them. 2. In a small bowl, whisk the egg whites with the salt until they are frothy. Add the vanilla and stir the mixture into the almond powder. Sift in the sugar, 1 cup at a time, and knead until it becomes a smooth, pliable dough. Divide the dough into 4 pieces, and wrap each one in foil. Chill until ready to use. The almond paste will keep up to 8 weeks if refrigerated in an airtight container. *Makes 4 cups*

Almond Cheesecake

½ cup sugar
4 ounces unsalted butter *or*
    margarine
6 eggs, separated
12 tablespoons (6 ounces) cream
    cheese
1 cup ground almonds
1 cup bread crumbs

Sour Cream Topping:

1 cup sour cream
½ cup sugar
1 teaspoon almond extract

1. Cream the sugar and butter together until light and fluffy. Add the egg yolks, cream cheese, almonds, and a little bit of the bread crumbs. 2. Whip the egg whites until they form soft peaks and fold them into the cake mixture. 3. Dust the bottom of a cake pan with a removable bottom with the remainder of the bread crumbs. Pour in the batter and bake in a preheated 350° oven for about 45 minutes, or until a toothpick inserted into the center comes out clean. 4. To prepare the sour cream topping, stir the sour cream, sugar, and almond extract until smooth. 5. Remove the pan from oven and spread on the sour cream topping. Return the cake to the oven and bake for 10 minutes (the cream will set when cool). *Makes 1 cake*

Spiced Almonds

½ cup confectioners' sugar
¼ cup cornstarch
1 teaspoon cinnamon
½ teaspoon allspice
½ teaspoon nutmeg

½ teaspoon ginger
2 tablespoons cold water
1 egg white
¾ cup (4 ounces) whole blanched
    almonds

1. Sift the sugar, cornstarch, cinnamon, allspice, nutmeg, and ginger into a shallow pan. 2. In a small bowl, add the cold water to the egg white and beat slightly. Moisten the almonds with tablespoonsful of the liquid mixture and roll them in the dry spiced mixture. When all the almonds have been coated, give the pan a good shaking to distribute them evenly. Bake in a preheated 250° oven for 1 to 1½ hours. *Makes ¾ cup*

Almond-Yogurt Soup

❦ ❦ ❦

2 tablespoons margarine *or* butter	4 cups hot water *or* consommé
2 onions, chopped	salt and pepper, to taste
2 tablespoons all-purpose flour	1 pint unflavored yogurt *or* sour
⅔ cup chopped almonds	cream
1 teaspoon ground fenugreek	⅓ cup roasted almond slivers

1. In a frying pan, melt the margarine or butter and sauté the onions until they are soft and golden. Add the flour, stirring until the mixture is smooth. Reduce the flame, add the almonds and fenugreek, and stir. Then add a ladleful of the hot liquid. Stir carefully, add the remainder of the liquid, and stir until it becomes smooth. Add the salt and pepper and check the taste. Bring the soup slowly to a boil; simmer covered for 15 minutes or until the flour has been thoroughly cooked and the soup begins to thicken.   2. In small bowl, beat the yogurt with a hand-held beater for 5 minutes. Add a ladleful of hot soup to the yogurt. Continue beating for a few minutes. Return the yogurt-soup mixture to the pan and beat the soup by hand. Allow it to cook over a very low heat. Do not boil, or it will curdle. Serve immediately garnished with roasted almond slivers. *Serves 4 to 6*

THE WALNUT (*Juglans regia*)

The walnut is mentioned only once in the Bible, in Song of Songs 6:11: "I went down to the garden of nuts." Although the walnut was known in Ancient Egypt, it was apparently not common in Israel in Old Testament times. It seems to have become widespread during the Second Temple period, however, when it was an important item in the country's economy.

Although many species are known in various parts of the world, only one species was cultivated in the Middle East; it was probably brought to Israel from Persia. Once developed, it was grown in most parts of the country, although there is evidence that it was mainly cultivated in the hills, especially in Galilee. The demand for walnuts was great. If there were not enough to go round, more were imported from Syria and Persia.

The walnut was also a source of oil used for cooking, heating, and lighting. Its outer husk provided a source of dye-stuff, while the branches and trunks of the tree were sturdy timber used for buildings and domestic furnishings. As in modern times, walnuts were grown in general fruit gardens, together with other fruits such as dates and pomegranates. Archeologists have discovered walnut shells dating back to biblical times.

The trunk of the walnut tree is smooth, and the rabbis used it as an example: If you climb to the top without due heed, you will fall down and be killed. So, too, if you govern Israel and take no heed how you govern, you must topple.

The tree is tall and broad, often growing to 25 feet. The leaves are large, odorous, and fall in the winter. The walnut tree blossoms in the spring and is pollinated by the wind. To the ancients, the structure of the nut symbolized fertility, while its solid cover and wholesome interior conveyed a sense of safety. This may have given rise to the custom of showering bride and groom with walnuts at the wedding ceremony.

Grafting is mentioned in ancient times as a method of reproduction, and is still used today. In modern Israel the growth of walnut trees has been neglected in favor of other cultivations regarded as more important; but single trees are to be found in all parts of the country.

Walnut-Cheese Olives

❦ ❦ ❦

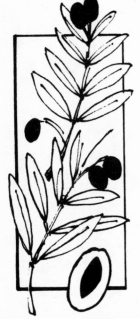

Olive

¼ cup butter
8 tablespoons cream cheese
4 tablespoons feta cheese, crumbled
2 tablespoons chopped shallots
2 teaspoons brandy

¼ teaspoon dry mustard
1 teaspoon ground hyssop
1 cup toasted walnuts, finely chopped
24 small stuffed olives

1. In a food processor or blender, process the butter, cheeses, shallots, brandy, mustard, and hyssop until well blended. Cover and refrigerate for 30 minutes, or until it is firm enough to hold its shape. If the mixture doesn't hold its shape, add a packet of powdered onion dip mixture or 2 tablespoons more cream cheese and chill a bit longer. 2. Put the walnuts into a shallow dish. Drain the olives and pat them dry with paper towels. Coat each olive with the cheese mixture and roll it in the walnuts. Transfer to a serving platter, cover, and refrigerate for 30 minutes or until quite firm. *Makes 24 hors d'oeuvres*

Walnut Salad Dressing

❦ ❦ ❦

This crunchy vinaigrette goes well with a fresh salad or over lightly steamed greens.

1½ tablespoons red wine vinegar
1 teaspoon Dijon mustard
¼ cup olive oil

salt and black pepper, to taste
1 clove garlic, minced
⅓ cup chopped walnuts

1. In a blender, combine the vinegar, mustard, oil, salt, pepper, and garlic.
2. Prepare the greens or salad and sprinkle the chopped walnuts on top. *Makes about ⅓ cup*

Walnut-stuffed Prunes

2¼ cups (1 pound) pitted prunes	2 tablespoons sugar
boiling tea	1 tablespoon lemon juice
1 cup walnuts, halved	confectioners' sugar (optional)
1 cup water	sweetened whipped cream (optional)

1. Put the prunes in a large bowl and pour the boiling tea over them. Allow them to soak overnight. Drain, pat dry, and stuff the prunes with the walnuts.   2. In a large saucepan bring the water, sugar, and lemon juice to a boil. Simmer for a few minues until it is syrupy. Carefully drop in the stuffed prunes. Simmer lightly for 30 minutes, adding a little water if necessary. The walnuts will absorb the syrup. Serve at room temperature with whipped cream sweetened with confectioners' sugar (optional). *Makes 2¼ cups*

THE PISTACHIO (*Pistacia vera*)

The tasty nuts of the small, deciduous pistachio tree are appreciated as much today as they were in biblical times, although pistachio nuts are mentioned only once in the Bible. In Genesis 43:11 Jacob tells his sons, who are about to go to Egypt, to take pistachios along as a gift to the regent (not realizing this was his son Joseph) as a choice fruit of Israel, which would presumably be regarded in Egypt as a special delicacy. Two species of pistachio were known to have grown in ancient Israel. Place names were called after them, because they grew plentifully in the vicinity. In later periods Arab place names in the country were also called after the pistachio tree.

Pistachio nuts can be enjoyed straight from the shell, or as an addition to other foods. They enrich the flavor of *baklava* (page 59) and filled semolina cakes (*ma'amoul*) (page 83).

THE CITRON (*Citrus medica*)

Citrus fruit is not mentioned in the Bible, although later Jewish tradition identified the "fruit of goodly trees" in Leviticus 23:40 with the citron. The citron looks like a lemon, but is larger, shaped more like a quince, and has a rough, thick skin.

The citron probably arrived in the Land of Israel during the Second Temple period, imported from its native India. It was cultivated for its use as one of the four species taken to the Temple (later to the synagogue) on the Feast of Tabernacles. Its individual shape and ceremonial usage led to its incorporation among the favorite artistic symbols of the Jewish people, and it is frequently depicted as a decoration in synagogue mosaics. Most vividly, it is recorded that when King Alexander Yannai acted contrary to rabbinical prescript in the Temple during the Festival of Tabernacles, "all the people pelted him with citrons"—which must have been like throwing ripe tomatoes at a bad actor in the theater.

The citron was a fruit of many uses. Its skin was eaten, either pickled or boiled to a pulp (in modern times, it has been preserved in brine, then cooked, and finally candied). Its peel was used as a perfume; and the fruit was regarded as an antidote to snakebite. Both sweet and sour varieties have been obtained by crossing citron with other citrus plants.

The citron today is used mainly in the Tabernacles ceremony (for which purpose Israel's citrons are widely exported to Jews in other countries), for the citronate extracted from its peel, and sometimes for making jam. For many centuries its descendants in the citrus family have taken pride of place. Its close relative, the lemon, provides all of citron's good culinary qualities without the same problems in growing and in having to remove a thick skin.

Citrus Peels Galore!

It seems a pity to throw away all those tasty, vitamin-packed lemon, orange, and grapefruit peels (if you have a compost pile, of course, you can throw them into it). The possibilities for using citrus peels are many—in making fruit drinks, fruit syrups, seasoning, and marmalade.

You'll find that adding rinds to cakes, stuffings, sauces, soups, and desserts will often change an ordinary dish into a gourmet treat. Lemon juice, in particular, is recommended as a flavor enhancer in a salt-free diet, and is often an alternative to vinegar.

If you keep a hand grater within reach, you can quickly grate peels to add the finishing touch to many dishes. Remember, the white pith beneath the peel is bitter; grate only the colored portion of the peel.

Citrus peels freeze well. In freezing they are softened, and ready for use in juice or marmalade.

Lemon Juice: Mix ½ teaspoon lemon peel with 2 teaspoons water as a substitute for fresh lemon juice.

Fresh Peel Lemonade: To make 1 glass of lemonade, mix the grated peel of 1 medium lemon with ¾ cup water and ½ teaspoon sugar. Allow the lemonade to sit for 10 minutes, then strain and serve.

Citrus Peels for Sauces: Remove the orange peel with a potato peeler and blanch for 3 minutes until the peel is limp. Wash in cold water. Chop finely and add it in small quantities to sauces and fruit drinks. Refrigerate the remaining peels for future use.

Citrus-flavored Sugar: Mix 2 tablespoons of grated citrus peel with 1 cup of sugar. Store in a covered jar in a cool place. Use it for flavoring compotes, icings, and puddings.

Candied Grapefruit Peels

❦ ❦ ❦

peels of 4 large grapefruits
3 cups sugar
1½ cups water

¼ cup honey
1 or 2 cups sugar, as needed

1. Quarter 4 large grapefruits. Carefully remove the peels, including the pith. Cut the peels into narrow strips. In a large saucepan, cover the peels with water. Bring the water to a boil over a high fire, reduce the heat, and simmer for 10 minutes. Drain. Repeat this process twice. Drain the peels on paper towels or clean cloth towels. 2. In a large saucepan, combine the sugar, water, and honey. Bring the mixture to a boil over moderate heat and let it boil for 30 minutes (push down any sugar crystals that cling to the sides of the pan). Stir in the grapefruit peels and simmer for 30 minutes, or until the syrup is thickened. Simmer the peels, stirring, for 15 minutes more, or until almost all the syrup has been absorbed by the peels. Be very careful not to let the syrup burn. 3. Cover several sheets of waxed paper with 1 or 2 cups of sugar, as needed. With tongs or a slotted spoon, transfer the peels to the waxed paper, and roll each candied grapefuit peel in the sugar. Let the peels dry at room temperature for 24 hours. Store covered in the refrigerator to keep fresh. *Makes 6 cups*

Party Lemonade

❦ ❦ ❦

There is no substitute for fresh fruit juice. If you are blessed with your own lemon tree, you can make use of the lemon leaves as well. Almost any stew or soup is enhanced by the addition of fresh lemon leaves. Dried, they can be used like bay leaves to flavor many dishes. If you are having a summer garden party, add lemon leaves to the punch or lemonade as you make it.

3 cups fresh lemon juice and the
squeezed lemons
3 or 4 lemon leaves
2 cups sugar

3 cups water
lemons, cut into paper-thin slices *or*
mint sprigs *or* pomegranate seeds
or strawberries, for garnish

1. Squeeze enough lemons to extract 3 cups lemon juice, and set aside. Make a syrup of washed lemon leaves and the squeezed lemon halves by adding the sugar and water and bringing to a boil. Simmer the liquid for 5 minutes, then remove it from the heat and allow the mixture to steep until it cools. Strain and combine with the fresh lemon juice. 2. In a large pitcher, combine the lemon mixture and about 6 cups of cold water. Refrigerate, covered, up to one day in advance. To serve, pour over ice cubes in a glass and garnish with lemon slices, sprigs of mint, pomegranate seeds, or strawberries. *Makes 10 cups*

Lemon and Ginger Sherbet

❦ ❦ ❦

Serve this tangy sherbet on a pineapple ring topped with grated chocolate. You can use orange juice, lime juice, or grape juice in place of the lemon juice.

1¼ cups water
¾ cup sugar
1 slice ginger root *or* ginger powder,
to taste
1 tablespoon (1 ¼-ounce package)
unflavored gelatin, soaked in ¼
cup water

1 teaspoon grated lemon rind
¾ cup lemon juice
2 to 3 eggs

1. Bring the water to a boil. Add the sugar and boil until syrupy. Put the slice of ginger root in syrup, or add ginger powder to your taste. Remove from the heat, add the gelatin, and allow the mixture to cool. Remove the slice of ginger. Stir in the lemon rind and lemon juice. Pour the mixture into an ice cube tray and freeze until the mixture becomes mushy. 2. In a large bowl or electric blender, beat or blend the mixture until it is smooth. Add 2 eggs (1 more if you would like a larger quantity of sherbet). Return the mixture to the ice cube tray and freeze for 1 hour or until solid. *Makes 1 pint*

Israeli Lemon Whip

juice of 2 lemons
peel of 2 lemons, grated
1 cup sugar
1 tablespoon (1 ¼-ounce package)
    unflavored gelatin, soaked in ¼
    cup cold water

4 large eggs, separated, *or* 6 medium
    eggs, separated

1. In a saucepan, heat the lemon juice and grated lemon peel. Add the sugar and stir until it is dissolved. Remove the mixture from the heat and allow it to cool. Add the gelatin.   2. Beat the egg yolks and gradually add the lemon mixture. Continue to beat until smooth. Refrigerate the mixture until it has thickened.   3. Beat the egg whites until they form stiff peaks. Fold them into the thickened lemon mixture. Serve in individual bowls, or in a large glass bowl. Top with whipped cream or freshly sliced bananas. *Makes 6 servings*

Lemon Curd

Lemon curd is good spread over matzo crackers, or as a topping for fresh fruit compote. You may also use it hot as a sauce.

1 cup sugar
1 cup margarine *or* butter
peel of 3 medium lemons, finely
    grated

juice of 3 medium lemons
3 eggs
1 teaspoon ground ginger

1. In the upper portion of a double boiler or in a Pyrex bowl over simmering water, combine the sugar, margarine or butter, lemon peel, and lemon juice. Mix well and stir occasionally until the margarine has melted and the sugar has dissolved.   2. In a small bowl, lightly beat the eggs. Stir some of the hot mixture into the eggs, add the ginger, and return the mixture to the pot. Continue stirring until the mixture begins to thicken. Lower the heat and cook without stirring for a few minutes, until the curd is thick but not curdled. 3. Ladle the hot curd into two sterilized ½-pint canning jars within ⅛ inch of the rims. Wipe the rims with a damp cloth, and close with scalded lids and screw-on bands. Cool. Refrigerate up to two weeks, or freeze up to one month. *Makes 1 pint*

Marmalades

Israel's Jaffa oranges belong to the Shamouti citrus family. They are sweeter than Spanish Seville oranges, and make excellent jams and marmalades. It is wise to make jams and marmalades when the fruit is slightly under-ripe. This ensures a good level of pectin, which is the jelling agent.

Jaffa Orange-and-Lemon Marmalade

4 oranges	4 quarts water
5 lemons	4 pounds granulated sugar, warmed

1. Scrub the oranges and lemons thoroughly. Cut them in half and slice into thin strips. Remove the pits and tie them in a bag made of cheesecloth or muslin, or a clean handkerchief.   2. In a preserving pan, combine the sliced fruit, water, and the bag of pits. Bring the mixture to a boil. Lower the heat and simmer gently for 2 hours, or until the peel has softened. Remove the bag of pits and add the warmed sugar to the pan. Stir with a wooden spoon until the sugar has dissolved. Bring the mixture to a boil and cook rapidly until the setting point has been reached, about 35 minutes.   3. Remove the pan from the heat and skim off any scum. Allow the marmalade to cool. Pour the marmalade into sterilized jars that are warm and dry. Seal with wax, or close securely with screw tops or circles of polythene transparent covers. *Makes about 9 pounds*

Easy Citrus-rind Marmalade

Fenugreek

1 cup orange rinds and grapefruit rinds, chopped	3 cups water
	3 cups sugar

1. Freeze the chopped rinds in a plastic bag.   2. In a saucepan, add the water to the frozen rinds and boil until the rinds are thawed. Continue boiling for another 15 minutes. (This is the basic marmalade stock. You can refrigerate it in a covered container and make the marmalade another day, or continue with the recipe.)   3. To make the marmalade, bring the stock to a boil in a 4-quart saucepan. Add the sugar and cook rapidly until a teaspoon of marmalade dropped on a cold saucer thickens.   4. Pour the marmalade into 2 warm, sterile ½-pint jars and seal, or allow to cool and cover with transparent polythene covers. *Makes 1 pint*

QUINCE (*Cydonia oblonga l.*)

Quinces have been available in the Middle East since long before apples and peaches were planted. Stuffed quinces are considered a delicacy. The sour quality of the fruit is a good companion to lamb. They also make an excellent paste, but more commonly are made into a jam. In Israel quinces are larger than those seen in Europe or the United States. Peeling and coring them is difficult, so they are sometimes parboiled before using them with meat or in making jams.

Quince Jam

6 pounds quinces	**6 pounds sugar**
2 cups water	**1 teaspoon ground ginger**

1. Peel, core, and quarter the quinces, reserving the peels and cores. In a large preserving pot, combine the fruit and water to cover. Simmer the fruit, covered, until it is tender. Remove the fruit with a slotted spoon and set aside.
2. Put the peels and cores into the pot and add the 2 cups water. Cover the pan and simmer until the peels are tender. Strain the juice, reserving the cooked fruit and peels. In the preserving pot, combine the juice and sugar. Cook, stirring carefully with a wooden spoon, until the sugar has dissolved and the syrup coats the back of spoon.   3. Return the fruit and peels to the pot and add the ginger. Boil gently, stirring constantly, for about 30 minutes or until the jam has set. If the fruit has not naturally puréed, mash it against the sides of the pot with the spoon and cook a little longer. Pour the jam into sterilized ½-pint jars and seal. *Makes 5 half-pints*

7 VEGETABLES AND GREENS

❦ ❦ ❦

> We remember the fish, which we were wont to eat in Egypt for nought; the cucumbers, and the melons, the leeks, and the onion, and the garlic; but now our soul is dried away; there is nothing at all; we have nought save this manna to look to.
> (Numbers 11:5-6)

In ancient times, men and women shared the quest for nourishment: men hunted animals for eating, and women gathered edible plants. Horticulture may well have begun thanks to the ingenuity of the women. Observing that certain edible plants had reseeded and then reappeared the next year, albeit at random, the gatherers collected the seeds and planted them in places near their dwellings, within easy reach.

The cultivation of vegetables was apparently limited in Old Testament times. A vegetable garden is only mentioned twice—once as a characteristic of Egypt (Deuteronomy 11:10) and once as developed by the king (1 Kings 21:2). Field vegetables were the rule, and garden vegetables the exception. They grew wild, were collected, and according to one account (2 Kings 4:38–40) were then boiled in water. It was only in the Second Temple period that vegetables seriously began to be cultivated in quantity, and now the choice became much more extensive.

Of the pulses, there is Bible reference to beans and lentils, while melons and cucumbers were found among the vegetables that grew wild. Sesame seeds had different uses, including the preparation of oil and to flavor stews. Garlic and onion also grew wild and were not cultivated in Old Testament times.

The chronic shortage of meat and poultry led to their use as vegetable stuffing. Eventually, this became an important method of using meat and poultry. Waterlogged, tasteless vegetables are not characteristic of modern Israeli cooking. Nor does vegetable cuisine fit a dictionary definition of the green stuff as "the lowest form of life." Neither are vegetables served platter-style. Israel has long had respect for the special character of each of the "fruits of the earth," in the words of the Jewish blessing said before eating vegetables.

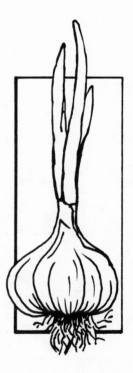

Garlic

How to Prepare Vegetables

Wash vegetables thoroughly. Do not allow them to soak in water either before or after cooking—the precious vitamins and flavors can be lost in this way.

Cook vegetables in their skins when possible. Save the cooking water for stock, soup, or cold vegetable juice.

Steam or cook vegetables in a small amount of boiling water until almost done. Add oil, margarine, or butter to finish the cooking (about 1 tablespoon fat for 2 cups of vegetables). Season with salt and spices during the end of the cooking time.

One of the best ways to cook many vegetables is the Chinese method of stir-frying, or slicing the vegetables into thin pieces and steaming them in a covered pan in a small amount of water until they are tender but still crisp. No objectionable odors develop this way, the cooking time is shortened, and the nutrition and taste of the vegetables are retained.

Vegetable Stew

❦ ❦ ❦

This hearty vegetable stew does not need meat to enrich it.

6 shallots, whole, with a portion of
    the stems
6 cloves garlic, unpeeled
3 turnips, peeled and diced
½ cup olive oil
½ head Boston lettuce, washed and
    sliced
2 cups cooked chickpeas or 1 can
    chickpeas (retain liquid)
heart of a young cabbage, cut in
    julienne strips
½ cup chopped fresh parsley, flat-
    leafed Italian if possible

Bouquet Garni*:

1 tablespoon chopped fresh parsley
2 bay leaves
1 teaspoon dry sage
1 teaspoon lemon balm leaves
salt and pepper, to taste
1 teaspoon turmeric

1. In a heavy iron saucepan or marmite, sauté the shallots, garlic, and turnips in ¼ cup of the oil. When the onions are soft add the lettuce. Add the bouquet garni. Cover the pan and cook over low heat, tossing vegetables from time to time with a wooden spoon, for about 30 minutes. Add the chickpeas and 1 cup of their cooking water (or the undrained can of chickpeas) and the remaining oil. Stir well.   2. When the vegetables are cooked, remove the bouquet, add

*Tie up ingredients for the bouquet garni in a clean cheesecloth bag. Remove the bag at the end of the cooking time.

the cabbage heart, and cook for 5 minutes more. Add a few tablespoons of liquid if the stew seems too thick. Garnish with parsley and serve in a tureen or right out of the pot to preserve the heat and aroma. *Serves 4*

ARTICHOKE (*Cynara scolymus*, Globe)

The artichoke is mentioned by the early rabbis. The wild artichoke (*Cynara syrica*) still grows in Israel. Because this magnificent, thistle-like plant can spread out its leafy base 6 feet wide, few private gardens here have room to accommodate it. It is grown commercially and sold with a portion of its long stem.

How to Prepare Artichokes

Select artichokes with tightly closed green leaves. Rinse the artichokes with cold water, slightly separating the leaves; or hold the artichokes by their stems and plunge them in and out of a bowl of salted water until they are clean. Drain. With a sharp stainless steel knife (other metals blacken the artichoke's flesh), cut off and discard the stems and tough outside leaves. Cut off the top third of each artichoke; cut away the tips of the remaining leaves with a kitchen scissors or sharp paring knife.

Place the artichokes upright in a pot just large enough to accommodate them. If the pot is too wide the artichokes will fall over. Add boiling water to cover, and 1 tablespoon lemon juice to preserve the green color. Cover and simmer for 40 minutes, or until the artichokes are tender but not mushy. Do not overcook. Turn artichokes upside-down on a plate until the water has drained out. Serve hot, with melted butter or olive oil and lemon juice; or at room temperature.

Middle Eastern Artichokes

Serve these artichokes at room temperature with the vinaigrette dipping sauce. They make a wonderful main course.

4 to 6 artichokes (1 artichoke per
    person)
juice of 2 lemons
1 onion, sliced
2 tablespoons olive oil
1 teaspoon all-purpose flour
1 teaspoon sugar
salt and black pepper, to taste
1 teaspoon basil

Vinaigrette Dipping Sauce:
4 tablespoons lemon juice *or* white
    wine vinegar
2 tablespoons artichoke cooking
    water *or* water
½ teaspoon mustard powder
½ cup vegetable oil
½ cup olive oil
⅓ cup chopped fresh parsley

1. Place the artichoke and all the ingredients in a pot. Cook according to the directions on page 149. 2. To prepare the sauce, combine the lemon juice, liquid, and mustard in a small bowl. Beat in the oils, adding them slowly in a stream, until the texture is smooth. Stir in the parsley. 3. Carefully remove the center leaves and choke of the cooled artichoke, scraping the heart until all fibers are removed. Spoon 2 tablespoons of sauce into the center of each artichoke and serve, or use as a dipping sauce. *Serves 4 to 6*

Stuffed Artichokes

❦ ❦ ❦

Serve this as an appetizer or first course.

6 small artichokes	1 egg beaten with 1 tablespoon water
6 ounces chopped beef	vegetable oil for frying
2 tablespoons bread crumbs	boiling water *or* soup stock
1 tablespoon fresh parsley, chopped	2 cloves garlic, crushed
salt and black pepper, to taste	juice of 2 lemons
2 tablespoons vegetable oil	hard-boiled eggs *or* fresh parsley and
1 egg, slightly beaten	lemon, for garnish
¼ cup all-purpose flour, or as needed	

1. Prepare the artichokes according to the basic instructions on page 149. Carefully remove the inner leaves and the chokes, and scrape the heart gently with a spoon until it is clean. 2. Combine the beef, bread crumbs, parsley, salt, pepper, and oil with the egg. Fill the artichokes with this mixture. 3. Roll each artichoke in flour, and dip it in the egg and water. Fry the artichokes quickly in hot oil, and arrange them in an ovenproof casserole. Fill the casserole half-way with boiling water or soup stock, and add the garlic and lemon juice. 4. Cover and bake in a preheated 350° oven for 1 hour, adding more water to the casserole if it becomes dry. Garnish with hard-boiled eggs or sprigs of fresh parsley and a slice of lemon. *Serves 6*

JERUSALEM ARTICHOKE OR SUNCHOKE
(*Helianthus tuberosus*)

The Jerusalem artichoke is not related to the Globe artichoke. It is part of the sunflower family, and is now called "sunchoke" in the United States. "Jerusalem" is thought to be derived not from the city in Israel, but from the Italian word *gerosol*, an earlier name for the sunflower.

Low in starch but rich in protein, sunchokes, like potatoes, are tubers and can be cooked and served in many of the same ways: in creamy soup, baked in casseroles, or cut up raw in salads. Sunchokes resemble ginger roots in appearance, and have a distinctive nutlike flavor that combines well with the taste of ginger. When washed well, there is no need to peel sunchokes.

Although not mentioned in the Bible or in talmudic literature, the Jerusalem artichoke has shared popularity in Israel with the common sunflower, which is indigenous to the Holy Land. (Sunflower seeds are to Israelis what popcorn is to Americans!) Sunflower seed oil is now used in making margarine, and is one of the treasured oils among health-food consumers.

Jerusalem Artichoke Soup

❦ ❦ ❦

2 pounds sunchokes, well scrubbed
2 quarts water
2 teaspoons lemon juice
4 stalks celery, sliced
3 tablespoons margarine *or* butter
1 cup chopped onions
1 clove garlic, minced
¼ teaspoon ground hyssop

¼ teaspoon black pepper
3 cubes vegetable soup flavoring
    dissolved in 3 cups hot water *or*
    3 cups vegetable stock
1 cup milk
salt, to taste
¼ cup chopped fresh dill *or* fresh
    parsley

1. Cut the sunchokes into ½-inch pieces and put them in a bowl of cold water to prevent discoloring.   2. In a large pot, bring the water and lemon juice to a boil. Add the sunchokes and celery and simmer, covered, for about 15 minutes or until the sunchokes are tender.   3. In a 5-quart saucepan, melt the margarine. Add the onion and garlic and cook slowly until the onion is soft. Add the hyssop, pepper, and vegetable soup mixture.   4. In a food processor or electric blender, purée the vegetable mixture. Then return it to the saucepan, stir in the milk, and add salt if needed. Heat the soup to boiling. Sprinkle with the chopped dill or parsley and serve. *Serves 4 to 6*

Jerusalem Artichoke Cocktail Balls

Dip these fried balls into *tahini* sauce for an unusual hors d'oeuvre.

2 pounds sunchokes, scrubbed
2 teaspoons olive oil *or* vegetable oil
1 cup dry bread crumbs
2 eggs, beaten
salt and pepper, to taste

1 teaspoon nutmeg
3 to 4 tablespoons vegetable oil for
    frying, as needed
tahini sauce (pages 212–13)
1 teaspoon lemon juice

1. Select artichokes of about equal size. Boil them in salted water to which 1 teaspoon of the oil has been added, until they are tender. Drain and toss lightly in a bowl with the remaining teaspoon of oil.   2. In a food processor, electric blender, or by hand, purée the artichokes. Add the bread crumbs, eggs, salt, pepper, and nutmeg, and combine well.   3. Heat the vegetable oil in a frying pan or a wok and drop the mixture by spoonfuls into the hot oil. Turn to cook on both sides. When golden brown, drain on a rack or on paper towels. Serve on a platter with cocktail forks or toothpicks, accompanied with a bowl of *tahini* sauce, to which a teaspoon of lemon juice has been added. *Makes 20 hors d'oeuvres*

Jerusalem Artichokes in Tomato Sauce

Saffron

This dish is a good accompaniment to fish or chicken breasts.

1 large onion, chopped
1 clove garlic, crushed
4 tablespoons olive oil *or* vegetable oil
2 pounds sunchokes, washed and
    peeled
1 6-ounce can tomato paste diluted
    with 2 cans water

juice of 1 lemon
1 tablespoon soy sauce
salt and pepper, to taste
1 teaspoon ground coriander
2 tablespoons chopped fresh parsley

1. In a large frying pan, sauté the onion and garlic in oil until golden. Add the sunchokes, tomato paste, and water. Season with the lemon juice, soy sauce, salt, pepper, and coriander. Bring to a boil, lower the heat, and simmer covered about 15 minutes (be careful not to overcook the sunchokes, or they will become mushy). Add the parsley.   2. Pour the sunchokes into a warmed casserole and serve. *Serves 4 to 6*

Sunchoke Slaw

2 cups water
2 tablespoons lemon juice
1 pound sunchokes
2 cups shredded carrots
¼ cup sliced scallions

½ cup mayonnaise
½ teaspoon grated lemon peel
2 tablespoons honey
½ cup roasted almonds, chopped

1. In a large bowl, combine the water and lemon juice. Peel the sunchokes and drop them in the water to prevent discoloring. Drain them and pat dry. Shred them into another bowl, and add two tablespoons of the water-lemon mixture. Add the carrots and scallions and mix well.   2. In a small bowl, combine the mayonnaise, lemon peel, and honey. Pour this dressing over the vegetables and stir well. Refrigerate, covered, for 1 hour. Top with the almonds and serve. *Makes 4 cups*

BEET SPINACH OR SWISS CHARD (*Beta vulgaris cicla*)

Beet spinach, also known as Swiss chard* or blette, has grown wild in this part of the world for centuries. It is related to the common beet. Easily cultivated, it became an important part of the Israelite diet.

Beet spinach was both easily accessible and esteemed for its high iron content. Talmudic literature praises it as being "good for the heart, eyes, and bowels." The following recipes illustrate its multiple uses in cooking.

How to Prepare Swiss Chard

Chard is grown in many home gardens, and is used in Israel interchangeably with spinach (it is also known as "Moroccan spinach"). To prepare chard, wash the leaves well. Remove the tough white veins and drain. Place the leaves in a covered pot, without any additional water. Cook on high heat for a few minutes, then remove the lid, lower the heat, and toss the leaves until they are almost limp. Chop them up and they are ready to use. (The white stems may also be eaten, but they take somewhat longer to cook.)

* When are chards not beet spinach? When they are young growths of globe artichokes. After a crop of artichoke heads have been taken, young growth pushes up. When they achieve a stretch of two feet they are blanched with straw to whiten the stems and leaves. They are then like chards.

Chard Appetizer

2 pounds fresh Swiss chard
2 medium onions, chopped or grated
juice of 1 crushed garlic clove
2 tablespoons butter *or* margarine *or*
    vegetable oil

1 tablespoon red pepper
½ teaspoon nutmeg
salt and black pepper, to taste
½ cup yogurt, drained
1 hard-boiled egg, chopped

1. Wash the chard and trim off the tough stems. Boil the chard in a small amount of salted water or steam until just tender. Drain and cool. 2. Sauté the onions and garlic in the butter or oil until golden. Allow them to cool. 3. Chop the chard finely, until it is almost puréed. Add the onions and garlic juice and press the mixture through a strainer. You may also process the chard mixture in a food processor or electric blender, being careful not to let the mixture become liquidized. Add the red pepper, nutmeg, salt, black pepper, and yogurt, mixing with a spoon. Serve on buttered toast garnished with chopped egg as an appetizer. *Serves 4*

Variation: To make a chard dip, follow the recipe above, but use 1 cup drained yogurt. Serve as a dip with crackers or fresh vegetables, or as a sauce over hard-boiled eggs.

Stir-fried Chard on Toast

2 pounds fresh Swiss chard
1 head lettuce, washed and shredded
2 tablespoons soy oil *or* vegetable oil
2 cloves garlic
10 shallots, including some green
    tops, chopped
salt and black pepper, to taste

1 large red pepper, seeded and sliced
1 teaspoon ground nutmeg
2 tablespoons soy sauce
2 tablespoons sherry
1 hard-boiled egg, chopped
4 toasted bread slices

1. Slice the chard, shred the lettuce, and set them aside. 2. Heat the oil in a large pan. Add the garlic, shallots, salt, and pepper. Sauté quickly for 1 minute. Add the red pepper and cook until the pepper is almost tender. Add the chard and lettuce gradually, tossing until they wilt. 3. Add nutmeg, soy sauce, and sherry, and toss the vegetables until they are coated with soy sauce and wine. Top with chopped egg and serve on toasted bread slices. *Serves 4*

Chard and Leftover Chicken

2 pounds Swiss chard
3 onions, chopped
2 tablespoons chicken fat *or* goose fat
    or margarine
1 cup leftover cooked chicken *or*
    turkey, cut in julienne strips
1 packet dry mushroom soup

1 cup cold water
⅝ cup white wine
1 tablespoon soy sauce
1 teaspoon nutmeg
black pepper to taste
paprika for garnish

1. Boil the chard in a small amount of salted water or steam until just tender. Chop it and set aside.   2. In a large frying pan, sauté the onions in the fat until they are soft. Add the chicken and chopped chard. Stir well until all the ingredients are coated with fat. Turn off the heat, and cover the mixture to keep it warm.   3. In a bowl, combine the dry mushroom soup mix with water, wine, and soy sauce. Stir until the soup is completely dissolved and add to the chicken and chard mixture.   4. Add the nutmeg and pepper and stir over low heat until tastes are well blended. Serve in vol-au-vent cases on toast or over rice, and sprinkle with paprika. *Serves 4*

Steamed Chard Salad

2 pounds fresh Swiss chard
½ cup vegetable oil
2 cloves garlic, pressed
3 tablespoons lemon juice *or* white
    wine vinegar
3 tablespoons Dijon mustard

½ teaspoon salt
¼ teaspoon black pepper
¼ teaspoon ground cumin
1 teaspoon sugar
¼ cup chopped scallions
1 or 2 hard-boiled eggs, chopped

1. Wash the chard and trim the tough white stems out of the leaves. Slice the stems into ¼-inch pieces and steam until tender, about 10 minutes. Cut the leaves into ½-inch strips and steam until tender, 5 to 7 minutes. Cool to room temperature.   2. In a small bowl, make the dressing: combine the oil, garlic, lemon juice, mustard, salt, pepper, cumin, and sugar. Beat vigorously until blended.   3. In a large bowl, toss the chard stems and leaves with the scallion. Pour the dressing over the chard mixture and toss well to coat.   4. Cover and refrigerate for at least 2 hours. Garnish with chopped egg. Serve chilled or at room temperature. *Serves 4*

Cumin

CABBAGE (*Brassica oleracea capitata*)

Despite the lowly place given to cabbage in legend and literature, and its destruction in the hands of institutional cooks, cabbage has served humankind for centuries. It represents one of nature's most ingenious designs, mentioned in 1 Kings 19:4–5 and Job 30:4 as "broom," as well as in talmudic literature. Rising out of the earth like a giant rose, its white, green, purple, or red leaves are a pleasure to behold. Among appreciative cooks its uses abound in seasonal menus. One can imagine how well it served the Hebrew people, and how appropriate it is to speak of "cabbages and kings."

Marinated Cabbage Salad

This salad is striking garnished with nasturtium or violet flowers.

½ pound radishes, grated
1 large head cabbage, finely shredded
salt

Marinade:

1 tablespoon dry mustard
1 tablespoon water
1 large egg
1 cup olive oil
¼ cup lemon juice *or* wine vinegar
1 or 2 cloves garlic, pressed
1 teaspoon caraway seeds
½ teaspoon black pepper
2 teaspoons sugar

1. In a colander, combine the radishes and cabbage. Sprinkle lightly with salt, mixing it in with your hands. Weight down the top with a heavy plate and let the mixture sit for 30 minutes. Shake the colander well and press out the liquid.
2. Combine all the ingredients for the marinade, and pour over the cabbage and radish mixture. Mix it well with a fork, cover, and refrigerate overnight. Check the seasoning before serving, and add more lemon juice or salt if necessary. *Serves 4*

Hearty Cabbage and Barley Soup

❦ ❦ ❦

1 medium cabbage, shredded	3 tablespoons pearl barley, washed
salt	1 teaspoon dill seed
1 large onion, chopped	1 teaspoon salt
1 tablespoon sesame oil	juice of 1 lemon
2 pints chicken soup stock (page 218)	

1. Put the shredded cabbage into a pot and salt thoroughly. Pour boiling water over it and return it to a boil. Remove the pot from the heat and pour the water off. 2. In a soup pot, gently cook the onion in the oil until soft. Add the chicken stock and bring to a boil. Add the cabbage and barley. Simmer over low heat for about 30 minutes or until the barley is soft. Add the dill and salt. Just before serving, stir in the lemon juice. *Serves 4*

Cabbage and Nasturtium Salad

❦ ❦ ❦

The peppery leaves and colorful, edible nasturtium flowers give the old standby cabbage an exotic look and taste.

1 medium cabbage	**Dressing:**
8 nasturtium leaves	⅓ cup lemon juice
2 tablespoons pickled capers *or*	1 cup olive oil
pickled nasturtium seeds	½ teaspoon dried mustard
nasturtium flowers	

1. Discard the outer leaves of the cabbage. Cut the cabbage in half and slice it with a bread knife. Put the cabbage slices in a bowl of cold water for a few minutes and drain in a colander. 2. With a kitchen scissors, cut the nasturtium leaves. Add the capers and cabbage. 3. To make the dressing, blend all the ingredients. Pour the dressing over the salad and toss. Decorate with nasturtium flowers. *Serves 6*

Stuffed Cabbage Leaves

❧ ❧ ❧

In the West cabbage is usually stuffed in chubby bundles. But cooks in Jerusalem and neighboring countries roll cabbage leaves delicately into slender cigar shapes. Serve them hot, as a main course, or cold as an hors d'oeuvre or first course.

1 medium white cabbage
salt
2 teaspoons vegetable oil
juice of 1 lemon
4 or 5 cloves garlic (optional)

Filling:

½ cup uncooked rice, washed
1 teaspoon salt
1 teaspoon allspice
freshly ground black pepper to taste
½ cup chopped scallion
¼ cup fresh mint *or* 2 teaspoons
    dried mint

1. Discard the ragged outer leaves of the cabbage. Carefully separate the remaining 15 to 20 large leaves, and drop them 4 or 5 at a time into a large pot of boiling salted water. Blanch about 3 minutes, until the leaves are pliable. Drain. Divide the leaf in two by removing the tough vein.   2. In a small bowl, combine the filling ingredients.   3. Lay the cabbage leaves flat and place a tablespoon of filling along the cut side of each leaf. Fold each side of the leaf over the filling toward the center, and roll up into a long cigar shape.   4. Line a casserole or large pot with the torn and unused cabbage leaves, to prevent scorching. Place the stuffed rolls close together, seam side down to prevent opening. Cover with another layer of stuffed leaves. Add water to almost cover the cabbage leaves, and sprinkle with salt, vegetable oil, and lemon juice. For an enticing aroma, tuck 4 or 5 garlic cloves among the cabbage leaves. Bring the water to a boil and cook, covered, on a low flame for about 1 hour. *Serves 4 as a main course*

Crustless Cabbage-and-Meat Pie

❧ ❧ ❧

Garlic

1 medium white cabbage
1¼ cups dry red wine *or* ⅝ cup dry
    red wine and ⅝ cup diluted
    tomato paste

Filling:

½ pound ground lamb *or* beef
½ cup uncooked rice
salt and black pepper, to taste
½ teaspoon ground cinnamon

1. Discard the ragged outer leaves of the cabbage. Carefully separate the remaining 15 to 20 large leaves, and drop them 4 or 5 at a time into a large pot of boiling salted water. Blanch about 3 minutes, until the leaves are pliable. Drain. Divide the leaf in half by removing the tough vein.   2. In a bowl, combine the filling ingredients well with your hands.   3. Line a greased deep, ovenproof dish with a layer of cabbage leaves. Spread a layer of filling over this. Repeat until you have used up the filling, ending with a layer of cabbage leaves.   4. Pour the wine over the cabbage and meat pie and bake, covered, in a preheated 350° oven for about 1 hour, or until the cabbage leaves are very tender and the filling is well cooked. Check the cabbage pie as it cooks. If it seems to be drying out add a little water flavored with lemon juice. Remove from the oven and allow it to settle for a moment, then carefully invert onto a serving platter. Serve upside down. *Serves 4*

CELERIAC, CELERY ROOT (*Apium graveolens*)

Celeriac belongs to the celery family. It is mentioned in the Bible as a garden vegetable, in contrast to vegetables that grow wild. This medium-height plant has medicinal properties, and is especially known for relieving rheumatic sufferers. Celeriac is grown for its large, rounded, edible root more than for its leaf stalk. Celeriac is identified as one of the greens dipped in salt water during the Passover Seder. (Ashkenazi Jews generally use parsley or celery leaves for this purpose.)

The roots of celeriac are washed well, peeled, fried or cooked, and served in a sauce. Grated, they add a tasty texture to salads.

Celeriac in Olive Oil

Served hot, this is a good accompaniment for chicken breasts. Served cold or at room temperature it is a refreshing salad on a warm day.

2 large celeriac roots	juice of 2 lemons
3 tablespoons olive oil	½ teaspoon ground sage
½ cup sliced onion	salt and black pepper, to taste

1. Peel and rinse the celeriac roots and cut them into ¾-inch cubes.   2. In a frying pan, heat the oil and cook the celeriac until it is more tender and lightly colored. Add the onions and cook for a few more minutes. Add the lemon juice and water to cover, season with sage, salt, and pepper to taste. Simmer 30 minutes or until the vegetables are tender and the liquid is reduced. *Serves 4*

Spiced Celeriac

❦ ❦ ❦

3 celeriac roots
6 cups water plus 2 tablespoons salt
1 medium apple
⅓ cup sliced onion
1 tablespoon vegetable oil

2 tablespoons all-purpose flour
½ teaspoon ground cumin
½ teaspoon salt
¼ teaspoon black pepper

1. Peel and rinse the celeriac roots and cut them into slices about ½ inch thick. Boil the slices in the salted water until just tender, about 15 minutes. Drain but reserve about ¼ cup of the water. 2. In a frying pan, sauté the apple and onions in the oil until soft. Push them to one side of pan. In the empty side, mix the flour and cumin and cook, stirring, for less than 1 minute. Add one tablespoon of celeriac water, and stir until the mixture is smooth. Mix in the apples and onions, and add the salt and pepper. Cook for 5 minutes, adding more water if necessary. Serve hot to accompany lamb or poultry. *Serves 4*

CUCUMBER (*Cucumis sativus*)

The origin of cucumber is not known, but it dates back at least three thousand years. Curiously, it is a fruit but has long been associated with the vegetable world—hence its inclusion here. The numerous varieties of cucumber have found many uses. In Israel and the Middle East small cucumbers for pickling and larger ones for salads are available all year round. The taste, texture, and cool color of the cucumber are especially welcome on hot summer days.

Peeled or scraped, sliced for salads, or halved and scooped out in boat shapes, the cucumber offers many serving possibilities. And if you've missed taking your vitamins, eating cucumber during the day will provide a rich supply of vitamin C and a moderate amount of vitamins A and B, along with potassium, iron, magnesium, silicon, and chlorine. Not bad for a seemingly water-packed vegetable!

Cold Cucumber Sauce

❦ ❦ ❦

1 pound cucumbers, peeled, seeded,
    and grated
1 tablespoon citrus vinegar
1 teaspoon salt
1 teaspoon ground coriander
1 small onion, grated

1 cup sour cream
½ cup heavy cream
juice of 2 lemons
½ cup chopped fresh dill
2 cloves garlic, minced
salt and pepper, to taste

1. In an electric blender or food processor with a steel blade, purée the cucumber, vinegar, salt, coriander, onion, sour cream, heavy cream, and lemon juice. Transfer the purée to a glass serving bowl. Stir in the dill and garlic. Serve with poached fish or over hard-boiled eggs. *Makes 2 cups*

Pickled Cucumbers

❦ ❦ ❦

Homemade dill pickles are so superior to most commercially prepared pickled cucumbers that it is worth the small effort it takes to preserve them. Home-grown, freshly picked cucumbers will be the most crisp, of course. If you don't grow your own, buy cucumbers that are as fresh as possible and not more than 5 inches long. Put them straight into the coldest part of the refrigerator for 24 hours before you put them into the brine.

12 green cucumbers, less than 5
    inches long
4 sprigs fresh dill
1 sprig basil
4 cloves garlic
6 black peppercorns, crushed

1 short spike fresh rosemary
1 fresh sage leaf *or* 1 dried sage leaf
2 fresh lemon leaves (optional)
1 tablespoon lemon balm
1 dried bay leaf
¾ cup Kosher salt *or* sea salt

1. In a large saucepan, cover all the ingredients except the cucumbers with boiling water. Add the cucumbers, cover the pan, and allow to cool.   2. When the mixture is cool, pour it into a large, sterilized screw-top jar. Be sure the brine completely covers the cucumbers. Store for 2 weeks. Remove any mildew that may have developed. Once the jar has been opened, keep it in the refrigerator. *Makes 12 pickles*

Dill

Unpeeled Cucumber Salad

You can improve the flavor of cucumber-based salads if you sprinkle the sliced cucumbers with salt and let them drain in a colander for at least 30 minutes. Remember to rinse the salt off before using!

2 unpeeled cucumbers, sliced
1 small onion, grated (optional)
chopped fresh dill *or* parsley, for garnish

Dressing:

1 tablespoon sugar
1 tablespoon citrus vinegar
4 tablespoons water
freshly ground black pepper, to taste
2 teaspoons dill seed

1. In a glass bowl, mix the dressing ingredients. Add the rinsed and drained cucumber slices. Mix in the onion if you like a salad with bite to it. Garnish with fresh dill or chopped parsley. *Serves 4 to 6*

Cheese-filled Cucumber Boats

6 medium cucumbers

Filling:

¼ pound cottage cheese
¼ pound feta cheese, crumbled
4 tablespoons mixed fresh herbs: dill, chives, and chopped fresh parsley, *or* 2 tablespoons dry mixed herbs
1 tablespoon prepared barbecue sauce

1. Wash the cucumbers, cut them in half lengthwise, and remove the seeds. Salt them and allow them to rest for 20 minutes. Rinse off the salt and pat dry with paper towels.   2. In a bowl, thoroughly mix the filling ingredients. Stuff each cucumber "boat" with filling. Serve immediately, or wrap in plastic wrap and refrigerate until serving time. *Serves 12*

Cucumber, Mint, and Yogurt Salad

❧ ❧ ❧

This salad is especially refreshing during the hot, dry summer months. It may be made in quantity for a cold buffet, served in small dishes, or as an accompaniment to grilled fish. For a cooling soup, increase yogurt to 4 cups and mix all the ingredients in the blender.

3 medium cucumbers
1 tablespoon salt
2 cloves garlic, crushed
½ teaspoon salt
2 cups plain yogurt *or* 2 cups sour
    cream

½ teaspoon pepper
½ cup chopped fresh mint *or* 1
    tablespoon dried mint

1. Peel the cucumbers, sprinkle with 1 tablespoon of salt, and allow them to rest for 30 minutes. Rinse the salt off, pat dry, and dice.   2. In a bowl, mix the garlic and ½ teaspoon of salt. Stir in the yogurt, pepper, and mint. Add the cucumbers and serve immediately, or refrigerate. *Serves 4 to 6*

Cucumbers-and-Greens Salad with a Bite

❧ ❧ ❧

It is worth growing radishes in a pot on your kitchen windowsill or balcony just for the leaves. They are good for you and give a healthy bite to a salad.

4 unpeeled cucumbers, chopped
1 bunch dandelion greens, chopped
1 cup chopped tender radish leaves
½ cup chopped fresh parsley
2 small radishes, thinly sliced

Dressing:
¼ cup olive oil
1 tablespoon lemon juice
2 tablespoons coriander seeds
2 tablespoons onion, chopped

1. In a glass bowl, mix the cucumbers, dandelion leaves, radish leaves, and parsley.   2. In an electric blender, combine the dressing ingredients. Blend at high speed until smooth. Pour the dressing over the greens, toss, and garnish with the radishes. *Serves 6 to 8*

Israeli
Cucumber-and-Bread Sauce

❦ ❦ ❦

This sauce is a great way to use up stale bread. Serve it over hard-boiled eggs, or as a dip.

3 slices stale bread
2 cloves garlic
4 tablespoons olive oil
juice of 1 lemon
1 egg *or* 2 eggs, if sauce is to be used
    as a dip

3 cucumbers, peeled and diced
salt and pepper, to taste
1 teaspoon marjoram *or* oregano
1 tablespoon chopped fresh parsley

1. Remove the crusts from the bread. In an electric blender, combine 1 slice of bread, garlic, oil, lemon juice, and egg, and blend on low speed until smooth. Add the second slice of bread and cucumbers and blend until smooth. Add the third slice of bread, salt, pepper, marjoram, and parsley. Blend until the sauce is smooth and creamy. *Makes 2 cups*

Sweet-and-Sour Cucumbers

❦ ❦ ❦

Serve this salad on a hot summer day with cold sliced meat or chicken.

4 unpeeled cucumbers, washed
salt
2 tablespoons sugar
2 tablespoons citrus vinegar

6 tablespoons cold water
freshly ground black pepper
1 tablespoon dill seed
chopped fresh parsley, for garnish

1. Slice the cucumbers as thinly as possible. Layer them in a glass serving dish, sprinkling salt on each layer. Let them rest for an hour. 2. In a large bowl, combine the sugar, vinegar, water, pepper, and dill. Rinse the cucumbers, drain, and toss them with the vinegar mixture. Garnish with parsley. *Serves 4 to 6*

Cucumber Relish

❦ ❦ ❦

This mild relish complements hamburgers or a yellow cheese sandwich, or you may mix it with white cheese to use as a spread or with broiled fish.

12 large cucumbers	½ cup sugar
6 green bell peppers	1 tablespoon mustard seeds
3 large onions	1 teaspoon celery seeds
½ cup salt	lemon juice, as needed
1 cup prepared horseradish	

1. Peel the cucumbers and remove the seeds. In a food processor or by hand, finely chop the cucumbers, peppers, and onions. Add the salt, mix well, and let rest overnight in a glass bowl to blend the flavors.   2. In the morning, drain the cucumbers and add the horseradish, sugar, mustard seeds, celery seeds, and enough lemon juice to cover the mixture. Mix well and pack in sterilized pint jars. Seal. *Makes 4 pints*

Dilled Feta Cheese
(*Pashtida*)

❦ ❦ ❦

Pashtida is a form of pie or quiche especially popular among the Sephardic Jews of Israel. It gives us a hint as to the way the early Hebrew people combined foods, particularly when there was not enough of one food for a family serving. *Pashtida* can be crustless, or the crust can be made from stale bread crumbs or a simple water-and-flour dough.

sanbusak pastry (pages 61–62)	2 tablespoons yogurt
1¼ cups feta cheese	1 teaspoon salt
½ cup cottage cheese	1 teaspoon chopped lemon peel
2 eggs, beaten	⅓ teaspoon ground nutmeg
⅓ cup chopped fresh dill	dried dill, for garnish

1. Make 1 *sanbusak* pastry to fit a 9-inch springform pan. Press the dough firmly to cover the bottom and sides of the well-greased pan.   2. In a food processor or by hand, blend the cheeses, eggs, fresh dill, yogurt, salt, lemon peel, and nutmeg. Pour the mixture into the crust and bake in a preheated 350° oven for 45 minutes, or until a toothpick inserted in the center comes out clean. *Serves 4 to 6*

GARLIC (*Allium sativum*)

Garlic is a vegetable that is primarily used as a spice. It is referred to in Numbers 11:5 and in talmudic literature as an important seasoning.

Garlic belongs to the lily family and is credited with health-rewarding powers of almost magical merit. It is counted as a stimulant, a diuretic, an antispasmodic agent, and an aphrodisiac. It has long been claimed that raw garlic eaten at bedtime will cure a cold (one of the side effects, however, is that you might lose your bedmate!).

Garlic is propagated by planting the cloves. It is the best pest-repellant to use in organic-based gardens. I plant garlic and nasturtiums whenever my fruit trees or flowering plants are threatened by some unwelcome pest.

How to Use Garlic

1. To substitute garlic powder for garlic: ⅛ teaspoon of garlic powder is equal to 1 clove of fresh garlic.   2. Garlic is easier to peel if it is first dipped in hot water.   3. Garlic skins added to gravy will thicken it. Remove the garlic skins before serving.   4. Plant garlic cloves around fruit trees to keep away leaf curl and pests, instead of using pesticides.   5. Garlic does not freeze well. It is better to add it when reheating frozen food.   6. When you cook onions and garlic together, cook the onions first so the garlic doesn't brown and become bitter.

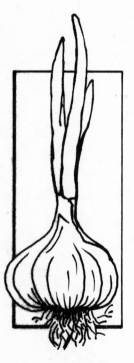

Garlic Pickles

❦ ❦ ❦

Pickled garlic cloves are last minute treasures to add to a green salad. They impart an unusual sweet-tart flavor.

1½ cups distilled vinegar	½ teaspoon salt
½ cup sugar	3 cups whole garlic cloves, peeled

1. In a 3-quart pan, combine the vinegar, sugar, and salt. Bring to a boil and stir until the sugar dissolves. Drop the garlic into boiling brine. Cook over high heat, stirring, for 1 minute. Allow garlic to cool. Store the pickled garlic in a tightly covered jar and allow to pickle for two days before using. The garlic pickles will stay good in the refrigerator for up to two months. *Makes 1½ pints*

Garlic

Garlic Spread
for French Bread

2 cloves garlic, finely minced
1 teaspoon fresh parsley, finely
   minced

1 teaspoon salt
½ cup softened butter *or* margarine
1 loaf French bread

1. In a small bowl, combine the garlic, parsley, salt, and butter. Mash with a fork until well mixed. 2. Cut the French bread into slices, but do not cut completely through the bottom crust. Carefully spread both sides of each slice with the garlic spread. Wrap the bread in aluminum foil and bake in a pre-heated 350° oven for 10 to 15 minutes. Serve hot from the oven. *Serves 4 to 6*

GARLIC CHIVES, GREEN GARLIC
(*Allium tuberosum*)

This beautiful plant, with its round head of purple flowers, adorns many flower gardens in Israel. Many people who have the plant growing in their yards have no idea that it is a wild garlic, and they can eat it! Like its relative, garlic, green garlic is also famed for fighting disease and keeping away evil spirits. Actually, for those who do not favor garlic in cooking, the flavor of this wild garlic is more subtle than its cousin and much easier to use. A scissor-cut snip or two has verdant effect in a mixed green salad. Added to vegetable soup toward the end of the cooking, it lifts the taste with a surprisingly pungent flavor.

Garlic Chives Spread

1 cup garlic chives, chopped
1 cup fresh parsley
½ cup olive oil

8 ounces cottage cheese
1 tablespoon mixed ground hyssop
   and sesame seeds

1. Blend the chives, parsley, and olive oil in a blender or food processor. 2. In a serving bowl, combine the blended mixture with the cottage cheese. Garnish with hyssop and sesame seeds. Serve as a spread or center it on a platter surrounded with scissor-cut lettuce leaves and sliced raw vegetables. *Makes 1 cup*

LEEK (*Allium porrum*)

Though described as a garden herb, this national emblem of Wales is a culti-vated member of the lily family. Leeks are mentioned in Numbers 11, and its references in talmudic literature are many. An easy plant to grow, its culture is similar to celery.

The leek looks something like an enormous scallion, to which it is related. Its long, flat, white and green leaves have many culinary uses that have long endeared the leek to chefs.

Leeks are among the five vegetables mentioned in the Bible as foods which the Israelites ate in Egypt and for which they longed in the wilderness of Sinai. Cook them in a small amount of salted water or chicken broth for 15 to 20 min-utes, depending on how young they are, then serve them with lemon juice and a sprinkle of chopped fresh parsley.

How to Clean Leeks

It is important to clean leeks thoroughly—their tight leaves often hide sand and dirt. Split the leek lengthwise. Holding it under cold running water, sepa-rate the leaves and rinse. You may need to rub with your fingers to get all the dirt off.

Curried Leek and Potato Soup

4 to 8 leeks	4 cups water
1 small onion	3 cups vegetable broth
5 medium boiling potatoes	½ cup heavy cream
2 tablespoons butter *or* margarine	salt and freshly ground black pepper,
2 tablespoons curry powder	to taste

1. Trim off the tough green leaves and cut the leeks into ½-inch cubes. 2. Cut the onion in half, and slice into very thin half-circles. 3. Peel the potatoes, cut them in half, and slice the halves into very thin half-circles. 4. In a soup pot, heat the butter or margarine and add the onion slices. Cook gently, stir-ring, until the onions are wilted. Add the curry powder and cook, stirring, for 1 minute. Add the leeks and cook about 5 minutes more, stirring often. Add the potatoes, water, and broth and bring to a boil. Simmer for 30 minutes. 5. Allow the soup to cool. Pour into the container of a food processor or an electric blender, and blend until smooth. Return the soup to a saucepan. Add the cream and salt and pepper to taste. Reheat gently (do not boil) and serve. *Serves 4 to 6*

Leeks with Olives

Leeks and olives make an interesting combination. Serve this dish warm, with fish or chicken breasts, or cold as a salad.

3 pounds leeks	**grated peel of ½ lemon**
2 tablespoons olive oil	**salt to taste**
½ pound tomatoes, quartered	**½ teaspoon paprika**
12 to 16 black olives, pitted	**½ cup chopped fresh parsley**
juice of 1 lemon	

1. Trim off the tough green leaves and cut the leeks into 1-inch lengths.   2. In a frying pan or saucepan, sauté the leeks in the oil. Then cover the pan and simmer for 15 minutes, or until tender. Add the tomatoes, olives, lemon juice, and lemon peel. Simmer for 10 minutes more. Stir in the salt and paprika. Put the mixture in a warm casserole and garnish with parsley. *Serves 6*

Leek-Olive Tart

Shortcrust Pastry:

2 cups all-purpose flour
pinch salt
4 ounces margarine *or* butter
4 tablespoons water

Press-in Pastry:

6 tablespoons margarine
1¼ cups all-purpose flour
1 egg

Filling:

2 pounds leeks
2 tablespoons olive oil *or* vegetable oil
2 tablespoons sliced stuffed olives
1 tablespoon grated lemon peel
½ teaspoon ground hyssop
½ teaspoon black pepper
2 eggs, beaten
½ cup Parmesan cheese, grated

1. First prepare either the shortcrust pastry or press-in pastry:

To prepare shortcrust pastry, sift the flour and salt into a mixing bowl and rub in the cut-up margarine or butter. Work the mixture with your fingers until the grains are pea-sized. Carefully sprinkle in the water, tossing the ingredients with a fork so that the dough is evenly moistened. Gather the pastry into a ball. Place the ball in a plastic bag or wrap in plastic, and allow it to rest in the refrigerator for 15 to 20 minutes while you prepare the filling.

To prepare press-in pastry, combine the margarine and flour in a food processor and process until the mixture becomes crumbs. Add the egg and process until it becomes a ball of dough. Or, work the margarine and flour with your

Olive

fingers until it is crumbly, add the egg, and knead until it forms a soft dough. Press the dough into a heat-proof glass pie pan or metal pie pan. Cover and refrigerate until ready to use.

2. To prepare the filling, trim off the tough green leaves and cut the leeks into 1-inch cubes. In a covered frying pan, simmer the leeks gently in the oil for 10 minutes. Add the olives, lemon peel, hyssop, and pepper. Cook gently, stirring occasionally, for 10 minutes. Remove the pan from the fire and stir in the eggs and cheese.   3. If you are using the shortcrust pastry, roll it out and press it into a heat-proof glass pie plate or metal pan. If you are using the press-in pastry, remove it from the refrigerator. Fill the pie shell with the leek-olive filling and bake in a preheated 350° oven for 30 minutes, or until a toothpick inserted in the center comes out clean. *Serves 4 to 6*

Sweet-and-Sour Leeks

Serve cold as a salad, or hot to accompany a relatively bland dish.

2 pounds leeks
3 tablespoons vegetable oil
3 cloves garlic, crushed

1 tablespoon honey
juice of 2 lemons

1. Trim the tough green leaves from the leeks and discard. Cut the leeks into 2 or 3 large pieces.   2. In a frying pan, heat the oil. Add the honey and garlic. When well blended, add the leeks and stir until the leeks are wilted and coated with honey and oil. Add the lemon juice and cook gently, covered, so that the leeks stew in their own juices for about 15 minutes. *Serves 4 to 6*

Leek Omelet

Serve this omelet garnished with parsley as an appetizer, or with grilled tomatoes and wedges of toast as a luncheon dish.

2 pounds leeks
butter *or* margarine *or* vegetable oil
juice of ½ lemon

salt and pepper
½ teaspoon ground allspice
6 eggs

1. Trim the tough green leaves from the leeks and discard. Cut the leeks into thin slices.   2. In a small saucepan, cook the leeks gently in butter or oil. Add

the lemon juice, salt, pepper, and allspice and allow leeks to cook in their own juices for a few minutes until partially done. 3. In a large bowl, beat the eggs well. Remove the leeks from the pan with a slotted spoon and stir them into the eggs. Oil or butter a skillet or frying pan. Pour in the eggs and leeks and cook on moderate heat until the underside is crisp and well done. Carefully flip the omelet over to cook, or place the skillet under the broiler for a minute until the top is brown. Cut into wedges and serve. *Makes 3 2-egg omelets or 6 1-egg omelets*

Leeks and Cheese

5 to 10 leeks (about 10 cups sliced leeks)	⅛ teaspoon grated nutmeg
4 tablespoons butter *or* margarine	¼ pound Swiss or Gruyere cheese, cut into ¼-inch cubes
3 tablespoons flour	1 egg yolk
1½ cups milk	½ cup heavy cream
salt and freshly ground black pepper, to taste	2 tablespoons grated Parmesan cheese

1. Trim the tough green leaves from the leeks and discard. Cut the leeks crosswise into 2-inch lengths. In a pot, barely cover the leeks with water. Bring to a boil and drain immediately. 2. In a saucepan, melt 2 tablespoons of the butter. Add the flour, stirring with a wire whisk. When blended and smooth, add the milk, stirring rapidly with the whisk. Add the salt, pepper, and nutmeg. Remove the sauce from the heat and add the cheese, stirring until the cheese melts. Stir in the egg yolk. 3. In an ovenproof casserole, combine the leeks and the remaining 2 tablespoons of butter. Add salt and pepper to taste, if needed. Cover and cook over low heat, stirring occasionally, for about 10 minutes. 4. Add the cream and stir. Heat to boiling, but do not boil. Pour the cheese sauce on top, and sprinkle with Parmesan cheese. Place under a preheated broiler till the top is browned. *Serves 4 to 6*

ONION (*Allium cepa*)

The onion is probably the most important vegetable in Israel's diet today. It is more than just a component of soups and stews; it is a major vegetable. The onion has a long history of enhancing all manner of good foods. Not a few Israeli mothers use the appetizing smell of fried onions to entice their children to eat. Onions, like lettuce, are sleep inducers if eaten raw. They are praised for their health value.

Many more people love to eat onions than to cook them! Fortunately, it is possible to peel an onion without crying. Here's how: peel off the top layer of the skin and carefully remove the translucent coating, which carries the strong scent and causes the eyes to water. If you do this near a sink with cold water running, you will remain dry eyed.

Cream of Onion and Cabbage Soup with Croutons

❧ ❧ ❧

This is a change from the popular French onion soup. It can be a meal in itself, served with garlic-coated French bread and a salad.

Soup:

3 cups shredded cabbage
3 cups sliced onions
¼ cup olive oil
¼ cup whole wheat flour
2 cups milk *or* water
¼ cup *tahini* sauce (pages 212–13)
¼ teaspoon celery seed
¼ teaspoon ground bay leaf
salt and black pepper, to taste

Herbed Croutons:

½ cup sunflower-oil margarine
4 cups stale whole wheat bread, cubed
1 cup brewer's yeast (optional)
1 tablespoon chopped fresh parsley
1 tablespoon mixed barbecue spices

1. Steam the cabbage until tender.   2. In a heavy-bottomed pot, gently cook the onions in ⅛ cup of the oil.   3. In a saucepan over low heat, whisk the remaining oil and flour together until they form a roux. Whisk in the milk or water until the mixture is smooth. Add the cabbage, onions, *tahini* sauce, celery seed, bay leaf, salt, and pepper. Simmer the soup for 10 minutes.   4. To prepare the croutons, melt the margarine in a frying pan and add the bread cubes. When the bread cubes have soaked up the margarine, add the yeast (if desired), parsley, and spices. Sauté for a few minutes. Put the croutons in a baking pan and toast in a preheated 350° oven for 10 minutes.   5. Serve the soup hot, garnished with the croutons. *Serves 4*

Onion-Apple Pie

This savory main-dish pie is a meal in itself.

Pastry:

sanbusak pastry (pages 61–62)

Filling:

3 medium turnips, peeled
3 medium apples, unpeeled
6 medium onions
8 hard-boiled eggs
½ teaspoon nutmeg
1 teaspoon freshly ground pepper
2 teaspoons salt

¼ pound sunflower-oil margarine
1 teaspoon lemon juice
6 tablespoons stock *or* water
1 egg beaten with 1 tablespoon water
   (optional)
sesame seeds (optional)

1. To prepare the pastry, double the recipe for *sanbusak* pastry and make enough for a 2-crust pie. Line a 9-inch pie pan with half of the dough.   2. To prepare the filling, thinly slice the turnips, apples, onions, and eggs. In a small bowl, combine the nutmeg, pepper, and salt.   3. Spread a layer of turnips on the pastry, followed by a layer of onions, a layer of apples, and a layer of eggs. Sprinkle with the nutmeg, pepper, salt mixture and dot with margarine. Repeat the layers until you use up all the ingredients. Sprinkle the top layer with the lemon juice and stock or water. Cover with the top crust and prick it with a fork. If you like, you may brush the top crust with the egg and water and sprinkle with sesame seeds. Bake in a preheated 375° oven for 1¼ hours.
Serves 4 to 6

Roast Onions

One of the easiest and tastiest ways to use onions is to roast them whole—in the kitchen oven or right in the hot barbecue coals. Roasted onions are onion-eating at its best. They deserve the status of a separate course. Put them in the oven to cook and forget about them while you prepare the rest of the meal.

4 cloves
4 medium to large onions, unpeeled
olive oil *or* vegetable oil

a little water
4 teaspoons thyme
salt and pepper, to taste

1. Stick 1 clove into each unpeeled onion, and put the onions in a greased baking pan with about 1 inch of water. Sprinkle each onion with 1 teaspoon of thyme and salt and pepper to taste.   2. Bake in a preheated 350° oven for about 1½ hours, or until the onions feel soft when pressed with a finger. The cooking time may be shortened by parboiling the onions for half an hour (whole and unpeeled) before you put them into the oven. To cook the onions in a barbecue, wrap them in foil and put them right in the hot coals. If you are also cooking potatoes, put the onions in the coals first. *Serves 4*

Baked Stuffed Onions

❦ ❦ ❦

4 large onions, unpeeled
stock *or* seasoned water
4 tablespoons butter *or* margarine
½ cup chopped almonds
2 tablespoons chopped fresh parsley
¼ teaspoon white pepper
¼ teaspoon salt

cloves (for a nice smell during the baking)
¼ cup bread crumbs
2 tablespoons vegetable oil
¼ teaspoon basil
parsley, for garnish

1. Blanch the onions in boiling stock or seasoned water for 25 minutes. Rinse them in cold water and drain. Turn the onions upside down, core them, and remove the peel. Hollow out the centers to make ½-inch-thick shells, reserving the onion centers for the next step.   2. In a bowl, combine the onion you just removed with the butter, almonds, parsley, pepper, and salt. Fill the onion shells with this stuffing and arrange the onions in a baking pan. Scatter some whole cloves in the pan.   3. Blend the bread crumbs, oil, and basil, and sprinkle over the onions. Cover the onions loosely with aluminum foil and bake in a preheated 350° oven for 20 minutes. Uncover and bake for 10 minutes more. Serve garnished with parsley. *Serves 4*

Batter-fried Herbed Onions and Sherry Dipping Sauce

1 pound pearl onions
vegetable oil for frying

Batter:

1 cup sifted all-purpose flour
1 teaspoon baking powder
½ teaspoon turmeric
½ teaspoon salt
½ teaspoon ground allspice
1 teaspoon sugar
1 egg, beaten
1 teaspoon soy sauce
⅔ cup milk *or* water

Sherry Dipping Sauce:

2 teaspoons mustard
2 teaspoons ketchup
2 teaspoons soy sauce
2 teaspoons vegetable oil
1 teaspoon garlic powder
1 teaspoon fennel powder
¼ cup sherry

1. To prepare the batter, sift together the dry ingredients in a medium bowl. Add the beaten egg, soy sauce, and milk or water, and mix until the batter is smooth.   2. Peel the onions (this is much easier if you parboil them for a minute or two in boiling water), slice them into rounds, and separate the rings. 3. In a deep frying pan, heat enough oil for deep frying. Coat the onion circles with batter. With a slotted spoon, drop them carefully into the hot oil. Fry the onions until they are brown and crisp (they will float to the top when cooked). Drain them on paper towels and serve hot, accompanied by sherry dipping sauce.   4. To prepare the dipping sauce, mix the dry ingredients and the mustard, ketchup, soy sauce, and vegetable oil to a paste with part of the sherry, then add the rest of the wine and mix well. *Serves 4*

Glazed Onions

2 pounds pearl onions, blanched and
   peeled
2 tablespoons unsalted butter

1½ teaspoons sugar
salt and pepper, to taste
water

1. In a saucepan, combine the onions, butter, sugar, salt, and pepper. Add enough water to barely cover the onions, and bring the water to a boil.   2. Cook the onions at a low boil over moderately high heat until the liquid is reduced to about ¼ cup and the onions are tender. Increase the heat to high and cook

the onions, shaking the pan to keep them from sticking, until they are golden and the liquid is reduced to a glaze. *Serves 6*

SHALLOT (*Allium ascalonicum*)

There is some confusion about whether the shallot and the scallion are the same plant with different names. Both are of the *Allium* family, but they are different: the scallion, *Allium fistolosium*, is a young onion which does not form a bulb (propagated by seeds); the shallot, *Allium ascalonicum*, is bulb producing, propagated by division of its small bulbs. Originally both plants had the same name, deriving from the ancient Philistine city of Ascalon. The Crusaders, who first brought them to Europe, called them after Ascalon where they discovered them growing. Finely chopped shallots add a piquant flavor to salads, soups, and sauces.

Shallot Sauce

Serve this sauce with sautéed patties or chops, and fillets of beef, lamb, chicken, or fish.

2 tablespoons meat drippings *or* **margarine** *or* **butter**
½ cup chopped shallots

½ cup white wine *or* **beef broth** *or* **chicken broth**
salt and pepper, to taste
lemon juice, to taste

1. Remove the sautéed meat from the pan and keep it warm. Add margarine or butter to the pan, if needed, to make 2 tablespoons drippings. (To make it without drippings, heat 2 tablespoons margarine or butter.) Add the shallots and sauté until limp. Stir in the wine broth, scraping up the brown bits in the pan with the spoon and mixing well.   2. Cook, uncovered, until the sauce is slightly thickened. Season to taste with salt, pepper, and lemon juice. *Makes about ¾ cup*

LETTUCE (*Lactuca sativa*)

This welcome garden vegetable with its many uses derives from an earlier wild species (*Lactuca scariola*). It is one of the plants upon which the commandment of eating bitter herbs at the Passover Seder can be performed. When wild lettuce is not available, a garden lettuce plant is left to go to seed. Its bitter roots are then chopped up and eaten raw.

Lettuce will grow in almost any soil, provided it is loose and well-drained. Because of Israel's long dry summers, which cause lettuce to bolt, lettuce seeds are planted in seed boxes or frames in the cool of early spring. Seedlings are transplanted to a partially sunny location.

Lettuce is a good source of vitamins A, B, and C. In Israel lettuce is usually served at every meal (including breakfast), and mixed with garden-mates such as cucumber, tomato, and parsley, without a salad dressing.

Lettuce leaves that are no longer crisp and presentable can be used to make soup stock and gravy. If that doesn't appeal to you, put the wilted leaves in the compost heap, or soak them in warm water; when the water cools use it to water your house plants.

Cos lettuce is the most popular variety of lettuce in Israel. It looks similar to romaine, and has the bitter taste of leafy endive. Dieters often use it instead of bread or rolls to wrap "sandwiches." Fillings can be made from low-fat cottage cheese mixed with chives, dill, or finely grated carrot. Non-weight-watchers have many options in the use of fillings, and Chinese egg-roll fillings are especially good.

Lettuce-based salads—upon which all manner of cheese, olives, chicken, tuna fish, or salami are layered, then topped with mayonnaise or fancy cream dressings—are not part of Holy Land cuisine. Here raw vegetables stand on their own merit; only occasionally are they moistened with a few drops of olive oil and lemon juice and a sprinkle of salt and pepper.

Lettuce and Egg Soup

🐞 🐞 🐞

6 cups chicken broth *or* vegetable
   broth
2 tablespoons cornstarch
2 tablespoons water
1 head lettuce, shredded

2 eggs, beaten with 2 tablespoons
   lemon juice
salt and pepper, to taste
1 teaspoon ground sage
chopped fresh parsley *or* radish
   leaves, for garnish

1. In a soup pot, heat the broth. In a small bowl, blend the cornstarch and water to make a paste, and stir it into the heated broth. Bring it to a boil, stirring. Add the shredded lettuce and cook for 5 minutes. Remove the soup from the heat.   2. Add the eggs beaten with the lemon juice to the broth, stirring constantly until blended. Season with salt and pepper to taste, and add the sage. Serve immediately, garnished with chopped parsley or tender radish leaves. *Serves 6*

Chicory

MELON

If ever "what's in a name" applied to a vegetable it is to the melon family, which includes marrows, squashes, cucumbers, gourds, zucchini, courgettes—*ad infinitum*. There are summer and winter squash, summer crookneck, and Turk's cap, to mention but a few names to confuse the gardener (less so the shopper, who more likely will pick out a desired squash without bothering about nomenclature).

The two melons mentioned in the Bible are the *Cucumis melo* varieties chate and watermelon. The chate melon was an essential ingredient in the early Hebrew diet, and is no less so today, especially as a stuffed vegetable. Stuffed vegetables are not specifically referred to in biblical or talmudic commentary, but it seems likely that when the Israelites lived in Egypt they enjoyed *mashchi*; during the later Persian presence here they undoubtedly ate *dolmas*; and, in more recent centuries, Jews learned the varieties of Turkish *dolma*. By whatever name, stuffing vegetables constituted an art and was a measuring rod of a woman's culinary skills.

The common filling for stuffed vegetables is a mixture of chopped onions, meat, rice, and parsley. In the past the amount of meat used indicated a family's financial status. In most cases the meat portion was used sparingly, to give flavor.

Spiced Watermelon Rind

1 large watermelon *or* 2 medium
    watermelons
½ cup salt
7½ cups sugar
2½ cups white wine vinegar *or* cider
    vinegar
⅓ cup distilled vinegar
2 lemons, unpeeled and thinly sliced

Spice Bouquet:
1 stick cinnamon
1 tablespoon whole cloves
1 tablespoon allspice
2 tablespoons grated fresh ginger root

1. Remove the pulp from the watermelon and reserve it for another use. Cut off and discard the green outer skin. Cut the white inner rind into 1-inch squares. 2. In a large bowl, cover the rind with 4 quarts of water and add the salt. Let mixture stand overnight. Drain the rind through a colander and wash the pieces under running water to remove the salt. 3. In a large enamel pot, combine the sugar, 3 quarts of water, and the vinegars. 4. To make the spice bouquet, wrap all the ingredients in clean cheesecloth and tie securely. Add the spice bouquet to the pot and cook the mixture for 1 hour. Remove from the heat and add the lemon slices. 5. Spoon the rind and lemon slices into sterilized jars (discard the spice bag) and seal. *Makes 6 pints*

Baked Summer Squash Casserole

1 large onion, chopped
2 tablespoons vegetable oil
2 pounds summer squash *or* zucchini
½ pound feta cheese
2 eggs, beaten

salt, to taste
½ teaspoon freshly ground black
   pepper
2 tablespoons chopped fresh parsley

1. In a large frying pan, gently cook the onion in the oil until soft.   2. Cut the squash into ½-inch slices, and trim off the ends. Steam them in a metal steamer, just until the peel is softened. Drain and layer them in a greased oven-proof serving dish. Crumble the cheese on top.   3. In a small bowl, combine the eggs, salt, pepper, and parsley. Stir well and pour over the squash. Bake in a preheated 375° oven for about 25 minutes. Serve warm, or at room temperature with yogurt. *Serves 4 to 6*

Batter-fried Summer Squash

2 pounds summer squash *or* zucchini
batter for fried vegetables (page 72)
vegetable oil for frying

lemon wedges for garnish
chopped fresh parsley, for garnish

1. Remove the ends from the squash or zucchini and scoop out the pulp, reserving it for summer squash omelet (page 180). Slice the squash or zucchini into rounds and drain in a colander and pat dry.   2. Prepare the batter.   3. In a frying pan, heat the oil until very hot. Dip the sliced vegetables in the batter and fry for 5 minutes, turning to cook on both sides. Drain on paper towels and keep them warm while you fry the remaining rounds. Serve garnished with lemon wedges and chopped parsley. *Serves 4 to 6*

Summer Squash Omelet

❦ ❦ ❦

squash pulp from batter-fried summer squash (page 179)
1 onion, chopped

1 tablespoon butter *or* vegetable oil
2 eggs, beaten
salt and pepper, to taste

1. Drain the pulp in a colander.   2. Sauté the onion in the butter until golden. Add the pulp, eggs, and salt and pepper to taste. Cook over moderately high heat until done. *Serves 1 or 2*

Stuffed Summer Squash in Yogurt

❦ ❦ ❦

Serve hot as a first course, or as a main luncheon dish.

1½ pints yogurt
1 tablespoon cornstarch
2 tablespoons milk
12 small summer squash *or* zucchini
vegetable stuffing (page 158)
2 to 3 tomatoes, sliced

5 cloves garlic
salt, to taste
1 teaspoon dry mint
1 tablespoon margarine *or* oil
½ teaspoon allspice

1. In a large pot, beat the yogurt until it is liquified. Combine the cornstarch and milk and stir it into the yogurt with a wooden spoon. Allow the yogurt to come to a boil, stirring in one direction only. Reduce the heat and let the yogurt simmer for about 10 minutes, uncovered (to ensure smoothness and prevent curdling).   2. Cut off one end of the squash and carefully scoop out the pulp, leaving the shell intact. Prepare vegetable stuffing and stuff the squash. Layer a pot with the sliced tomatoes and place the stuffed squash on top of them. Add 2 cups of water, and bring to a boil. Simmer for about 30 minutes, or until the squash is almost cooked. Pour the cooked yogurt over the squash. Cover the pot and simmer until the squash is tender.   3. Put the garlic cloves through a press, and mix the pulp with the salt and mint. In a small frying pan, sauté the mixture in oil or margarine. Stir in the allspice. Carefully add this mixture to the squash and yogurt. *Serves 12*

Garden Sorrel

Cold Summer Squash-and-Barley Soup

❦ ❦ ❦

This is a meal-in-a-bowl summer soup. With bread, cheese, and a green salad, it makes a refreshing meal on a hot night.

1 cup pearl barley, rinsed
2 pounds summer squash *or* zucchini, sliced
½ cup chopped onions
½ cup chopped celery
2 tablespoons vegetable oil
2 tablespoons whole wheat flour

4 cups vegetable stock
2 teaspoons ground cumin
1 cup plain yogurt
1 egg, lightly beaten
1 teaspoon salt
chopped fresh dill, for garnish, *or* parsley

1. In a medium saucepan, bring 1½ cups of water to a boil. Stir in the barley. Cover the pan and simmer about 45 minutes or until the water has been absorbed and the barley is tender.   2. In a large, heavy saucepan, sauté the onions, squash, and celery in oil for 2 minutes. Blend in the flour gradually and slowly pour in the stock. Continue to cook, stirring, until the mixture thickens slightly and comes to a boil. Stir in the barley and cumin. Cover, lower the heat, and simmer the mixture for 15 minutes, or until it is very thick.   3. In a bowl, combine the yogurt, egg, and salt. Remove the pan from the heat and slowly stir in the yogurt mixture. Reheat the soup over very low heat, stirring only until the soup is heated through. Ladle the soup into bowls and garnish with chopped dill or parsley. *Serves 4*

Pumpkin Pie Squares

1½ cups all-purpose flour
2 cups barley flakes
1½ cups brown sugar
¾ cup margarine
3 eggs
1 pound cooked pumpkin, drained
    and mashed, *or* 1 16-ounce can
    pumpkin purée
1 can evaporated milk
½ teaspoon ginger
½ teaspoon nutmeg
½ teaspoon cloves
½ teaspoon salt
1 teaspoon cinnamon
1 teaspoon vanilla extract
2 cups chopped walnuts

Topping (optional):
2 cups sour cream
2 tablespoons sugar
½ teaspoon vanilla

1. In a large bowl, mix together the flour, barley flakes, and half the sugar. Cut the margarine into chunks and put it in a food processor with the flour and barley mixture, or work it with your fingers until the grains are pea-size. Press the dough into a 10 × 15-inch rimmed baking pan. Prick the dough with a fork to prevent puffing. Bake on the lowest rack of a preheated 350° oven for 20 minutes. 2. In a large bowl, beat the eggs and add the pumpkin, milk, ginger, nutmeg, cloves, salt, cinnamon, vanilla, and the remaining sugar. Stir until smooth. 3. Pour the pumpkin mixture into the partially baked crust and smooth the top with a knife. Bake another 20 minutes, until the filling is almost set. Remove from the oven and sprinkle with the walnuts. 4. To make the topping, combine the topping ingredients in a small bowl. Remove the pie from the oven after the final 20 minutes, spread the topping over it, and bake 10 minutes more. Then top with walnuts. Cool, cut into squares, and serve. *Makes 1 10-inch pie*

Cold Pumpkin Pudding

❦ ❦ ❦

You may serve this as pudding topped with whipped cream, or use it as a pie filling for a baked pastry shell such as *sanbusak* pastry (pages 61–62). Cover the bottom of the pastry shell with a layer of raw chickpeas or foil so that the crust will remain crisp during baking.

4 pounds pumpkin, seeded, pared, and cut into 1-inch pieces (about 4 cups)
2 cups brown sugar
1 cup water
½ teaspoon ground cloves

½ teaspoon ginger
½ teaspoon cinnamon
2 eggs, beaten
2 tablespoons butter
1 cup heavy cream, whipped (optional)

1. In a large saucepan, combine the pumpkin and sugar. Add the water and cook over medium heat until tender, about 30 minutes (or pressure-cook for 10 minutes). Remove from the heat. 2. In a food processor, electric blender, or by hand, blend the pumpkin mixture with the cloves, ginger, and cinnamon. Stir in the eggs and butter. Cook, stirring, for 5 minutes over medium heat until thickened. Put the pudding into a serving bowl and refrigerate for a few hours. Spread the walnuts over the pudding, cover with whipped cream if you desire, and serve. *Serves 6*

Pumpkin Pancakes

❦ ❦ ❦

These pancakes are sometimes served instead of potato pancakes at Chanukah time.

3 cups mashed cooked pumpkin
1½ cups all-purpose flour
½ teaspoon baking powder

½ teaspoon allspice
vegetable oil for frying

1. In a large bowl, mix all the ingredients well. 2. Drop by tablespoonsful onto a heated, greased griddle or into a pan filled with hot oil for deep frying. Turn over to cook both sides until golden. Drain the pancakes on paper towels. Sprinkle with sugar, confectioners' sugar, or salt, and serve with applesauce. *Serves 4*

Syrian Marjoram

Pumpkin-Ginger Relish

1 6-pound pumpkin, quartered,
    seeded, strings discarded, and
    peeled
4 cups sugar
2 teaspoons cinnamon
2 teaspoons ground ginger

2½ cups fresh lemon juice
3 teaspoons grated lemon peel
2 cups water
½ teaspoon salt
3 tablespoons marmalade

1. Dice the pumpkin into ⅓-inch cubes. In a large bowl, combine it with the sugar, cinnamon, and ginger. Add the lemon juice and lemon peel and combine well. Let it stand overnight, uncovered, stirring occasionally.   2. Transfer the mixture to an enameled or stainless steel pan. Stir in the water and salt. Bring the mixture to a boil and simmer, covered, for 10 minutes, stirring occasionally until the pumpkin is tender. Stir in the marmalade, and cook for a few minutes more.   3. With a slotted spoon, transfer the relish to sterilized pint jars and fill within ½ inch from the top. Seal. *Makes 6 pints*

MUSHROOM (*Boletis*, etc.)

Mushrooms grow wild in Israel mainly in the hills around the roots of pine trees. They show up after the first rains of winter. Some varieties of cultivated mushrooms are dried for later use. Mushrooms have almost no calories and are vested with magic! One measure of their magic is the presence of glutamate, a flavor-enhancer used by the Chinese for centuries but only newly discovered by Westerners. The uses for mushrooms are endless. They can be quickly sautéed in butter or oil, chopped up and added to many dishes, or stuffed with a variety of fillings.

Stuffed Mushrooms

12 large mushrooms
1 cup bread crumbs
2 ounces butter *or* margarine
½ cup chopped fresh parsley
1 egg

½ teaspoon oregano
salt and pepper, to taste
2 tablespoons grated Parmesan cheese
chopped fresh parsley, for garnish

1. Wash the mushrooms carefully and remove the stems (save them for another dish).   2. To prepare the stuffing, combine the bread crumbs, butter, parsley,

egg, oregano, and salt and pepper. Fill each cap with stuffing and sprinkle with grated cheese. Place the mushrooms in a greased baking pan or ovenproof dish. Bake in a preheated 350° oven for 30 minutes. Serve hot, garnished with parsley. *Serves 6 for hors d'oeuvres*

Cream of Mushroom and Barley Soup

3 tablespoons butter *or* margarine
2 tablespoons flour
1 teaspoon salt
½ teaspoon pepper
4 cups milk *or* chicken stock *or*
    vegetable stock *or* meat stock

1 cup cooked barley
1 cup fresh mushrooms *or*
    reconstituted dried mushrooms
1 tablespoon grated onion
juice from 2 cloves garlic
paprika

1. In a heavy saucepan over a low flame, blend the butter, flour, salt, and pepper. Remove from the heat and stir in the liquid. Bring the soup to a boil, stirring until it is smooth. Add the barley, mushrooms, onion, and garlic juice. Serve hot with a sprinkle of paprika. *Serves 4 to 6*

Marinated Raw Mushroom Salad

½ pound button mushrooms
½ cup chopped fresh parsley
3 tablespoons olive oil
juice of 1 lemon

½ teaspoon ground oregano *or*
    marjoram
2 garlic cloves, pressed

1. Wash the mushrooms and wipe dry. Thinly slice them vertically, to preserve their special shape, and put them in a glass bowl or pottery dish. 2. In a small bowl, mix the parsley, oil, lemon juice, oregano, and garlic, and pour over the mushrooms. Marinate the mushrooms in the refrigerator for a few hours. To serve, lift mushrooms out with a slotted spoon and place in a glass dish, or serve in small dishes on a buffet table with wooden toothpicks. *Serves 4*

No-Crust Mushroom Quiche

3 ounces butter *or* margarine
3 tablespoons chopped onion
1 pound fresh mushrooms *or*
    4 ounces dried mushrooms,
    reconstituted

½ teaspoon nutmeg
1 tablespoon cornstarch
1 teaspoon or more water
3 eggs, beaten

1. In a large frying pan, melt the butter. Sauté the onions until golden. Add the mushrooms and nutmeg. Cook, stirring occasionally, until the mushrooms are tender. 2. Make a paste of the cornstarch and water, and stir into the mushroom mixture. Add the beaten eggs. Pour the mixture into a greased oven-proof pie dish. Bake in a preheated 375° oven for 30 minutes, or until a toothpick inserted into the center comes out clean. *Serves 4 to 6*

Mushrooms in Sour Cream

2 medium onions, finely chopped
4 tablespoons butter *or* margarine *or*
    vegetable oil
4 cups sliced fresh mushrooms
1 tablespoon flour

1 cup sour cream *or* yogurt
1 teaspoon ground nutmeg
salt, to taste
pepper

1. In a frying pan, sauté the onions in butter until translucent. Add the mushrooms and continue cooking over medium heat, stirring constantly, until the mushrooms and onions are tender. 2. In a small bowl, stir the flour into the sour cream or yogurt; add the nutmeg and salt. Pour this mixture over the mushrooms and blend with a wooden spoon. Cover the pan and simmer for 5 minutes. Serve on toast, with a grind of black pepper or as a filling for vol-au-vent pastry. *Serves 4*

RADISH (*Raphanus sativus*)

No wonder the early Hebrew people enjoyed radishes—they are easy to harvest, require no cooking, and are good mixed with other vegetables in salads and sauces. Radish is a new gardener's best friend. Easy to grow, radishes are especially satisfying in a child's first garden. They are sharp to the palate but pleasing to the eye.

Radish and Spiced Mushroom Salad

2 teaspoons ground hyssop
2 teaspoons sesame seeds
1 tablespoon vegetable oil
½ teaspoon honey
1 tablespoon lemon juice
1 cup yogurt
¼ pound red radishes, grated (about 2 cups)

2 ounces dried mushrooms, reconstituted and drained
4 shallots, with some green tops, chopped
salt and pepper, to taste
lettuce, torn or shredded

1. In a small saucepan, combine the hyssop, sesame seeds, oil, honey, and lemon juice. Cook over low heat for 5 minutes. 2. When the mixture is cool, combine it in a large bowl with the yogurt. Add the radishes, mushrooms, and shallots. Toss well and add salt and pepper to taste. Serve the salad on a bed of shredded or torn lettuce. *Serves 4 to 6*

Spiced Radish, Mushroom, and Shallot Salad

You can use this salad to stuff tomatoes or cucumber boats, or serve on lettuce leaves.

½ pound red radishes
3 shallots, with some green tops
½ pound small, firm white mushrooms
½ teaspoon ground coriander
½ teaspoon cayenne pepper
½ teaspoon fennel seeds
½ teaspoon ground cumin

½ teaspoon turmeric
½ teaspoon salt
1 tablespoon olive oil
1 tablespoon honey
½ teaspoon fresh lemon juice
1 cup sour cream
24 lettuce leaves *or* endive leaves
paprika, for garnish

1. Slice the radishes into thin semicircles. Slice the shallots into thin circles.

Slice the mushrooms lengthwise into thin sections.   2. In a small saucepan, combine the coriander, cayenne, fennel seeds, cumin, turmeric, and salt. Add the oil, honey, and lemon juice. Cook the mixture over low heat, stirring, for 3 minutes. Allow to cool for 10 minutes.   3. In a large bowl, whisk together the cooled spice mixture with the sour cream. Add the radishes, shallots, and mushrooms, and toss well.   4. Select lettuce leaves of equal size, or cut off the leaf tops to equalize them. Spoon mounded tablespoons of salad on each leaf. Sprinkle paprika on top. *Makes 24 servings*

Radish and Turnip Salad

1 pound red radishes
1 pound unpeeled turnips
⅓ cup chopped onions

3 tablespoons olive oil
salt and pepper, to taste
18 black ripe olives

1. Grate the radishes and turnips, and combine in a serving bowl.   2. Gently cook the onions in the oil until soft. Combine them with the radishes and turnips, and add salt and pepper to taste. Garnish with the olives and serve. *Serves 4 to 6*

Radishes in
Sour Cream or Yogurt

30 small red radishes
1 tablespoon honey
1 cup sour cream *or* yogurt

2 tablespoons white wine vinegar
1 teaspoon herb salt
½ cup chopped fresh dill

1. Slice the radishes into thin circles and put them into a serving bowl.   2. In an electric blender, or with a fork, slowly blend the honey and sour cream or yogurt. Gradually add the vinegar. Stir mixture into radishes and add the salt. Serve garnished with dill. *Serves 4 to 6*

Radish Preserve

❧ ❧ ❧

This prized Passover preserve is traditionally spread on matzot.

1 pound red radishes, peeled and cut
   in julienne strips
¼ cup water
¼ cup honey

1¼ cups sugar
1 teaspoon ground ginger *or* minced
   fresh ginger root
½ cup slivered blanched almonds

1. In a saucepan, bring the radishes to a boil in 1 quart of water and drain in a colander. Repeat and drain again.   2. In a saucepan, mix the water, honey, sugar, and ginger, and bring to a boil. Add the radishes. Simmer over very low heat until the radishes are almost transparent. Add the almonds. Cook until the preserve is thick. Pour into 2 8-ounce glass jars. *Makes 16 ounces*

SORREL (*Rumex acetosa*)

Sorrel is not mentioned in the Bible, but is an important vegetable in rabbinic literature. It resembles spinach, although the leaves are slightly longer and the taste is not as pungent. Because its growing season is longer than that of spinach, sorrel leaves have been appreciated by many ancient peoples, who used the raw young leaves in salads and the mature leaves in vegetable dishes and in soups. The French *bonne femme* soup is made with sorrel leaves. See the recipe for grilled quail and chicken livers (page 260) for another way to use sorrel.

Sorrel Soup

❧ ❧ ❧

1 cup shredded sorrel leaves
1 tablespoon olive oil *or* butter
1 tablespoon all-purpose flour
4 cups hot water *or* vegetable stock

½ teaspoon salt
2 cups milk
1 egg, beaten
croutons, for garnish

1. In a saucepan, steam the sorrel with the oil or butter. Cover the pan and cook until the sorrel leaves have wilted.   2. Add the flour to the pan; mix well. Slowly add water or stock and salt, stirring constantly. Simmer over low heat about 15 minutes.   3. Mix the milk and beaten egg; add to the soup. Stir well and reheat, but do not let the soup boil. Serve immediately in a soup tureen and garnish with croutons, or offer sliced French bread spread with garlic and butter (see page 167). *Serves 4 to 6*

Garden Sorrel

Raw Sorrel Omelet

❦ ❦ ❦

1 cup packed sorrel leaves, stems and
    ribs removed, *or* spinach
4 eggs

2 teaspoons chopped garlic chives
2 teaspoons nutmeg
1 tablespoon margarine

1. Wash, dry, and finely slice the sorrel leaves or put them through a food processor. 2. In a bowl, beat the eggs and add the sorrel, garlic, and nutmeg. 3. In an omelet pan, heat the margarine until it sizzles. Stir the egg mixture and pour it into the pan. Stir briskly with a fork, so that the omelet is evenly heated. Lift the corners of the omelet, fold over, and transfer to a hot serving plate. *Makes 2 2-egg omelets or 4 1-egg omelets*

SPINACH

Spinach and Lentil Soup

❦ ❦ ❦

1 pound fresh spinach *or* ½ pound
    frozen spinach
½ pound green lentils (about 2 cups),
    rinsed and picked over
2 medium onions

2 cloves garlic, minced
2 tablespoons olive oil
1 teaspoon ground nutmeg
salt and pepper, to taste
slice of lemon, for garnish

1. Wash the fresh spinach thoroughly and drain in a colander. If you are using frozen spinach, thaw it and squeeze out any excess moisture. 2. In a large saucepan, cover the lentils with 6 cups of water. Bring to a boil and simmer 1 hour, or pressure-cook until done. 3. Sauté the onions and garlic in the oil until soft. Add the nutmeg, and salt and pepper to taste. Cover and cook on low heat for about 5 minutes. Add the spinach and cook over very low heat. Cover the pan and continue to cook slowly for a few minutes longer. 4. Add the spinach mixture to cooked lentils. Simmer gently, adding more water if necessary. Serve garnished with a slice of lemon. *Serves 6 to 8 as a first course, 4 to 6 as a main course*

Lentil

Spinach Omelet

1 pound fresh spinach *or* ½ pound
    frozen spinach
1 tablespoon butter *or* margarine *or*
    vegetable oil

½ cup onions (optional)
salt and pepper, to taste
½ teaspoon nutmeg
6 eggs

1. Wash the fresh spinach thoroughly. If you are using frozen spinach, allow it to thaw. In a skillet, sauté the spinach in ½ tablespoon of the fat for 2 or 3 minutes. Do not overcook. Drain it thoroughly and chop. If you are using onions, sauté them in the remaining butter or oil until soft. Add salt and pepper and nutmeg to taste.   2. In a large bowl, beat the eggs and stir in the spinach mixture (add onions, if you are using them). Pour the mixture into a well-oiled skillet, and fry until the underside is crisp. Place the skillet under the broiler for a minute and cook until the top is brown, or carefully turn the omelet over and cook the other side in the pan.   3. Cut into wedges and serve with yogurt.
Makes 3 2-egg omelets or 6 1-egg omelets

Fresh Spinach Salad

3 bunches fresh spinach
1 cup crumbled feta cheese

Herbal Dressing:
½ teaspoon rosemary
½ teaspoon thyme
1 teaspoon basil
1 teaspoon hyssop
salt and pepper, to taste
1 tablespoon water
3 tablespoons lemon juice
1 cup olive oil

1. Wash the spinach thoroughly and drain in a colander. Tear into bite-size pieces.   2. In a small bowl, mix the rosemary, thyme, basil, hyssop, salt, and pepper with the water and let it sit for a few minutes. Add the lemon juice and olive oil. Pour the dressing into a jar with a close-fitting top and shake well. 3. In a large salad bowl, toss the spinach with the dressing and crumble feta cheese over it. Serve immediately. *Serves 6 to 8*

Fresh Spinach and Mushroom Salad

❧ ❧ ❧

3 bunches fresh spinach
herbal dressing (page 191)
1 cup thinly sliced fresh mushrooms

1. Follow steps 1 and 2 in fresh spinach salad (page 191). 2. In a small bowl, pour the dressing over the mushrooms and let them steep for 10 to 15 minutes. 3. In a large salad bowl, toss the spinach with the mushrooms and serve. *Serves 6*

TURNIPS (*Brassica rapa*)
RUTABAGAS (*Brassica napobrassica*)

Before potatoes were introduced as a crop in Israel, turnips were used in their place. They don't stand up, in preference, against the competition with root crops such as carrots and beets. But given enough space in the garden they are a faithful winter standby.

Quicker growing than other root crops, turnips reach maturity within forty to sixty days. Turnips planted at the end of summer can be harvested in the fall, and a second planting any time between September and October will be ready for hearty, cold-weather meals. Not a few gardeners here grow turnips or their relatives, rutabagas, for their attractive appearance. They also make inexpensive house plants. Plant them in pots, or cut off the top of a turnip or rutabaga and place it in a soup bowl filled with pebbles and water.

For some reason, many people think they don't like turnips and rutabagas. The seasoning makes the difference. Diners who first taste turnips and rutabagas without knowing what they are eating will quickly learn to appreciate them!

Curried Rutabaga Balls

2 cups cooked mashed rutabagas *or*
    turnips
1 cup sifted all-purpose flour
2 teaspoons double-acting baking
    powder
1 teaspoon salt

½ teaspoon freshly ground black
    pepper
½ teaspoon ground ginger
2 eggs, beaten
vegetable oil

1. In a bowl, combine the rutabagas with the flour, baking powder, salt, pepper, and ginger. Beat in the eggs.   2. Heat ½ inch of oil in a large heavy-bottomed frying pan or wok. Drop the batter by the tablespoonful into the oil. Fry over medium to high heat, turning the balls until they are golden. Drain on paper towels. Serve with a savory dip, such as *tahini* sauce (pages 212–13). *Serves 4 to 6*

Dilled Turnips and Sausage

3 pounds turnips, peeled and
    quartered
1 teaspoon sugar
1 teaspoon salt
1 teaspoon dill seed

⅓ cup meat stock *or* 1 bouillon cube
    dissolved in ⅓ cup hot water
¼ teaspoon black pepper
2 teaspoons lemon juice
½ pound sliced salami *or* 12
    frankfurters, sliced

1. In a large saucepan, cover the turnips with water and add the sugar, salt, and dill seed. Cover, bring to a boil, and simmer 10 minutes.   2. Mix the turnips with the meat stock, pepper, and lemon juice. Bake in a covered, greased casserole for 20 minutes, or until the turnips are tender.   3. While the turnips are baking, lightly sauté the sliced salami or frankfurters. Remove the lid from the casserole and top with the meat. Bake for 5 minutes more. Serve with Dijon mustard. *Serves 6 to 8*

Turnip

Turnip-Apple Salad

2 medium turnips, grated
2 medium cooking apples, grated
1 onion, grated
2 stalks celery, chopped

Dressing:

1 teaspoon soy sauce
1 tablespoon lemon juice
2 tablespoons olive oil
1 teaspoon sugar

1. In a large bowl, combine the turnips, apples, onion, and celery. 2. Mix the dressing ingredients and toss with the salad until well mixed. Serve immediately in small bowls, or on a bed of lettuce. *Serves 4 to 6*

WILD GREENS

Some of my best friends are weeds. They are not just winners, they are survivors. They link generations of vegetable growth, much of which is edible. Though a long prejudice persists against weeds, it has more to do with fear and with a sense of things "looking right" than with how these veterans taste. Too many people would prefer to eat nice-looking embalmed fruits and vegetables than to taste nature's seasonal freshness. They overlook the fact that most of today's edible flora originally were derived from wild plants.

Tidiness has been the order of the day, sponsored by an exaggerated concern for weed-free home gardens and public landscapes. In the main, this has been achieved by massive doses of weed killers and insecticides. Sadly, without weeds the general flora and fauna will suffer. The more chemicals used to destroy weeds and pests, the less oxygen there is in the air for humans and animals. Interfering with nature, in many instances, is an attempt to play God. Remember: before God, the small ant and the big elephant are the same; so too a self-sowing weed and a cultivated rose.

Good and evil exist side by side in all living things. If there are poisonous plants and animals among us, let them wage their own battle for survival. They have done so long before chemical stink bombs disturbed the elements! Our job is to learn from nature, not to destroy its balance. If a weed bothers you, pluck it out before it goes to seed and put it in the compost pile. Let the chemistry of the pile cope with it. But before you do that, make sure that it isn't worth eating! Instead of going out to dinner, try picking your supper from among the neighboring fields. Good luck!

Almost every country in the world has been blessed with a food basket of wild plants. These have been especially known to women, who have foraged for them in their role as food providers for their families. Israel's small size is in no way a measure of its fertility. More eloquently perhaps than a scholar's research or an archeologist's dry evidence, the edible wild plants of Jerusalem in particular are testimony to the good earth of Jerusalem and the Judean hillside. The green presence is a living museum of humankind's early food basket. Climate and the geographical position between the Mediterranean basin and the Middle East have endowed it with a natural habitat of Mother Nature's edible bounty. Weeds feel at home here.

CAPER (*Capparis spinosa*)

We have discussed the caper at length in Herbs and Spices (pages 29–41). Now let's look at some recipes for this tiny bud.

Pickled Capers

2 cups capers	6 lemon slices *or* lemon leaves *or* 3
¾ cup coarse salt	peppercorns *or* 4 bay leaves
3 quarts water	

1. Soak the capers in water for two days, changing the water each day.   2. Prepare a basic brine of the salt and water. To this brine add your choice of flavoring: lemon slices, lemon leaves, peppercorns, or bay leaves.   3. In a large sterilized glass container, pack the capers and pour the brine over them. Make sure the capers are covered with brine—otherwise they will spoil. Remove the scum and add more brine when necessary. Ferment for 1 month, then pack the capers with brine in sterilized glass jars and seal. *Makes about 3 cups*

Caper Sauce

The caper flowers' buds ripen in early summer. After pickling, they are ready to eat. They yield a piquant sauce, which is especially delightful in such cold summer dishes as hard-boiled eggs, cold fish, and cold chicken salad.

2 tablespoons pickled capers	juice of 1 lemon
6 anchovy fillets, drained	freshly ground black pepper
¼ cup olive oil	

1. Pound the capers and anchovies in a mortar, or process in a blender or food processor until they form a paste.   2. Beat in the olive oil in a slow stream, as for mayonnaise. Add the lemon juice and pepper to taste. *Makes 1 cup*

Caper

CHICORY (*Cichorium intybus*)

We found chicory growing wild in our garden. It is one of the five bitter herbs which can be used on the Passover Seder menu.

Chicory is a strikingly beautiful plant when in bloom, showing cornflower-blue blossoms. A limestone-loving plant, long resident in the hills of Judea, it is called *chicouryeh* in Arabic, from which the English name is probably derived.

The roots are boiled, more often by the Arab population than the Israelis, nor do Israelis roast the roots to make a coffee substitute. But the young leaves can be eaten in a salad, or cooked as a vegetable with mustard sauce.

Steamed Chicory Leaves

Chicory

With the addition of beaten eggs, these tender greens can turn into an omelet.

4 cups young chicory leaves
1 onion, chopped
2 cloves garlic, minced
olive oil *or* butter *or* margarine

1. In a saucepan, steam the chicory leaves, covered, for 15 minutes. 2. In a small frying pan, sauté the onion and garlic in the olive oil. Stir in the cooked greens and serve. *Serves 4*

Raw Chicory-Dandelion Green Salad

2 cups chicory leaves, washed, dried, and torn
1 cup dandelion greens, washed, dried, and torn
1 onion, chopped
1 tablespoon fresh parsley, chopped

3 tablespoons olive oil
3 tablespoons freshly squeezed orange juice
½ teaspoon curry powder
salt and pepper, to taste
1 cup sliced green olives (optional)

1. In a salad bowl, combine the chicory leaves, dandelion, onion, and parsley. Dress with the olive oil and orange juice. Season with curry powder, and salt and pepper to taste. Add the olives if you like. *Serves 4*

FENNEL (*Foeniculum vulgare*)

I did not find fennel growing in my garden when we first settled here. But, on a summer's walk around the neighborhood, my eye caught a landscape swaying with the graceful feathery stalks of this ancient plant. In Israel it flowers from May until the first rains fall and the plant goes to seed.

I didn't trust my talents, or the garden's capacity to produce plants from seeds. So, with large garden fork in hand, I set out to dig up some rooted plants. They have fared well and lend a lingering color to the garden in late summer, when garden color dims. My fennel plants have stood up to the not infrequent droughts we suffer—they seem to be weatherproof!

The possible uses of fennel seeds are legion. Not the least of them is a strong infusion which, when imbibed daily, is said to aid the battle of the bulge. Fennel seeds are especially associated with fish—quite conveniently, they grow near sea coasts as well as in hilly areas.

A branch placed in a bottle of salad oil will give a surprisingly fresh taste to the simplest dressing. Seeds scattered on barbecue coals will soon give evidence that something is cooking and ready to eat. *Pita* bread (pages 56–57) topped with fennel seeds makes good eating, and is an aid to digestion.

Ground fennel seed added to a simple white sauce goes well with steamed fish or hard-boiled eggs. You can make an easy fennel-seed tissane by steeping 2 tablespoons of seeds in boiling water. Strain, serve, and sweeten to taste.

A fennel face pack is made by mixing yogurt, strong fennel tea, honey, and leaves of fennel. Applied to the face it cheers up the skin, smooths the wrinkles, and gives a tonic effect to tired skin. If your feet are tired, add strong fennel-seed tea to a pan of water, soak your feet, and feel soothed.

Fresh fennel complements fish well. See the recipes for broiled red mullet with orange sauce (page 270) and red bream with fennel, thyme, and white wine (page 273).

MALLOW (*Malva rotundifolia*)

No discussion of nature's gifts to humanity would be complete without common wild mallow. It graces every earth-bed in gardens, dump heaps, and roadsides; and even in tiny wall crevices, stone walls, and fences, where enough earth and dust have collected to bed a root of this aristocrat of wild greens. So volatile is its growing strength that it survives in diverse climates and soils. It is the Esperanto of the weed world, growing in the chilly climates of Europe and the Americas, as well as the warm environment of the Middle East, and the southern and western United States.

Spring is the best time to cut mallow, when the leaves are tender and before the plant flowers and goes to seed. The tender leaves make a sharp-tasting salad, or they can be made into a casserole consisting of layers of rice and mallow on a bed of dried onions. Mallow pancakes seasoned with nutmeg and yogurt make a wonderful brunch offering.

In Arabic mallow is called *khubbesai*, which means bread—an indication of how much it was considered daily bread. In Hebrew it is called *halamit*, bread to starving Israelis during the Siege of Jerusalem in 1948.

A soldier on guard near the frontier dividing Jerusalem during the Siege of Jerusalem told me of a sight he saw during a short cease-fire between the warring Jews and Arabs of the City of Jerusalem. When the coast seemed clear, Jewish women rushed out to cut mallow on one side of the dividing line; and, almost in the same growing patch, Arab women too made a dash to pick mallow. No wonder a near holiness surrounds this plant—it is neutral. Today, mallow is served by many Israelis as part of the Passover Seder, in thanksgiving and in memory of things past.

A few years ago, I visited my family in Menlo Park, California. Leaving my sleeping brothers, I set out for the post office. As I turned a corner, I noticed a gardener fast at work weeding out a lovely garden. As I approached, I almost tripped over a big pile of mallow in the street. I was shocked. I went to the front door of the charming house and rang the doorbell. I said to the woman who answered it, "Good morning, madam. Excuse me for disturbing you, but I wanted to tell you that the gardener is throwing out your lunch."

"I beg your pardon," the startled woman replied. "What lunch?"

This was my cue to tell her about how mallow could be made into a rice-and-onion casserole. Also, that if she made it now and wrapped the pot in newspapers and an old pullover, it would keep warm until lunch time. She clearly thought I was a nut, but gently mentioned that she already had prepared lunch. "Well," I replied, "why don't you freeze that and eat the mallow while it is young and tender? You see, I'm from Jerusalem, where mallow is not considered a weed. It has meant bread to many peoples there."

Upside-down Barley and Common Mallow Ring

When the mallow plants are young, in early spring, the leaves may be eaten raw in a salad. As the plants mature and flower the leaves may be cooked as spinach, layered with rice or barley. Mallow buds may be sautéed gently in oil, seasoned with allspice, and used as a garnish.

If you cannot find mallow, you may substitute spinach or swiss chard in this recipe.

Mallow

2 pounds mallow leaves *or* spinach,
   washed and drained (about 8
   cups, packed)
2 onions, chopped
2 cloves garlic, crushed
2 tablespoons vegetable oil
1 teaspoon ground coriander
1 teaspoon allspice
salt and pepper, to taste
3 cups steamed barley
juice of 1 lemon
½ cup roasted almonds

1. Steam the mallow leaves and drain. 2. Fry the onions and garlic in oil until brown. Add the coriander, allspice, salt, and pepper. Mix with the mallow leaves. 3. Line a greased baking dish with a layer of the mixed greens and onion mixture. Cover with a thick layer of barley and moisten with lemon juice. Repeat the layers until done. Bake uncovered at 350° for 30 minutes, or cook on top of the stove, covered, for 45 minutes. 4. Remove the casserole from the oven and allow it to set for two minutes. Then turn it upside down onto a warmed, round platter. Garnish with roasted almonds. *Serves 6*

Note: Add leftover cooked chicken or turkey to the onion mixture for a more substantial dish.

MUSTARD (*Aren arvensis*)

Mustard *arvensis*, a wild green, is very good in a mixed salad when the leaves are young and tender. Later, as they mature, they become pungent and should be cooked. Fried onions go well with them, and they can be used as a filling for pastries or served with sliced hard-boiled eggs. They lend a sharp taste to an otherwise bland vegetable soup. All the mustards are rich in minerals and in vitamins A, B, B_1, B_2, and C. If you are not given to foraging for mustard plants, seeds are available in many nurseries throughout the United States, some of which have a mail order seed service.

STINGING NETTLE (*Urtica* species)

The leaves of the stinging nettle have small spines that inject silicic acid into the skin, which makes picking painful unless you wear gloves. But picking is worth the effort. Young nettle greens are high in vitamin C, especially the tips, and make a good cooked salad (miraculously, during the cooking the sting disappears).

Although the nettle leaves are at their best when freshly gathered, it's wise to pick more than the day's food requirement so that they can be dried for later use. But remember, they are only valuable dried if they retain their green color. Old leaves are rich in protein and esteemed by farmers for feeding livestock and poultry—that is, if the family doesn't eat them first, or use them for a herbal tea.

The cooked and cooled tips of the nettle are best for making a salad, to which sorrel, raw shallots, and parsley can be added. A dressing of lemon juice, olive oil, and ground dried hyssop enhances the taste considerably.

Spring Tonic Nettle Soup

❦ ❦ ❦

½ cup nettle leaves
1 quart chicken stock *or* vegetable
    stock
2 shallots, chopped
1 tablespoon olive oil
1 pound potatoes *or* turnips, peeled
    and diced

1 teaspoon basil
1 teaspoon sage
1 teaspoon parsley
2 tablespoons cream
2 tablespoons butter *or* margarine

1. Wearing gloves, pick the young nettle leaves. Wash and lightly dry them, and cook them in a saucepan with the stock until tender. Let them cool.   2. In a large pan, sauté the shallots in the oil. Add the potatoes and sauté again. Pour in the boiling stock. Add the nettles, basil, sage, and parsley, and simmer 15 minutes. Let sit, covered, for 10 minutes. Mix in the cream and butter, and serve. *Serves 4 to 6*

ROQUETTE (*Eruca sativa*)

This "what's in a name" herb is also called arugula, rocket, or orquette. An easy and fast grower, roquette served the ancient Hebrew people well. According to tradition, the sages suggested that roquette, considered an aphrodisiac, should be eaten on the eve of the Sabbath to foster love and banish jealousy. No wonder it continues to be a popular vegetable today! A salad of mixed greens including chicory, parsley, and lettuce dressed with vinaigrette is improved with the inclusion of roquette which has a sharp, nutty flavor. The plant tends to seed early, but in turn self-sows readily. Continual cutting of the leaves keeps it intact. It is available in seed packets and worth a place in the garden, since the flower buds and flowers can also be eaten and taste just like the leaves. They make an attractive garnish to a simple salad of the roquette leaves on their own.

TURNIP LEAVES (*Brassica rapa*)

When Meir and I thinned out over-planted turnips seeds, we found the taste of the young leaves earthy and similar to radish leaves. Mixed with sliced cucumber and chopped tomatoes, and dressed with olive oil and lemon juice, they were really delicious—a salad worth serving with fish and chips, English style.

    As the root turnips are swelling under the ground, the top leaves can be snipped for a mixed green salad combined with raw spinach and raw thinly sliced mushrooms, served with a sweet-and-sour dressing and a sprinkle of sesame seeds.

Garden Roquette

Wilted Greens and Turnips

¼ cup vegetable oil
¼ cup orange juice
2 teaspoons red wine vinegar
¼ teaspoon paprika
salt and pepper, to taste

5 cups mixed greens: lettuce, raw
    spinach, or radish tops
1 pound turnips, cooked, peeled, and
    quartered
1 cup walnuts *or* cheese-flavored
    cocktail tidbits *or* croutons

1. In a small bowl, mix the oil, orange juice, vinegar, paprika, salt, and pepper.   2. In a salad bowl, combine the greens and turnips. Pour the dressing over it and toss. Top with walnuts or your choice of garnish. *Serves 4 to 6*

Sour Cream
or Yogurt Dressing

½ teaspoon dry mustard
½ teaspoon wine vinegar
salt and pepper, to taste

1½ cups sour cream *or* yogurt
½ cup chopped fresh parsley

1. Combine all ingredients and mix well. Toss with a green salad. *Makes about 2 cups*

Sweet-and-Sour Dressing

¼ cup olive oil
2 tablespoons citrus vinegar
2 tablespoons wine vinegar
1 tablespoon chutney

1 tablespoon brown sugar
salt and pepper, to taste
¼ cup dried onion

1. Combine all the ingredients and mix well. Marinate until the onion is reconstituted. *Makes about ½ cup*

Fresh Cress
and Roquette Salad

❧ ❧ ❧

2 cups cress, chopped
2 cups roquette, chopped
5 tablespoons olive oil

1½ tablespoons wine vinegar
1½ tablespoons Dijon mustard
2 hard-boiled eggs, sliced

1. Wash the greens and pat dry. Chop them or scissor slice, and combine in a salad bowl.   2. In a small bowl, beat the oil, vinegar, and mustard with a fork until well mixed.   3. Toss the salad with the dressing and top with the sliced eggs. *Serves 4*

8 STOCKS, SAUCES, SALAD DRESSINGS, SOUPS, AND STEWS

❦ ❦ ❦

A cook's culinary distinction is often evaluated by the quality of his or her soups and sauces (except by family members who judge the cook's talents by the dessert course). Soups and stews, along with bread, have sustained generations of people in the Lands of the Bible, including peasants, priests, and prophets.

One portion of the daily diet always included soup. It was served in a bowl, mug, or soup plate; hot, cold, or room temperature.

Because of the chronic, centuries-long shortage of meat in the Land of the Bible, it was necessary to stretch meat as far as possible. Meat soups and stocks based on bones were the mainstay of protein nourishment: often they were closer to stews and meal-in-a-bowl suppers.

Israel's main meal is served in the early afternoon; a light meal is served in the evening. Depending on the season, it may consist of dairy foods, salads, fruit soups, and bread; during the cold, rainy season the family enjoys a rich hearty soup followed by fruit as a sweet.

STOCKS

A well-made stock is the basis of many soups and sauces. Stocks are wonderful ways to use meat bones and poultry carcasses, and vegetables just past their prime.

To Clarify Stock

In general, a properly made stock is clear. But if you desire a cold jellied consommé or an aspic, it is necessary to further clarify the stock.

Remove the fat from 1 quart of stock. Stir a slightly beaten egg white, along with the crumbled whole shell of the egg, into the cooled stock. Carefully bring the stock to a boil, without stirring. The egg will rise to the top, bringing

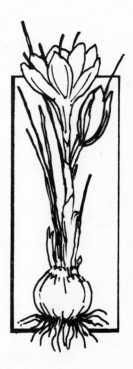

Saffron

with it a thick scum which is part of the clarifying action. Simmer the stock for about 10 minutes more over low heat. Allow the stock to cool for 1 hour.

Wet a cloth in hot water, wring it out, and place it over the top of a large pot as a strainer. Push the egg scum to one side of the stock to make room for a soup ladle. Ladle out the stock and gently pour it through the strainer cloth. Allow the clarified stock to cool, uncovered. Then pour it into a container with a tight-fitting cover and refrigerate.

Consommé

Consommé may be made from white, brown, fish, or vegetable stock. After the stock is degreased and clarified, you will have a clear, mild consommé ready to serve as hot broth, or as a chilled consommé Madrilene or clear aspic. In the last two cases, more body is required. This can be achieved in the following manner:

To 1 quart of degreased stock add ¼ pound lean beef, 1 egg white, and its crumpled shell. Place in the stock pot uncooked chicken carcasses and more vegetables, if desired (if the stock is brown, use tomatoes or tomato skins). Mix these, adding the stock to the pot. Bring the stock slowly to the simmering point (do not allow it to boil) for about 15 minutes. Remove the pot from stove. When the stock has cooled and rested, ladle it through a cloth strainer. Cool it, uncovered, and refrigerate in a tightly closed container.

Basic Brown Stock

❦ ❦ ❦

4 pounds veal knuckle *or* beef
    knuckle *or* a combination of
    knuckles and marrow bones
2 large onions, coarsely chopped
2 carrots
6 black peppercorns *or* 1 teaspoon
    ground pepper
1 teaspoon coarse salt

Bouquet Garni*:

2 bay leaves
2 or 3 sprigs parsley
½ teaspoon thyme
1 teaspoon marjoram
¼ cup celery leaves *or* 1 celeriac root
    or leaves of celeriac
2 cloves garlic

1. Brown the cut-up knuckles and marrow bones briefly in a large stock pot. Combine and add all the ingredients except the salt and cover with 8 to 10 cups of water. Slowly bring to a boil, reduce the heat, and allow the stock to simmer on very low heat for at least 2 hours, uncovered. Stir from time to time. Near the end of the cooking time, add the salt.   2. Strain the stock (you may reserve the bonus to make a second brown stock, page 204), and leave uncovered

*Tie up ingredients for the bouquet garni in a clean cheesecloth bag. Remove the bag at the end of the cooking time.

to cool. You can store the stock in the refrigerator, covered. The congealed fat that rises to the top of chilled stock acts as an extra protection; remove it before you use the stock. The stock will keep, frozen, for several months. If you do not freeze it, keep it fresh by bringing it to a boil every third day. *Makes about 2 quarts*

Second Brown Stock

You can make a second stock from the knuckles and marrow bones removed from the first stock. Use it for sauces and gravies, or as the basis of a soup to be eaten the same day, serve it as a broth, or thicken it with cornstarch for a heartier soup.

bones from basic brown stock (page 203)
1 quart water
½ cup celery leaves

5 to 10 fresh parsley stems
1 teaspoon turmeric
1 teaspoon salt

1. In a large soup pot, combine all of the ingredients except the salt. Bring to a boil and simmer, uncovered, for 1 or 2 hours. Add the salt near the end of the cooking time. Strain and use the stock immediately, freeze, or store covered in the refrigerator. 2. To make this stock with a pressure cooker, combine all the ingredients (but add water so that the pressure cooker is not more than half full). Pressure cook at 15 pounds for about 30 minutes. Reduce the pressure, and strain the stock after the pot has cooled off. *Makes about 1 quart*

White Stock

4 pounds veal knuckles *or* chicken
    parts (neck, giblets, chicken feet,
    and uncooked chicken carcasses)
    or 1 large chicken
8 cups water
2 carrots, cut in chunks
1 turnip, sliced
2 stalks celery, cut in large slices
1 teaspoon turmeric
salt to taste

Bouquet Garni*:
4 white peppercorns
2 bay leaves
1 teaspoon thyme
6 whole cloves
2 or 3 parsley stems
2 or 3 sprigs fresh coriander *or* 1
    teaspoon crushed coriander
    seeds
handful of celeriac leaves

1. In a large stock pot, combine the veal knuckles or chicken parts and water. Cover and bring to a boil. Add the carrots, turnip, celery, turmeric, and salt. Tie the bouquet garni ingredients in a cloth bag and add to the pot. Simmer gently for at least 3 hours. Skim the surface during the cooking time. If you use a whole chicken, remove it when it has been cooked (about 1½ hours). Reserve the meat for another use, and return the bones to the broth for the rest of the cooking time.   2. Strain the stock and cool it, uncovered, in the refrigerator. Store as for basic brown stock (page 205). *Makes about 2 quarts*

*Tie up ingredients for the bouquet garni in a clean cheesecloth bag. Remove the bag at the end of the cooking time.

Fish Stock I

You can use this fish stock as a basis for soups and sauces.

2 tablespoons olive oil *or* vegetable oil
2 pounds inexpensive whole fish,
    cleaned, *or* fresh fish bones,
    heads, tails, and skins, washed
1 cup chopped onions
2 celery stalks with their leaves, cut
    in large slices
1 cup chopped fresh parsley leaves
1 carrot, cut in large chunks

2 sprigs fresh thyme *or* 1 teaspoon
    dried thyme
1 teaspoon ground nutmeg
1 teaspoon sea salt *or* salt
1 teaspoon lemon juice
3 cups water and 2 tablespoons
    vinegar *or* 2 cups water and 1
    cup dry white wine
4 black peppercorns

1. In a large stock pot, heat the oil. Add the fish, onions, celery, parsley, carrot, thyme, nutmeg, and salt, and sauté until the vegetables are soft. Add the lemon juice, water and vinegar (or wine), and peppercorns. Heat, uncovered, until the liquid comes to a boil. Simmer for 20 minutes. (If you overcook the fish stock, it will taste bitter.)   2. Cool the stock and strain through a fine sieve. Freeze the stock for later use, or use immediately. It will keep covered in the refrigerator for only a few days. *Makes about 1 quart*

Fish Stock II

❦ ❦ ❦

You can use this stock as a basis for a sauce or soup to be served with the fish the stock is made from.

1 whole fish	**1 sprig parsley**
1 carrot, cut up	**3 black peppercorns**
½ onion, coarsely chopped	**1 tablespoon olive oil *or* vegetable oil**

1. Steam the fish on a steamer top or rack over a pot containing all of the other ingredients and 2 cups of water. Cover and steam the fish for 20 minutes.   2. Transfer it to a warm plate, ready for serving. Strain the stock and use immediately as a basis for a quick soup or sauce. *Makes 1 pint*

Vegetable-Herb Stock

❦ ❦ ❦

Vegetable stock is important to the growing number of Israeli vegetarians, and to those Jews who observe the Jewish dietary laws. Israel's dramatic advancement in vegetable production has made a new world in vegetable taste and presentation. And although the custom here is to eat as many vegetables as possible raw, there is still a demand for a cooked-vegetable stock enhanced by the exceptional choice of fresh herbs. Vegetable-herb stock, as the basis for milk sauces for fish and egg dishes, yields a subtle dimension to the taste bouquet.

Garden Roquette

3 tablespoons vegetable oil *or*
    margarine
3 carrots, sliced in large chunks
2 onions, quartered *or* 3 to 5
    scallions, sliced in large pieces
3 stalks celeriac *or* celery stalks with
    their leaves, sliced in large pieces
2 tomatoes, quartered
1 teaspoon ground mace
6 peppercorns
2 cloves garlic, unpeeled
2 quarts water
1 teaspoon salt

Bouquet Garni*:

4 to 5 sprigs parsley
1 sprig fresh thyme *or* 1 teaspoon
    dried thyme
3 bay leaves
1 teaspoon ground sage

1. In a large stock pot, heat the oil. Add the carrots, onions, and celery and stir well. Cover the pot and cook slowly until vegetables are soft. Then add the tomatoes, mace, peppercorns, garlic, and bouquet garni. Cover with water, add salt, and bring to a boil. Remove the scum and allow the stock to simmer for at least 1 hour, covered.   2. Strain the stock and refrigerate or freeze. *Makes about 2 quarts*

Note: To make a thick or creamed vegetable soup, purée the non-leafy cooked vegetables in a food or electric blender, and combine with the stock.

*Tie up ingredients for the bouquet garni in a clean cheesecloth bag. Remove the bag at the end of the cooking time.

Basic White Sauce

❧ ❧ ❧

1 tablespoon butter *or* margarine
1 tablespoon flour
1 cup milk *or* water
salt and pepper, to taste

1. In a heavy saucepan, melt the butter or margarine over a low flame. Slowly add the flour and mix to a paste with a wooden spoon or wire whisk. Gradually add the milk or water, stirring constantly. Season with salt and pepper. Cook on a low flame, stirring until thickened (about 10 minutes). *Makes 1 cup*

Note: For a thicker sauce, increase the flour and fat to 2 tablespoons each for the same amount of liquid. For a really thick sauce, use 3 tablespoons each of flour and fat.

Béchamel Sauce

2 tablespoons butter	salt and pepper, to taste
2 tablespoons flour	½ teaspoon nutmeg
1 cup warmed milk	1 bay leaf (optional)

1. In a heavy saucepan, melt the butter over a low flame. Slowly add the flour and mix to a paste. Gradually add the milk with a wooden spoon or wire whisk. Add the seasoning and cook, stirring constantly until smooth.   2. You can put the sauce in a slow oven to keep warm and set while you finish cooking, or place the saucepan in a pan of hot water. The sauce should be kept warm for about 20 minutes. *Makes 1 cup*

Variations: To make velouté sauce, substitute wine for the milk. To make sauce mornay, add 2 tablespoons grated cheese. To make sauce aurore, add 1 tablespoon of tomato paste.

Mayonnaise

Although the origin of mayonnaise is French, it has long been an important part of Middle Eastern cuisine. It is a standby for serving over hard-boiled eggs, cold fish, and cold chicken, and is the basis for three other important sauces: sauce tartare, aioli, and skordalia.

Israel markets a good-quality ready-made mayonnaise, but many home-makers prefer to make their own. Traditional recipes and methods of making mayonnaise call for using the slow, steady, hand-beating method of mixing the egg and the oil, which requires skill, practice, and patience.

Some cooks opt for the easier method of making mayonnaise in the blender, and some use vinegar instead of lemon. That is the real scandal! If you can, try the traditional method—you can't beat it for texture and flavor. For the best results, the ingredients should be at room temperature.

2 egg yolks	½ teaspoon dry mustard
1½ cups olive oil	salt and freshly ground black pepper,
2 tablespoons lemon juice	to taste

1. In a bowl, beat the egg yolks with a wooden spoon until they thicken. Add the oil drop by drop, beating constantly. After you have added about ½ cup, the mixture should begin to have body—you'll know you're on the right track! Drizzle in the remaining oil, still beating. The mixture should now have the

consistency of mayonnaise.   2. Beat in the lemon juice, mustard, and salt and pepper.   3. If the mayonnaise should curdle, don't worry—you can save it. In a clean bowl, beat 1 egg yolk until it is thick. Beat in the curdled mayonnaise. *Makes 2 cups*

Blender Mayonnaise

❦ ❦ ❦

1 egg
1 teaspoon dry mustard
1 teaspoon salt
freshly ground black pepper, to taste

1 teaspoon honey *or* sugar
1 cup olive oil *or* ½ cup olive oil and
    ½ cup safflower oil
2 tablespoons lemon juice

1. In an electric blender, blend the egg well. Add the mustard, salt, pepper, and honey, and blend until the mixture begins to thicken.   2. Remove the top of the blender container. With the blender running, slowly drizzle in the oil until you have blended ½ cup. Add the lemon juice and the rest of the oil in a stream until the mayonnaise is thick and fluffy. *Makes 1½ cups*

Easy Hollandaise Sauce

❦ ❦ ❦

This sauce goes well with such vegetables as cooked broccoli or cauliflower, or poached fish.

½ cup butter *or* margarine
1½ tablespoons lemon juice *or* citrus
    vinegar
2 tablespoons boiling water

3 egg yolks
½ teaspoon salt
freshly ground black pepper

1. In a small saucepan, melt the butter or margarine.   2. In a heat-proof glass bowl over a pan of hot water, combine the lemon juice or vinegar and the boiling water. Add the egg yolks and beat with a wire whisk or with one beater of an electric hand beater until the eggs begin to thicken.   3. Remove the bowl from the water, and slowly beat in the butter. Season with salt and pepper, to taste. *Makes 1 cup*

Safflower

Blender Hollandaise Sauce

Purists insist this blender-made sauce is less tasty than the handmade sauce, but it is much easier to make and can be frozen and reconstituted over hot water. Add turmeric to give it a stronger color, but don't add too much or you will have a bitter flavor.

1 cup butter *or* margarine
3 egg yolks
2 tablespoons lemon juice
freshly ground black pepper, to taste

1. In a small saucepan, melt the butter or margarine. In an electric blender, blend the egg yolks, lemon juice, and pepper on high speed. Remove the lid after a few seconds and slowly pour in the butter. Blend for 30 seconds, or until the sauce is well blended. Serve immediately, or place the container in a pan of warm water to keep the sauce warm. *Makes about 2 cups*

Jerusalem Sauce Tartare

Serve this sauce on cold fish.

1½ cups mayonnaise (page 210) *or* prepared mayonnaise
1 small dill pickle, chopped
3 green olives, chopped
2 scallions, chopped
1 tablespoon capers, drained and chopped

1 handful chopped parsley leaves
1 teaspoon ground coriander
½ teaspoon sugar
salt and pepper, to taste
1 tablespoon lemon juice

1. In a bowl, mix all the ingredients until smoothly blended. Taste, and add more lemon juice if needed. *Makes about 2 cups*

Tarator Sauce for Fish

❧ ❧ ❧

2 slices white bread, crusts removed
8 ounces pine nuts *or* 6 ounces
    ground almonds

2 cloves garlic, crushed
juice of 2 lemons
fish stock

1. Soak the bread in water and squeeze out the surplus moisture.   2. In a mortar, pound the pine nuts. Add the bread and crushed garlic and pound again. Add the lemon juice and enough fish stock to make a firm, fluid sauce. Mix well. Put the sauce through a sieve for a smooth consistency. *Makes about 1 cup*

Egg-and-Lemon Sauce

❧ ❧ ❧

Serve this sauce with stuffed vegetables and cold meats. When you serve it with fish be sure to use a fish stock.

1 tablespoon margarine
2 level tablespoons flour
1 cup hot stock
1 tablespoon hot sauce

2 egg yolks
juice of 2 lemons
1 tablespoon cold water
salt and pepper, to taste

1. In the top of a double boiler, melt the butter or margarine. Add the flour, stirring constantly with a wooden spoon or wire whisk. Slowly add the hot stock, stirring constantly.   2. In a bowl, beat the eggs until they are light and creamy. Slowly add the lemon juice and water. Beat 1 tablespoon of hot sauce into the eggs and lemon. Pour this mixture into the hot sauce. Be careful not to overcook the sauce, as it may curdle. *Makes about 1½ cups*

Tahini Sauce

❧ ❧ ❧

Tahini sauce makes a wonderful dip for cocktails. It can be served on small plates garnished with chopped egg and parsley as a first course, or as an accompaniment to cold dishes, meatballs, hard-boiled eggs, *kibbi*, chickpeas, and *hummus*.

3 cloves garlic (or less, according to taste)
½ cup prepared *tahini* paste

½ cup lemon juice
½ teaspoon ground cumin
½ cup chopped fresh parsley

1. In an electric blender, blend the garlic, *tahini* paste, and lemon juice on high speed until the garlic is crushed. Keep blending, adding enough water to make a smooth cream. Add the cumin and taste.   2. Pour the sauce into a bowl and garnish with parsley. *Makes 1 cup*

Tahini-Yogurt Dip

3 cloves garlic
½ cup prepared *tahini* paste
½ cup yogurt

juice of 2 medium lemons
salt, to taste

1. In an electric blender, blend all the ingredients until they are smooth. 2. Pour the dip into a bowl and set it on a tray with wedges of *pita* bread or crackers for dipping, or use it as a dressing for a mixed vegetable salad. *Makes 1 cup*

Walnut and Tahini Sauce

¼ pound walnuts (1 cup shelled)
2 cloves garlic
salt, to taste

3 to 4 tablespoons prepared *tahini* paste
juice of 2 lemons
4 tablespoons chopped fresh parsley

1. In a food processor or electric blender, grind the walnuts, garlic, and a little salt until the walnuts are almost ground to a paste.   2. Add the *tahini* paste; gradually add the lemon juice and parsley. Serve with fried or baked fish, or with boiled vegetables. *Makes 1 cup*

Taklia Sauce
for Vegetable Soups

4 cloves garlic, crushed
½ teaspoon salt
2 tablespoons oil

1 tablespoon whole coriander seeds *or*
1 teaspoon ground coriander seeds
cayenne pepper
juice of 1 lemon

1. In food processor or electric blender, combine all ingredients and blend until smooth. *Makes ½ cup*

Yemenite Paste (*Zhug*)

Yemenite Jews are among the most colorful and popular immigrants to Israel. Their diet has been low in sugar and rich in meat, which they prefer fried. They use highly spiced sauces that are related to oriental seasoning, and prefer them on bread to jam! Add this paste to any sauce that requires a hot, spicy flavor. One tablespoon goes a long way!

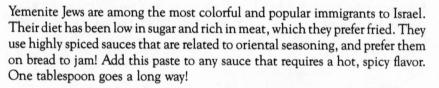

3 cloves garlic, crushed
1 teaspoon freshly ground black
    pepper
1 teaspoon caraway seeds
4 whole cardamom pods

4 dried red chili peppers
½ cup chopped fresh coriander leaves
½ teaspoon salt
juice of ½ lemon

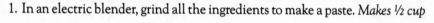

1. In an electric blender, grind all the ingredients to make a paste. *Makes ½ cup*

Coriander

Hillbeh

Add this blend to Indian and Chinese sauces for "hot" dishes. For a spread with an oriental flavor, blend *hillbeh* to your taste with cottage cheese.

2 tablespoons ground fenugreek seeds
1 teaspoon tomato paste
1 teaspoon freshly ground black
    pepper
1 teaspoon caraway seeds

4 whole cardamom pods
4 dried red chili peppers
6 cloves garlic
1 teaspoon *zhug* (page 214)

1. Soak the fenugreek seeds in water for 2 hours. Strain them and combine with tomato paste in a bowl.   2. Grind the pepper, caraway seeds, cardamom pods, chili pepper, and garlic. Add them to the fenugreek seed mixture along with the *zhug*, and mix well. *Makes ½ cup.*

Hawayij

Hawayij is one of the sauces used for seasoning meat and soups. It is usually made in a large quantity and is kept handy the way Americans use ketchup.

2 tablespoons ground black pepper
1 tablespoon caraway seeds
1 teaspoon cardamom seeds

1 teaspoon saffron *or* ground turmeric
2 teaspoons turmeric

1. Grind all the ingredients to a fine powder. Store in a sealed jar. *Makes ¼ cup*

Pesto Sauce

Pesto comes from the Italian "to pound." Like many sauces, the traditional pounding in a mortar both blends the flavors and grinds the ingredients to a paste. Today this can be done more quickly in the electric blender. This sauce freezes well, or stays fresh for some time in the refrigerator. Use it on pasta, or to give a delightful flavor to tomato sauce, soups, and stews. The substitution of *tahini* for cheese will give this sauce a decidedly Middle Eastern flavor!

1 cup fresh basil
2 garlic cloves, crushed
¾ cup grated Parmesan cheese *or* ½ cup prepared *tahini* paste

½ cup olive oil *or* vegetable oil
salt and freshly ground black pepper, to taste

1. In an electric blender, food processor, or mortar, combine the basil leaves and garlic until they are finely ground. Add the cheese and oil. Blend thoroughly until the mixture is a thick paste. *Makes about 2 cups*

Fresh Herb Vinegar

½ gallon white wine vinegar
2 dozen black peppercorns
6 shallots, chopped, *or* 1 bunch scallions
¾ cup fresh basil, chopped
8 sprigs fresh rosemary

8 sprigs fresh thyme
1 handful celery leaves, chopped
½ cup parsley root, chopped
½ cup fresh parsley, chopped
1 teaspoon saffron

1. Combine all the ingredients in a large bottle. Place it in a sunny window for 2 weeks to blend the flavors. Strain the liquid through a cloth.   2. Refrigerate —the vinegar will last a long time. *Makes ½ gallon*

Herb Dressing Vinaigrette

1 cup olive oil *or* vegetable oil
⅓ cup vinegar
1 cup fresh mint, chopped
1 bunch scallion tops, chopped
½ teaspoon basil
½ teaspoon marjoram

salt and pepper, to taste
½ teaspoon honey
1 teaspoon soy sauce
1 teaspoon dry mustard mixed to a paste with water
2 cloves garlic

1. Combine all ingredients and mix well. Let the mixture rest for a few minutes to allow the flavors to blend.   2. Remove the garlic cloves and use immediately, or refrigerate. *Makes about 1½ cups*

Almond-Vinegar Sauce

This is a very good fish sauce. It also goes well with hard-boiled eggs and stuffed vegetables.

⅔ cup (¼ pound) ground almonds   water
1 cup wine vinegar   salt and pepper, to taste
1 teaspoon dry mustard

1. Blend the almonds, vinegar, and mustard to a smooth paste.   2. Add water, if necessary, to thin the sauce. Season with salt and pepper to taste. *Makes 1½ to 2 cups*

Mint-Yogurt Dressing

1 tablespoon finely chopped fresh
    mint
5 ounces yogurt
salt and pepper, to taste

1. Mix the mint with the yogurt and season with salt and pepper to taste.
2. Pour the dressing over a green salad or over thinly sliced cucumbers. (Serve immediately, or the juices of the cucumber and yogurt will run together.) *Makes ⅔ cup*

SOUPS

Legend holds that Sabbath food tastes the best of all the week's food because it contains a special "Sabbath spice." The Sabbath meals—Friday evening, and lunch after the morning Sabbath service—are mostly family occasions. The streets of Jerusalem on Friday morning are permeated with the aroma of chicken and chicken soup—a testament to their place of honor in the Israeli diet! There is no doubt as to what's cooking for the Sabbath.

Golden Chicken Soup

The delight of chicken soup–"Jewish penicillin"–has been recorded in folklore– and confirmed by modern medicine!–as a cure for all kinds of ailments.

1 stewing chicken, skinned feet, and
  gizzard
3 quarts cold water
3 carrots, scraped and sliced
1 handful celeriac leaves *or* white
  celery leaves
½ cup chopped fresh parsley, leaves
  and stems

1 large onion, sliced
1 bay leaf
1 tablespoon salt
1 teaspoon turmeric *or* ½ teaspoon
  saffron
½ teaspoon black pepper

1. In a large stock pot, combine the chicken and water. Bring the water to a boil, skim, and add the vegetables, bay leaf, and salt. Simmer, covered, until the chicken is tender (about 1 to 1½ hours). Remove the chicken from the pot and reserve it for another use.   2. Add the turmeric and pepper and simmer the stock for another hour. Strain; allow the soup to cool until a layer of hard fat forms on the surface.   3. Remove the rendered chicken fat and reserve it for use in other recipes. Reheat the soup, adding the cooked chicken if you wish. Serve with rice, dumplings, or matzo balls (page 52), and a garnish of chopped parsley. *Makes 3 quarts*

Chicken Carcass Soup

A good soup can also be made from leftover cooked chicken or turkey carcasses.

1 chicken carcass *or* turkey carcass
4 or 5 cups water
1 handful celeriac leaves *or* celery
  leaves
2 onions, sliced
2 unpeeled carrots, cut in large
  chunks

1 bay leaf
1 handful fresh parsley leaves and
  stems, chopped
1 teaspoon marjoram
½ teaspoon nutmeg
salt and pepper, to taste

1. In a stockpot, combine all the ingredients. Simmer, covered, for 1 hour. 2. Strain the soup and refrigerate. Remove most or all of the fat from the top, and serve. *Makes about 1 quart*

Chicken Soup and Matzo Balls

The most important family meal in the Jewish cycle of festivals is the Passover Seder meal. Before the meal the family reads the Haggada, which tells the history of Passover (*Pesach*) and celebrates the Exodus of the Hebrew people from Egypt and their liberation from slavery.

During the eight days of Passover, observing Jews do not eat leavened bread; instead, they eat unleavened bread (*matzo*) to symbolize the bread made in haste by the Israelite women in preparation for their departure from Egypt. Jewish homemakers rely heavily on crushed matzo and potato flour for baking and cooking the holiday meal. Spiced matzo balls are served along with the traditional chicken soup. Use the recipe for golden chicken soup on page 218, and the recipe for spiced matzo balls on page 52.

Sorrel and Turnip Soup

1 pound sorrel leaves, stems and
    center veins removed
1½ cups chopped onion
3 tablespoons butter *or* margarine
1 teaspoon turmeric
6 cups chicken stock *or* vegetable
    stock
3 cups grated turnips *or* potatoes

2 tablespoons fresh coriander leaves,
    chopped, *or* 2 teaspoons
    coriander seeds
⅔ cup sour cream *or* nondairy cream
    or yogurt
salt and pepper, to taste
2 tablespoons chopped fresh parsley

1. Stack several layers of sorrel leaves and cut them crosswise into fine strips. In a large soup pot, cook the onions in butter over moderate heat until soft. Add the turmeric, stock, turnips, and coriander.   2. Bring the liquid to a boil, and simmer covered over low heat for 15 minutes. Stir in the sour cream and return the soup just to the boiling point, but do *not* boil. In a food processor with a steel blade or an electric blender, blend the liquid in batches, adding sorrel with each batch. Return the blended mixture to the soup pot, and season with salt and pepper to taste. Heat the soup, but don't let it boil. Serve in a soup tureen and garnish with chopped parsley. *Serves 6 to 8*

Turnip

Shavuot Soups

The festival of Shavuot (Pentecost) falls in May-June. According to the Bible, it celebrates the wheat harvest; later descriptions state that it was the time of the giving of the Law on Mount Sinai. According to tradition, Shavuot food is primarily made from milk and dairy products. One reason given is that when Moses and the Hebrew people returned to their tents, after the giving of the Law and the Ten Commandments, the people were too tired to prepare an elaborate meal; instead they ate a quickly prepared meal of dairy products. Another legend holds that dairy food was eaten to celebrate the comparison of the Law to milk in the Song of Songs. Whatever the reason, milk-based products are consumed in volume here on Shavuot, and during the spring and summer months as well. Cream of sorrel soup is a most popular soup.

Hot Cream of Sorrel Soup

1 pound sorrel *or* Swiss chard *or* spinach
2 tablespoons vegetable oil *or* margarine
1 teaspoon ground coriander *or* ¼ cup fresh coriander leaves, chopped

salt and pepper, to taste
5 medium potatoes, peeled and diced
6 cups water
½ cup sour cream *or* stabilized yogurt (see page 276)
1 lemon, thinly sliced, for garnish
chopped fresh parsley, for garnish

1. Wash and drain the sorrel.   2. In a stock pot, heat the oil. Sauté the sorrel with the coriander, salt, and pepper until the leaves are well coated with oil and almost tender. Add the potatoes and water and bring to a boil. Simmer, covered, until the potatoes are cooked.   3. Cool the soup. In a food processor or electric blender, blend until the soup becomes a smooth purée.   4. Put the sour cream into a soup tureen, or put a dollop in individual soup bowls. Pour the soup over it, and garnish with the lemon slices and parsley. *Serves 4 to 6*

Lentil Soup
with Spinach and Lemon

❦ ❦ ❦

1½ cups green lentils, washed and
    picked over *or* brown lentils
8 cups water plus soup seasoning
    powder *or* 2 cups soup stock plus
    6 cups water
1½ pounds spinach *or* Swiss chard
2 medium onions, finely chopped
3 cloves garlic, crushed

4 tablespoons olive oil *or* vegetable oil
4 freshly milled coriander seeds *or* 1
    tablespoon ground coriander
½ teaspoon salt
¼ teaspoon pepper
¼ teaspoon ground cumin
2 tablespoons lemon juice
sliced lemons for garnish

1. In a large soup pot, combine the lentils with water and bring to a boil. Cover and simmer for 15 minutes. 2. Wash the spinach well, and drain. Shred the leaves and put them into the soup. Simmer for 45 minutes. 3. Shortly before the soup is finished cooking, sauté the onions and garlic in the oil. Add the coriander, salt, pepper, cumin, and lemon juice. Cook for 10 minutes more. Serve garnished with lemon slices. *Serves 8*

Melokhia Soup
and *Taklia* Sauce

❦ ❦ ❦

Melokhia (*corchorus olitorius*) is one of the earliest recorded plants in the areas of Israel, Jordan, and Egypt. Scenes showing how to make the soup and stew from it have been depicted in Pharaonic tomb drawings, indicating the importance of the plant in ancient times. Arab farmers in the region surrounding Jerusalem and Bethlehem utilize much of the available land for growing melokhia as a summer standby. The leaves are also dried for winter use.

It is difficult to compare the tall, graceful melokhia with any other edible plant, except to say that its dark green leaves resemble members of the mallow family. Its taste is unique, with an earthy, glutinous quality.

Dried melokhia leaves are available in many shops specializing in Middle East foodstuffs. A reasonably good substitute can be made with spinach leaves, but it's worth the effort to look for the real thing.

Lentil

2 pounds fresh melokhia leaves *or* 4
 ounces dried melokhia leaves
2 quarts chicken stock *or* rabbit stock
 or beef stock *or* duck stock

salt and pepper, to taste
1 tablespoon *taklia* sauce (page 214)

1. Remove the leaves from the fresh melokhia stalks. Wash well, drain, and chop. If you are using dried melokhia leaves, rub a quantity of them between the palms of your hands until they resemble ground parsley leaves. In a bowl, cover them with water. When the leaves have absorbed all the water, they are ready to use. 2. In a large stock pot, bring the stock to a boil. Add the melokhia and boil for a few minutes. Simmer, covered, for 20 minutes. Salt and pepper to taste, and add the *taklia* sauce. Simmer 5 minutes more and serve. *Serves 8*

Vegetable Soup

❦ ❦ ❦

2 cups water
2 cups vegetable stock (pages 207–8)
2 large onions, chopped
2 tablespoons olive oil *or* vegetable oil
2 carrots, sliced
1 cup fresh parsley, chopped
1 handful celery leaves *or* celeriac
 leaves
3 bay leaves

½ teaspoon turmeric
1 tablespoon fresh sage leaves *or* 1
 teaspoon ground sage
1 teaspoon salt
1 teaspoon black pepper
4 whole tomatoes *or* 1 6-ounce can
 tomato paste
3 small summer squash

1. In a large pot, bring the water to a boil. Add the vegetable stock. 2. In a frying pan, sauté the onions in the oil until golden. Add the carrots, parsley, celery leaves, bay leaves, turmeric, sage, salt, and pepper. When the carrots are tender, add them to the stock. Add the tomatoes and squash and simmer, covered, for about 45 minutes. Remove the bay leaves. Serve with *pita* bread (pages 56–57) or whole wheat bread. *Serves 4 to 6*

Curried Leek
and Potato Soup

❧ ❧ ❧

4 to 8 leeks
1 small onion
5 medium potatoes
2 tablespoons margarine *or* butter
2 tablespoons curry powder

4 cups water
3 cups vegetable broth
½ cup heavy cream
salt and freshly ground black pepper,
    to taste

1. Trim the tough green leaves from the leeks and cut them into ½-inch cubes. Cut the onion in half, and thinly slice the onion halves. Peel the potatoes, cut them in half, and thinly slice the potato halves.   2. In a soup pot, heat the margarine and add the onion slices. Cook, stirring, until wilted. Add the leeks and cook about 5 minutes, stirring often. Sprinkle on the curry powder and mix well. Add the potatoes, water, and broth, and bring to a boil. Lower the heat and simmer, covered, for 30 minutes.   3. Cool the mixture and pour it into the container of an electric food processor. Blend until smooth. Return the mixture to the saucepan and add the cream, salt, and pepper to taste. Reheat gently and serve. *Serves 8 to 10*

Easter Soup
and *Avgolemon* Sauce

❧ ❧ ❧

The largest Christian community in Israel belongs to the Greek Orthodox church. Easter, not Christmas, is the most important religious feast of the year among the Greek Orthodox in Jerusalem and the Holy Land. Easter Soup is served at the meal which breaks the Holy Week fast. Made from lamb or sheep, it combines a rich meat base and Greek *avgolemon* sauce. Traditionally, the soup is made from a lamb's head, sheep bones, or the heart, liver, lungs, and intestine of a young lamb. This recipe calls for the lamb's head, liver, and knuckles.

1 lamb's head (from a 12-pound lamb)
4 quarts water
1 lamb's liver
1 pound lamb knuckles
2 onions, quartered
2 carrots, cut in large chunks
2 sprigs fresh parsley
2 bay leaves
1 celeriac root *or* 1 handful celery
    leaves

½ teaspoon turmeric
salt and pepper, to taste
2 tablespoons raw rice
fresh mint sprigs, for garnish

Avgolemon Sauce:

4 eggs
juice of 2 lemons
1 cup reserved broth

1. Have the butcher split the head in half. Soak the halves in cold water for 2 hours. Pour off the water and rinse well. Rinse and drain the liver and knuckles.   2. In a large stewing pot, cover the head halves with water. Add the liver, knuckles, vegetables, and seasoning. Cover and simmer for 20 minutes. Remove the liver and put it aside. Simmer the stock for 1 hour, skimming off the scum that rises to the surface. Add the rice during the last 20 minutes of cooking.   3. Strain the broth into another pot, reserving 1 cup for the *avgolemon* sauce.   4. To prepare the *avgolemon* sauce, beat the eggs in a bowl until they are light and lemon colored. Slowly add the lemon juice, beating until the mixture thickens. Add the reserved broth and beat until well blended. 5. Pour the broth into a warm soup tureen. Carefully stir in the *avgolemon* sauce and serve. *Makes 2 cups*

Tahini Soup (*Tahinosoupa*)

Tahini, a peanut butter–like paste made from sesame seeds (see pages 212–13), is a Middle Eastern favorite. Christians here use it to advantage in this Lenten Soup.

2 quarts water
salt to taste
1 cup raw rice
1 cup prepared *tahini* paste

½ cup water
juice of 2 lemons
2 cloves garlic, crushed (optional)
fresh parsley, for garnish

1. In a soup pot, bring the water and salt to a boil and add the rice. Simmer, covered, for 20 minutes.   2. While the rice is cooking, prepare the *tahini*. In a bowl or in an electric blender, mix the *tahini* and water. Slowly add the lemon juice and blend until smooth. Add the garlic for a stronger-tasting soup. Blend in 1 ladleful of rice-cooking water, and stir this mixture into the rice and water. Serve garnished with parsley. *Serves 8 to 10*

Cold Soups

Cold soup is a delightful way to add liquids to the body on a hot day. Cold soups are nourishing, colorful, and allow you to get the vitamins from fruits or vegetables that don't measure up to eating raw. Fruit soups are often served at the end of a meal, like dessert. Whatever the ingredients or the occasion, fruit soups bring the garden straight into the dining room.

Summer-fresh Fruit Soup

❦ ❦ ❦

3 cups mixed fresh fruit in season
    (apples, cored and seeded but not
    peeled; grapes; loquats; melons;
    raisins)
peel of 1 lemon, grated
8 cups water
sugar to taste, depending on
    sweetness of fruit

3 tablespoons cornstarch
3 cups fresh fruit juice
1 teaspoon cinnamon
juice of 1 lemon
fresh mint for garnish *or* sour cream
    or yogurt

1. In a large soup pot, combine the fruit, lemon peel, and water, and bring to a boil. Sweeten to taste with sugar. When the fruit is tender, strain the liquid. In an electric blender, purée the fruit. 2. In a small bowl, combine the cornstarch and a few teaspoons of the uncooked fruit juice. Add this to the rest of the fruit juice. 3. In the soup pot, bring the juice to a boil and add the blended fruit pulp. Mix well. Add the cinnamon and lemon juice. Serve in glasses or bowls garnished with mint, or sour cream or yogurt topping. *Serves 6*

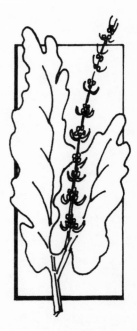

Cold Cucumber-Mint Soup

❦ ❦ ❦

2 large cucumbers, peeled
3 to 4 sprigs fresh mint, chopped
6 pitted green olives
1 teaspoon olive oil *or* vegetable oil
salt and pepper to taste

¼ teaspoon allspice
2 scallions
1 cup milk
6 ounces yogurt
freshly chopped mint, for garnish

1. Slice the cucumbers in half lengthwise and remove the seeds. Chop the cucumbers and put them in the container of an electric blender. Add the mint, olives, and oil. Blend on high speed until well blended but not liquefied.

Spinach Beet

2. Add the salt and pepper, allspice, scallions, milk, and yogurt. Blend until smooth and refrigerate until chilled. Serve in soup bowls or glasses, garnished with mint. *Serves 4*

Calf's Feet Jelly (*Cholodyetz*)

❦ ❦ ❦

Calf's feet jelly, like jellied consommé or aspic, is especially welcome on a hot summer day.

2 calf's feet
5 pints water
1 onion
2 shallots *or* scallions
2 whole carrots, cooked tender-crisp
2 stalks celery
6 peppercorns
salt, to taste
grated peel and juice of 1 lemon
whites and shells of 2 eggs
2 tablespoons white wine vinegar
½ cup sherry
2 hard-boiled eggs
6 lettuce leaves

Bouquet Garni*:

2 cups parsley
1 tablespoon thyme
4 bay leaves

1. Wash and blanch each foot, and divide into at least 4 pieces. In a stewing pot, combine the feet and the water . Bring to a boil, and skim off the scum. Add the onion, shallots, carrots, celery, bouquet garni, and peppercorns. Add salt to taste. Bring to a boil again and simmer on low heat for 4 hours. Strain and refrigerate. Carefully remove the congealed fat and discard.   2. In the stewing pot, combine the stock, lemon juice, peel, egg whites, eggshells, wine vinegar, and sherry. Bring to a boil, stirring, for about 10 minutes.   3. Arrange the sliced hard-boiled eggs in a 13 × 9-inch loaf pan and pour the strained stock over them. Refrigerate to set the aspic. If the aspic does not jell, remove the eggs and reboil the liquid, adding ½ ounce unflavored gelatin. Serve cold on a lettuce leaf with vinegar, hot mustard sauce, or horseradish. *Serves 6*

*Tie up ingredients for the bouquet garni in a clean cheesecloth bag. Remove the bag at the end of the cooking time.

Dumplings to Accompany Soups

Did the taste for dumplings originate in the East and move West, or was the basic need to reinforce soups and stews with a tasty lump of dough common to many cuisines? We'll probably never know. Each nation boasts its particular distinction in making a soup accompaniment, whether it is dumplings, croutons, or meatballs. One thing is certain: the Old World taste for dumplings implies heartiness and satisfaction.

In the Middle East cracked wheat (bulgur) and semolina flour are the common denominators. Matzo meal is used during Passover when the use of leavened flour is forbidden. Whichever ingredient is used, and whether the dumplings are plain or stuffed, the important factor is good taste and lightness —"sinkers" are definitely out!

Meat-filled Bulgur Dumplings

1½ cups bulgur, finely ground
1 onion, chopped
2 tablespoons vegetable oil
½ pound beef, chopped
2 tablespoons fresh parsley, chopped

salt and pepper, to taste
¼ teaspoon allspice
¾ cup flour
¼ cup water

1. Wash the bulgur in hot water, rinse in cold water, and drain. Place on a towel to dry. 2. In a frying pan, sauté the chopped onion in the oil. Add the beef and cook, stirring, until the meat is no longer red. Add the parsley, pepper, and allspice. 3. In a bowl, combine the bulgur with the flour and add enough water to make a smooth dough. Allow the dough to rest in a cool place until firm, about ½ hour. 4. With moistened hands, form a dumpling-size ball. Insert a finger into it and work the dough to firm it. When all the dumplings are prepared, fill them with the meat filling and pinch the dough closed, flattening them a little. Cook in boiling soup for 15 minutes, covered. Uncover and check for doneness. Serve with soup or stew. *Serves 12*

Flour Dumplings

4 heaping tablespoons all-purpose
    flour, sifted
2 heaping tablespoons grated suet *or*
    margarine *or* butter

¼ tablespoon baking powder
1 tablespoon chopped fresh parsley
1 tablespoon mixed ground sage, salt,
    pepper, nutmeg

1. In a bowl, mix the flour and grated suet or margarine. Add the rest of the ingredients and enough water to make a stiff paste. Let the mixture rest in a cool place for at least 30 minutes.   2. Knead the dumpling dough on a floured board. Shape into marble-sized balls (they will swell, so keep the balls small). 3. In a soup pot, bring water, stock, or soup to a boil. Poach the dumplings, covered, in the simmering liquid for 15 minutes. Test for doneness (they should be light and cooked through). Drain and serve in soup or stew. *Serves 10*

Bread Crumb and Parsley Dumplings

❧ ❧ ❧

These dumplings offer a perfect opportunity to use up old bread.

1 onion, finely chopped	1 tablespoon chopped fresh dill
1 tablespoon butter *or* margarine	3 medium eggs, slightly beaten
3 cups medium-fine dry bread crumbs	salt and pepper, to taste
¼ cup chopped fresh parsley	

1. In a small frying pan, sauté the onion in butter or margarine until transparent.   2. In a bowl, combine the bread crumbs with the parsley and dill. Add the eggs, salt, and pepper.   3. In a soup pot, bring water, stock, or soup to a boil. Drop the mixture by tablespoonsful into the boiling liquid. Simmer, covered, for 25 minutes. Serve with soup or stew. *Serves 12*

STEWS: MEALS-IN-A-BOWL

Homemade soups based on tasty, substantial stocks can easily be made into stews and served with rice or potatoes. They can be made into meals-in-a-bowl, for those busy days when a three-course menu isn't possible.

Chickpea Soup with Sausage

❦ ❦ ❦

2 tablespoons butter *or* margarine *or*
    vegetable oil
2 onions, chopped
2 cloves garlic, crushed
2 teaspoons curry powder
1 teaspoon turmeric
½ teaspoon cayenne pepper
1½ cups uncooked chickpeas *or*
    1 1-pound can chickpeas

2 quarts water
1 teaspoon salt
juice of 2 lemons
1 small jar cocktail sausages *or* ¼ cup
    Parmesan cheese
½ cup chopped fresh parsley,
    for garnish

1. In a large soup pot, melt the fat over medium heat. Add the onions, garlic, curry powder, turmeric, and cayenne. When the onions are soft, lower the heat and cook 10 minutes.   2. Soak the uncooked chickpeas overnight in cold water with 1 teaspoon salt. Drain off the water in the morning. In a large pot, cover the chickpeas with 2 quarts of water and 1 teaspoon salt. Bring to a boil, removing scum as it rises to the surface. When the water is clear, continue. If you use canned chickpeas, rinse and drain them. Put them in the pot with the salted water and continue.   3. Add the onions to the chickpeas. Simmer, covered, for 2 hours, or pressure cook for 30 minutes (do not fill the cooker more than halfway with water).   4. In an electric blender, coarsely purée the chickpeas in their liquid. Reheat and add the lemon juice. Add the cocktail sausages and heat until they are warmed through. Garnish with parsley and serve. If you are using Parmesan cheese, sprinkle it over the soup before you add the parsley garnish. *Serves 8 to 10*

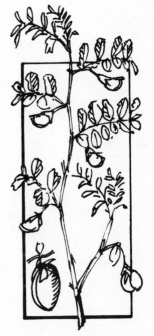

Chickpea

Sheep's Head Meal-in-a-Bowl

❦ ❦ ❦

It's most unlikely that you will find a sheep's head in your supermarket. In Israel, however, meat products are usually purchased from a long-patronized family butcher who enjoys the honor due the family doctor! The oriental tradition of men doing the shopping persists, and many families buy food wholesale.

Many modern Moslem women substitute frozen brain, tongue, and marrow bones to make a substantial soup-stew to be eaten at the end of a fast. However, many traditional Moslems continue to serve sheep's head or lamb's head stew. Depending on how accommodating your butcher is, you may wish to experiment with sheep's head for a large autumn cookout!

1 sheep's head (tongue and brain
    removed)
salt
lemon juice
3 quarts water
3 carrots, thickly sliced
3 onions, coarsely chopped
1 celeriac root, chopped, *or* the leaves
    and stems of 1 celeriac root,
    chopped
8 to 12 boiled potatoes, quartered
    (optional)
10 to 12 slices bread, cut up
    (optional)

Bouquet Garni*:
½ cup parsley leaves
½ cup marjoram leaves
salt and pepper to taste
¼ cup coriander seeds
3 cloves garlic, crushed
3 bay leaves

1. Unless you are game enough to do it yourself, ask the butcher to remove the brains and tongue (pickle the tongue for a special occasion). Wash the head well, and blanch it in boiling water until the scum rises. Drain. Lightly salt the head, and wipe it with a clean cloth soaked in lemon juice and a little water. 2. Tie the two sections of head together with string. In a large soup pot, cover the head with water and bring to a boil. Simmer, loosely covered, for about 3 hours. Add the carrots, onions, celeriac, and bouquet garni, and simmer until the vegetables are tender. 3. Remove the head, cut it into pieces, and add it to the soup. If you are serving it as a stew, add the potatoes or bread. Simmer for 10 to 15 minutes, and serve. *Serves 12*

*Tie up ingredients for the bouquet garni in a clean cheesecloth bag. Remove the bag at the end of the cooking time.

Oxtail Meal-in-a-Bowl Soup

❦ ❦ ❦

This is another substantial soup that is especially welcome in the winter months or on cool autumn evenings. Serve with bulgur dumplings (page 73) or dumplings made from flour (pages 227–28).

1 oxtail, disjointed (about 2 pounds)
2 quarts water
¼ to ½ cup all-purpose flour
2 medium onions, chopped
1 tablespoon margarine *or* vegetable
    oil
salt, to taste
6 peppercorns
4 bay leaves
1 teaspoon basil
1 teaspoon ground cumin

2 cloves garlic, crushed
¼ cup celeriac leaves *or* white celery
    leaves
parsley for garnish

Roux:

1 tablespoon cornstarch *or* flour
2 tablespoons animal fat *or* margarine
2 tablespoons tomato paste
¼ cup sherry *or* dry red wine
    (optional)

1. Rinse the oxtail and place it in a pot with salted water. Bring to a boil, strain, and discard the water. Roll the oxtail pieces in flour.   2. In a soup pot, brown the onions in the fat. Add the oxtail pieces. Cover with 2 quarts of water. Add the salt, the peppercorns, bay leaves, basil, cumin, and garlic. Bring to a boil, uncovered. Simmer slowly for 2 hours. Add the celeriac leaves and parsley and simmer for 30 minutes longer. Strain, chill, and degrease. Reheat the stock. 3. In a small pan, brown the cornstarch or flour and whisk in the fat to make a roux. Slowly add the stock and tomato paste to the roux and stir until smooth. Add the roux to the soup and check the seasoning.   4. Cut up the oxtails and add them to the soup. Stir in the sherry or wine, if you desire. Add dumplings or slices of lemon. *Serves 8 to 10*

9 MEAT AND FOWL

❧ ❧ ❧

The Bible is certainly not a vegetarian document, but meat eating is not a high priority except in a ceremonial context. It was not part of the staple diet of the Israelites, which consisted mainly of agricultural products. Meat was a luxury item regarded as highly desirable, as by the Israelites in the wilderness who yearned for the "fleshpots" of Egypt (Exodus 16:3).

One of the problems was the many restrictions imposed on meat eating. Animals were carefully divided into the pure and the impure, which immediately ruled out many species for eating purposes. The blood had to be meticulously removed before the meat could be eaten. Most significantly, the eating of animals was linked with special festive and ritual occasions, and the killing of animals for eating outside this framework was forbidden. However, there is evidence that this proscription was often ignored, and the ban was removed in the period of the kings.

Permitted animals could be hunted or grown domestically. Generally, the Israelites were too busy working the soil or looking after the herd to go out hunting; those who did were generally after the various kinds of deer that roamed wild. Most of the meat eaten was from domestic animals—cattle and sheep. Nevertheless, because of their value, these were rarely killed for private consumption—and when they were, it was more likely that the less-costly sheep would be slaughtered.

Fowl was not subject to the same restrictions as meat and could be freely eaten, but it was not an important food in Old Testament times—fowl were not raised in Israel. Birds consumed were generally the result of hunting and were in consequence quite a rarity. Only under Persian rule (from the sixth to the fourth centuries B.C.) were domestic fowl, such as hens and pigeons, raised. In the New Testament we read of fowl fed by the Heavenly Father (Matthew 6:26); fowl that picked up newly sown seed (Matthew 13:4); and the cock that crew after Peter's denial (Mark 14:30, 72). Until the domestication of fowl, there was little egg consumption; and most eggs that were eaten were gathered wild and found by chance.

Garden Sorrel

Of course, in modern Israel, meat, poultry, and eggs are plentiful. When my children were small, I obtained a couple of hens and made a small chicken run in the garden. But the neighbors (and my husband) objected, especially to being awoken around dawn, and the experiment was short-lived.

LAMB

Paschal Lamb

Lamb is generally favored for the Passover meal. It is symbolic of the year-old lamb sacrificed in the Temple of Jerusalem to commemorate the eve of the Exodus from Egypt. It is the custom today to place a roasted shank bone on the Passover table as a symbol of the Paschal lamb, whether lamb is served or not.

Easter and Passover dates frequently occur in close proximity. Christians also prefer lamb on the feast of Easter. The Paschal lamb offering symbolizes Christ as the Lamb of God.

Whole roast lamb or sheep is still prepared in villages on special ceremonial occasions and family festivities. The outdoor barbecue spit is set up in the garden or rigged up on the beach. If the kitchen oven is large enough, it may well accommodate a baby lamb of 15 to 18 pounds!

1 baby lamb, 15 to 18 pounds	saffron *or* turmeric, for color
2 pounds rice	½ pound raisins
3 onions, chopped	½ pound ground almonds
2 tablespoons vegetable oil	sprigs of fresh mint and thyme, *or*
salt and pepper, to taste	rosemary

1. Have the butcher prepare the lamb for roasting.   2. Cook the rice. Sauté the onions in the oil until they are golden, and mix them with the rice. Add salt and pepper to taste, and a small amount of saffron or turmeric for a golden color. Stir in the raisins and almonds until evenly distributed.   3. Stuff the lamb, sew it up, and place it in a hot, preheated oven which is reduced to 350°. Place sprigs of mint and thyme or rosemary on the roasting pan. Roast for about 25 minutes to the pound for a tender, underdone roast. Or, barbecue on a spit over hot coals until done. *Serves 20*

Oven-roasted Leg of Lamb with Herb Paste

This oven-roasted leg of lamb is much easier to prepare than a whole, stuffed lamb—and it will certainly fit in your oven!

1 leg of lamb, 4 to 5 pounds
parsley, for garnish

Herb Paste:

2 cloves garlic, crushed
1 teaspoon ground rosemary
salt and papper, to taste
1 jigger brandy *or* sherry
juice of 1 lemon
1 cup chopped fresh mint

1. In a small bowl, mix all the ingredients for the herb paste. Remove any excess fat from the leg of lamb, and discard. Rub the lamb all over with the herb paste. If possible, wrap it in a plastic bag and leave it in the refrigerator for a few hours. 2. Preheat the oven to 450°. Roast the lamb for about 2 hours. Turn off the heat, and let the roast rest for 15 minutes. This allows the juices to congeal, and makes carving easier. 3. Slice the lamb and serve with pan juices as a gravy. Or, thicken the gravy with cornstarch and water mixed into a paste, or with a prepared gravy mix. Garnish with parsley. *Serves 10 to 12*

Lamb Stew and Chickpeas

4 cups cooked chickpeas (about 2
    cups raw) *or* 2 16-ounce cans
    chickpeas
3 pounds lamb shoulder, cut into 2-
    inch cubes (bones included)
¼ cup vegetable oil
4 onions, chopped

3 teaspoons ground coriander seed
2 teaspoons ground cumin
1 tablespoon crushed garlic
1 tablespoon meat-flavored soup mix
salt and pepper, to taste
1 teaspoon chopped fresh mint
3 cups water *or* broth

1. Cook the chickpeas according to the recipe on page 100, or use canned chickpeas, rinsed and drained. 2. In a large Dutch oven, brown the lamb in batches in the oil. Put the pieces on a warmed plate and keep them warm. In the same pot, sauté the onions until golden. Add the coriander, cumin, garlic, soup mix, salt and pepper, mint, lamb, and the water or broth. Bring to a boil and lower the heat. Add the chickpeas and simmer gently, covered, for 1 hour,

or until the lamb is tender.   3. Refrigerate overnight and remove the congealed fat. Reheat the stew on top of the stove, or in a casserole in a preheated 350° oven for about 30 minutes. Serve with a mixed salad. *Serves 6 to 8*

Shish Kebab

❦ ❦ ❦

Cooking in the open air goes back to the beginning of human survival, and the discovery that meat cooked over embers doesn't shrink as much as meat roasted over a roaring flame. Tribal nomad desert peoples perfected the means of making small fires out of twigs and dry wood. Eventually they used charcoal, which produced the welcome low embers.

The origin of shish kebab can be traced to Turkish soldiers who, during the long Ottoman Empire, lived out of doors with few amenities. They discovered the usefulness of charcoal cooking, using long skewers to roast a meal. They also sought ways to make the available tough meat more tender. Lemon juice, oil, and spices were made into a marinade into which the meat was put before cooking. One of the marinades used today among Arabs consists of mixing onion juice, yogurt, garlic, and salt. A more common marinade is the one in this recipe. Start marinating the lamb first thing in the morning, or before bed at night.

2 pounds boned lamb *or* beef	**Marinade:**
4 to 6 large tomatoes	2 tablespoons olive oil
2 to 4 green peppers	3 tablespoons lemon juice
2 to 4 medium onions *or* scallions	1 large onion, grated
	salt and pepper, to taste
	1 tablespoon crushed thyme

1. Cut the meat into 1-inch cubes.   2. In a large bowl, mix all the marinade ingredients. Add the meat and stir well, so that each piece of meat is coated. Refrigerate for 5 to 6 hours or overnight. Remove from the refrigerator 2 hours before cooking time.   3. Arrange the meat on long skewers alternately with wedges of tomatoes, thick slices of green peppers, and thickly sliced onions or scallions.   4. Broil in a preheated broiler, or over a charcoal fire 3 inches above red-hot coals. Broil 5 minutes on each side (or longer, if you are barbecuing). Place the skewers on serving platters, and serve with rice, chips, or *pita* bread (pages 56–57). *Serves 4 to 6*

Note: For a sharper marinade, add to the oil, lemon juice, and onion the following: 2 teaspoons ground coriander seed, 1 teaspoon ground cumin, 3 teaspoons paprika, ½ teaspoon ground ginger, ¼ teaspoon garlic powder, and a generous portion of finely chopped fresh parsley.

Broiled Lamb Kidneys and Onions

8 to 12 lamb kidneys (2 to 3 per
    person)
salt and pepper, to taste
juice of 4 lemons
4 tablespoons mixed dried and crushed
    rosemary, mint, and bay leaf

2 to 4 medium onions, sliced and
    simmered until tender, for
    garnish
chopped fresh parsley, for garnish

1. In a large pot, bring water to a boil. Put in the kidneys and boil a few minutes, uncovered. Drain off the water and rinse the blanched kidneys immediately in cold water. Cut them in half, and sprinkle with the lemon juice and mixed herbs. Put them on skewers for broiling. 2. Layer the cooked onions in a broiler pan and cover them with the skewered kidneys. Place the pan about 6 inches from the flame. Broil 5 minutes, turn, and broil 5 minutes more, or until the kidneys are tender. Serve on triangles of toast as an appetizer, topped with onions and parsley; or omit the onions and serve the kidneys with cocktail forks. *Serves 4*

Curried Chopped Lamb Kebabs

Lamb kebabs go a long way, so they're good to serve to a large group for an outdoor supper. These highly spiced kebabs go well with a mixed green salad. Children often enjoy the contents off the skewer served on a hot dog roll.

1½ pounds ground lamb *or* beef *or*
    veal
1 onion, finely chopped
2 ounces fresh white bread crumbs
½ teaspoon dry mustard
salt and pepper, to taste
2 teaspoons curry powder
1 egg, beaten
½ pound fresh button mushrooms *or*
    1 large can button mushrooms
3 unpeeled cucumbers, sliced
2 onions, cut into quarters and
    separated into layers
olives, for garnish

Oregano Sauce:

2 ounces margarine *or* butter
2 tablespoons vegetable oil
2 teaspoons ground oregano

1. In a large bowl, combine the lamb and onion. Add the bread crumbs, mustard, salt, pepper, and curry powder. Bind the mixture with the egg.   2. With floured hands, shape the mixture into small, egg-size ovals. Thread on skewers alternately with the mushrooms, cucumbers, and onions.   3. To prepare the oregano sauce, melt the margarine in a small frying pan. Add the oil and oregano and stir well.   4. Baste the skewered kebabs with the sauce and broil in a preheated broiler or on a charcoal fire for about 10 minutes, or until done. Turn the skewers frequently and baste with the sauce during cooking. Garnish each skewer with a stuffed olive, if you desire. *Serves 4 to 6*

BEEF

Spiced Veal Goulash

5 tablespoons vegetable oil	1 tablespoon soy sauce
2 onions, chopped	1 clove garlic, crushed
½ pound mushrooms, thinly sliced	1 teaspoon allspice
1½ pounds stewing veal, cut in strips	1 cup white wine
2 tablespoons flour	¼ cup chopped fresh parsley
salt and pepper, to taste	½ cup nondairy cream *or* heavy cream

1. In a heavy skillet, heat 2 tablespoons of the vegetable oil. Sauté the onions until translucent. Add the mushrooms, and cook on low heat until just tender. Put them in a dish and keep them warm.   2. Sprinkle the veal with the flour. Heat the remaining oil, add the veal, and brown for 5 minutes over high heat. Add the salt, pepper, soy sauce, garlic, allspice, mushrooms, onions, wine, and parsley. Lower the heat and cook, covered, until the veal is tender. Add the cream and heat through. Serve with pasta or rice. *Serves 4 to 6*

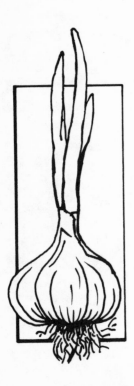

Garlic

Brisket of Beef

3½ to 4 pounds boneless beef brisket	2 bay leaves
3 onions	1 handful fresh parsley
2 cloves garlic	1 handful celery leaves
salt and pepper, to taste	10 whole cloves

1. In a large, heavy-bottomed pot, brown the brisket on both sides. Drain off the fat and add enough water to cover the meat. Add the rest of the ingredients

and bring to a boil. Cover the pan and reduce the heat. Cook the meat for 3 hours or until it is tender.   2. Remove the meat from the pot and let it rest before you carve it. Strain the cooking juices and use 1 or 2 cups to make gravy. *Serves 8 to 10*

Fruit-glazed Brisket of Beef

3½ to 4 pounds boneless beef brisket	2 tablespoons brown sugar
1 8-ounce can whole apricots	¼ teaspoon salt
1 teaspoon lemon juice	10 whole cloves
	apricot sections, for garnish (optional)

1. Cook the brisket according to the brisket of beef (pages 238–39). Put the cooked beef in a shallow baking dish, and keep it warm while you make the glaze.   2. To prepare the glaze, combine the apricots, lemon juice, brown sugar, and salt in a saucepan. Heat until the sugar is dissolved. Pour the glaze over the brisket. Decorate the brisket with whole cloves and sections of apricots, if you wish. Bake at 350° for 15 minutes, or until the glaze is set. *Serves 8 to 10*

Pickled or Corned Beef

3 pounds brisket of beef

Marinade:

1 tablespoon powdered mustard	1 teaspoon ground coriander
3 tablespoons water	1 teaspoon ground allspice
1 bay leaf	3 unpeeled garlic cloves
1 teaspoon black peppercorns	2 tablespoons brown sugar
1 ounce saltpeter *or* 2 teaspoons salt	1 cup water
2 whole cloves	juice of 1 lemon
1 teaspoon ground ginger	

1. In a small bowl, mix the mustard and water. Allow it to rest for about 10 minutes.   2. In a saucepan, mix the mustard with the remaining ingredients and bring to a boil.   3. Put the meat in a bowl just large enough to contain the marinade and the meat. Pour the marinade over the meat and cool. Cover and

refrigerate for 10 days, turning the meat twice a day.   4. Begin this step 1 day before you plan to serve the meat, if possible. Remove the meat from the marinade, but reserve the marinade. Drain the meat and wipe dry. In a heavy pot or Dutch oven, brown the meat. Add water to cover, cover the pot, and bring to a boil. Simmer 3 to 4 hours, or until the meat is tender when tested with a fork. Skim off the fat.   5. Reheat the meat. Add potatoes or dumplings to be eaten with the beef. While the beef is reheating, make a gravy. In a small bowl, make a paste of 2 tablespoons flour and 1 tablespoon water. Slowly stir in 1 cup strained marinade and 1 cup cooking juices. Cook the gravy briefly until it thickens.   6. Serve the sliced beef with the gravy, and with potatoes or dumplings cooked in the same pot during the time the beef is being reheated. *Serves 8*

Cold Pickled Tongue

Cold tongue goes very well with cold boiled or roasted chicken on a party meat platter, accompanied with homemade mustard.

1 beef tongue, approximately
    3 pounds

Marinade:

1 tablespoon powdered mustard
3 tablespoons water
1 bay leaf
1 teaspoon black peppercorns
1 ounce saltpeter *or* 2 teaspoons salt
2 whole cloves
1 teaspoon gound ginger
1 teaspoon ground coriander
1 teaspoon ground allspice
3 garlic cloves, unpeeled
2 tablespoons brown sugar
1 cup water
juice of 1 lemon

1. In a small bowl, mix the mustard and water. Allow it to rest for about 10 minutes.   2. In a saucepan, mix the mustard with the remaining ingredients and bring to a boil.   3. Put the tongue in a bowl just large enough to contain the marinade and the tongue. Cover and refrigerate for 8 to 10 days.   4. Drain the tongue, and cook it in simmering water for 3 hours, until tender when tested with a fork. Turn off the heat and allow the tongue to cool in its cooking juices.   5. Remove the tongue and drain. Pull off the skin, and return the tongue to the cooking pot to cool further. Shape the tongue into a round, tie

Coriander

with heavy string, and place in a small ovenproof glass bowl or earthenware crock. Cover with a piece of cheesecloth and aluminum foil. Weight the tongue down to hold the shape. Refrigerate overnight. 6. Thinly slice the tongue, and serve with lettuce and pickles. *Serves 12 to 20*

Marinated Beef Casserole

❦ ❦ ❦

3 pounds lean stewing beef
½ pound pitted green olives
3 carrots, sliced
¼ cup chopped fresh parsley
1 tablespoon chicken fat *or* margarine
4 tomatoes, chopped

Marinade:

¼ cup olive oil
1 carrot, sliced
1 onion, sliced
½ celeriac, thinly sliced, *or* ½ head
　　celeriac leaves
½ cup red wine
¼ cup wine vinegar
¼ cup chopped fresh parsley
2 scallions
2 cloves garlic, crushed
2 bay leaves
1 sprig fresh rosemary
5 black peppercorns
salt to taste

1. To prepare the marinade, heat the olive oil in a saucepan. Add the carrot, onion, and celeriac and brown slightly. Pour in the wine and wine vinegar. Add the herbs and spices, and simmer gently for 30 minutes. 2. Put the meat in a glass or ceramic bowl and pour the marinade over it. Marinate for 8 hours or overnight. 3. Remove the beef from the marinade and cut it into large serving pieces. Put the beef into a large, greased ovenproof earthenware tureen or oven casserole. Pour strained marinade over it. Add the olives, carrots, parsley, and cut up pieces of chicken fat or margarine. Cover the casserole or tureen with a sheet of waxed paper and a tight-fitting lid. Cook in a preheated 300° oven for 3 hours, or until the meat is tender. Add the cut-up tomatoes to the stew. Ladle the stew into bowls and serve. *Serves 6 to 8*

Beef Liver and Apple

1½ pounds beef liver	4 unpeeled green cooking apples,
all-purpose flour	cored and sliced
1 tablespoon olive oil	2 tablespoons chopped fresh parsley
¼ cup margarine	salt and pepper, to taste
2 medium onions, chopped	4 tablespoons sherry
2 cloves garlic, crushed	parsley, for garnish

1. Freeze and partially thaw the liver to make slicing easier. (If you observe *kashrut*, place the cut-up liver under the broiler to allow the blood to drain.) Slice the liver into strips and roll them in flour.   2. In a frying pan, heat the oil and margarine and sauté the onions and garlic. Put them on a warm platter and keep them warm. Sauté the liver for a few minutes. Lower the heat and add the onions, garlic, and apples. Stir in the parsley, salt and pepper, and sherry. Cover the pan and cook slowly until the liver is tender—be careful not to overcook, or the liver will be tough. Serve with rice and garnish with more parsley. *Serves 4*

Chopped Meat Pie with *Tahini* Sauce

2 pounds beef *or* lamb *or* veal,	1 teaspoon ground allspice
chopped	vegetable oil *or* margarine
2 onions, grated	1 cup *tahini* sauce (see pages 212–13)
2 cloves garlic, crushed	chopped fresh parsley
salt and pepper, to taste	

1. Grind the chopped beef in a grinder or food processor until it is smooth. Mix in the onions, crushed garlic, salt, pepper, and allspice.   2. Oil a round baking tray or large ovenproof plate. Spread the meat mixture evenly to a thickness of 1 inch, and brush the surface with oil. Bake in a preheated 375° oven for 45 minutes, or until the surface of the meat is browned.   3. Remove the meat from the oven, and pour the *tahini* sauce over it. Bake for 10 minutes more, or until the *tahini* sauce is firm. Cut the meat pie into wedges and garnish each portion with parsley. Serve with chips and a mixed salad for a hearty supper dish. *Serves 4 to 6*

Braised Oxtail Joints
with Onions and Mushrooms

ぎ ぎ ぎ

3 pounds oxtail joints
½ cup all-purpose flour
salt and pepper, to taste
2 tablespoons drippings *or* vegetable
　　oil
1 4-ounce can button mushrooms
1 pound pearl onions, peeled
fresh parsley for garnish

Bouquet Garni*:
6 parsley stalks
1 teaspoon thyme
3 bay leaves
4 peppercorns

1. Roll the oxtail joints in ¼ cup of the flour seasoned with salt and pepper.
In a large pan, brown the oxtails in the fat. Pour off the drippings. Add the bouquet garni and the mushrooms plus their liquid. Bring to a boil, and skim away
the froth that rises to the top. Reduce the heat and cover the pan. Simmer
gently for about 3 hours.　2. In a saucepan, cover the onions with cold water
and bring to a boil. Simmer for 5 minutes, and drain. Set them aside until the
oxtails are almost tender. Add the onions to the pan. Simmer 1 hour, covered,
or until the oxtail joints are tender. (You may also put the oxtails and onions
into a covered casserole and bake in a preheated 350° oven for 2 hours, or until
the meat falls from the bone.) Refrigerate, and remove the congealed fat.
3. Remove the meat, mushrooms, and onions and thicken the liquid with the
remaining flour. Return the meat mixture to the pan. Serve with a sprinkle of
fresh parsley. *Serves 4 to 6*

* Tie up ingredients for the bouquet garni in a clean cheesecloth bag. Remove the bag at the end
of the cooking time.

Oven-fried Beef Liver
with Mushroom and Onion Sauce

ぎ ぎ ぎ

Oven-fried liver is a shortcut to preparing supper. Cook the liver in onion-soup
sauce and serve with baked tomato halves for a complete meal.

2 pounds beef liver
3 tablespoons olive oil
1 tablespoon chopped fresh parsley
1 teaspoon crushed bay leaves

1 teaspoon crushed hyssop leaves
salt and pepper, to taste
3 medium tomatoes
1 package dry onion soup mix

1. Trim off and discard the liver's membrane. Slice ½ inch thick. (Frozen liver partially thawed is easier to slice.) If you observe *kashrut*, place the liver under the broiler to allow the blood to run out.   2. Put the oil in a large, rimmed, ovenproof glass baking dish, add the parsley, bay leaves, hyssop leaves, salt, and pepper. Add the liver, spooning the mixture over it. Bake, uncovered, in a pre-heated 400° oven for 15 minutes.   3. While the liver is baking, cut the tomatoes in half. Place them in a pan with 1 cup of water. Remove the herb seasoning from the liver dish and spoon it over the tops of the tomatoes. Cover and steam on top of the stove until almost done. Put the tomatoes in an oven-proof dish, reserving the liquid, and put them in the oven to keep warm. 4. Add the onion soup mix to the water in which the tomatoes were cooked. Bring to a boil and simmer 5 minutes. Pour over the baked liver for a gravy. *Serves 6*

Brain Salad Appetizer

❦ ❦ ❦

Brains have long been considered a delicacy in the Middle East, as have all organ meats. Because they are in short supply women in Jerusalem go to the market early to buy their choice of brain, spleen, lungs, penis, udder, intestines, and hearts.

3 sets calves brains *or* 4 sets lambs' brains	salt and pepper, to taste
	juice of 2 lemons
4 cups water plus 1 teaspoon salt plus 1 tablespoon vinegar	vegetable oil
	1 teaspoon basil
1 large onion, chopped	chopped fresh parsley, for garnish

1. Wash the brains under cold running water. Cook for 1 hour in cold water to which 1 tablespoon of vinegar has been added. Wash in cold water and carefully remove the outer membranes. Wash again and drain.   2. In a large pot, bring the water, salt, and vinegar to a boil. Add the brains and simmer, uncovered, for 20 minutes.   3. While the brains are cooking, marinate the chopped onion in the salt, pepper, and lemon juice for 15 minutes.   4. Drain the brains and cool. Slice crosswise ½ inch thick, and place the slices in a shallow serving dish. Add vegetable oil to the marinated onions and mix. Gently pour over the brains. Sprinkle on the basil and garnish with chopped parsley. Serve cold as an appetizer with rye bread or savory crackers. *Serves 4*

FOWL
Stewed Chicken

1 3- to 3½-pound stewing fowl *or*
    roasting chicken
½ lemon
½ teaspoon thyme
½ teaspoon saffron *or* 1 teaspoon
    turmeric
2 stalks celery *or* celeriac, with leaves

2 carrots, scraped
1 small onion, halved
1 teaspoon salt
4 sprigs parsley
2 bay leaves
1 clove

1. Wash the chicken, pat dry, and rub the inside of it with the lemon and thyme. In a large pot, barely cover the chicken with water. Add the remainder of the ingredients. Bring the water to a boil and lower the heat. Simmer, covered, for 1 to 1½ hours or until the chicken is tender.   2. Put the chicken on a warmed plate and strain the stock. Let cool, and remove the fat which rises. Reheat the stock and serve. *Serves 4*

Poached Cold Lemon Chicken

1 large chicken
½ lemon
salt and pepper to taste
1 sprig fresh mint
½ pound carrots, peeled
½ pound onions, peeled
peel of 1 lemon, grated

juice of 1 lemon
¼ cup sherry
1 tablespoon cornstarch *or* arrowroot
    or ½ ounce unflavored gelatin
1 tablespoon chopped fresh parsley
chopped fresh mint leaves, for garnish
1 lemon, thinly sliced

1. Wash the chicken and pat dry. Rub it inside and out with the lemon. Sprinkle with salt and pepper, and place a sprig of mint in the cavity of the chicken. 2. In large pot, barely cover the chicken with water. Poach until done, 1 to 1½ hours. Halfway through the cooking, add the carrots and onions. Turn the chicken occasionally, and cook until tender.   3. Let the chicken cool in its stock. Remove, and slice the flesh into medium-size pieces.   4. Strain the stock. In a saucepan, heat 2 cups of stock. Stir in the lemon peel, lemon juice, and sherry. Simmer. Mix the cornstarch with cold water to form a paste, and add to the simmering stock to make a thickened sauce. Put the sliced chicken

Saffron

in the sauce along with the chopped parsley, and let cool in the pan.   5. Arrange the sliced chicken and sauce in a glass dish. Garnish with mint leaves and thinly sliced lemon. *Serves 6*

Cold Stuffed Chicken

❦ ❦ ❦

Although one school of thought frowns on stuffing a chicken before it is cooled, this stuffing is excellent for a poached-baked chicken. It makes a nice change from the conventional chicken salad served to a large group.

1 3½- to 4-pound chicken
½ lemon

Stuffing:

2 hard-boiled eggs, coarsely chopped
⅔ cup blanched almonds, chopped
3 eggs, beaten
1 teaspoon salt
½ teaspoon black pepper
½ teaspoon ground cinnamon
rose petals, chopped, *or* marigold
      petals
½ teaspoon allspice
¼ teaspoon saffron *or* ½ teaspoon
      turmeric

1. To prepare the stuffing, combine the hard-boiled eggs, almonds, and beaten eggs. Add the rest of the ingredients and mix well.   2. Wash the chicken and pat dry. Rub the inside with the lemon. Stuff and truss the chicken.   3. In a large pot, bring 3 cups of water to a boil. Put in the chicken, cover, and reduce the heat. Simmer until tender, about 1 hour. Remove the chicken, and reserve the liquid for soup.   4. Drain the chicken well and roast it in a preheated 300° oven until crisp.   5. Remove the neck, wings, and feet, and thinly slice the chicken with its stuffing. Serve cold. *Serves 6*

Chicken with Olives

❦ ❦ ❦

1 4-pound stewing chicken
2 tablespoons chicken fat *or*
    vegetable oil
2 medium onions, sliced
salt and pepper, to taste

½ teaspoon ground cumin
¾ cup water
1 teaspoon paprika
½ pound pitted green olives *or* pitted
    black olives
juice of 1 lemon

1. Wash the chicken and pat dry. In a deep heavy pot, heat the fat or oil. Add the onions, salt, pepper, cumin, and paprika. Gradually add ¾ cup water. Place the chicken on top. Cover the pot and reduce the heat. Cook the chicken for 1 to 1½ hours, turning the chicken during cooking. 2. In a small pot, cover the olives with cold water. Boil and pour off the water. Repeat until all the salt has been removed from the olives. Add the olives to the chicken at the end of cooking and warm through. 3. Serve the chicken on a warmed platter, encircled with the olives. Squeeze the lemon juice over the chicken. Serve with plain boiled rice or *couscous* (pages 79–80). *Serves 4 to 6*

Rice-stuffed Roast Chicken

❦ ❦ ❦

1 4-pound roasting chicken

Rice Stuffing:
¼ pound chicken giblets
salt and pepper, to taste
1 cup cooked rice
½ cup raisins
½ cup blanched almonds, chopped
¼ cup chopped onions
½ cup chopped fresh parsley
2 ounces margarine *or* butter
1 sprig fresh basil
1 egg, beaten

1. Boil the giblets in 2 cups of water seasoned with salt and pepper to taste. When they are done, remove them from the stock with a slotted spoon and chop. In a large bowl, mix all the stuffing ingredients except the egg, working in the margarine until a good consistency is reached. Now work in the egg. Stuff and truss the chicken. 2. Wash the chicken and pat dry. Roast the chicken, uncovered, in a preheated 350° oven for about 1½ hours, or 20 min-

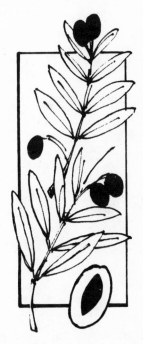

Olive

utes to the pound. Baste occasionally with pan juices. Or, cover chicken with foil, roast the chicken, and remove the foil for the last 30 minutes, basting twice. 3. To make a gravy, boil the pan juices until reduced. Mix 2 tablespoons of flour and 2 tablespoons of margarine. Stir in small pieces until smooth. *Serves 4 to 6*

Variation: Make a basting sauce of 1 cup grape juice, 1 tablespoon hot prepared mustard, and 1 tablespoon tomato paste. Baste the chicken and roast it in a roasting bag until done. Make the gravy with juices from the roasting bag.

Turkish Pilav

Four hundred years of a Turkish presence in the Land of Israel affected the diet and cuisine of the many peoples living here. Not only did the special style of black coffee become known as Turkish coffee, but the whole range of *pilavi* are associated with the best of Turkish cooking. If the sauce test was the ultimate for a good French cook, the pilav remains today a test of the homemaker's reputation as a good cook. Pilav dishes are cooked with beef or chicken broth instead of water. Here is a popular chicken and rice pilav.

2 pounds chicken, disjointed, cut into medium pieces	1 teaspoon pepper
5 onions, chopped	1 teaspoon allspice
¾ cup raw long-grain rice	5 cups chicken stock *or* beef stock
1 teaspoon salt	1 tablespoon boiling water
	2 teaspoons chopped nuts

1. In a strong, flat pan or top-of-the-stove casserole, layer half of the chicken pieces. Arrange a layer of onions over the chicken, and half the rice over the onions. Arrange another layer of chicken pieces, onions, and rice. Add the salt, pepper, and allspice, and pour the stock over all. Sprinkle with the boiling water. 2. Cover and cook on low heat for 1 hour, or until done. Remove the lid and add the nuts. *Serves 4*

Pomegranate Chicken

❧ ❧ ❧

Pomegranate chicken is served here during the Jewish New Year holiday, when the pomegranates are ripe. First cut the pomegranates in half and squeeze out the juice. With care, the shells can be cleaned of the tough membranes and used as dessert bowls for fruit salad.

1 large broiler-fryer chicken *or* 2
    smaller chickens
vegetable oil
chopped fresh parsley for garnish

Sauce:

2 onions, grated
½ cup margarine *or* butter
⅔ cup almonds *or* walnuts
1 cup fresh pomegranate juice
1 ounce powdered rose hips
1 cup chicken stock
salt and pepper, to taste
1 teaspoon honey

1. Disjoint the chicken and cut it into pieces. Sauté in the oil, turning often so that the pieces are evenly browned. 2. To prepare the sauce, sauté the onion in the margarine or butter until soft, in a large frying pan or top-of-the-stove casserole. Add the nuts, stirring until well mixed. Add the pomegranate juice, rose hip powder, and stock. Stir until the sauce thickens. Season with salt, pepper, and honey. 3. Pour the sauce over the chicken. Cover and cook in a preheated 325° oven for about 40 minutes or until done. Serve in the casserole or on a hot platter. Garnish with parsley. *Serves 4*

Barbecued Broilers

❧ ❧ ❧

After the long period of "boiling chickens only," small young chickens—both for home and terrace cooking and for picnics—have become favorites here. Men who won't go into the kitchen to cook seem to think outdoor cooking, especially barbecueing, is a manly chore worthy of their talents. Perhaps it is a throwback to more primitive times, when women were the gatherers of wild greens and men the hunters and fire-makers. Whatever the reasons, women often welcome playing second fiddle to the outdoor chef as he orchestrates the menu and shops for the ingredients. Cheers for outdoor chefs!

Pomegranate

3 broiler chickens, split in half

Barbecue Sauce:

1 6-ounce can tomato paste diluted
    with 2 cans water
¼ cup honey
¼ cup lemon juice
2 tablespoons vegetable oil
2 tablespoons soy sauce *or*
    Worcestershire sauce
1 teaspoon spicy oriental tomato
    sauce *or* Tabasco sauce
½ teaspoon salt
1 teaspoon prepared mustard

1. Wash and pat dry the split chickens. In a bowl, combine all the barbecue sauce ingredients. Brush the halved broilers with the sauce and place them cut side down on a greased grill over glowing coals. 2. Grill until tender, about 30 minutes, turning and basting with the remaining sauce. Serve with a mixed vegetable salad and toasted halves of Arab *pita* bread (pages 56–57) or hamburger rolls for a hearty meal. Don't forget to applaud the chef! *Serves 6*

Marinated Ginger Chicken

1 2½-pound broiler chicken
2 teaspoons honey
1 teaspoon cornstarch
chopped fresh parsley, for garnish

Marinade:

5 tablespoons finely chopped peeled
    ginger root *or* 1 tablespoon
    ground ginger root
¼ cup soy sauce
3 tablespoons sesame seed oil
2 tablespoons finely chopped
    scallions
½ cup sherry
dash of salt and pepper

1. Split the chicken at the breast and lay it flat in a large, ovenproof glass baking dish. 2. Combine the marinade ingredients, pour over the chicken, and marinate for at least 1 hour. 3. Drain the chicken, reserving the marinade. Place the chicken in an oiled roasting pan, skin side down, and baste with the marinade. Bake in a preheated 350° oven for about 45 minutes. 4. To prepare the sauce, combine the remaining marinade with the honey and cornstarch. Stir well, and cook in a pan over low heat until it thickens. 5. Cut the chicken into at least six serving pieces. Lay them on a hot platter and pour the

sauce over them. Garnish with chopped parsley. Baked fruit—unpeeled apple rings, or dates stuffed with walnuts—makes a good accompaniment to this dish. *Serves 4*

Steamed Stuffed Chicken Breasts

❦ ❦ ❦

This low-calorie recipe may seem complicated, but it can be partially made beforehand. The steaming process can be done between courses—let the diners wait, not the chicken breasts!

3 1-pound chicken breasts, skinned, boned, and halved
salt and pepper to taste
6 large lettuce leaves, cos or endive, washed and drained
chopped fresh parsley, for garnish

Poaching Liquid:

1 cup lemon balm *or* melissa leaves (available in herb and spice shops)
4 shallots, with some of the green tops
1 cup white wine

Stuffing:

3 cups dry bread crumbs
2 cups pistachio nuts, chopped
1 cup chopped fresh basil leaves
1 cup chopped chives
1 egg, beaten
salt and pepper, to taste
1 teaspoon Tabasco sauce

Sauce:

2 cups poaching liquid
2 teaspoons arrowroot

1. Put the chicken breasts between 2 sheets of wax paper and pound flat. Sprinkle with salt and pepper.   2. To prepare the stuffing, combine all the stuffing ingredients in a large bowl. Make a slight incision along the side of each breast. Put about 3 tablespoons of the stuffing into each incision. Roll up the chicken tightly to hold the filling and secure with kitchen string. Place each breast seam side down in the center of a lettuce leaf. Turn in the ends and roll the leaf sides together to make a parcel. Place the rolls in a heat-proof glass baking dish large enough to hold 6 rolls. (At this point, you can cover and refrigerate the rolls a few hours or overnight—but no longer—until you are ready to complete the meal.)   3. Combine the ingredients for the poaching liquid and pour it over the chicken rolls. Carefully set the plate into a roasting bag (not an ordinary plastic bag!) and place it on a steamer rack set over boiling water. Steam rolls for 5 minutes.   4. Turn off the heat. Open up the bag, turn the rolls, baste them with poaching liquid, and close the bag. Let the rolls finish cooking in the lingering steam. After 3 minutes, remove the bag from the steamer. Open the bag and pour its liquid into a sauce pan. Put the breasts on a warm serving plate while you make the sauce.   5. To prepare a sauce, boil 2 cups of the poaching juices (add wine or steaming water to make 2 cups). Mix the arrow-

root with 3 tablespoons of water and stir into the liquid until thickened. Pour the sauce over the chicken breasts and serve immediately with a sprinkle of chopped parsley. *Serves 6*

Marinated Chicken Breasts

❦ ❦ ❦

Chicken breasts are handy for outdoor grilling, especially when marinated beforehand. Marinating is one chore that can be done in advance, and which improves the flavor.

3 whole chicken breasts, split

Herb Marinade:

½ cup red cooking wine
1 sprig fresh rosemary *or* ½ teaspoon dried rosemary
1 sprig thyme *or* ½ teaspoon dried thyme

½ teaspoon turmeric
½ cup chopped parsley
2 scallions, finely chopped
salt to taste
2 tablespoons olive oil *or* vegetable oil

Sauce:

1 tablespoon arrowroot *or* cornstarch
½ cup marinade

1. Put the chicken breasts between 2 sheets of wax paper and pound flat. 2. In a bowl, combine the marinade ingredients. Pour the marinade into a large plastic bag, add the chicken breasts, and close securely. Place the bag in a bowl or pan and marinate for several hours or overnight in the refrigerator. Drain in a colander, reserving the marinade for a sauce. 3. Place the marinated chicken breasts over hot coals and broil for about 5 minutes on each side. Taste the marinade, adding soy sauce or powdered mustard if you wish. Serve as is, or make a sauce. To make a sauce, combine 1 tablespoon of arrowroot or cornstarch with ½ cup marinade. Stir until smooth and heat until the sauce is thickened and smooth. Pour over the chicken. *Serves 6*

Quick-fry Breasts of Chicken

❦ ❦ ❦

This poultry dish can be cooked at the table in an electric frying pan, or in a pan over an open grill. The taste is superb, the cooking fast, and diners have the fun of seeing the chicken being prepared. Served with grilled bananas or pineapple rings, this is an elegant dish.

3 whole chicken breasts, split	3 teaspoons chopped chives *or* green
salt and pepper, to taste	scallion tops
olive oil	½ cup chopped fresh parsley
3 tablespoons margarine	2 teaspoons soy sauce
1 teaspoon dry mustard	juice of 1 lemon

1. Put the chicken breasts between 2 pieces of wax paper and pound flat. Season the meat with salt and pepper to taste, and brush lightly with olive oil.
2. In a frying pan, heat 2 tablespoons of the butter or margarine over low heat. Add a few drops of olive oil, the mustard, and chives. Sauté the chicken quickly, turning the meat after 4 minutes. Cook 2 minutes on the second side or until done but not overcooked. Put the chicken on a warm platter. To the remaining pan juices add the parsley, soy sauce, 1 tablespoon of the margarine, and lemon juice. Blend and pour immediately over chicken. Serve. *Serves 6*

Bachelor
Chicken Breast Flambé

❦ ❦ ❦

Some obliging husbands in Israel are agreeable to giving their wives a night off from preparing supper. They usually insist on doing something special, and rarely agree to preparing a poached egg on toast! This recipe is a favorite among the men in our family.

2 pounds boned chicken breasts	salt and pepper, to taste
4 tablespoons margarine	2 tablespoons water
2 tablespoons brandy	1 cup nondairy cream
1 teaspoon arrowroot *or* cornstarch	½ cup chopped fresh parsley
½ teaspoon dry mustard	1 cup button mushrooms, cooked
1 teaspoon curry powder	

1. Slice the chicken breasts diagonally into 2-inch strips. In a heavy skillet or frying pan, melt half the margarine. Sauté the breasts on both sides. Pour the brandy over the meat and ignite. When the flame dies down, transfer the meat to a warm plate.   2. Add the remaining margarine to the pan and mix it with the existing pan juices. In a small bowl, mix the arrowroot, mustard, curry powder, salt, and pepper with 2 tablespoons of water to make a smooth paste. Add to the pan and slowly pour in the cream. Heat through. Return the meat to the pan, and stir gently until it has absorbed all the gravy. Serve at once sprinkled with parsley. You may stretch the dish by adding the button mushrooms when the chicken is returned to the pan. Serve with rice, or with canned fruit that has been drained and sprinkled with nutmeg and warmed. *Serves 4 to 6*

Breasts of Chicken in Wine and Herb Sauce

1½ pounds chicken breasts
salt, to taste
all-purpose flour
½ pound onions, sliced (about 3)
3 tablespoons olive oil
2 tablespoons tomato paste
3 tomatoes, peeled and sliced
½ pound mushrooms, sliced

1 cup dry white wine
15 stuffed olives, sliced
salt and pepper, to taste
1 tablespoon lemon balm leaves, dried
1 teaspoon paprika
chopped fresh parsley
3 hard-boiled eggs, sliced

1. Slice the chicken breasts. Lightly salt and flour them. In a large frying pan, sauté the onions in the olive oil until golden. Add the chicken, tomato paste, tomatoes, and sliced mushrooms. Pour the wine over all, stir well, and simmer for about 15 minutes on medium heat, or until the chicken is tender. Do not overcook. Add the olives, salt, pepper, lemon balm leaves, the paprika, and parsley. Serve garnished with sliced hard-boiled eggs over boiled rice. *Serves 4*

Almond Chicken Wings

Although chicken wings are often given short shrift—they are used for stock making when bones are in short supply—many people, given the choice, select wings for their tenderness and delicacy of taste. These spiced fortified wings are good finger food.

12 chicken wings
salt and pepper, to taste
¼ cup all-purpose flour
½ teaspoon ground allspice
1 cup stale bread crumbs
1 cup ground almonds

4 tablespoons chopped fresh parsley
1 teaspoon chopped fresh mint
2 eggs beaten with 2 tablespoons water
vegetable oil for frying
parsley sprigs, for garnish
lemon wedges, for garnish

1. Halve each chicken wing at the joint and discard the tip. Wash and pat dry. Sprinkle with salt and pepper. Place them four at a time in a brown paper bag containing the flour and allspice.   2. In a bowl, combine the bread crumbs, ground almonds, parsley, and mint. Dip 2 to 3 floured wings at a time in the egg-water mixture, then roll them in the crumb-almond mixture. Transfer them to a large dish. Refrigerate, covered, for about 1 hour.   3. In a large pan or deep fryer, heat the oil and fry the wings until they are lightly browned. Turn them

to cook evenly. Drain on a rack and on paper towels. To keep them moist and warm, divide them between two brown paper bags or oven roasting bags and put them in a warm oven until ready to serve. Garnish with parsley and wedges of lemon. *Makes 24 appetizers*

Spiced Sesame Chicken Wings

🐞 🐞 🐞

These spicy chicken wings can be grilled quickly to offer a sharp bite when you need appetizers and barbecued morsels. Enriched with sesame seed, they are protein packed.

12 chicken wings
3 tablespoons sesame seeds
1 teaspoon ground cumin
1 teaspoon paprika
1 teaspoon sage
½ teaspoon salt
2 eggs beaten with 1 tablespoon water

Basting Sauce:

½ cup vegetable oil
1 clove garlic, crushed
3 tablespoons white wine *or* citrus
    vinegar
1 tablespoon soy sauce
salt and pepper, to taste
¼ teaspoon dry mustard
1 teaspoon brown sugar

1. Halve each chicken wing at the joint and discard the tip. Wash and pat dry.   2. In a bowl, combine the sesame seeds, cumin, paprika, sage, and salt. Dip the wings in the egg-water mixture, and coat them with the sesame seed mixture. Place the wings on a barbecue rack about 5 inches from glowing coals.   3. Combine the ingredients for the basting sauce. Cook the chicken wings about 10 minutes, turn, and baste. Broil 10 minutes more, baste, and cook 5 minutes more or until done. Serve with the remaining sauce for dipping. Serve with a mixed green salad, or grilled sliced onions. *Makes 24 appetizers*

Liver Paté

🐞 🐞 🐞

This is a dramatic focal-point dish for a *mezze* service, or it can be the centerpiece for a cocktail-buffet table. Serve with savory crackers, sliced rye bread, or wedges of toasted bread.

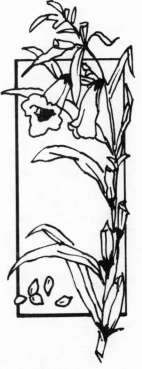

Sesame

½ pound chicken livers
1 pound calf's liver
1 onion
2 slices white bread, soaked in water
    and drained
3 eggs, beaten
1 cup cream (nondairy for *kashrut*
    observers)

½ cup chicken fat *or* margarine
⅓ cup cognac
3 teaspoons salt
1 teaspoon soy sauce
1 teaspoon ground ginger
1 teaspoon nutmeg
2 teaspoons white pepper
lettuce leaves
1 hard-boiled egg, chopped

1. Wash the livers and pat dry. If you observe *kashrut*, place the livers under the broiler to drain out the blood.   2. Lightly grease a 3-quart mold or heat-proof glass bowl that will fit into a pressure cooker.   3. In a meat grinder, grind the livers, onion, and bread. Put in a bowl and add the eggs, cream, and fat. Blend until smooth, and add the rest of the ingredients except the hard-boiled egg.   4. Pour the liver mixture into the mold. Cover with a lid or a double thickness of aluminum foil. Tie the cover down with string. Place the mold in a pan and bake in a preheated 350° oven for 1 hour. Or, place the mold on a rack in a pressure cooker and steam for 45 minutes. Allow the paté to cool, and put it in the refrigerator overnight.   5. Invert the mold on a plate of lettuce leaves and top with the chopped hard-boiled egg. *Makes 1½ pounds*

Chopped Chicken Liver

1 pound chicken livers
3 tablespoons chicken fat *or*
    margarine
3 medium onions, chopped

salt and pepper, to taste
1 teaspoon nutmeg
3 hard-boiled eggs, chopped
½ cup chopped fresh parsley

1. Wash the livers and pat dry. If you observe *kashrut*, place the livers under the broiler long enough for the blood to drain out.   2. In a large skillet, melt the fat. Sauté the onions until golden. Add the livers and sauté until tender, about 3 minutes.   3. Grind or chop the livers and onions until smooth. Add the salt, pepper, nutmeg, and chopped eggs. On a platter, arrange the chopped liver into a mound with a fork. Garnish with parsley. Serve as a spread with savory crackers or as an appetizer on a leaf of lettuce. *Makes 1 pound*

Apple-stuffed Roast Goose

Geese are mainly raised in Israel for their luscious livers, which are used in *paté de foie gras*. The local population seldom sees goose liver in the shops, because Israel exports it; but geese are sometimes available. Apple stuffing contrasts well with the robust taste of the goose.

1 6- to 9-pound goose	1 pound cooking apples, peeled,
salt and pepper, to taste	cored, and sliced
1 teaspoon ground marjoram	1 cup (6 ounces) raisins
	3 tablespoons bread crumbs

1. Wash the goose thoroughly, pat dry, and rub inside with the salt, pepper, and marjoram.   2. Mix the apples, raisins, and bread crumbs. Stuff the goose and sew up the neck and belly.   3. In a large saucepan, pour water over the goose until it is almost covered. Boil for 10 minutes to release some of the fat.   4. Preheat the oven to 425°. Remove the goose from the saucepan and allow it to cool on a draining board. Pat dry with paper towels. Put the goose breast down on a rack, with a pan underneath the bird to catch the fat drippings. Reduce the oven to 350°, and roast the goose until done (about 25 minutes to the pound). After about 30 minutes pierce the drumsticks with a fork to allow the fat to run off. Pour it off as it accumulates. After about 1½ hours turn the goose. When it seems almost done, brush the goose with salted water to make the skin crisp. Roast for 20 minutes more. Serve with a pan gravy seasoned with ginger. *Serves 6*

Roast Partridges

3 to 4 young partridges	4 pimento-stuffed green olives, halved
vegetable oil	peel of 2 lemons, grated
salt, pepper, and ground sage, to taste	juice of two lemons

1. Wash the partridges and pat dry. Split them completely in half. In a large frying pan, sauté the halves in a little oil for 10 minutes. Remove from the pan and season with salt, pepper, and sage. Let cool.   2. Prepare a square of aluminum foil for each half bird, and rub with oil. Lay each partridge cavity up on a square of foil. Put the halved olives and 1 teaspoon of lemon peel into each cavity. Spoon the pan juices and the lemon juice over the filling. Fold over the silver foil to make an airtight bundle. Place the birds on oven racks and roast in a preheated 350° oven for 10 to 15 minutes, or until done. Open up the foil at the table (watch out for the steam!) and serve with shallot sauce (page 176). *Serves 4*

Braised Pigeons

1 2-pound cabbage
2 tablespoons chicken fat *or*
    margarine
6 pigeons, plucked and dressed
2 bay leaves

1 teaspoon ground thyme
juice of 1 lemon
2 tablespoons all-purpose flour
chopped parsley, for garnish

1. Remove the discolored outer leaves of a head of cabbage, shred, and rinse. In a large saucepan, cover the cabbage with hot water. Cook for 5 minutes on medium heat. Drain, saving 1 cup of the liquid.   2. Grease an ovenproof casserole and line it with cabbage leaves. Melt the fat in a frying pan and brown the pigeons. Put them in the casserole and add the remaining cabbage leaves, bay leaves, thyme, and lemon juice.   3. In the frying pan, mix the flour with the remaining fat until slightly brown. Add the reserved cabbage water and cook for 3 minutes, or until the sauce thickens. Pour the sauce into the casserole, and carefully mix the sauce and pigeons. Cover the casserole and bake in a preheated 325° oven for 2 hours or until the pigeons are tender. Serve as a separate course, garnished with chopped parsley. *Serves 6*

Marinated Picnic Pigeons

Fava
(Broad Bean)

A mixed green salad or vegetable salad is just the thing to accompany these grilled pigeons.

3 pigeons plucked, dressed, and split
    in half
2 cups lemon juice
1 cup olive oil
1 teaspoon salt

1 teaspoon pepper
branches of thyme
olive oil
3 *pita* breads (pages 56–57) *or*
    hamburger rolls, sliced in half

1. Marinate the pigeons in the lemon juice, oil, salt, and pepper for a few hours or overnight.   2. Prepare a charcoal fire. When the coals are hot and grey, place branches of thyme over the greased rack or grid. Place the pigeons on the rack, cut side down, over the hot coals. Baste occasionally with olive oil. Turn the pigeons frequently to ensure even browning. Cook for 20 to 25 minutes, or until done. Slightly toast the *pita* halves on one side and brush with remaining marinade. Serve half a pigeon on toasted *pita* with a sprinkle of parsley. *Serves 6*

QUAIL (*Phasianidae*)

The phenomenal migrations of quail were documented in biblical times. According to the ancient historian, Josephus, "They came flying over this stretch of sea, wearied, they skimmed the ground and settled in the Hebrews' camp" (Antiquities III:25). Although their comparatively short wings slow down their initial ascent, quail are outstanding long-distance fliers once they are airborne.

Large flocks of quail passed over the Mediterranean Sea during their migrations back and forth from Europe to Africa in the fall and spring. They rested mainly in the south of the country, along the shores of Gaza and El Arish and sometimes along the Red Sea shores. They were easy to catch in their wearied state. "Some were eaten fresh, the rest spread out on the ground to dry in the sun" (Numbers 11:31–33). With their high reproductive capacity, they produced as many as twelve to fifteen eggs in one clutch. Today quails, as in biblical times, breed in cereal and fodder fields and build their nests on the ground. They are caught today and eaten as a delicacy in Israel.

Quail and Spiced Pilav

These simply prepared quail are an elegant accompaniment to pilav.

6 quail
salt and pepper, to taste
2 tablespoons olive oil *or* margarine

1. Wash the quail and pat dry. Carefully remove the breast bones and back bones. Flatten the birds by pounding them with a mallet. Rub with salt and pepper, and baste with oil or melted margarine before broiling. 2. Place a rack over the charcoal fire, 4 inches above the hot but not flaming coals (or cook in a preheated broiler). Broil the birds 8 to 10 minutes on each side. Turn only once. The birds are better slightly underdone, but not *too* rare. 3. Arrange rice pilav (page 248) on an oval platter, and top it with the quail. Serve with a salad of cucumbers and chopped dill and sliced lemons. *Serves 6*

Grilled Quail
and Chicken Livers

6 medium quail
salt and pepper, to taste
olive oil
1 pound chicken livers
1 pound sorrel leaves, washed and cut
    in half

1 tablespoon olive oil
juice of 1 lemon
wedges of 3 lemons

1. Wash the quail and pat dry. Carefully remove the breast bones and back bones. Flatten the birds by pounding with a mallet. Rub with salt and pepper, and baste with oil. Rinse and drain the chicken livers and cut them in half. Pat dry.   2. Place the quails on a rack over smoldering red charcoals. Grill for 10 minutes and turn over. Grill 7 minutes more. At the same time, set the chicken livers on a rack or on skewers and place them over the hot coals. Turn them after 7 minutes, and grill 5 minutes more.   3. While the quail and livers are grilling, gently cook the sorrel leaves in a saucepan with the olive oil. Cover the pan and cook until the sorrel leaves have nearly wilted.   4. Squeeze the juice of 1 lemon over the quails and chicken livers. Remove the sorrel leaves to a heated platter, and place the quails and chicken livers on the sorrel leaves.   5. Serve immediately with lemon wedges and toasted triangles of light rye bread and freshly ground pepper. *Serves 6*

10 FISH

Although the Bible often refers to fish, it never once mentions a particular species. Even the most famous example—the one which swallowed Jonah—is called only "a big fish," and the identification with a whale was only a popular later tradition. In fact, the fish in Israel today have probably changed little since Bible days. Over twenty species are indigenous to Israel, more than half of them in the Jordan river and its tributaries.

In the wilderness of Sinai, it is recorded, the Israelites longed to eat the fish they had known in Egypt (where the Nile is a rich source of fish, as is conveyed most vividly in the first plague spoken of in Exodus 7:21). In Moses' dietary laws, fish had to have fins and scales to be permitted for food, and this has excluded from the Jewish diet all shellfish.

For Israelites living along the coast, fishing was an important livelihood. Fish was taken inland to Jerusalem, one of whose entrances was the Fish Gate (Nehemiah 3:3), so called because it was next to a fish market. It is doubtful if fresh fish would still have been edible after the journey to Jerusalem; presumably the fish was salted or smoked near the scene of the catch.

Fishing took various forms: spearing the fish, probably with a harpoon (Job 41:7); angling on a line (Amos 4:2; Matthew 17:27); casting a net, which was usual in the Sea of Galilee (Luke 5:4–9; Matthew 13:47–50); and with a small hand net (Habakkuk 1:15).

Fish, especially in the area surrounding the Sea of Galilee, play an important role in the New Testament. Jesus asked the fishermen Peter, Andrew, James, and John to leave their occupation, to follow him, and become fishers of men. Several of his miracles involved fish (Luke 5:1–11; Matthew 17:27); the miracle of the loaves and fishes (Luke 9:13–17 and elsewhere), one of his most famous miracles, is commemorated in an ancient mosaic floor which can still be seen at Tabgha, on the shores of the Sea of Galilee.

Although the Land of Israel is small, its supply of fish has been drawn from three seas: the Mediterranean, the Red Sea, and the Sea of Galilee. To increase the supply, fish ponds were developed. Carp were the major fish used for pond

Caper

breeding, especially in the early days of modern settlement in Israel. As Israel's fish industry developed, more fish became available. Carp breeding was improved by the introduction of the Far Eastern silver carp. The pond-bred St. Peter's fish (John Dory or *tilapea galilaea*), which has been crossed with an African variety, has seen even greater success. It's easy to prepare for pan frying or outdoor grilling, and its popularity has grown.

Legend holds that the flat St. Peter's fish is so called because of its markings, which were said to have been left there by the fingers of St. Peter. It seemed to him that the fish made a crying sound as he grasped it, so he threw it back into the sea.

During the winter of 1985 to 1986, the rains in Israel were considerably less than average. As a result the level of Israel's major water supplier, the Sea of Galilee, fell alarmingly low. The water flow to the agricultural fields of the country and to the household taps was threatened.

The Sea of Galilee was a sight to behold. People stopped vacationing around the sea because they were saddened to view it. Then one day an odd-looking stick began to protrude from the shallow depth of the sea. All eyes turned to it. Upon inspection, the upright stick was found to be the mast of a fishing vessel dating back two thousand years. The boat was intact, if somewhat fragile. Kitchen utensils had survived their long water imprisonment; they bore evidence of the time of their use, and many local and foreign marine archeologists rushed to Galilee to inspect this quaint vessel and to evaluate its survival state.

The fishing vessel was carefully removed from the muddy water of the Sea of Galilee. Today it is on view in the lakeside *kibbutz* of Ginnosar, as a small but significant underwater find attesting to the importance of the fishing trade to the dwellers of Galilee.

In recent years Catholics have been relieved of the obligation to eat fish on Friday; but in the Holy Land the custom remains firm among Christian communities. Eating fish on Friday, and as the last meal on the Sabbath, is common practice in Jewish communities as well.

The simple factor of availability has contributed to the inclusion of so many fish dishes in Jewish cooking. And although Jewish dietary rules forbid the consumption of certain types of fish, unlike meat and fowl they do not have to be slaughtered ritually; nor is it required that the blood be drawn from the fish. Many fish dishes, therefore, are easy and quick to prepare. They are a boon to the barbecue chef, especially when strewn with rosemary or sage leaves.

Red mullet, sole, hake, grey mullet, haddock, and turbot are favorite Mediterranean fish. Red mullet is a particularly choice fish. It is one of the few fish that is cooked whole and not gutted. The liver and cheeks are considered delicacies, and are removed and prepared separately.

Because fresh fish decomposes quickly, it should be cooked as soon as possible. Broiling is the most popular method, depending on the type and size of the fish. The cook guts, cleans, washes, and scores the sides of the fish, and lightly brushes them with oil. Fish sprinkled with oregano or dill and broiled over charcoal are hard to beat. The diner squeezes fresh lemon wedges over the fish and enjoys. Another common method of preparing fish fillets is to dust them with flour or bread crumbs and fry them in hot olive oil. Small fish such as sardines and herrings can be dipped in an egg bath, then rolled in crumbs or flour and quickly fried in deep oil and drained. Large stuffed fish are generally baked for festive family meals. Fish stew is usually made from a large seasonal fish or cheap cuts of fish. These are used especially in making fumet (page 265), fish stock (pages 206–7), or gefilte fish (pages 264–65).

Herring Salad Appetizer

Traditionally, herring dishes are served to break the fast of Yom Kippur, to replace the salt excreted. But herring salad is good any time—for lunch, as an appetizer before dinner, or with cocktails.

2 fresh herrings (about 1¼ pounds) *or* 1 16-ounce jar herring fillets in oil
2 dill pickles, chopped
1 tablespoon chopped onion
½ pound apples, cut up
1 teaspoon honey *or* sugar
½ cup mayonnaise mixed with ½ cup sour cream
4 tablespoons vinegar
1 tablespoon chopped fresh parsley
black pepper, to taste
chopped lettuce leaves for garnish
stuffed olives for garnish

1. If you are using fresh herrings, soak them in water overnight. Clean, fillet, and chop them into small pieces. If you are using prepared herring, rinse them and chop into small pieces. 2. In a bowl, mix the herring with the pickles, onions, and apples. To this mixture add the honey or sugar, mayonnaise and sour cream, vinegar, and parsley. Add pepper to taste. Mound the herring salad on a dish, and surround it with a ring of chopped lettuce leaves and stuffed olives. *Makes about 2 pounds*

Herring Salad

Herring in many forms was very much a part of the early Israelite diet. In modern times, the early Jewish settlers realized too how important it was to replace the salt excreted during the hot months of the year. Herring salads like this one are often served for breakfast, both in *kibbutz* dining rooms and in the best hotels in Israel. Try this as a main course.

3 fresh herrings *or* 1 16-ounce jar
    pickled herrings
1 onion
6 to 8 black peppercorns
1 cup citrus vinegar
1 tablespoon sugar
2 teaspoons prepared horseradish
lettuce
cucumbers, sliced
2 teaspoons capers

Sauce:
4 hard-boiled eggs
juice of 2 lemons
1 cup sour cream
2 tablespoons tomato paste
2 tablespoons horseradish
1 tablespoon prepared mustard
1 teaspoon soy sauce

1. Clean the fresh herrings and soak them overnight in cold water. Skin the fish and bone it, filleting the flesh from the backbone. Slice into small pieces. If you are using pickled herring, rinse them and slice into small pieces. Arrange the herring in a shallow glass or crockery dish.   2. Slice the peeled onion in thin rings and spread them over the fish. Add the peppercorns. Mix the vinegar, sugar, and horseradish and pour carefully over the fish. Refrigerate for a few hours.   3. To prepare the sauce, mash the egg yolks with the lemon juice in a small bowl. Add the chopped egg whites and the remaining ingredients. 4. Remove the herrings from the marinade with a slotted spoon. Chop them and mix with the sauce. Spread the herring salad over a bed of lettuce and surround the salad with slices of cucumber. Scatter the capers on top. Serve with brown bread and butter as a luncheon dish. *Serves 4*

Gefilte Fish

❦ ❦ ❦

Fenugreek

3 pounds fresh fish (use at least two
    varieties, lean and fat, such as
    pike and carp or halibut, *or*
    whitefish with carp)
2 large onions, quartered
2 eggs, well beaten
1 cup bread crumbs *or* matzo meal
1 teaspoon salt
½ teaspoon black pepper

1 tablespoon water
1 tablespoon vegetable oil
1 quart fumet (page 265) *or* vegetable
    stock (pages 207–8)
2 carrots, sliced in rounds
lemon slices, for garnish
1 cup chopped fresh parsley, for
    garnish

1. Have the fishmonger clean and fillet the fish. Save the head, bones, and skin for the fumet. Grind the flesh in a grinder; add the onions and regrind.   2. In a large bowl, combine the beaten eggs, bread crumbs, salt, and pepper. Add the water and oil and knead the mixture well. Form the mixture into flat ovals (you may have to add more meal or water to make a firm cake).   3. Prepare the fumet or vegetable stock. In a large pot, bring the fumet to a boil. Carefully

lower the fishcakes into the stock, and top each with a sliced carrot. Bring the stock to a boil again, lower the heat, and cover the pot. Simmer for 2 hours. The stock will jell. **4.** Spoon some of the jellied stock onto a serving platter, and carefully arrange the fishcakes on the platter. Garnish with lemon slices and chopped parsley. Serve cold as an appetizer with beet horseradish (page 35). *Makes 3 pounds*

Variation: Gefilte Fish Balls. Form the fish mixture into small balls and simmer for 1 hour in boiling fumet. Serve with beet horseradish and toothpicks for cocktail appetizers. Strain the remaining soup stock, which will jell when it is chilled. It makes a delicious jellied fish consommé. Serve with lemon wedges.

Fumet

Fumet is a stock made from fish heads, bones, and skin. Use it as a basis for fish sauce, or as a poaching liquid.

4 cups water *or* **2 cups water and 2 cups wine**	**2 cloves garlic**
2 tablespoons lemon juice *or* **2 tablespoons wine vinegar**	**1 teaspoon ground thyme**
1 handful celeriac leaves *or* **celery leaves**	**2 tablespoons chopped fresh parsley**
2 carrots	**2 bay leaves**
1 onion	**1 teaspoon coriander seeds** *or* **1 tablespoon chopped fresh coriander leaves**
	1 pound fish heads, bones, and skin

1. In a stock pot, combine all ingredients except the fish heads, bones, and skin. Simmer for 20 minutes, then add the fish and simmer 30 minutes more. Jellied stock left after cooking the fish may be reheated, strained, and recooked until it is reduced. Use as a basis for a fish sauce. *Makes about 1 quart*

Cocktail Fish Fingers in Sherry Sauce

2 pounds fresh fish *or* frozen fish
2 cups bread crumbs
2 eggs
salt and black pepper, to taste
2 teaspoons ground cumin

1 cup vegetable oil
4 cloves garlic, crushed
1 cup sherry wine
1 cup wine vinegar
1 cup chopped fresh parsley

1. Finely grind the fish. In a bowl, combine it with the bread crumbs, eggs, salt, pepper, and cumin. With wet hands, roll the fish mixture into finger-shaped pieces.   2. In a frying pan, heat the oil. Carefully fry the fish fingers until they are golden. Remove them with a slotted spoon, drain, and arrange them in a large square or oblong ceramic dish.   3. To the remaining oil add the garlic, and fry until golden. Add the sherry and wine vinegar, and bring to a boil. Pour this sauce over the fish and sprinkle with parsley. Serve with toothpicks. *Serves 20 for cocktails*

Salt Cod in Milk

Serve this dish as an appetizer or as a luncheon meal with boiled potatoes.

2 pounds salt cod
2 tablespoons coriander seed
½ teaspoon ground black pepper
⅛ cup olive oil mixed with ⅛ cup
    vegetable oil

1 cup milk
2 cloves garlic, crushed
1 tablespoon mixed ground cumin,
    ground coriander, and cinnamon

1. To desalt and refresh the salt cod, soak it in water for at least 24 hours, changing the water several times. Rinse well.   2. In a large saucepan, cover the cod with cold water. Bring it to a boil and lower the heat. Poach the fish, covered, for 15 minutes. Drain the fish and refresh it under cold water. Remove and discard the skin and bones.   3. Cut the cod into medium-size pieces and sprinkle with the coriander and pepper. In a frying pan, heat the oil. Fry the cod until golden. Cover with the milk, add the garlic, and simmer for 10 minutes. Serve hot or cold, sprinkled with the cumin, coriander, and cinnamon mixture. *Serves 6*

Creamed Salt Cod

2 pounds salt cod
1¼ cups olive oil
1 cup thin cream, warmed
1 garlic clove, crushed

salt and freshly ground black pepper,
    to taste
12 slices French bread

1. Desalt and refresh the cod as described in salt cod in milk, step 1 (page 266).
2. In a glass container over hot water, warm the oil. In a saucepan, warm the cream. Pour a small amount of the oil into a saucepan, add the crushed garlic, and lower the heat. With a wooden spoon, mash the fish into the oil and garlic mixture. Continue to mash the fish, alternately adding 2 tablespoons each of the warmed oil and cream, being careful that the mixture does not simmer. When all the liquid has been absorbed, add the salt and pepper.   3. In a frying pan, heat the oil and fry the bread slices. Serve the creamed cod in a warmed dish surrounded with the fried bread. A mixed green salad is a good accompaniment. *Serves* 6

Marinated Fried Fish in Beer Batter

2 pounds fish fillets, flounder *or* hake
vegetable oil for frying
salt to taste
lemon wedges, for garnish
chopped fresh parsley, for garnish

Marinade:

¼ cup lemon juice
¼ cup vegetable oil
⅓ cup soy sauce
¼ teaspoon black pepper
¼ teaspoon ground coriander

Beer Batter:

2 tablespoons vegetable oil
2 cups all-purpose flour
¼ teaspoon salt
1 egg, beaten
½ teaspoon turmeric
1 can flat beer

1. Wash fish and pat dry. Cut into serving pieces.   2. In a bowl, mix all the marinade ingredients. Marinate the fish for a few hours or overnight.   3. To prepare the beer batter, stir the oil into the flour in a large bowl. Add the salt, beaten egg, and turmeric. Slowly add the beer and beat with a hand-held beater until smooth. Let the batter rest for 2 hours.   4. Drain the fish, reserving

the marinade for another time. In a frying pan, heat the oil. Dip pieces of fish into the beer batter, and deep fry them in the hot oil until golden (turmeric enhances the color). Drain on a rack or on paper towels. Sprinkle with salt. Serve hot, garnished with lemon wedges and parsley. *Serves 6*

Variation: Substitute drained sardines for the fillets. They do not have to be marinated first. Simply dip them in batter and fry. Serve with tartare sauce (page 212).

Cold Fried Fish Fillets

Fried fish is one of the classic Sabbath dishes. It's served as a first course on Friday night dinner, or as a main course for the Sabbath lunch.

1½ pounds fish fillets (sole, sea bass, *or* whiting)	1 teaspoon ground cumin
1½ cups bread crumbs *or* matzo meal, mixed with 1 tablespoon cornstarch	2 eggs beaten with 2 tablespoons water
	vegetable oil for frying
salt and pepper, to taste	lemon wedges, for garnish

1. Wash the fish fillets and pat dry with paper towels. In a flat dish, mix the bread crumbs with salt, pepper, and cumin. In a second dish, beat the eggs and water. 2. In a frying pan, pour the oil to a depth of ⅛ inch. Heat. Dip the fillets, one at a time, first into the beaten egg and then into the bread crumbs. When the oil is hot but not smoking, place the fillets in the pan. Fry on one side until golden, then fry on the second side. 3. Drain the fried fillets on a rack or on paper towels. Serve cold or at room temperature with lemon wedges. *Serves 4 to 6*

Deep-fried Fish

12 whole small fish (red mullet *or* mackerel) for 6 servings	salt and pepper, to taste
1 lemon	1 teaspoon oregano
vegetable oil *or* fat for frying	2 eggs beaten with 2 tablespoons water
1 tablespoon all-purpose flour	lemon wedges, for garnish

1. Have the fishmonger clean and scale the fish. If you do it at home, soak the fish in water for a few minutes to soften it. Scale with a fork, remove the intestines, and wash in cold water. Rub inside and out with a cut lemon and sprinkle with salt.   2. In a deep frying pan, heat the oil or fat. In a flat dish, combine the flour, salt, pepper, and oregano. In another dish, beat the eggs and water. Roll the fish first in the seasoned flour, then dip in the egg. Roll again in flour, and shake off surplus flour. Arrange a few fish at a time in a frying basket, and fry them in hot oil for 5 to 8 minutes. The fish is done when it rises to the surface. Drain on a rack or on paper towels. Serve hot with lemon wedges or tartare sauce (page 212). *Serves 6*

Fish Fillets
in Grape Sauce

ఴ ఴ ఴ

With a rich soup to start, and fruit and cheese for dessert, this recipe makes an easy supper.

3 to 4 pounds fillet of hake *or*
    flounder
2 cups all-purpose flour
salt and pepper, to taste
1 teaspoon allspice
2 tablespoons butter *or* **margarine** *or*
    vegetable oil
2 tablespoons chopped fresh parsley
juice of 2 lemons

Sauce:
1½ pounds seedless grapes
1 tablespoon butter
2 tablespoons water
½ cup dry white wine
1 tablespoon sugar

1. Wash the fillets and pat dry. In a flat pan, mix the flour, salt, pepper, and allspice.   2. In a frying pan, heat the butter. Sauté the fillets over moderate heat for about 5 minutes. Fry 5 minutes more on the other side. Put the fillets in a warm, ovenproof dish and keep them warm.   3. Allow the butter to brown. Stir in parsley and lemon juice, and pour over the fish.   4. To make the sauce, put the grapes (reserve some for garnish) in a saucepan with the butter and water. Cover the pan and cook until the grapes are soft. Put them in a colander and press out the juice. Return the grape juice to the pan. Add the wine and sugar, and stir until the mixture is smooth. Cook, stirring, until the sauce thickens.   5. Pour the sauce over the fish. Broil the fish for a few minutes, or bake them in a preheated 350° oven for 5 minutes. Garnish with uncooked grapes and serve. *Serves 6*

Fried Fish
with *Tahini* Sauce

2 pounds grey mullet *or* halibut *or*
    haddock
all-purpose flour
vegetable oil for frying
1 tablespoon freshly ground
    coriander seeds
½ cup chopped fresh parsley

Tahini Sauce for Fish:

juice of 2 lemons *or* 2 tablespoons
    wine vinegar
¼ pint prepared *tahini* paste
½ cup water
2 cloves garlic, crushed
salt and pepper, to taste
1 teaspoon ground cumin

1. Wash the fish and pat dry. Dust them with flour, and shake off the excess.
2. In a frying pan, heat the oil. Fry the fish until just golden. Put them on a warm ovenproof dish. 3. To prepare the sauce, stir the lemon juice or wine vinegar into the *tahini* paste in a small bowl. Mix until smooth. Thin with water and add garlic. When the mixture is smooth, add the salt, pepper, and cumin. 4. Pour the remaining pan juices over the fish. Spoon the *tahini* sauce over the entire dish and sprinkle with ground coriander. Broil on medium (if possible) for 5 minutes or until the sauce is just slightly browned. Garnish with parsley and serve immediately. *Serves 6*

Broiled Red Mullet
with Orange Sauce

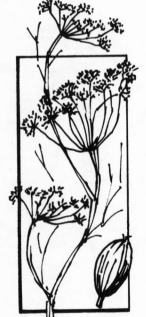

Fennel

3 large or 6 small red mullets *or* red
    snappers
salt
4 teaspoons chopped fresh fennel
    leaves *or* 2 tablespoons dried
    fennel
2 tablespoons rosemary
1 large bunch fresh fennel, including
    stalks
4 tablespoons vegetable oil
salt and pepper, to taste
half-slices of orange, for garnish
chopped fresh parsley, for garnish

Orange Sauce:

3 tablespoons butter
3 tablespoons all-purpose flour
juice of 2 oranges (about 1 cup)
1 bouillon cube dissolved in 1 cup
    hot water

1. Clean and scale the fish. Wash, pat dry, and salt inside and out. Fill the fish with the chopped fennel and rosemary. In a broiling pan, make a bed of fennel branches. Brush the fish with oil on both sides and place on a wire rack above the broiling pan.   2. Broil under medium heat, if possible. Don't let the fish burn. Turn the fish and brush again with oil. Put on a warm serving platter. 3. To prepare the sauce, stir the butter and flour together in a saucepan over medium heat. When well blended, stir in the orange juice and add the bouillion cube. Cook a few minutes more, then pour the sauce over the fish. Decorate with slices of oranges and chopped parsley. *Serves 6*

Marinated Fish Steaks

6 fish steaks (hake *or* cod *or*
    swordfish)

Marinade:

½ cup soy sauce
½ cup orange juice *or* pomegranate
    juice
3 tablespoons oil
2 tablespoons tomato paste
1 tablespoon lemon juice
½ teaspoon pepper
½ teaspoon oregano
1 teaspoon ground ginger
2 cloves garlic, chopped
3 tablespoons chopped fresh parsley

Sauce:

marinade
1 tablespoon butter *or* margarine
2 tablespoons all-purpose flour

1. Wash the fish and pat dry. Place them in 1 layer in a baking pan or large ovenproof glass dish. In a bowl, combine the ingredients for the marinade and pour it over the fish. Refrigerate for 1 hour; turn and marinate for 1 more hour.   2. Pour off the marinade and reserve it. Broil the fish under medium heat (if possible) for 10 minutes on each side, or grill the fish over red-hot coals for 8 minutes on each side.   3. To make a sauce, strain the marinade. In a saucepan, melt the butter and whisk in the flour. Add the marinade slowly and stir until smooth and thickened. Serve the steaks with sauce or lemon wedges. *Serves 6*

Baked Hake Au Gratin

❦ ❦ ❦

3 pounds hake fillets
salt and pepper, to taste
1 teaspoon olive oil
2 onions, chopped
2 cloves garlic, crushed
juice of 2 lemons
1 4-ounce can button mushrooms,
    halved, or 1 ounce dried
    mushrooms, reconstituted

10 sliced olives
2 hard-boiled eggs, chopped
2 sprigs fresh parsley, chopped
2 tablespoons bread crumbs or matzo
    meal
1 cup cooked chickpeas
¼ cup butter or margarine, cubed
parsley, for garnish

1. Wash the fish fillets and pat dry. Season with salt and pepper, to taste. Pour the oil over the bottom of a baking dish. Add the chopped onions and garlic. Place the fillets on top and season with the lemon juice. 2. In a bowl, chop together the mushrooms, olives, eggs, parsley, and bread crumbs (reserve 1 teaspoon of bread crumbs for topping). Scatter the chickpeas and chopped mixture over the fish; dot with butter or margarine. Sprinkle on the remaining bread crumbs. Bake in a preheated 350° oven for 30 minutes. Garnish with chopped parsley and serve. *Serves 6*

Fish and Turnip Stew

❦ ❦ ❦

This stew is a main course. It uses a selection of fish, and is characterized by its sharp, hot taste. Here Mediterranean fish are combined with Sea of Galilee fish.

⅝ cup olive oil
6 cloves garlic, crushed
1 chili pepper, chopped
3 medium tomatoes
½ cup chopped fresh parsley
1 large onion, chopped
salt, to taste

4 cups fumet (page 265)
1 pound turnips, peeled and cut into
    ½-inch slices
3 pounds fish (2 or 3 varieties,
    including carp, halibut, turbot,
    grey mullet, hake)
lemon wedges

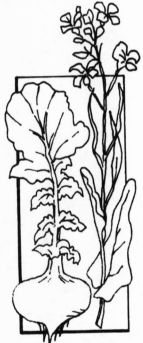

Turnip

1. In a stewing pot, heat the oil. Add the garlic, chili pepper, tomatoes, parsley, and onion. Cook for about 10 minutes. 2. Prepare the fumet, strain, and add to the pot. Bring to a boil and add the turnips. Cover and cook on medium heat for 10 minutes, or until the turnips are tender. Add the cut-up pieces of fish or fish steaks. Lower the heat and simmer for about 10 minutes. Serve in soup bowls garnished with wedges of lemon. *Serves 6*

Fish Filling
for *Sanbusak* Pastry

1 pound fish (carp, pike, hake),
    ground
1 medium onion, grated
½ cup bread crumbs *or* matzo meal
black pepper, to taste
½ teaspoon ground cumin
1 teaspoon soy sauce

1 teaspoon celery salt
1 teaspooon vegetable oil
1 egg
sanbusak pastry (pages 61–62)
yolk of 1 egg beaten with 1
    tablespoon water for basting
sesame seeds, for garnish

1. In a large bowl, mix the fish, onion, bread crumbs, pepper, cumin, soy sauce, celery salt, vegetable oil, and egg. Blend until smooth.　2. Make the *sanbusak* pastry. Roll out the dough thinly and cut it into 4-inch rounds with a pastry cutter or glass. Put 1 heaping teaspoon of filling in the center of half of a round. Fold over the second half to make a half-moon shape. Seal by pinching the edges tightly with your fingers or a fork. Baste with the egg yolk mixture and sprinkle with sesame seeds. Bake in a preheated 350° oven for 40 to 45 minutes, or until brown. *Makes about 24 pastries, serves 4 to 6*

Red Bream with Fennel,
Thyme, and White Wine

2-pound red bream *or* 6 ¼- to ½-
    pound fish (you may also use
    halibut)
3 sprigs of fresh thyme
¼ cup butter
salt and pepper, to taste

3 sprigs fresh fennel
2 onions, grated
½ cup chopped fresh parsley
1 tablespoon olive oil
1¼ cups dry white wine
1 or 2 lemons, sliced in thin rounds

1. Wash the fish and pat dry. Stuff the cavity with sprigs of thyme, knobs of butter, salt, and pepper. Make an incision in the fish's back and insert the fresh fennel sprigs.　2. Place the fish on a greased oven rack over an oven pan layered with grated onions and chopped parsley. Pour the oil and wine over the fish. Place the rounds of lemon on top of fish.　3. Bake in a preheated 350° oven for 20 to 25 minutes, basting once with pan juices during this time. Pour the pan juices over the fish and serve immediately. *Serves 6*

11 DAIRY AND EGGS

🐛 🐛 🐛

"A land flowing milk and honey" was a phrase first applied to the Holy Land by two of the spies sent by Moses to gauge its desirability for settlement. The fact that these two products were singled out for their abundance attests to the high regard in which they were held. "Milk and honey" has since become a synonym for affluence.

DAIRY

Although the milk drunk in the Land of Israel in biblical times came primarily from sheep and goats, cow's milk was also consumed. (The camel was considered ritually unclean and the Israelites did not accept its milk, although this was the principal drink of the Bedouins in the deserts of the area.) Milk was considered a "safe" drink, unlike water, which could be contaminated. Milk could not be kept fresh for long; but sour, curdled milk was regarded as a delicacy, something special for an esteemed guest—in fact, it was brought by Abraham to his three unexpected visitors (Genesis 18:8). Out of protest against a Canaanite sacrificial custom of making a charm by boiling a kid in the milk of its mother, such a practice was strictly forbidden to the Israelites; this ban was taken so severely by later rabbis that they insisted on a waiting period of several hours between the eating of meat and milk products. Milk is mentioned only four times in the New Testament—and three of these are metaphorical.

Yogurt
Yogurt is the one food common to all communities of cooking in the Middle East. It seems to go with everything, depending on family custom and religious tradition. Milk products, including sweet cream, sour cream, low-fat yogurt, and a broad assortment of cheeses, are eaten in at least one meal of the day. One festival in the Jewish calendar very much associated with milk products is the feast of Pentecost (Shavuot), which celebrates the revelation on Mount

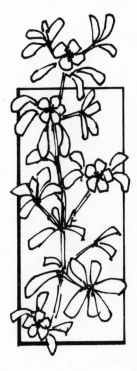

Purslane

Sinai. During that time all manner of milk dishes are served, and most of them are accompanied by yogurt or sour cream.

There is some controversy about who invented the yogurt process. Probably it happened by chance, when nomadic goatkeepers poured milk into goatskin containers. The warm sun changed the character of the milk, causing lactic acid–producing bacteria to ferment the milk. The result had a light, custardy consistency—namely, yogurt.

Making yogurt for the family is a cherished, personalized operation. The tastes differ, depending on how sour family members like their yogurt.

Although today there are many gadgets and bits of equipment on the market to facilitate the process, yogurt making is quite uncomplicated. The principle involved is similar to that in making sourdough bread: it requires a starter. A yogurt starter or activator (culture of the bacteria *bularis*) is the main requirement. You can buy it dry in a health food store, or you can use fresh, live yogurt. Once you start making your own yogurt, put aside a portion of it for the next batch.

Homemade Yogurt: In a heavy enamel saucepan, bring 4 cups of milk to a boil until the froth begins to rise. Lower the heat and let the milk simmer for 2 minutes. Turn off the heat and allow the milk to cool slightly. Put one finger in, and leave it there while you count up to 10. If you have to pull it out, it's too hot. Milk cooler or hotter than this test will not produce a good yogurt. Remove any scum from the top.

In a large glass or earthenware bowl, beat 2 tablespoons of activator or plain yogurt until liquefied. Slowly add a few tablespoons of the warmed milk in a stream, beating with one hand and adding the rest of the milk with the other until the mixture is thoroughly blended.

Cover the bowl with a sheet of plastic wrap and fasten it with a rubber band. Wrap the bowl in a woolen blanket or shawl and place it in a warm place free from drafts for 8 hours or overnight.

When it is ready, refrigerate it. It will remain fresh up to a week, but if you succeed in making it there probably won't be much left after a few days. Remember to save part of it to use as a starter for a new batch.

Stabilized Yogurt for Cooking: To stabilize yogurt for cooking, combine 2 tablespoons of yogurt with 2 teaspoons of cornstarch. In a heavy saucepan, uncovered, bring to a boil 2 cups of yogurt mixed with the cornstarch mixture. Simmer it over low heat for about 10 minutes. Stir, in one direction only, until it has thickened. Allow the yogurt to cook before using.

Cheese

Butter as we know it was not made in biblical times, but cheese was popular. The Bible has only two references to cheese—Job 10:10 and 1 Samuel 17:18—where it refers to a cottage cheese. However, by the New Testament period, there was a guild of cheesemakers in Jerusalem who gave their name to the Valley of the Cheesemakers near the Temple.

Many cheeses developed out of the basic yogurt process. The popular Middle Eastern feta cheese is similar to the white cheese eaten in ancient times. The cheese was pressed and then put into brine to preserve it.

Feta-type cheeses were made from goat's or sheep's milk as well as cow's milk (the latter were used less and had the blandest taste). Whereas the cream cheeses melt in baking, the white pressed cheeses do not; they are therefore used in many pastry recipes and dishes combining vegetables and cheese.

Labna Cheese: You can make a simple cheese from sour milk or yogurt. Pour the sour milk or yogurt into a sieve or colander lined with cheesecloth, or into a dampened cotton tea cloth placed over a bowl. Allow the whey to drain; this takes at least 8 hours, or overnight. When dry, shape the curds into a ball, or press into a bowl. Season with salt or sugar if you wish.

Herb and Cheese Filling
for *Sanbusak* Pastry

½ pound feta cheese
½ pound cottage cheese
2 tablespoons chopped fresh parsley
2 tablespoons chopped chives

pepper, to taste
1 egg, beaten
sanbusak pastry (pages 61–62)

1. In a bowl, mash the feta cheese with a fork. Add the cottage cheese, parsley, chives, pepper, and egg. Mix well.   2. To make pastry, see fish filling for *sanbusak* pastry (page 273), step 2. Cut the pastry into triangles or crescents. Fill with cheese filling and close up pastry.   3. Bake in a preheated 350° for 40 minutes, or until brown. *Makes about 24 pastries, serves 4 to 6*

Chard and Feta Cheese Filling
for *Sanbusak* Pastry

2 pounds Swiss chard
1 large onion, chopped
1 tablespoon olive oil
3 eggs
2 teaspoons dried parsley
½ teaspoon ground nutmeg

½ teaspoon black pepper
2 cups crumbled feta cheese
sanbusak pastry (pages 61–62)
1 egg, lightly beaten
sesame seeds, for garnish

1. Wash the chard. Cook it in boiling water or steam until the stems are limp. Drain. Cool slightly and chop or scissor-cut the leaves.   2. In a pan, cook the onion in 1 tablespoon of the olive oil. Cover and stir occasionally until the onion is limp.   3. In a large bowl, beat the eggs. Add the chard, onion, parsley, nutmeg, pepper, and feta.   4. To make and fill the pastry, see fish filling for *sanbusak* pastry (page 273), step 2.   5. Arrange the crescents on an ungreased baking sheet. Brush the surfaces with the egg and sprinkle on sesame seeds. Bake in a preheated 400° oven about 40 minutes, or until nicely browned. Serve soon after baking. *Makes about 24 pastries, serves 4 to 6*

Cottage Cheese Soufflé

1½ pounds cottage cheese
3 eggs, separated
6 tablespoons margarine, melted
3 tablespoons all-purpose flour

16 ounces yogurt
salt and pepper, to taste
½ teaspoon oregano
½ cup grated Parmesan cheese

1. In a bowl, beat the cheese, egg yolks, and margarine until well blended. Add the flour, yogurt, salt, pepper, and oregano. Beat the egg whites until they form soft peaks and carefully fold them into the mixture.   2. Pour into a well-greased casserole or soufflé dish. Sprinkle the top with Parmesan cheese. Bake in a preheated 350° oven until golden and well risen. Serve immediately. (Keep your guests waiting, but not the soufflé!) *Serves 4 to 6*

Sesame

Potato-Cheese Pancakes (Latkes)

❦ ❦ ❦

2 pounds potatoes (3 cups, peeled and
    cut up)
1 medium onion, grated
3 eggs separated
salt and black pepper, to taste
½ teaspoon nutmeg
3 tablespoons matzo meal

3 tablespoons all-purpose flour (if not
    using matzo meal, increase flour
    to 6 tablespoons)
4 ounces Gruyere cheese, grated
    (about 1 cup grated)
2 tablespoons vegetable oil

1. Grate the potatoes by hand on the fine or medium holes of a grater. Or, grate the potatoes with the onion in an electric blender. Drain in a colander.   2. In a large bowl, mix the potatoes and onion with the egg yolks, salt, pepper, nutmeg, matzo meal, and flour. Grate the cheese into the potato mixture. If the batter is too liquid, add more flour or matzo meal. Beat the egg whites until they form stiff peaks and fold them into the mixture.   3. In a large skillet, heat the oil. When the oil is moderately hot, drop in the potato batter by tablespoonsful. Fry until medium brown on both sides. Drain on paper towels and serve with applesauce. *Serves 4 to 6*

Blintzes with Cheese Filling

❦ ❦ ❦

vegetable oil for frying

Batter:

4 eggs
1 cup water
salt, to taste
2 tablespoons vegetable oil
1 cup all-purpose flour

Cheese Filling:

2 cups cottage cheese
½ teaspoon salt
2 tablespoons sugar
1 tablespoon all-purpose flour
1 tablespoon butter *or* margarine,
    melted
¼ cup seedless raisins (optional)

1. To prepare the batter, mix all ingredients by hand or blend until smooth in an electric blender.   2. Lightly grease a 7-inch skillet and heat it until hot but not smoking. Pour about 2 tablespoons of batter into it, and quickly tilt the skillet so that the batter thinly covers the bottom of pan. When the underside is lightly browned, carefully turn the pancake out on a large napkin or tea towel, browned side up. Continue to make pancakes, stacking them, until the batter is used. Cover the *blintzes* with plastic wrap and finish cooking later, or

continue the recipe. 3. To prepare the filling, beat all the ingredients until well mixed. (Use the raisins if you are making blintzes for dessert.) Spread a heaping tablespoon of filling along one side of the pancake, turn in the ends, and roll up. 4. Fry the *blintzes* in oil in a hot frying pan, or bake them in a preheated 425° oven until browned. Serve with sour cream or cinnamon sugar (½ teaspoon cinnamon mixed with ⅓ cup fine sugar). Seasoned applesauce also makes a nice accompaniment. *Makes about 20 blintzes*

Milk Puddings

Fresh, warm milk was considered to be a remedy for chest pains. Some believed that girls who drank milk would become fairer! The special pudding-custard made from orchid roots (page 40) was served warm or cold.

Although the following milk-based puddings generally are served cold, especially in summer, this type of pudding was undoubtedly served at room temperature in ancient times.

Oriental Milk Pudding

2 tablespoons quick-cooking rice
   cereal
½ cup sugar
1 tablespoon cornstarch *or* potato
   flour
2½ cups milk
¼ teaspoon almond extract

2 teaspoons rose water
½ cup blanched almonds, ground
crystallized rose petals, for garnish, *or*
   fruit in season *or* whipped cream

1. In the upper part of a double boiler or a heat-proof glass bowl over a pot of hot water, mix the rice, sugar, and cornstarch. Stir in some of the milk. Heat the remaining milk, and pour it into the rice mixture. Cook over a medium flame, stirring until well-mixed and thickened. 2. Stir in the almond extract, rose water, and almonds, leaving some for a garnish. Cover and chill. Garnish with almonds and rose petals, fruit, or whipped cream. *Serves 4*

Almond Milk Pudding

This pudding was once considered a royal delight.

2 heaping tablespoons all-purpose
    flour
2 heaping tablespoons rice flour
½ cup cold water
4 cups milk

1 cup sugar
⅔ cup finely ground blanched
    almonds
1 tablespoon rose water *or* almond
    extract

1. In a bowl, mix the flour, rice flour, and water to a smooth paste.   2. In the upper part of a double boiler, combine the milk and sugar and stir gently. (If you use a regular pan, stir constantly, being careful not to scrape the bottom of the pan in case the milk has scorched.) When the milk comes to a boil, gradually add the rice-and-flour paste and continue stirring. Cook 30 minutes, stirring occasionally, or until the mixture has thickened enough to coat the back of the spoon. Add the ground almonds and stir well. Cook 5 minutes more.   3. Remove the pan from the heat and stir in the rose water. Cool and serve in individual glass bowls, or in a large glass bowl. Garnish with blanched almonds, if you wish. *Makes 6*

Variation: Rose Water Milk Pudding. Make almond milk pudding, but use ¾ cup water and 2 tablespoons rose water. Pour the pudding into a flat, square glass dish (the pudding should be about 1 inch deep) and refrigerate overnight. Serve in the same dish, or cut into serving portions. Just before serving, put ¼ cup confectioners' sugar into a strainer and shake it over the pudding. Sprinkle on a little rose water and garnish with blackberries or strawberries.

Pears Filled
with Cheese and Mint

3 large pears
1 8-ounce package cream cheese
½ cup sweet cream
½ cup fresh mint leaves

1 jigger crème de menthe (if serving
    for dessert)
nasturtium *or* geranium leaves, for
    garnish
6 fresh mint leaves, for garnish

1. Peel the pears, cut them in half, and scoop out the middle.   2. In a bowl, mix the cheese and cream by hand. Blend the mint leaves with the crème de menthe (omit the liqueur if you are serving the pears as part of a salad platter)

and add to the cheese mixture. 3. Fill the pears with the cheese mixture. Serve on glass plates, with pears placed on nasturtium leaves or large geranium leaves. Place 1 mint leaf on each serving as a garnish. *Serves 6*

Custard

This basic custard is a basis for many variations.

5 egg yolks
½ cup castor sugar
2 cups milk

1. In a bowl, beat the egg yolks with the sugar until light. 2. In the top of a double boiler or in a heat-proof glass bowl over hot water, bring the milk just to a boil. Add the beaten yolks and lower the heat. Cook, stirring, until the mixture thickens. 3. Pour into individual serving dishes and refrigerate, use warm, or use as the basis of a recipe such as apricot mousse (below). *Makes 2 cups*

Apricot Mousse

½ cup heavy cream, whipped
1 cup prepared custard (above)
½ cup roasted almonds, ground
½ teaspoon vanilla extract
½ teaspoon almond extract
1 3-ounce package lemon gelatin

1 cup hot water
3 egg whites
3 tablespoons sugar
1 pound fresh, ripe apricots, pitted
peeled, sliced apricots, for garnish
6 cherries, for garnish

1. In a bowl, combine the whipped cream, custard, almonds, vanilla extract, and almond extract. Blend until smooth. 2. Dissolve the gelatin in the hot water. Cool, and refrigerate until it is slightly thickened. 3. Beat the egg whites with the sugar until stiff peaks form, and fold into the gelatin. Fold this into the whipped cream mixture until evenly blended. Refrigerate until set. 4. Pour this mixture into 6 sherbet glasses, filling them about ¾ full. Purée the unpeeled apricots in an electric blender. Refrigerate until set. Pour the apricot purée over the mousse when it has set, and garnish with slices of peeled apricots and cherries. *Serves 6*

Chocolate-Almond Mousse

6 ounces bitter chocolate
3 eggs, separated
2 teaspoons unflavored gelatin
    softened in 3 tablespoons cold
    water
⅛ teaspoon salt
⅛ teaspoon cream of tartar

3 tablespoons sugar
3 tablespoons cognac
1½ cups heavy cream, whipped
½ cup chopped, blanched almonds
1 square semisweet chocolate, melted
    and cooled
½ teaspoon instant coffee

1. In the top of a double boiler, melt the chocolate over low heat. In a small bowl, beat the egg yolks slightly. Beat some of the melted chocolate into the egg yolks, then stir the egg yolk mixture into the pan of chocolate. Cook and stir, without boiling, until the mixture thickens. Stir the softened gelatin into the chocolate mixture until the gelatin is dissolved. Cool.   2. In a small bowl, beat the egg whites with the salt and cream of tartar until it forms stiff peaks. Gradually mix in the sugar.   3. Stir the cognac into the cooled chocolate mixture, and fold in the stiff egg whites. Fold in 1 cup of the whipped cream and add the chopped nuts. Refrigerate for at least 8 hours or overnight.   4. Just before serving, mix the melted semisweet chocolate and coffee together. Blend with the remaining whipped cream. Serve the mousse in individual dishes, topped with a dollop of this flavored whipped cream. *Serves* 6

Devorah's Quick Blender Chocolate Cream

This is the easiest dessert I know. Serve it in demitasse cups, because it is rich, or in small dessert bowls topped with whipped cream or roasted nuts.

4 ounces bitter chocolate *or* 4 ounces
    cooking chocolate
1 teaspoon strong coffee

½ cup sugar
3 eggs
1 jigger orange liqueur *or* Sabra
    liqueur

1. In the top of a double boiler, melt the chocolate. Stir in the coffee and sugar, and cool.   2. In an electric blender, blend the eggs until thick. Add the chocolate mixture and the liqueur and blend until smooth. *Serves 8*

EGGS

The Bible has little to say about the egg. There is a reference in Deuteronomy 22:6 to birds' eggs and the compassionate command to drive away the mother before taking the eggs from the nest. However, rabbinical commentary concerning eggs is fuller. Eggs are said to be permitted food, with one exception: an egg that shows a blood-spot on the yolk, an indication that the embryo is beginning to form and as such is a living form. Religious law does not allow Jews to eat part of a living animal.

Eggs were used in ancient times as a standard measure of volume, not only in Jewish law but as a common denominator. It seems, however, that the egg scale was that of a desert chicken, which is considerably larger than today's largest chicken egg. Two present-day eggs are considered equal to one of the earlier desert vintage.

Folklore has described the egg as having laxative qualities, and as being capable of exciting sexual stimulation. It is associated with mourning, in that it is "round and has no mouth." One must not open one's mouth to complain of one's fate. It is described as a wheel encircling the earth, ever revolving.

A roasted egg is one of the symbolic items of the Passover Seder plate. It symbolizes the paschal sacrifice, which came to an end with the destruction of the Temple in Jerusalem. Hard-boiled eggs, in a bowl of salted water, are also served in many communities for the Passover-eve meal.

Although modern dietary recommendations suggest eating only three eggs a week to ensure a low cholesterol level, few people in Israel follow that advice. Eggs supply an important portion of the week's food intake, especially in a diet that leans heavily on dairy food, vegetables, and cereals.

Eggs are easy to prepare in many forms: boiled, poached, fried, or scrambled. Combining vegetables, cheese, or leftover meats with eggs is a cook's standby. In the Middle East *pashtida*, an egg-based dish, glorifies any leftovers. No matter how humble the ingredients may be, they are well seasoned. In fact, the recipe is often made from fresh ingredients.

Baked Eggs and Spinach

1 pound spinach, lightly steamed	1 egg
1 tablespoon margarine	1 tablespoon béchamel sauce (page
2 tablespoons cheddar cheese, grated,	209)
or cottage cheese	

1. Combine the cooked spinach and margarine and make a bed of them in the bottom of an individual ovenproof dish. Sprinkle lightly with the grated cheese, and break the egg on top. Cover the egg with the béchamel sauce, and

Spinach Beet

bake in a preheated 350° oven about 10 minutes, or until the egg is set. Serve as is, or sprinkle with 2 additional tablespoons of cheese and brown under broiler for a few minutes. *Serves 1*

Hard-boiled Brown Eggs
(*Hamindas*)

Cooking eggs in this manner goes back centuries. *Hamindas* continue to be an important part of Sephardic cuisine in Israel and in Sephardic communities around the world. Ground coffee is sometimes added to the water, to obtain a darker egg color. *Hamindas* are sometimes cooked in the *cholent* pot (see pages 94–95). The lengthy cooking changes the color of the egg albumen to brown, and darkens the yolks, which become wonderfully creamy.

12 raw eggs in their shells	**water to cover**
onion skins from 6 onions	**¼ cup vegetable oil**

1. Place the eggs and onion skins in a large saucepan and cover with water, several inches above the eggs. Pour the oil on top of the water to slow down the evaporation process during the long cooking.   2. Cover the pan and simmer over very low heat for 8 hours or overnight. Or put the eggs into a large casserole or glass pot, cover with brown wrapping paper, and bake in a preheated 200° oven for 10 hours or overnight. Serve hot or cold. *Serves 12*

Leek Omelet

1 pound leeks *or* **1 pound spinach**	**salt and pepper, to taste**
butter *or* **margarine** *or* **vegetable oil**	**½ teaspoon ground allspice**
juice of a ½ lemon	**6 eggs**

1. Wash the leeks (see page 168) and remove the tough green leaves. Cut into thin slices. In a frying pan, cook the leeks gently in margarine or oil. Season with lemon juice, salt, pepper, and allspice, and allow the leeks to cook in their own juices until partially done.   2. In a bowl, beat the eggs well. Add the leeks. Pour into a well-oiled skillet and cook until the underside is crisp and well done. Turn the omelet and cook the other side, or place the skillet under the broiler until the top is brown. Cut into wedges and serve with yogurt. *Makes 3 2-egg omelets, or 6 1-egg omelets*

Chicken, Rice,
and Egg *Pashtida*

This *pashtida* is a main course. Serve it with a substantial salad of mixed greens and a fruit dessert. It is an easily made, tasty supper.

2 tablespoons olive oil
1 medium onion, chopped
1 garlic clove, crushed
2 or 3 cardamom pods, crushed
salt and pepper, to taste
¼ teaspoon turmeric
4 eggs

2 cups cooked chicken, cut-up
2 cups cooked white rice *or* brown
   rice
1 15- or 16-ounce can chickpeas,
   drained
2 tablespoons chopped fresh parsley

1. In a large skillet, heat the oil over medium-high heat. Sauté the onion and garlic until soft. Stir in the cardamom pods, salt, pepper, and turmeric until well combined.   2. In a large bowl, beat the eggs. Add the chicken, rice, chickpeas, and the onion and garlic mixture. Mix well.   3. Pour the *pashtida* mixture into a greased ovenproof dish. Cover and bake in a preheated 350° oven for 5 minutes. Remove the cover and bake 15 minutes more, or until the top browns. Garnish with parsley and serve in the baking dish. *Serves 4*

Vegetable and
Herb *Pashtida*

1 pound spring onions, finely
   chopped
1 pound fresh spinach, finely
   chopped, *or* Swiss chard
1 tablespoon fresh hyssop, finely
   chopped, *or* oregano
1 tablespoon fresh coriander leaves,
   finely chopped, *or* 1 teaspoon
   ground coriander seed

1 bunch fresh chives, finely chopped
4 eggs, beaten
salt and pepper, to taste
½ cup finely chopped walnuts *or*
   almonds
5 tablespoons softened margarine *or*
   butter
½ cup finely chopped fresh dill

1. In a large bowl, mix all the ingredients.   2. Pour the mixture into a greased ovenproof dish. Cover and bake in a preheated 350° oven for 30 minutes. Remove the cover and bake 15 minutes more, or until it forms a brown crust. Cut into wedges and serve, accompanied by yogurt mixed with chopped fresh dill. *Serves 12 as an appetizer, or 6 as a main dish*

12 COOKING WITH BIBLICAL FLOWERS

❦ ❦ ❦

The three flowers mentioned in the Bible are bulbous. Two of them belong to the *Liliaceae* family: the white madonna lily (*Lilium candidum*) and the coastal white sand lily (*Pancretium maritimum*). The Rose of Sharon is described in the Song of Solomon: "I am the Rose of Sharon, a lily of the valleys, as the lily among brambles, so is my love among maidens." "Rose of Sharon" is a mistranslation, and people have wrongly assumed that the brambles were those of the rose bush. Actually, the rose (*rosa* in Latin and *vered* in Hebrew) is *not* mentioned in the Bible. However, there is no doubt that roses grew wild in the Holy Land. These wild roses have five petals, whereas the lily flowers have six. (Post-biblical literature suggests that the Hebrew word for lily, *shoshan*, derives from the Hebrew word for six, *shesh*.)

The third biblical flower mentioned is the narcissus (*Narcissus tazetta*), with which the popular daffodil is often confused. A wild plant with small-cupped white-and-yellow flowers in clusters, it is often called paper-white narcissus.

Although the identified flowers of the Bible are so few, biblical vegetables, fruits, and herbs are crowned with edible blossoms and seeds. Many of these plants were used extensively in medicants, flavorings, and scent. It is reasonable to assume that the ancient Hebrew people, as farmers and wild plant gatherers, enjoyed blossoms and seeds as well. Therefore we will extend the cast of biblical flowers to include all manner of food-providing blossoms and seeds. As it has been written in Revelation 22:2, "the leaves of trees are for the healing of nations." How much more so might fragrant and sweet-tasting blossoms soothe the terror among warring peoples!

Most people rarely eat flowers. One reason is a lack of knowledge concerning edible flora among many gardeners and chefs. Not a few home gardeners are reluctant to pick flowers for indoor arrangements, and are less enthusiastic about picking flowers for soups, teas, fruit salads, or jams. The garden show is the prime thing! However, some gardeners enjoy both the flower show and the

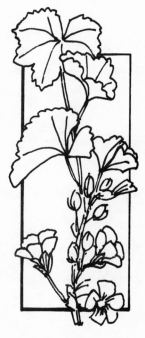

Mallow

opportunity to dip into nature's floral basket for their daily dose of vitamins and minerals. This is easily realized by using the leaves and stems of flowering plants long after their flowers are no longer beautiful to behold.

Much descriptive discourse has been derived from flora and fauna sources in nature, not all of them complimentary. For example, "going to seed" has long carried a derogatory connotation. In general, it is true that flowers should be picked before they go to seed; otherwise, as the plant expends its energy in seed production, its strength is drawn away from the plant's capacity to produce more flowers. However, it is possible, depending on the size of the garden, to leave a few perennial plants to complete their cycle of growth and reproductive action. The ensuing seeds are storehouses of natural, health-giving properties. When we consider that the seed-bearing plants are the highest in the evolutionary scale, why not enjoy them?

If no garden or terrace planting area is available to you—and even if it is—why not go out with the children and some friends on a combined picnic and wild plant search? You may pick some greens to go with your sandwiches, or some blossoms to add to your dessert. Of course, it is helpful to have a friend who is knowledgeable about edible weeds and wild plants. Don't eat every lovely plant you see—many are quite toxic!

SOME USES FOR THE BLOSSOMS, SEEDS, AND LEAVES OF BIBLICAL PLANTS

Flower Garnishes

Before using blossoms and leaves, rinse them well. Drain them carefully on paper towels in the fresh air until they are dry. Then add color and excitement to your meals by using flowers and leaves as garnishes. Here are a few suggestions:

- When you make sunchoke cocktail balls (page 152), trim the border of the serving plate with sunchoke flowers; or add sunchoke flowers to the frying pan after cooking the cocktail balls.
- Add sunchoke flower petals to the sunchoke slaw (page 153).
- Add za'atar (ground hyssop and sesame seeds) to chopped chard and garnish with hyssop blossoms.
- Garnish the top of the crustless cabbage and meat pie (page 158) with rosemary flowers.
- Serve the sweet and sour leeks (page 170) dressed with the blue blossoms of garlic chives.
- Insert fresh sage sprigs in baked whole stuffed onions (page 174) during the last 10 minutes of baking.
- Garnish turnip-apple salad (page 194) with young blue chicory flowers to lift the color of the salad.
- When serving nettle soup (page 200), add mallow buds as you would croutons.

- Decorate individual servings of grape and lemon sorbets (page 121) with pomegranate blossoms.
- Decorate raisin cake roll (pages 122–23) rounds with orange blossoms.
- Place a date blossom on the mound of hard sauce accompanying individual servings of steamed date and nut pudding (pages 125–26).
- Scatter the petals of climbing rose buds over date and cream tart (pages 127–28). Add a cup of almond blossoms to the almond cheesecake (page 136) mixture.
- Scatter lemon blossoms over a bowl of Israeli lemon whip (page 143).

Flower Infusions

Use flower and seed infusions as you would herbal teas. They promote well being and are free from caffeine.

Flower infusions are best made in a china or glass teapot to avoid any hint of a metallic taste. Wash the flowers and leaves carefully in case they have been sprayed. Cover dried or fresh flowers with boiling water and allow them to steep for about 10 minutes. For a stronger infusion, use more flowers rather than steeping the contents longer.

Seed infusions can also be made and used as a broth. Bruise the seeds slightly to bring out the oil. Put the seeds in an enamel pot and pour boiling water over them. Simmer over high heat for 10 minutes. Strain and serve hot.

Sprouting Seeds

Not a few health-minded cooks have learned about the benefits of seed sprouting. The most popular sprouting seed is the mung bean, but many biblical seeds and beans sprout easily. You may happily sprout seeds of sesame, millet, radish, parsley, mustard, and fenugreek, as well as wheat, barley, lentils, chickpeas, and fava beans.

Rinse ⅓ cup of seeds, and place them in a wide-mouthed quart jar. Cover the top with a layer of cheesecloth or mesh-like material, or use quart jars with wire-mesh tops. You want some air to circulate, so do not cover further. Place the jar in a warm place—under the sink near the hot water pipe, or at the back of the refrigerator top where the warm air is released. Rinse the seeds at least twice a day—you do not want to grow mold!

The sprouts are ready when they are about 2 or 3 inches long, depending on the size of the seed. Be careful to use the sprouts before they go beyond their developing period, or they will have a slightly stinging taste. Tasting them as they grow is the best way to establish your preference. Add them to raw salads, white-cheese spreads, scrambled eggs, or Chinese fried rice. They are good on their own for munching, as a change from carrots and celery.

Seed Tissanes

You can make a pleasant drink from a combination of equal amounts of caraway seeds, fennel seeds, and anise seeds. This drink is considered an antiflatulent. If necessary, drink a cup after meals. In any case, it is a pleasant, warming drink.

Crush the seeds with a pestle or grind them in a coffee grinder. Put them in a glass or ceramic bowl and pour boiling water over them. Allow time for the seeds to impart their goodness and flavor, about 20 minutes. Strain.

THE WHITE MADONNA LILY (*Lilium candidum*)

The lily is a bulbous plant of stately growth, bearing a long, green leafy stem. The six petals form a trumpet flower, which remains open day and night for four to five days. Its scent is strongest at night.

In Christian tradition, the lily is a symbol of purity. As such, it has been associated with the Virgin Mary. A papal edict issued in the seventeenth century gave recognition to the spiritual qualities attributed to the white lily, as seen in artistic representations of the Annunciation. The works of Botticelli and Titian especially highlight the white and graceful form of the flower. These interpretations have contributed to the popular name of the flower as the madonna lily.

Oriental appreciation of lily flowers for their beauty, scent, and taste is apparent in the Chinese proverb, "If you have two loaves of bread, sell one and buy a lily." Chinese cooking especially makes use of dried and fresh lily buds. If you have a large bed of lilies and can spare some buds, add them to the oil in which fish has been fried, stir quickly, drain, and serve with the fish and sliced lemons.

Summer Supper, Al Fresco

For an exciting but simple supper of flowers from your garden—not far from the scent of lilies, I hope—try this menu, accompanied by a dry white wine:

A soup of seeds (page 291)
Lily-blossom omelet (pages 291–92)
Salad of fresh mint, cucumber salad, and yogurt (page 163)
Blender-made rose petal gelatin and rose petal jam (pages 296, 297)

Saffron

A Soup of Seeds

Many French chefs advise using unpeeled garlic cloves in soups and sauces that are to be strained, because the garlic skins add a thickening agent.

2 bay leaves	2 cups prepared *tahini* paste
2 lemon leaves, crushed, *or* 2 lemon balm leaves	1 pound fresh cooked pumpkin *or* 1 1-pound can pumpkin purée
10 unpeeled garlic cloves	2 teaspoons *zhug* (page 214) *or* 1 teaspoon chili powder
1 teaspoon caraway seeds	
1 teaspoon fennel seeds	rosemary flowers, for garnish, *or*
1 teaspoon olive oil	violet flowers

1. In a large pot, combine the bay leaves, lemon leaves, unpeeled garlic cloves, caraway seeds, fennel seeds, and olive oil. Cover with 8 cups boiling water and simmer gently for 30 minutes. Strain.   2. In a small bowl, mix 1 cup of the broth with the *tahini* paste until smooth. Stir into the broth. Add the pumpkin and *zhug* and stir. Heat to serve warm, or refrigerate and serve chilled. Top with the floral garnish. *Serves 8*

Lily-blossom Omelet

The Tiger Lily or Humboldt Lily (*Hemerocallis fulva*) grows wild in many warm areas of the United States. This tuberous plant is associated with Chinese cooking, which uses fresh and dried buds in meat broths and vegetable stews. The lily tubers, thinly sliced, are used in salads the way sunchoke tubers are.

12 lily blossoms	2 tablespoons water
4 scallions with 4-inch green stems	salt and pepper, to taste
2 tablespoons margarine	violet flowers, for garnish, *or* chopped fresh parsley
3 eggs	

1. Pick the lily blossoms in the morning. Wash them well. Slice each blossom crosswise 3 times. Set aside. Slice the scallions crosswise.   2. In a frying pan, melt the margarine and sauté the scallions for 5 minutes. Add the lily blossoms and sauté 3 minutes. With a slotted spoon, remove the contents from the pan to a warmed platter.   3. In a bowl, beat the eggs until fluffy. Add 2 tablespoons of cold water and continue beating. Pour the egg mixture into the frying pan, and put the scallions and lily blossoms into the center. Lower the heat and cook slowly. When the eggs are set, fold the omelet in half. Serve immediately

on warmed plates. Garnish with violet flowers or chopped parsley. *Makes 1 3-egg omelet or 3 1-egg omelets*

Rainbow Rice Mold

❦ ❦ ❦

1 cup short-grain white rice
1 cup brown sugar, packed
2 cups lily flowers, sliced crosswise,
 or ¾ cup dried lily buds
1 cup blanched almonds
1 cup orange blossoms

1 cup raisins
1 cup mixed candied, colored citrus
 peels
fresh mint leaves, for garnish
glacé cherries, for garnish, *or* sliced
 pineapple

1. Cook the rice in boiling water for 15 minutes, or until tender. Drain any extra water and stir in the sugar.   2. In the base of an oiled 1½-pint glass mold, layer the rice mold: begin with a layer of rice, add a layer of lily flowers or buds, and cover with a layer of almonds. Press down well after each addition. Add a second layer of rice, and top this with a layer of orange blossoms, raisins, and citrus peels. Continue layering until all ingredients have been used. The final layer should be rice.   3. Press the top down very firmly, and tap the glass bowl. Cover the bowl with wax paper or aluminum foil, and place it on a steamer over boiling water that reaches halfway up the side of the bowl. Cook for 35 to 40 minutes.   4. Unmold and serve hot, or refrigerate and serve cold. Set the rice mold on a round plate decorated with mint leaves and glacé cherries or sliced pineapple.

Note: For more color, add ½ teaspoon of saffron or 1 teaspoon of turmeric to the water in which the rice is cooked.

THE ROSE (*Rosa* species)

Although it is uncertain when rose cultivation began, it seems to have emerged in Mediterranean lands. Tall rose plants in Jericho are referred to in the Apocrypha (Ecclesiasticus 24:14). Four species have been identified in the region of the Holy Land: the Phoenician Rose (*Rosa phoenicia*), which only grows in eastern Mediterranean lands; the dog rose (*Rosa canina*), which can also be found in other temperate lands; and two small alpine shrubs, one found on Mount Hermon to the north of Israel, and one on mountains in Sinai to the south. Both were cultivated in ancient times for cosmetic or ornamental purposes.

Cultivated roses were introduced from Persia and Syria in the later biblical period. The damask rose (named after Damascus) was an early arrival, and probably graced the spacious gardens renowned in the late Second Temple times, particularly in the area around Jerusalem and Jericho. The rabbis reported that no greenery was permitted in Jerusalem, but an exception was made for a single rose garden which had grown in the city since the time of the early prophets. Perhaps the ban was due to the odor involved in manuring plants, whereas roses were excepted because they emitted a pleasing fragrance. It has been suggested that they were grown near the Temple so that their petals could be mixed in the ritual incense. Other references establish that in late Bible times pink, red, and white roses grew in Israel—but not the yellow variety.

Rose Petals and Rose Water

Throughout the biblical Near East people regularly ate roses and rose products. Rose petals were used for making jams, with pride of place going to the sweet-smelling pink petals of the damask rose. The sweet confection was highly popular, and unbeknownst to the ancients was rich in vitamin C. If fresh petals were not available, dried petals could be substituted. (This could not be done with the rose hips, however, which had to be fresh.)

Rose water had many uses, but it was primarily mixed into pastries, cakes, and biscuits. It was said that neither in summer or winter were roses absent from the table of King Solomon—and if they were not available in Israel, they were duly imported from Egypt or Ethiopia.

How to Prepare Rose Petals: Roses are best picked in the early morning, after the night's dew has dried but before the heat of the sun is at its peak. Remove the petals, leaving the heel, which has a bitter taste. Wash the petals lightly in water to remove dust and any insecticide. (It is better not to cook with roses that have been sprayed with insecticide.) Partially dry in paper toweling. The petals are then ready to use.

Many varieties of roses are suitable for preparation. The color of the rose is generally a good guide to its flavor, although today changes in rose culture have improved the appearance of the flowers at the expense of the scent. The important thing is to use the petals as soon as they are ready in order to realize their full flavor and scent.

Rose Water: You can purchase rose water in import stores, health food stores, and even some grocery stores. If you have roses you can make your own! The easiest way to make rose water is to fill a kettle or pot ¾ full with petals and cover them with water. Allow the petals to simmer below the boiling point for about 1 hour. Strain. Save the water, and to it add a new batch of petals. Repeat the process at least three times, or until you smell a strong rose scent. Bottle the rose water and seal tightly in sterilized containers.

Rose Petal Potpourri

Layer as many rose petals as you have in a large, covered dish, and lightly sprinkle each layer with salt. Shake the contents every morning for about 10 days. Transfer the petals to a glass or crockery jar, in the bottom of which you have

Purslane

placed 2 ounces of ground allspice and pieces of cinnamon stick. Partly cover the jar and let it rest for 6 weeks. At this point you may add other flower petals, and dried herb leaves such as sage, mint, or basil for a more pungent scent. Use the potpourri to fill sachet bags, or keep it for beauty and scent in a clear glass jar.

Rose Hips

The small red, orange, or green berries at the base of the withered roses constitute the fruit of the rosebush. Their prestige has greatly increased with the popularity of rose hip tea and the awareness of the high vitamin content of the rose hips: C, A, B, E, K, and P! But there is more to rose hip consumption than drinking tea. For gardeners, the drawback of homegrown rose hips is having to leave the roses on the stems long enough to produce the hips. Not all gardens are planned to conceal roses going to seed. Fortunately, you can purchase rose hips in health food and herbal stores. They are sold in three forms: the whole dried berry for preserving or making syrups; powdered for making puddings, soups, and teas; and pressed into tablets.

How to Prepare Rose Hips: When you use rose hips from your own garden, remove the blossom ends, stems, and leaves. Wash the hips very carefully to remove any harmful spray or insect life, then refrigerate until thoroughly chilled (chilling inactivates the enzymes which might otherwise cause a loss of vitamin C). Use as soon as possible, as the hips quickly spoil. Grind the hips in a food processor or coffee grinder.

Rose Hip Jam

The old fashioned damask rose is a favorite rose for cooking purposes. Its size and scent add quality to all rose preparations. In general, dark red roses have a strong taste as well, whereas the lighter shades lend a more delicate flavor. When there are not enough rose hips in your garden, you may supplement the supply with store-bought hips or for jam, add an orange, lemon or apple. Here is a basic recipe for rose hip jam. The ratio of sugar and fruit is about equal.

1 cup water
1 pound rose hips
1 pound warmed sugar, or as needed

1. In a heavy stainless steel pan, combine the water and rose hips. Bring to a boil and simmer until the fruit is tender. Press through a strainer or colander. 2. Weigh the pulp. Add 1 pound of sugar for each pound of pulp. Simmer until the jam thickens. Pour into sterilized ½-pint jars, cover tightly, and store. *Makes 2 pints*

Rose Petal Jam

❦ ❦ ❦

1 pound rose petals, washed and dried	juice of 1 lemon
2 pounds sugar	1 teaspoon ginger
1¼ cups water	

1. In a bowl, combine the rose petals and 1 pound of the sugar. Mix well. Let the mixture rest for 1 day, stirring twice during that period.   2. Transfer the mixture to a large enamel or stainless steel pot. Add the remaining sugar and the water. Slowly bring it to a boil—don't raise the flame until the sugar is completely dissolved.   3. Boil until the mixture becomes a firm syrup. Add the lemon juice and ginger. To test readiness, drop a spoonful of jam on a saucer and allow it to cool slightly. If it thickens to a honey-like consistency, the jam is ready.   4. Pour the jam into sterilized ½-pint jars; seal tightly with screw-on tops or transparent plastic lids secured with rubber bands. *Makes 3 pints*

Rose Hip Syrup

❦ ❦ ❦

Rose hip syrup has a number of uses: to sweeten tea or punch, or to top puddings.

½ pound rose hips	½ pound sugar
water to cover	juice of 1 lemon

1. Wash and dry the rose hips. Simmer gently in water, covered, until they are soft.   2. Strain and set aside the water. Return the pulp to the pan and cover with water. Bring to a boil and simmer 10 minutes. Strain through a jelly bag or a heavy cotton-lined strainer. Combine the two lots of juice, pour into the washed jelly bag or cotton-lined strainer. Allow the juice to drain 6 hours or overnight to ensure a clearer juice.   3. Add sugar and lemon juice and boil until it is reduced to 1½ quarts. *Makes 1½ quarts syrup*

Rose Hip Syrup Wine Punch

🐞 🐞 🐞

1 bottle rose wine, approximately
    1 quart
¼ cup rose hip syrup (page 295)

juice of 1 lemon *or* pomegranate
thinly sliced lemons, for garnish
rose petals, for garnish, *or* mint leaves

1. Combine the wine, syrup, and lemon juice. 2. Serve the punch in a large bowl with thinly sliced lemons and scattered rose petals or mint leaves. *Makes 1 quart*

Wild Rose Petal Jam

🐞 🐞 🐞

The *Rosa canina* is known by many names: wild rose, dog rose, and cockbramble, to mention but a few. People the world over have been delighted to behold patches of these rose shrubs, whose white flowers grow in clusters. For those gardeners who don't want to leave their garden roses on the stems until they go to seed, using the wild *Rosa canina* in rose hip production is one answer. Although the scent of wild roses is more delicate than the cultivated species, a very tasty rose petal can be made from them, especially if some garden rose petals are added. The jam is exceedingly sweet—a bit of it goes a long way.

2 cups wild rose petals, packed
½ cup water
1 tablespoon lemon juice

1 tablespoon orange juice
2 cups sugar

1. Wash the wild rose petals well. 2. Mix the water with the lemon juice and orange juice and dissolve the sugar in it. Combine the sugar water and petals in an enamel pan. Cook over a very low flame. Stir often during the 15 minutes of cooking, then only occasionally until the sugar is thoroughly dissolved and the petals are soft. 3. Pour the jam into a small glass jar and cover tightly. *Makes 1 pint*

Garden Roquette

Rose Petal and Apple Chutney

1 pound rose petals, washed and dried
3 pounds tart apples, peeled and cut up
½ pound raisins (about 2 cups)
1 pound brown sugar
2 pounds onions, peeled and chopped
2 cups cider vinegar *or* citrus vinegar

2 ounces fresh ginger root, peeled and finely chopped, *or* 2 teaspoons ground ginger
2 tablespoons mustard seeds
1 tablespoon salt
grated rind and juice of 1 lemon
grated rind and juice of 1 orange
¼ teaspoon pepper
½ teaspoon cinnamon

1. In a stainless steel stewing pot, bring all the ingredients to a boil. Lower the heat and cook very gently until the fruit and petals are tender. 2. Pour into warm, sterilized ½-pint jars. Seal tightly when cool. Store in a cool, dry place. *Makes about 5 pints*

Rose Petal-Honey Gelatin Dessert

This is a good addition to a three-part dessert made up of two fresh fruits or three flavors of gelatin, allowing the diner to taste several "goodies."

2 cups rose petals, washed and dried
3 cups water
juice of 2 lemons

1½ cups honey *or* 4 cups sugar
2 packages unflavored gelatin
1 teaspoon rose water

1. In an electric blender, blend the rose petals with 1½ cups of water and the lemon juice, until smooth. Slowly add the honey or sugar. 2. In a saucepan, heat 1½ cups of the water with the gelatin. Bring the mixture to a boil. Boil for 1 minute, stirring constantly. Pour the gelatin mixture into a blender, and blend with the rose petal mixture for 1 minute. Cool slightly. Add the rose water. Pour into sterilized ½-pint jars and seal, or pour into dessert bowls and refrigerate. *Makes 2 pints*

Rose Petal-Rose Water Surprise

🌹 🌹 🌹

5 large roses
5 cups water
2½ cups sugar
⅔ cup fresh lemon juice

1 teaspoon rose water
5 cups chopped fresh pineapple *or*
    drained canned pineapple chunks
2 cups crushed ice

1. Wash the roses carefully and separate the petals. Put the petals in a bowl, cover them with the water, and let rest for 4 hours.   2. Drain the petals in a colander, reserving the water. To the strained water add the sugar and lemon juice. Stir well until the sugar dissolves. Add the rose water, pineapple, and ice. Fill sherbet glasses with the iced mixture, and top with a rose petal. For an unusual cocktail-dessert, pour 1 ounce dry gin into the sherbet glasses before you add the rose petal drink. *Serves 6*

Rose Petal Syrup

🌹 🌹 🌹

4 cups rose petals, packed
3 cups sugar

1. Wash and dry the rose petals. In an enamel pan, combine them with water to barely cover.   2. Bring to a boil over a medium flame. Gradually add the sugar and continue boiling slowly for 10 minutes, or until it becomes a syrup.   3. Strain the syrup into a sterilized bottle, cork tightly, and let rest for 2 weeks before using. *Makes 1 quart*

OTHER FLOWER RECIPES
Chicken and Marinated Mallow Buds with Rice or Chinese Rice Noodles

❦ ❦ ❦

1½ cups dried mushrooms
1 cup small mallow buds
3 tablespoons oil
1 cup sliced chicken breast
2 cups Chinese rice thread noodles
    or rice

Marinade:

1 teaspoon chopped lemon peel
1 teaspoon salt
2 teaspoons sugar
1 tablespoon sherry
1 tablespoon soy sauce

1. In a small bowl, reconstitute the dried mushrooms in warm water to cover. 2. In another bowl, combine the marinade ingredients. Add the mallow buds and mushrooms, and marinate for ½ hour. 3. In a frying pan or wok, heat the oil. Add the chicken and sauté 1 minute. Drain the mallow buds and mushrooms and add them to the pan. Pour in the marinade, mix well, and stir-fry for 2 minutes. Serve over rice or Chinese rice thread noodles. (To reconstitute noodles, pour 1 cup boiling water over 2 cups rice thread noodles and let rest until the noodles have absorbed the water.) *Serves 2 to 4*

Batter-fried Squash Blossoms

❦ ❦ ❦

Male squash blossoms tend to fall off the plant without maturing. They are easy to harvest and make an attractive first course. You can also use them to garnish a platter of fish or mixed vegetables.

10 squash blossoms
3 tablespoons margarine

Batter:

2 eggs, separated
⅔ cup water
1 tablespoon vegetable oil

1 cup all-purpose flour
1 tablespoon wheat germ
¼ teaspoon salt
1 teaspoon ground cumin

1. Harvest the squash blossoms when they are wide open, in the cool of morning before the sun causes them to close. Remove the stems. Open the flowers on one end and wash them carefully. Put them into a bowl of water and refrigerate for as long as three days. Pat the blossoms dry just before using them

Mallow

(remember—the batter should rest at least 1 hour).   2. To prepare the batter, beat the egg yolks, water, and oil in a large bowl. Mix the flour, wheat germ, salt, and cumin, and combine with the liquid. Allow the batter to rest for 1 hour.   3. Beat the egg whites until they form stiff peaks. Fold into the batter when you are ready to begin frying.   4. In a heavy frying pan, melt the margarine. Dip each blossom into the batter and fry until golden brown on both sides. Drain on paper towels. Serve warm with applesauce or rose petal chutney (page 297). *Serves 4*

Stuffed Squash Blossoms

❦ ❦ ❦

For this recipe, select a stuffing from the rice stuffing for cabbage leaves or the beef and bread crumb stuffing for artichoke hearts. If you use the stuffing for artichoke hearts, partially cook the stuffing before you fill the blossoms. Only the rice has to be precooked in the recipe for stuffed cabbage leaves.

10 squash blossoms
rice stuffing for cabbage leaves (page
    158) *or* beef and bread crumb
    stuffing for artichokes (page 150)
juice of 1 lemon

1. Carefully rinse the squash blossoms and dry them on a towel.   2. Make the stuffing of your choice. Open each blossom and fill it lightly so that it closes easily. Place the blossoms side by side in an ovenproof baking dish. Sprinkle the lemon juice of one lemon over them. Bake the blossoms in a preheated 350° oven until heated through, about 5 minutes. Don't over-bake them! *Serves 4*

13 EDIBLE THORNS AND THISTLES

❦ ❦ ❦

Two edible prickly plants that we have mentioned before deserve attention: the blackberry bush (*Rubus sanctus*) and the caper plant (*Capparis spinosa*).

Israel is rich in prickly plants, as I can attest from the period before I began to cultivate my garden! The country has over seventy species—and I seemed to have all of them. They often take over the landscape, reminding one of the curse of Genesis 3:17–18: "Cursed is the ground for thy sake . . . Thorns also and thistles shall it bring forth to thee."

The Bible mentions more than twenty thorns and thistles, but identification is uncertain—one often cannot tell whether the reference is to a specific plant or is a general term. It is doubtful if the different kinds were separately identified in biblical times (and indeed, to most Israelis today a thorn is a thorn is a thorn). Many of them are unparalleled in the West, but we can hazard some guesses. The bramble in Jotham's parable (Judges 9:14–15) may be the buckthorn bush, common in this part of the world. The crown of thorns which the Romans placed on Jesus' head may be the plant identified in Latin as *Ziziphus spina-christi* (the Christ thorn), a tall evergreen found in Samaria and other regions of the country.

To add to the general confusion, English versions of the Bible give different names to the same plant. The briar and the bramble, the thorn and the thistle, can turn out to be identical—and the translation in many cases is no guide. Most problematic is the identification of the burning bush—which was not consumed—before which Moses had his first revelation of God (Exodus 3:12–4). Many suggestions have been offered. One identifies it with the above mentioned *Ziziphus*, which would provide a floral link between Moses and Jesus. Another proposal is that it was the senna bush (*Cassia senna*)—the very word senna comes from the Hebrew *sneh*, which is used here for the bush.

On the traditional site of Mount Sinai stands the famous Monastery of Saint Catherine, which incorporates an ancient bush revered by the monks as the original "burning bush." It is the shrub *Colutea istria*, which has bright

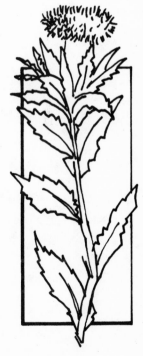

Safflower

yellow flowers. When I visited the monastery in 1971, one of the monks overturned a stove in his apartment. It caught fire and the blaze began to spread. Panic seized the monks, as their sole source of water was a well in the courtyard. Their library contains one of the most famous and precious collections of ancient manuscripts and icons, and this was near the sight of the blaze. However, it was not the library that was uppermost in the minds of the monks, but their precious shrub! They established relays to bring water from the well so that the burning bush should not catch fire.

Another tradition regarded the bush as a bramble or blackberry. This was accepted in early times, and many rabbinic legends and homilies are based on this identification.

BLACKBERRIES

Blackberries have a kind of magic. They accommodate the city dweller's notion of country life and nature's bounty just waiting for the forager to pick. Even when scratches and cuts are the price of the picking, urban dwellers feel they have overcome some of nature's hazards in their quest for dining in the wild. So widespread is the presence of blackberries that their delicious taste has been enjoyed in many countries for generations. Their seeds have even been found in the stomach of Neolithic man.

Part of their virtue is that they ripen at the end of summer, just when a change of fruit is so welcome. Blackberries make a natural dessert on a picnic when near their habitats. The clever picker knows that you start at the lower stalks of the branches to find the fully ripe ones, the sweetest among the berries. The upper berries, which are in easy reach, are not as good until later in the season at the end of September. Of course, having them growing in your garden is a great way to cover unsightly places or to use in fence-facing.

Blackberry lovers each have a favorite recipe for using them—that is, if the children don't eat them raw first! Here are a few suggestions for enjoying our international fruit friend.

Blackberry Yogurt

1 cup fresh blackberry juice
1 cup yogurt
½ teaspoon ground cloves

1. Wash the berries and extract their juice with a fruit juicer, or by pressing them through a strainer lined with a double thickness of muslin. Let the juice stand in a warm place for 1 hour.   2. Blend the yogurt with the juice and cloves. *Serves 2*

Note: For a pleasant summer drink, mix ½ cup blackberry juice with lemonade to taste.

Blackberry Soup

This soup can be served cold, as a prelude to a summer meal, or as a dessert (in which case you may increase the sugar content). Decorating the dessert soup with blackberry flowers enhances the presentation. If those are not available, mint leaves are a good substitute.

1 cup fresh blackberry juice
⅓ cup sugar
1 teaspoon grated orange rind
2 cups water
2 cups dry red wine

2 cups blackberries
1 teaspoon arrowroot powder
blackberry flower blossoms, for
    garnish, *or* fresh mint *or*
    whipped cream

1. Extract the juice according to the recipe for blackberry yogurt, step 1 (page 302).   2. In an enamel pan, combine the sugar and orange rind and cover with water. Cook about 5 minutes, or until the rind is soft. Add the wine and berries. Blend the arrowroot with a little water and stir into the soup for about 2 minutes. Refrigerate. *Serves 4 to 6*

Blackberry Jam

I've rarely had the chance to make this jam, since the Wigs would dash out each morning to pick the berries to eat with cereal—or, if they were in a hurry, just "as is." Some day, when the vines take over all the wire fencing, we'll have enough berries to satisfy each person's taste. Here is an easy recipe to try.

2 quarts ripe blackberries, crushed
1 3-ounce package liquid pectin
7 cups sugar

1. To avoid having too many seeds in your jam, put half of the crushed pulp through a sieve. The result should be about 5 cups of pulp.   2. In a large pot, combine the pulp and pectin and bring the mixture to a boil. Add the sugar and again bring to a boil. Raise the heat and boil hard for 1 minute. Pour into warm, sterilized, ½-pint jars and seal at room temperature. *Makes 1 quart*

Blackberry Cobbler

❦ ❦ ❦

3 to 4 cups ripe blackberries
3 tablespoons cornstarch
1 cup brown sugar, packed
⅛ teaspoon salt
1 teaspoon allspice
½ cup heavy cream

Shortcake Dough:
2 cups all-purpose flour
2 tablespoons sugar
3 teaspoons baking powder
1 teaspoon salt
3 ounces margarine
⅔ cup milk

1. Put the berries in an ovenproof glass casserole. Mix the cornstarch, sugar, salt, and allspice, and sprinkle the mixture over the berries.   2. To prepare the dough, sift the dry ingredients into a large bowl. Cut in the margarine and work with your fingers to make a soft dough. Add the milk, and knead lightly. 3. Drop the dough by spoonfuls onto the fruit. Bake in a preheated 350° oven for 30 minutes or until the dough is nicely browned. Serve warm with cream. *Serves 4 to 6*

Variation: Pat half of the dough into a well-greased 8-inch round layer pan. Dot with butter or margarine. Pat the other half of the dough on top. Bake in a preheated 350° oven for 30 minutes. Split the layers apart and spoon the berries between the layers and on top. Serve as is or with whipped cream.

WILD GREENS

CAPER (*Capparis spinosa*)

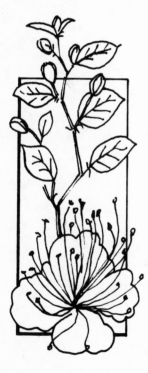

The flowering caper plant is of rare beauty, displaying a prism of colors on stringlike petals. It grows among the rocks and walls including the Western Wall and in mountainous terrain. Ecclesiastes 12:5 speaking of the caper's fruit says, "The almond tree shall blossom . . . and the caperberry shall fail; Because man goeth to his long home. . . . " This symbolizes how short man's life is. Soon after the plant blossoms, the seeds are scattered and the flowering part of the plant dies.

Fortunately, the plant produces new fruit every day. The flower buds are picked when they are quite young and pickled in salt or vinegar. After the plant completes its flowering, it develops a small cucumberlike fruit pod, which is also pickled and served with pickled vegetables as a delicacy.

Caper

Pickled Capers

1 pound capers	1 cup Kosher salt
lemon slices *or* lemon leaves *or*	
peppercorns *or* bay leaves	

1. Soak the capers in water for 2 days, changing the water each day. Prepare a basic brine of 1 cup Kosher salt (or sea salt) to 12 cups water. To this brine add either lemon slices, lemon leaves, peppercorns, or bay leaves. 2. Pack the capers in a large sterilized glass container. Again add your choice of lemon slices, lemon leaves, peppercorns, or bay leaves. Pour the brine over the capers, making sure they are completely covered. Remove the scum and add more brine when necessary. Pickle for 1 month, and seal in jars with the brine. *Makes 2 quarts*

Caper Sauce

Capers yield a piquant sauce, which is especially good in cold summer dishes: hard-boiled eggs, cold fish, or cold chicken salad.

2 tablespoons pickled capers (above)	juice of 1 lemon
6 anchovy fillets, drained	freshly ground black pepper
¼ cup olive oil	

1. In mortar or food chopper, pound the capers and anchovies to a paste. Beat in the olive oil by drops as for mayonnaise. Beat in the lemon juice and pepper to taste. *Makes about 1 cup*

Caper-Egg Sauce for
Boiled Lamb, Mutton, or Chicken

4 egg yolks
1 teaspoon cold water mixed with
   1 teaspoon all-purpose flour

1 tablespoon capers and some juice

1. In a saucepan, beat the egg yolks. Beat in the flour and water mixture.   2. Cook over medium heat to thicken, stirring constantly to prevent curdling. Stir in the capers and their juice, and mix until smooth. *Makes about 1 cup*

GLOSSARY

❧ ❧ ❧

Aravah Desert area in southern Israel.

Ashkenazi (plural **Ashkenazim**) Jews who originated in northwest Europe; later mostly concentrated in eastern Europe.

baklava Turkish pastry made with honey and nuts.

Beth Din Jewish law court.

Beit HaKerem Suburb of Jerusalem, founded by teachers and writers in the early 1920s.

bitter herbs Herbs eaten on Passover eve to remind the Jews of the bitter lot of their ancestors in Egypt. According to the early rabbis wild chicory, chicory, compass lettuce, yellow star thistle, and sow-thistle were eligible to be eaten as bitter herbs on this occasion.

blintze Filled pancake.

boreka Small filled pastry, savory, or sweet.

bulgur Wheat that has been prepared for cooking by cracking, steaming, and toasting; also called cracked wheat.

challah Sabbath egg-bread loaf.

Chanukah Feast of Light, celebrated in December–January, commemorating the victories of the Maccabees over the Syrian persecutors in the second century B.C.

cholent Sabbath dish; a slow-cooking stew prepared on Fridays and kept warm in the oven until Saturday lunch.

couscous Fine semolina made from wheat grain.

Sesame

couscousier Special pot for making *couscous.*

dolmas Stuffed vine leaves; also stuffed cabbage leaves.

felafel Appetizer made from chickpeas and spices, fried in deep fat.

feta cheese Salted white soft cheese made from sheep's or goats' milk, kept in whey.

filo Paper-thin sheets of pastry.

fumet Stock made from fish heads and fish bones added to a vegetable-based stock.

gefilte fish Stuffed fish; chopped fish made into fish cakes.

Haggadah The text of the Passover-eve home ritual.

hamin Equivalent of *cholent* among Sephardic Jews.

Havdalah End-of-Sabbath service.

hillbeh Yemenite herb paste.

hummus Savory cream paste made from chickpeas and *tahini.*

kashrut Jewish law concerning ritual fitness of foods.

kebab Portions of meat skewered and grilled or broiled.

kibbi Bulgur pounded to a paste and formed into egg-shaped forms for frying in deep fat or spread on tray for grilling.

kibbutz Israeli village commune. A member is popularly known as a "kibbutznik."

kosher Food that is ritually fit.

kugel Form of pudding using noodles or potatoes as base.

machshi Stuffed vegetables.

matzo (plural **matzot**) Unleavened bread, eaten at Passover.

matzo meal Matzot ground into a meal.

melokhia Spinach-like vegetable, peculiar to the Middle East.

mezze Collection of small dishes with a variety of foods, similar to hors d'oeuvres.

mikveh Ritual bath.

mitzvah A commandment; performance of a commandment or righteous deed.

moshav (plural **moshavim**) Cooperative smallholders' village.

Negev Israel's southern area, mostly desert.

New Year Jewish tradition enumerates four new years: In the spring, for the religious calendar; in the fall, a new year for tithing cattle and a civil new year (the one generally referred to); and at the end of the winter, new year for trees.

parve According to Jewish law, a "neutral" food containing neither meat nor milk and which may be eaten with either.

pashtida Pie or pancake, made of vegetables or cooked meats, held together with eggs.

Passover Spring festival commemorating the exodus from Egypt.

pilav Spiced rice casserole.

pita (plural **pitot**) Arab round flat bread with pouch inside.

Rosh Hashanah Jewish New Year.

sanbusak Overall word for pastry in Arab countries. It is usually in half-moon shapes and filled.

Seder The Passover-eve home ritual.

Sephardi (plural **Sephardim)** Strictly, Jews originating from Spain and Portugal; also applied to all non-Ashkenazi Jews.

seven species The foods which the spies sent by Moses to the Land of Canaan found growing in abundance: wheat, barley, olives, grapes, pomegranates, figs, and dates.

Shavuot Feast of Pentecost or Weeks, a harvest festival, also commemorating the giving of the Law to Moses on Mount Sinai.

shochet Jewish ritual slaughterer.

tabouleh Salad made of bulgur and vegetables.

tahini Paste made of ground sesame seeds.

War of Independence War fought by Israel with surrounding Arab nations in 1948–1949, after it had declared its independence.

Western Wall Section of western supporting wall of Temple compound, still standing in Jerusalem and venerated by Jews.

Yom Kippur Day of Atonement, annual Jewish fast day.

za'atar Combination of ground hyssop with salt, sumac, or sesame seeds added.

INDEX

❦ ❦ ❦

For ease of use, all page references to recipes have been underlined.

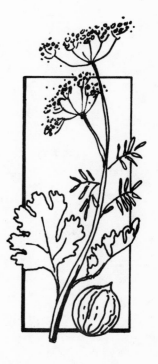

Coriander